CHURCH AND STATE
IN RUSSIA

CHURCH AND STATE IN RUSSIA~ *The Last Years of the Empire*~ *1900-1917*

By JOHN SHELTON CURTISS

1972

OCTAGON BOOKS

New York

Reprinted 1965
by special arrangement with Columbia University Press
Second Octagon printing 1972

OCTAGON BOOKS
A DIVISION OF FARRAR, STRAUS & GIROUX, INC.
19 Union Square West
New York, N. Y. 10003

LIBRARY OF CONGRESS CATALOG CARD NUMBER: 65-16770

ISBN 0-374-92014-1

Printed in U.S.A. by
NOBLE OFFSET PRINTERS, INC.
NEW YORK 3, N. Y.

To My Wife

EDNA SUTTER CURTISS

Preface

ACCORDING to the original plan, this work was to deal chiefly with the relations between Orthodoxy and Autocracy in Russia. The reader will quickly discover, however, that in its present form this study has a much broader scope than the title at first suggests. Not only does it treat of the political relations between the church and the state, but it also includes a discussion of the economic position of the church. This was included, in part because the state treasury gave the church substantial revenues, and partly because the church's attitude toward the state was affected in a variety of ways by its economic condition. The discrimination of the state against the religious groups which were rivals of the church for the spiritual allegiance of the Russian part of the population has been discussed in some detail. Moreover, a consideration of the culture and the morals of the clergy, their education, and the part which they played in the education of the people, has been included, as these were important factors in determining the church's ability to give support to the state.

In the section dealing with the church during the revolutionary years, 1905–7, much has been said of the movement for ecclesiastical reform, since this movement was in part an attempt to alter profoundly the relations between the church and the civil government. Even those phases of the ecclesiastical reform movement which did not directly involve the relations between the church and the civil power have been discussed, as they throw light upon the inner strengths and weaknesses of the church, and therefore upon its ability to render effective assistance to the state.

The chapters on the period of the Revolution of 1905 have, of course, touched on the attitude of the church and its clergy toward the Revolution, and toward the state under attack. The liberalism as well as the conservatism of some sections of the church has been noted, and in some cases the extreme reaction of other sections. In the succeeding chapters the topics under consideration are the failure of the movement for ecclesiastical reform after the Revolution of 1905, the continued dominance of the Over Procurator, and the relations between the church and the later Dumas. Also included in the later chapters are topics which were touched on in the preceding chapters—namely, the campaign of the clergy for increased subsidies from the treasury, and the attitude of lay society toward the church. The final chapter covers the Rasputin episode and its effect upon ecclesiastical life, as well as the stand taken by the church during the World War.

On the other hand, the book does not discuss the theological system or creed of any of the religious denominations, and no attempt has been made to discuss the moral precepts and teachings of the Orthodox Church or of other religious bodies—other than those precepts that related specifically to the state and the duties of the subject to the government. Nothing has been said about church architecture, painting, or music, or about the influence of these religious arts upon the thought or the life of the people.

It is possible that adverse criticism may be elicited by the lack of detailed discussion of the position of certain non-Orthodox religions which existed within the Russian Empire—the Catholic, Lutheran, Jewish, Armenian, Moslem, Lamaite, and other faiths. The reason for this omission is that Catholicism and Lutheranism were confined chiefly to the Polish and the Baltic provinces, and were of little importance in Russia proper. As for the others, their adherents were also national minorities living, for the most part, on the periphery of the Russian state. The handling of problems connected with these faiths played a relatively small part in the relations between the Russian Orthodox Church and the Imperial Government.

This volume is chiefly concerned with the period from 1900 to the "first revolution" of 1917. In the first five years of the twentieth century the Russian Church was still under the authority of the man who typified rigid control over the ecclesiastical establishment— K. P. Pobedonostsev. During this period we still see in the affairs of the church the nineteenth-century system, not yet substantially modified by the revolutionary events of the twentieth century. In the years between 1905 and 1917 the church was confronted with changed conditions, and yet in spite of the October Manifesto and other conces-

sions, during these years the autocratic Tsar still controlled it. The
terminal date for the volume is February (old style), 1917, when the
autocratic regime of Nicholas II collapsed. For the Russian Church,
that event meant the end of one epoch and the beginning of another
very different one.

The Russian words employed in this volume have been trans-
literated according to the system of the Library of Congress, with the
diacritical marks omitted.

All dates of events in Russia are given in the old style (according
to the Julian Calendar).

In writing this book I have been exceptionally fortunate in the
valuable assistance which I have received from many sources. First
among these is Professor Geroid T. Robinson of Columbia University.
With his help many pitfalls have been avoided; without it, the worth
of my book would have been much less. He has been unsparing of his
time and energy, and unfailingly helpful with suggestions. The years
which I have spent on this work have been made fruitful by his assistance. Professors John H. Wuorinen and Clarence Manning, and
Michael T. Florinsky, all of Columbia University, have also been of
great help with their criticism and advice.

Grateful acknowledgment must be made to the members of several
institutions. The generous financial assistance rendered by the American Council of Learned Societies made it possible to complete this
study. The staffs of the Columbia University Library, the New York
Public Library, and the Widener Library of Harvard University have
unfailingly done their part to make easier the routine work of re-
search. Finally mention must be made of the kindness and courtesy
of the members of the staffs of the Leningrad Division of the Central
Historical Archive of the U.S.S.R. and of the Special Reading Room
of the Leningrad Public Library, who went to great lengths to assist
my search for obscure source material.

My sincere thanks go to my wife, who never failed to give aid and
encouragement in season and out of season.

JOHN SHELTON CURTISS

BROOKLYN COLLEGE
January, 1940

Contents

PART I

A Thousand Years of
Church and State

CHAPTER I

An Outline of Russian Church History to the Year 1900; Moscow as "The Third Rome"

WHEN OLGA, wife of the Varangian Prince Igor of Kiev, adopted Christianity about the middle of the tenth century, it was the Eastern Orthodox form which she accepted, the faith introduced into the land of Rus by Varangians who had learned to cherish it while serving under the emperors in Constantinople. Already a church had been established in Kiev, and doubtless, with Olga's example to follow, many of the hardy Varangians and numbers of the Slavs accepted the new belief. But Olga's son and Igor's successor, Sviatoslav, was an ambitious fighting man, who cared more for the glory to be won in battle than for the chanting of priests. So it was not until the time of Vladimir, Sviatoslav's son, that the men of Rus were urged by their ruler to accept the Gospel, the worship of the Greeks of Constantinople, Tsargrad the great.[1]

Legend has it that Vladimir, curious about the faiths professed in neighboring lands, sent messengers to the Moslem Bulgars of the Volga, to the Jews, to Catholic Germany, and to the Greeks. The envoys were not greatly impressed by what they had learned on their first three visitations; but those who went to Constantinople came back still enthusiastic about their experiences. Their words, as related by the chronicler, were:

Then we went on to Greece, and the Greeks led us to the edifices where they worship their God, and we knew not whether we were in heaven or

[1] E. E. Golubinskii, *Istoriia Russkoi Tserkvi*, I (part 1), 74 ff.

on earth. For on earth there is no such splendor or such beauty, and we are at a loss how to describe it. We only know that God dwells there among men, and their service is fairer than the ceremonies of other nations. For we cannot forget that beauty. Every man, after tasting something sweet, is afterward unwilling to accept that which is bitter, and therefore we cannot dwell longer here.[2]

Unfortunately it cannot be determined whether this was merely the legendary or the actual manner in which Christianity came to Russia. It may be that Vladimir was persuaded to accept this faith by fellow Varangians who had become Christians while serving in Constantinople. Nevertheless, the important fact is that it was from Constantinople that this creed came.

By the end of the tenth century the Byzantine Church had established a tradition which differed radically from the theory developed in the Roman Church by Hildebrand. This churchman, later Pope Gregory VII, gave powerful reinforcement to the doctrine that the pope was the lineal successor of Peter, with absolute and final jurisdiction over Christendom. The pope, Gregory maintained, could "depose kings and emperors, and absolve subjects from their oath of allegiance to unworthy sovereigns";[3] indeed Gregory VII actually did exert his power over lay rulers. He rebuked the sovereigns of France, Spain, Denmark, Poland, Hungary, and other states, and in 1077 had the satisfaction of seeing the proud Holy Roman Emperor come to Canossa.[4]

Quite different was the position of the patriarch of Constantinople in the tenth and eleventh centuries. From the days of Constantine, who called the Council of Nicea, the Eastern Church had to reckon with the emperors. Constantine set the pattern for later rulers by presiding at the Council, and by arresting and imprisoning Arius and his followers; later in his reign he showed his power over the church by recalling Arius and some of his most ardent supporters, and by removing several of those who had participated in the adoption of the Nicene Creed.[5] The Emperor Theodosius imitated Constantine to the extent of calling an Ecumenical Council in 381, at which he

[2] S. H. Cross, *The Russian Primary Chronicle*, p. 199.
[3] P. Schaff, *History of the Christian Church*, V, 29–32.
[4] *Ibid.*, V, 32–33, 55–56.
[5] A. A. Vasiliev, *Histoire de l'empire byzantin*, I, 68–70.

interfered by removing his ecclesiastical opponents from the dominant positions.[6] The tendency toward imperial domination of the Eastern Church was carried much further by Justinian, who established the system often known as caesaropapism.

, . . . Justinian not only made it his aim to keep in his hands the government of the clergy and to preside over their destinies (not excepting their most eminent representatives), but also considered it his right to rule the life of the clergy, to name men at will to the most elevated posts in the hierarchy, to impose himself as mediator and as judge in ecclesiastical debates. On the other hand, Justinian . . . exerted all his efforts to establish unity of faith among his subjects, frequently participating in dogmatic debates and imposing final solutions in disputed questions of dogma.[7]

Caesaropapism did not die with Justinian. Heraclius I interfered in a religious conflict in 638 A. D.; when the pope condemned this action, the succeeding emperor, Constantine II, had the pope arrested, brought to Constantinople, and subjected to terrible indignities.[8] " 'I am emperor and priest,' wrote Leo III to Pope Gregory II" in the eighth century. He was "a convinced representative of this [caesaropapist] political conviction."[9] The Emperor Leo VI (the Macedonian), whose reign began in 866, even issued ordinances on strictly ecclesiastical matters without calling a church council; his rulings forbade women to receive communion for forty days after childbirth, enjoined the observance of Sunday, set the feasts and the holidays of the Church, and the like.[10]

Caesaropapism was not, however, the only theory held in the Byzantine empire concerning the relations between church and state. In the ninth century Emperor Basil the Macedonian published his *Epanagogue,* which repeated the theory of the "symphony," or harmonious equality of patriarch and emperor, which had been proclaimed at the Seventh Ecumenical Council in the preceding century.[11] This principle was generally accepted in theory, and under later emperors it continued to be accepted. In actuality, however, the relations between church and state in Byzantium continued to be

[6] *Ibid.,* I, 101–3.   [7] *Ibid.,* I, 195–96.
[8] *Ibid.,* I, 294–95.   [9] *Ibid.,* I, 341–42.
[10] W. Moeller, *History of the Christian Church,* II, 231.
[11] P. S. Troitskii, *Tserkov' i Gosudarstvo v Rossii,* p. 17.

dominated by caesaropapism. The patriarch did not attain equality with the emperor; as before, the latter was dominant. Even the greatest of the patriarchs, Photius and Cerularius, were deposed by the emperors. Alexis I deposed Cosmas in 1081, and three years later removed Eustratius. Under Manuel I (1143–80) there were ten patriarchs, of whom several were deposed by the emperor. Isaac II, who became emperor in 1185, set up five patriarchs in six years; of these the first three were deposed by Isaac. This ruler even went so far as to despoil the church of sacred objects; heavily jeweled chalices from the sanctuaries were used on his table, for he declared himself the equal of the apostles, and stated that in relation to him there was no difference between things profane and divine.[12] Indeed a chronicler of this period stated: "There does not exist on earth any difference between the power of God and that of the Emperors; they may use as their own the possessions of the Lord, for they have received their power from God." [13]

A Patriarch of Constantinople had more and more to limit himself to being merely the faithful servitor of the Emperor, and in some fashion the repository of a power which did not belong to him in reality. One can almost say that the Emperors had succeeded in uniting in their hands the two supreme powers—the civil and the religious power . . .

since the leaders of the church were merely the instruments of the emperors, and could not be named or hold office without their consent.[14]

This, then, was the church to which the Russians belonged—a church renowned for the splendor and the beauty of its rituals and adornments, but subject to the civil power. This church in more than full measure rendered unto Caesar.

Quite in keeping with this characteristic of the Orthodox Church was the manner of its introduction into Rus, for it was imposed on the people by the Prince Vladimir. After personally accepting the new faith in 987, he induced the heathen Kievans to submit to christening. Certainly not all of the pagans could be converted; but the old worship of Perun, god of the thunder, was made illegal and was driven

---

[12] L. Œconomos, *La Vie religieuse dans l'empire byzantin au temps des Comnènes et des Anges*, pp. 104–7, 118–24.

[13] Vasiliev, *op. cit.*, II, 121–22.   [14] Œconomos, *op. cit.*, p. 117.

underground. Some of the more obstinate of the heathen are believed to have been killed to quench the opposition to Christianity.[15]

Although Christianity was introduced into Rus by the action of Vladimir independently of the Byzantines, this independence of the Russian Church was very short-lived. Constantinople, known to the Russians as Tsargrad, so far overshadowed them in wealth, glory, prestige, and learning that it easily followed that the Russian Church became subject to the patriarch of Constantinople. The service books, the rules of canon law, and all the other elements of the newly adopted faith were imported from the Greeks, probably by way of their converts, the Bulgarians, so that when the prince felt the need for a head for his church he was ready to accept a Greek metropolitan appointed by the patriarch.

For more than two centuries after that the Greeks dominated the Russian Church; until the coming of the Mongols in the thirteenth century, the metropolitans of Rus were all Greeks, named and consecrated in Constantinople.[16] To be sure some of the bishops were Russians, even in fairly early times; but the Greek influence was very strong. Nor could the Russian princes do much to control the churchmen, for the constant wars among the princes kept their position so unstable that the metropolitan of Kiev was a tower of strength compared with most of them.[17] Consequently the Russian bishops and metropolitans were accustomed to look to Constantinople for guidance; like the churchmen in that city, they bowed before the Byzantine emperors as the elect of God. The name of the emperor was mentioned in the prayers said in the Russian churches. Even as late as 1389 Patriarch Antonius of Constantinople wrote to the Grand Prince Vasilii complaining of the Prince's lack of respect for him and for his master, the emperor. Said the patriarch:

With sorrow . . . have I heard that thou dost not permit the Metropolitan to mention in the liturgy the godly name of the Emperor, saying, forsooth, "We have the Church, but the Emperor we do not have, and do not wish to know." This is not well. The holy Emperor holds a high place in the Church. He is not like other rulers—the local princes and potentates. The Emperor in the beginning established and confirmed the

---

[15] Golubinskii, *op. cit.*, I (part 1), 163–75.
[16] *Ibid.*, pp. 272–74.   [17] *Ibid.*, pp. 548–51.

true faith for all the world. The Emperors called the Ecumenical Councils. They also confirmed by their laws the observance of what the godly and holy canons declare to be the true dogmas and the orthodoxy of Church life. . . . It is not possible for a Christian to have the Church and not the Emperor. For the Church and the Empire are in close union, . . . and it is not possible to separate the one from the other.[18]

In the century when the Western Church was headed by Innocent III, who claimed and exacted submission from kings and emperors, the Russian Church was imbued with the spirit of submission to the Greek emperor, to the leading civil ruler of the Orthodox world. Of course that principle as yet benefited the princes of Russia not a whit; but the time was to come when to them and not to Constantinople would be given the allegiance of the churchmen.

With the princes of Rus the metropolitans and bishops had great influence. Before the coming of the Mongol hordes the metropolitans could stand boldly forth, condemning the lawlessness and the bloodshed of the times, and pacifying the warring princes. "We were established in the Russian land by God, in order to restrain you from bloodshed," said Metropolitan Nikifor to the Prince of Kiev, Rurik, at the end of the twelfth century.[19] Bishops and metropolitans often acted as ambassadors and envoys between hostile factions, and their advice and arbitration were frequently accepted. When treaties were ratified the signers solemnized their pledges by "kissing the cross" of a prelate.[20] Moreover the clergy took little part in the incessant intrigues of the princes, but used their power to save the humble folk from suffering.[21]

The hierarchs had wide power in supervising the morals of the people. Their courts were given jurisdiction over cases concerning morals—those involving marriage, illegitimate children, sexual offenses, and the like, as well as crimes in general against women and children.[22] Thanks to these powers and to their moral sway over the people, the hierarchs were able to root out heathen practices such as polygamy and marriage by capture. Moreover the Orthodox monasteries in Russia had a certain educational influence; they were almost the sole abodes of learning, and few literate men could be found out-

[18] I. S. Berdnikov, *Kratkii Kurs Tserkovnago Prava*, p. 826.
[19] *Ibid.*, p. 828.   [20] Golubinskii, *op. cit.*, I (part 1), 548.
[21] *Ibid.*   [22] *Ibid.*, pp. 412–27.

side the church.[23] It is no accident that at least until the time of Peter the Great the name for a clerk, even in the civil government, was *diak,* or deacon.

The church's prestige was high in the land before the Mongol hordes overran it in the first half of the thirteenth century. After that calamity the church's influence was even more important, for with the collapse of the civil government the church remained the most vital cohesive force. Vast damage was undoubtedly done to the church's organization and property by the nomad hordes; but after the fighting was over the church was allowed to raise its head almost unmolested. As a matter of policy, the Mongol khans were decidedly benevolent toward Orthodoxy. Perhaps it was superstitious fear of all religions; perhaps it was political considerations which moved them; whatever the cause, they recognized the existing rights of the clergy— self-government of the church, freedom to practice and to propagate religion, the ownership of property, freedom from taxation, and judicial powers.[24] Moreover, when local Mongols troubled the church, the khans of the Golden Horde—the westernmost of the units into which the great Mongol Empire disintegrated—were usually ready to grant protective charters to the metropolitans. Said one such charter, from Mengu-Timur to Metropolitan Peter: "Let no one in Rus offend the Church of the Metropolitan and his people. . . . Peter the Metropolitan . . . alone judges and rules his people in all things. . . . Let all be obedient and submissive to the Metropolitan." [25]

In return the church coöperated with the Mongols. A special diocese was set up at Sarai, the capital of the Golden Horde, in 1261.[26] Metropolitan Feognost especially served the Mongols: when the prince of Tver killed the ambassadors of the Khan Uzbek-Shevkal and fled to Pskov for refuge, the metropolitan excommunicated the people of Pskov for their refusal to surrender the offending prince; [27] and on several occasions the churchmen saved the people from much suffering by inducing them to submit to the powerful Mongols, who would otherwise have devastated the land.

Although the temporal authority of the grand princes was very

[23] *Ibid.,* pp. 738–41.   [24] *Ibid.,* II (part 1), 17–40.
[25] Troitskii, *Tserkov' i Gosudarstvo v Rossii,* p. 30.
[26] Golubinskii, *op. cit.,* II (part 1), 60.   [27] *Ibid.,* p. 153.

low during the earlier part of the Mongol period and though the spiritual authority of the church remained strong, the metropolitans did not try to set themselves up as temporal overlords (as did the popes in the West after the break-up of the Carolingian Empire), but rather aided in the growth of temporal unity under the grand princes of Moscow, which developed as the Mongol power declined. Kiev had been abandoned about the middle of the twelfth century by the grand princes, who settled in Vladimir; before long the metropolitans did likewise. However, the Metropolitan Peter was constantly at odds with the grand prince, and instead of living in Vladimir the prelate resided most of the time in the second-rate city of Moscow, where he later was buried. Peter's successor, Feognost, likewise made Moscow his residence, and when the grave of Peter gained fame as the scene of miracles, which led to his canonization, "this . . . had an extraordinarily important political significance for Moscow." [28] The city gained greatly in prestige, and was embellished with a number of churches, so that it was made worthy of being the capital of the Russian land. In 1362 Ivan, Prince of Moscow, was made grand prince by the Mongols: in this triumph the ecclesiastical support of the city played a part.

Another supporter of Moscow was Metropolitan Aleksii, appointed in 1353 at the request of the reigning grand prince. This churchman was a veritable Richelieu—"a most zealous protector of the possessions and the authority of the Princes of Moscow against external enemies. . . ." In 1362, having won the favor of the Mongols, he succeeded in having Moscow proclaimed as the permanent seat of the grand princes. In like fashion the authority of the patriarch of Constantinople was invoked in behalf of the rising state. When the princes of Tver and Lithuania attacked Moscow, Metropolitan Aleksii excommunicated them and obtained from the patriarch a decree confirming the penalty and commanding all the lesser princes of Russia to obey their metropolitan. Moreover in 1361 Lithuania was made subject in religious matters to the metropolitan of Moscow[29] —a severe loss of prestige for a dangerous enemy of the Muscovites. Unfortunately this was only a temporary victory; but it indicates that, thanks to the efforts of this churchman, as well as for other

[28] Golubinskii, *op. cit.*, II (part 1), pp. 137–51.   [29] *Ibid.*, pp. 175–206.

reasons of weight, Moscow was coming to be recognized as first in the land.

A further important consequence of the coming of the Mongols was that the Russian Church was becoming more and more independent of the Greeks. After the onslaught of the nomads in 1240, in which the metropolitan of Kiev was killed or driven into exile (it cannot be determined which), the Russians were for a time without the services of a Greek as head of their church. Consequently Russians were chosen locally by the grand princes, with the help of the Russian bishops, and later were sent to the patriarch of Constantinople for his confirmation, so that for some time no Greek metropolitans came to Russia.[30] To be sure several Greek metropolitans came later; none the less the Russians were feeling surer and surer of themselves. Constantinople, beset by Latins and by the Turks, was obviously declining, while Moscow was in the ascendant; this fact had its influence on matters spiritual. Likewise the Russians were coming to feel that the Greeks were no longer pure in faith and in morals. In the latter part of the fourteenth century the grand prince felt that he had been tricked by the highest spiritual authorities in connection with the consecration of a Russian metropolitan, so that he and his successors lost faith in the righteousness of the Greeks. Moreover, when the Greek metropolitan Isidor of Moscow returned from the Council of Florence in 1439 and proclaimed the union with Rome, the grand prince had him imprisoned for heresy, and only his timely escape saved him from death. The Russians thereupon installed as metropolitan a Russian bishop, Iona by name,[31] who did not even go to Constantinople for confirmation by the patriarch. From that time on many of the Russians were convinced that the Greeks were morally bankrupt and that only the Russians were truly Orthodox. The fall of Constantinople in 1453 at the hands of the "unclean Turks" only confirmed their suspicions of a moral blight upon the Greek world.

Furthermore the position of the grand princes of Moscow was becoming increasingly strong. They were gradually bringing under their

[30] *Ibid.*, pp. 50–54.
[31] N. F. Kapterev, *Kharakter Otnoshenii Rossii k Pravoslavnomu Vostoku v XVI i XVII Stoletiiakh*, pp. 5–6; Golubinskii, *op. cit.*, II (part 1), 454–88.

sway all of the lesser princes of the Russian land, and even the great trading city of Novgorod had finally to submit to their rule. In addition the authority of the grand princes was being extended over the vacant lands of the north and east by the migration of settlers, in which pioneering the hermits and the monasteries of the Orthodox Church played no small part. Moreoever in the fifteenth century the grand princes felt strong enough to challenge the overlordship of the Mongols, and to proclaim themselves the sole masters in their own land. The relations between the Russian Church and the state of Muscovy reflected the new order of things. The grand princes now assumed the position formerly held by the Eastern emperors—that of protectors and guides of the church. After the naming of Iona (and in some cases, even before) the bishops and metropolitans were Russians appointed directly by the grand princes, or, *pro forma*, by the church councils called by them; no longer were the metropolitans of Moscow chosen in Constantinople. Unwelcome candidates named by the councils not infrequently were rejected by the princes. Thus the councils did not really elect the prelates; they met to give formal approval to the choices made by the civil rulers and to consecrate the men named by the latter.[32]

It cannot be said that the men of the church struggled very hard against the authority of the grand princes; in many cases the ecclesiastics even asked the intervention of the civil power. When Novgorod refused to submit to the wishes of Metropolitan Kiprian, of Moscow, the grand prince intervened, and not in vain. After threats had proved unavailing, troops were sent, and the people of Novgorod were soon induced to make peace with the metropolitan.[33] In 1490, when the Judaist heresy developed in Novgorod, Bishop Genadii insisted on rigorous action by the government and repeatedly urged the grand prince to follow the example of the Spanish rulers by cleansing the land with fire and sword.[34] And although Vasilii, father of Ivan the Terrible, met with strong opposition from many churchmen when he proposed to take the lands of the monasteries—his supporters Vassian and Maxim the Greek aroused such strong antagonism (voiced by Joseph of Volokolamsk) that the matter had to be dropped—still

[32] Berdnikov, *op. cit.*, pp. 845–49.
[33] Golubinskii, *op. cit.*, II (part 1), 314–17.   [34] *Ibid.*, pp. 560–82.

Vasilii had little further difficulty in keeping the churchmen in submission. When Archbishop Serapion incurred his displeasure, Vasilii had him deposed, excommunicated, and sent to a monastery, where he died.[35] This example served to frighten the rest, and there was little further trouble with the bishops. During the sixteenth century only Metropolitan Varlaam challenged the authority of the grand prince, and he was deposed, exiled, and replaced by Metropolitan Daniil in 1522; Daniil was as submissive as the grand prince might wish.[36]

After 1440 the Russian Church was independent of Constantinople in all but name. Theoretically it still remained one of the metropolitanates of the Greek Church; actually it was autocephalous. The higher clergy were enthroned at the behest of the grand princes, and no longer was it thought necessary to have the metropolitans consecrated at Constantinople. Indeed Moscow, rather than the fallen capital on the Bosphorus, now was looked upon by Russians as the holy city of God. After Muscovy threw off the Mongol yoke, late in the fifteenth century, the metropolitan of Moscow, Zosima, spoke of Ivan III as "the child of God, shining in Orthodoxy, the truly-believing and Christ-loving Grand Prince Ivan Vasilevich, Sovereign and Autocrat of all Rus, the new Emperor Constantine over Constantine's new city, Moscow, and over all the Russian land." [37] The fall of Constantinople in 1453 and the subjection of the Eastern patriarchs to the Ottoman sultans greatly lowered the prestige of these prelates in the eyes of the Russians, while Ivan III's marriage with Sophia, niece of the last emperor of Byzantium, added to the glory of Moscow. A certain monk, Filofei by name, writing at the end of the fifteenth century, proclaimed that the first and the second Romes (the latter being Constantinople) for their heresies had fallen to the barbarians, and that their place as capital of the Christian world was now filled by Moscow: ". . . for two Romes fell, and the third stands, and a fourth there will not be. . . ." [38] This theory so inspired the Russians that from then on they looked on Moscow rather than Constantinople as the true abode of Orthodoxy. Even as early as the

---

[35] *Ibid.*, pp. 627–43.   [36] *Ibid.*, pp. 697–99.

[37] P. V. Verkhovskoi, *Uchrezhdenie Dukhovnoi Kollegii i Dukhovnyi Reglament*, I, 16.

[38] Kapterev, *op. cit.*, p. 15.

reign of Vasilii the Dark, who became grand prince in 1425, the Russian scribes began to proclaim the grand prince as "the God-sent bringer of truth"; Ivan the Terrible was hailed as "the unshakable pillar," "the immovable foundation of the Christian Church," "the holder of the reins of the holy Church of God, which is the throne of all bishops and priests, the sage helmsman of the ship of this world." [39] It is interesting, however, to note that when in 1547 Ivan IV took the title of Tsar, previously applied by the Russians to the Byzantine emperors and the Mongol grand khans but not regularly used by the Russian rulers, he valued the prestige of the patriarch of Constantinople sufficiently to send an abbot to that city to ask the patriarch to call a council to approve his new title. This approval the patriarch and his council gave; but when the patriarch tried to establish the rule that in future all the Tsars must be approved by the patriarchs of Constantinople, this pretension was disregarded by the Muscovites, who, after the initial consent had been secured, no longer felt the need for the sanction of the Greek churchmen. [40]

It is not strange that the Tsars, with their consciousness of power and prestige as successors to the Byzantine emperors as protectors of the Orthodox Church, should feel that theirs was the duty of supporting and guiding the church. Whereas Ivan III had been reluctant to interfere with church matters, his grandson, Ivan IV, known as Ivan the Terrible, was not slow to assert himself. When in 1551, at the advice of Metropolitan Makarii, he summoned the great council of the Russian Church which came to be known as the *Stoglav Sobor,* he told the assembled clerics that he was the guardian of the purity of the church and of Orthodoxy. And as this was the generally accepted view of both clergy and laymen, he heard no dissent. [41] At this council the Tsar made the opening address, in which he indicated the evils within the church. Moreover the hundred questions submitted to the council (from which the name *Stoglav* was derived), which specified the problems to be dealt with, came ostensibly from the Tsar, although actually Makarii had drawn up the list. Thanks to the efforts of Tsar and metropolitan, this council instituted some needed reforms

[39] M. Reisner, *Dukhovnaia Politsiia v Rossii,* pp. 10–13.
[40] Kapterev, *op. cit.,* pp. 27–30.
[41] Verkhovskoi, *op. cit.,* I, 23–26.

in the church; but, sad to relate, almost immediately after the death of Makarii all its good work was undone and forgotten.[42]

Under the influence of this metropolitan, Ivan manifested all reverence and esteem for the church, but in the interest of morality intervened unchallenged in its affairs. However, when Ivan the Terrible, like his father and grandfather before him, tried to deal with the great and increasing landholding of the monasteries, he met with so much latent opposition that he did not venture to do more than forbid further bequests or sales of land to the monasteries without the imperial consent.[43] But the church retained what it had. This problem remained, to receive final solution only in the eighteenth century.

In the early years of his reign, under the influence of his first wife, Afanasia, and of Metropolitan Makarii, Ivan IV did not abuse his power. However, when these two had died the Tsar soon began to earn his sobriquet "the Terrible." He surrounded himself with ruthless men, and no man of God could restrain him. In fact Ivan himself made and unmade metropolitans freely, and churchmen as well as many laymen must have breathed sighs of relief when he was succeeded by his young son, Feodor. Unfortunately the latter's reign was a period of disorder and decline, until Boris Godunov rose to power under the Tsar. It was in this latter period of Feodor's reign that the Russian Church became fully independent of Constantinople, thanks to the naming of a Russian patriarch.

Characteristically the establishment of the patriarchate was brought about by the Tsar and Boris Godunov, rather than by the church. The Tsar decided upon it and, after taking counsel with the great of the land (the *Boiars'* Duma), began negotiations with the Eastern patriarchs. Only after patriarchal approval in principle had been received from Ieremei of Constantinople was a Russian church council summoned to ratify this significant step.[44] It proved somewhat difficult to obtain the active coöperation of the Greeks in this matter. Fortunately Patriarch Ieremei came to Russia in 1589 to receive benefactions and was induced to meet with the Russian bishops to name three candidates for the patriarchate and to sign a manifesto

[42] Golubinskii, *op. cit.*, II (part 1), 773–95.

[43] *Ibid.*, pp. 796–98.   [44] Berdnikov, *op. cit.*, pp. 853–54.

naming Moscow as "the Third Rome." From the three Tsar Feodor picked Iov, who became the first of the Russian patriarchs.[45]

It cannot be said, however, that the church always flourished during the century and more of the patriarchate. At first Patriarch Iov was influential in the state. He it was who urged Boris Godunov to mount the throne after Feodor's death. But so noted a supporter of the new Tsar was he that when the people of Moscow rose against Godunov, in behalf of the pretender Dmitrii, they fell on Iov, dragging him from the church, and after beating him plundered his mansion, shouting, "Rich, rich is Iov the Patriarch; let us . . . despoil him."[46] Nor did his early successors fare much better. During the Time of Troubles, the period of civil war and foreign invasion lasting from 1604 to 1613, patriarchs were made and broken by the various claimants to the throne. Russia was invaded by Catholic Poles, who tried to convert the Russians to loyalty to the pope; when the Orthodox clergy opposed them, the invaders turned upon the hostile hierarchs. After some years of turmoil the Russian Church played a part in the rallying of the forces of the land once more to establish an Orthodox Tsar and the Orthodox faith in a firm position.

When the new Tsar, Mikhail Romanov, was finally joined in Moscow by his father, Patriarch Filaret, long a prisoner in Poland, the Russian Church was in a sorry state indeed. Education and morality had sunk to such low levels that it was felt by some that the recent calamities were a merited punishment from God. Monasteries and churches had been plundered, their lands laid waste, and their superiors in many cases carried into captivity. Moreover the distressed government had burdened many of the monasteries with levies of money and likewise with the full support of many fighting men. Then too the civil and criminal jurisdiction over the clergy was no longer in the hands of the bishops; during the Time of Troubles it had been transferred to the Monastery Office (*Prikaz*), a department of the civil administration. But Filaret, a strong character, became practically co-ruler with his son; together they received ambassadors and performed other important acts of state; together they set about

---

[45] Makarii (Metropolitan), *Istoriia Russkoi Tserkvi*, X, 7–35; Kapterev, *op. cit.*, pp. 38–51.

[46] Makarii, *op. cit.*, X, 85–93.

the difficult work of restoring church and state to their former strength and well-being.[47]

Except for Patriarch Filaret, the first patriarchs after the Time of Troubles were not powerful figures. They were generally submissive to the Tsars and contented themselves with administering the church to the satisfaction of the temporal rulers. Patriarch Ioasaf, successor to Filaret, was indeed consulted about important matters of state, but Ioasaf declared that his duty was to pray for the Tsar, not to advise him, for the Tsar was autocrat over all.[48]

In 1652 Nikon, archbishop of Novgorod, was made patriarch. He was a man of strong character and enjoyed the favor of Tsar Aleksei. Perhaps because he foresaw a struggle with the Tsar over power, Nikon many times refused to take the patriarchal office and accepted it only after Aleksei and all the notables had taken a solemn oath that Nikon was to be head of the church and that they would uphold him and defer to him in the interpretation of all matters of dogma and the rules of the apostles and the church fathers.[49]

Armed with this pledge, Nikon was in a position to make a stand against the civil power; but before doing this he dealt with another matter close to his heart. The Russian service books, originally translated from Greek texts, had during the centuries become filled with mistakes which had become sanctified by usage. Moreover in some points of the ritual the Russians differed from the Greeks—the use of two instead of three fingers in making the sign of the cross, the twofold rather than the threefold alleluia in the liturgy, the spelling of the Savior's name *Isus* in place of *Iisus*, and the direction of the movement of processions around the church. The two-fingered crossing and the twofold alleluia had been sanctioned, and the usages of the Greeks condemned, by the *Stoglav* Council in 1551, so that when Nikon, with the support of the Council of 1655, attempted to establish the three-fingered crossing and the threefold alleluia, he was offering, in place of what was established and accepted, certain changes based upon the books of the Greeks, who for a very long time had not been highly respected in Russia. To make matters worse, Nikon's strongest supporters in the revising of the service

[47] *Ibid.*, X, 229–31; XI, 67–71.   [48] *Ibid.*, XI, 92–94.
[49] *Ibid.*, XII, 1–7.

books were the Ukrainian scholars from Kiev, whom the Muscovites suspected of close relations with the Polish Catholics. Furthermore a tradition of holiness had been woven around the time-hallowed practices, and some feared that the proposed changes marked a first weakening of the faith which would precede the coming of Antichrist.[50] Hence the resulting reaction was strong.

Probably economic distress played a part in the popular opposition that followed. The peasants were falling more and more into the power of the heavy-handed lords and like the merchants they were burdened with taxes. Bad harvests and plagues added to the distress. To many of the ignorant humble folk the changing of the service books meant that the Tsar and the patriarch, who were in league with their oppressors, had forgotten the true faith. Those who dared to oppose the reforms were largely from the lower ranks of society— peasants, common soldiers, village priests, monks (notably in the Solovetskii Monastery in the far north), and those picturesque outlaws of the frontier, the Cossacks, as well as a number of burghers.[51] Certain it is that in spite of the severity of the measures against them and in spite of the fact that they recognized the basic doctrines of the Orthodox Church, the Old Believers—those who clung to the old ways—were determined in their opposition to what they regarded as the innovations of Nikon.

Nikon moved quickly to crush the opposition shown by some of the clergy by exiling the leaders to distant monasteries. In this he had the full support of the Tsar; indeed during the first years of Nikon's patriarchate the relations between these two were of the best. The control which the civil government exercised through the Monastery Office, so disliked by the men of the church, was not extended to the patriarchal domains, which were greatly enlarged by gifts from the Tsar.[52] Furthermore the patriarch assumed a great place in the state. He was given the title of "Great Lord," which since the time of Filaret only the Tsar had borne. He dined often at the Tsar's table,

[50] V. O. Kliuchevskii, *Kurs Russkoi Istorii*, III, 367–68; 399–400; Kapterev, *Patriarkh Nikon i Tsar' Aleksei Mikhailovich*, I, 447.

[51] N. M. Nikol'skii, "Raskol v Pervoi Polovine XIX Veka," *Istoriia Rossii v XIX Veke*, IV, 44–45.

[52] Makarii, *op. cit.*, XII, 266–68.

and not infrequently entertained the latter at his own board. When Aleksei was at the front fighting the Poles, the patriarch acted almost as emperor, issuing decrees to all and sundry, summoning the Tsar's ministers, and receiving *boiars* (nobles) and military men, who were careful to be properly humble before him. Truly Nikon was so haughty and arrogant, even to the highest in the land, that *"boiars and men of rank did not fear the Tsar as much as they feared the Patriarch, and in several instances they feared the latter vastly more."* [53]

This high position, far above that of any of the patriarchs since Filaret, did not last. After the Tsar Aleksei returned from the wars it was not long before Nikon quarreled with him, and, when the Tsar showed signs of coldness to the patriarch, the latter publicly renounced his office and putting on a simple cassock retired to one of his monasteries. He did not, however, admit that the patriarchal office was vacant, and stubbornly refused to resign and allow another patriarch to be chosen. Apparently Nikon hoped that this step would lead the Tsar to beseech him to return to his former high estate, but if so he was disappointed. Aleksei showed no readiness to humble himself, and during the ensuing years Nikon grew more and more hostile to the emperor. The patriarch's claims in the dispute were never clearly defined, for at different times he gave different reasons for his actions. However, important incidents in the quarrel had been the beating of one of Nikon's supporters by an underling of the Tsar in 1658 and the failure of the emperor to come to church when Nikon invited him—which latter fact seems to show that the struggle was designed to establish the prestige of the patriarch in the face of the powerful Tsar. Later Nikon declared that he had acted as he did because the Tsar took away the church's jurisdiction over the clergy and judged them himself; again he said that it was because the Tsar, who had promised to hear and to defer to him (Nikon), began to turn away and to act according to other advice.[54] Moreover Nikon's rage when Aleksei adjudicated a boundary dispute between Nikon's Voskresenskii Monastery and a neighbor points to a fear of state encroachments on the great landed wealth of the church.[55] But whatever the reason

[53] *Ibid.*, XII, 230–40.   [54] Kapterev, *Patriarkh Nikon*, I, 398–403.
[55] Makarii, *op. cit.*, XII, 368–75.

for the dispute, the famous prelate was defeated. The Tsar never took him back into favor, and when the patriarch publicly read a curse against his enemies, which men interpreted as directed against the Tsar, the latter took steps to depose him.[56] A council of the Russian Church, called in 1665, urged the election of a new patriarch who would discipline Nikon.[57] Finally the thorny problem was settled by a council held in Moscow in 1666–67, attended by the patriarchs of Antioch and Alexandria and the legates of those of Constantinople and Jerusalem, as well as by Russian clergy, at which time Nikon was solemnly deposed and a new patriarch named by the council and the Tsar. [58]

This was a great victory for the civil power as represented by the Tsar Aleksei. However he was not to have a one-sided triumph, for while the patriarchs supported him fully, many of the Russian bishops were not so disposed. When it came to signing the conciliar decree drawn up by the patriarchs confirming the full power of the Tsar over the church, the Russians demurred. The opponents of Aleksei's autocracy cited a passage from one of the church fathers, referring to "the priesthood, which surpasses all other walks of life as the soul surpasses the body." Several of the Russian bishops dared to dispute with the foreign patriarchs on this point, and almost all of the Russian churchmen seemed to be hostile to recognition of the power of the emperor over the church.[59] The Russian clergy were quite willing to have Nikon humbled, for he had been highhanded in his dealings with many of them. His disciplinary measures had often been harsh and he had taken land and monasteries away from several of the dioceses to add to the patriarchal holdings. However the prelates had no desire to see the power of Nikon replaced by civil authority. Only after the Greek patriarchs had threatened them with anathema did the Russian bishops accept a formula saying that while the Tsar was supreme in the state, the patriarch was supreme in the church. This arrangement was not clearly defined; only in one particular was the dividing line plainly marked. The Tsar agreed to restore to the church jurisdiction over the clergy, which had previously been exercised by the Monastery Office, an institution of the government; how-

[56] Makarii, *op. cit.*, XII, 448–69.   [57] *Ibid.*, XII, 505–13.
[58] *Ibid.*, XII, 683–765.   [59] Kapterev, *Patriarkh Nikon*, II, 229–45.

ever, this office was not abolished and until 1675 it retained control over the lands of the church.[60]

This conflict between the Greek patriarchs and the Russian bishops, after Nikon's fate had been decided, was fundamentally a conflict between the tradition of the parent Byzantine Church and an attitude of suspicion toward the intentions of the civil power, which had occasionally appeared in the Russian Church during the Muscovite period. For the most part the prelates of the Russian Church had been loyal supporters of the power of the civil rulers; but when Vasilii III and Ivan IV had attempted to limit or to lay hands on the lands of the church they found that the churchmen were no longer meek. This was also true in the reign of Aleksei; if the Russian bishops were unwilling to go as far as Nikon went in attacking the temporal power, his aggressiveness perhaps helped to stimulate in them an unusual vigor of spirit. They were willing to support the Tsar against Nikon and to accept the revision of the service books as the Tsar desired; but when the latter tried to retain his control over the lands of the church and his judicial powers over the clergy, the churchmen showed a rebellious spirit. Thus the attitude of the Russian clergy toward the state was not at the moment as subservient as that held by most of the earlier Russian churchmen, who for the most part had been truer to the Byzantine tradition.

This was the outcome of Nikon's conflict with Aleksei. But while the Council of 1667 condemned Nikon for quarreling with the Tsar, it did not condemn the revision of the service books, but on the contrary approved it. It also approved the threefold alleluia, *Iisus* as the spelling of the Savior's name, and the rule that processions were to go around the church against the sun and not with it. Furthermore the council solemnly pronounced anathema upon all of the Old Believers who clung to the rejected forms and urged the civil government to deal with them.[61] Indeed it was high time. During the years when Nikon had been sulking in his tent, the Old Believers had had a chance to carry on their propaganda with little fear of punishment and had grown greatly in numbers. Nor could they be easily converted to the official church. When the Tsar took measures to im-

[60] *Ibid.*, II, 250; Berdnikov, *op. cit.*, 861–63.
[61] Makarii, *op. cit.*, XII, 770–77.

prison the leaders of the schismatics, this had little effect upon the mass of their followers.[62]

In view of the stubbornness of the Old Believers and their zeal in denouncing the Orthodox Church and its clergy, another council of the Russian clergy was summoned at Moscow in 1681. The Tsar was urged by this council to use stern measures with the schismatics, as milder forms of punishment had proved ineffectual.[63] Consequently troops were sent against the schismatics, and it went hard with those who were caught. In 1685 the Tsarevna Sofia issued an *ukaz* ordering still more drastic measures. Stubborn enemies of the church were to be burned after having been subjected to threefold tortures, while those who accepted the Orthodox faith under compulsion were to be imprisoned in monasteries under guard.[64] Thus with the prompting of the church the state dealt with the erring sons of Orthodoxy. Many fled, others were executed, while numbers of the schismatics burned themselves alive rather than be taken by the government. But while the church was successful in bringing great force to bear against its enemies, it could not but be affected by the loss of these sincere and devout Christians. The church was weakened, and by its appeals to the state for aid it surrendered the possibility of resisting the encroachments of the civil power.

These new encroachments did not begin at once after Nikon's fall; Aleksei did nothing to arouse the hostility of the clergy. However the patriarchs who succeeded Nikon could do little to widen their powers, although they strove to win concessions from the state.[65] Moreover as new ideas seeped into Russia from the West, especially in the reigns of Aleksei and Peter, there was a tendency among laymen to consider religious matters less important than secular interests. The churchmen, however, were thoroughly steeped in the ideas of the Nikonian period and for the most part opposed the trend toward intensive secular control, in spite of the earlier Byzantine tradition of submissiveness to the civil ruler. Hence the hand of the reforming Tsar Peter fell heavily upon the church. However, when Peter assumed the power he did not at once interfere with the church. In fact throughout the life of Patriarch Adrian the Tsar refrained from

[62] Makarii, *op. cit.*, XII, 592–610.
[63] Berdnikov, *op. cit.*, 1005–6.
[64] *Ibid.*, p. 1006.
[65] Verkhovskoi, *op. cit.*, I, 104–5.

drastic measures, in spite of the fact that the patriarch was definitely opposed to the new tendency. Even Adrian's first message to the faithful, in which he claimed that he was above the Tsar's authority, did not spur Peter to action. Nor did the hostility of many of the clergy at the time of the revolt of the *Streltsy*, nor their connection with the plot of Peter's son, Aleksei, lead to decisive steps on the part of the energetic Tsar.[66] Peter bided his time.

When Patriarch Adrian died in 1700 Peter was in the midst of a campaign against the Swedes and could devote little time to the church, although several of his German and Russian advisers urged him to set up a collective form of control over its affairs. Instead he temporized: Metropolitan Stefan Iavorskii was installed as exarch over the spiritual affairs of the church, while the Monastery Office was to administer its lands.[67] However, as time went on there were many infringements of what the clergy regarded as their interests. The Monastery Office not only controlled the lands of the monasteries but also diverted some of their funds for purposes of state—a change unwelcome to many churchmen. In a variety of other ways Peter antagonized the churchmen: by extending limited toleration to Old Believers, by attempting to reform the discipline of the clergy, by issuing edicts against abuses by the bishops, and the like.[68] In addition, Stefan Iavorskii, who had viewed his position as exarch as a stepping-stone to the patriarchate, found that the years were passing without bringing the realization of this hope any nearer; hence he began to show hostility to Peter in small ways, although he did not dare to make an open protest. This seems to have had the effect of making Peter lose patience with the clergy as a group, for he decided to institute a "Religious College" to administer the church, instead of having a patriarch named.[69]

This Religious College, which almost immediately was given the title of "the Most Holy Synod," was established in 1721 "by an *ukaz* of the Monarch according to the decision of the Senate." Although the Synod was made up of bishops, abbots, and other clergy, these were appointed and removable by the Tsar, so that the Synod was not a representative body. Indeed it was patterned after the state-

[66] *Ibid.*, I, 104–8.   [67] *Ibid.*, I, 112.
[68] *Ibid.*, I, 112–13.   [69] *Ibid.*, I, 113–15.

controlled synods of the Lutheran Church in Sweden and Prussia.[70] And to exercise due restraint upon this new body, Peter told the Senate to find for him a good man among the army officers "who will have boldness and will know the administration of the Synod and can be Over Procurator." [71]

The decree of the "all-powerful Monarch" gave nine reasons for creating the Synod. Among them were the supposed impartiality of a Synod, its collective wisdom, due to the interplay of several minds, the permanence of its corporate membership, and so on. The real reason, however, was the seventh, which stated that the existence of a patriarch might cause disaffection among the people, as there might conceivably develop a conflict between the civil and the spiritual authorities.[72] Here was the heart of the matter; the Tsar did not want another Nikon. To ensure that the members of the Synod should not be opposed to the interests of state, they were required to swear, "I recognize and confirm with my oath that the supreme judge of this Holy Synod is the Emperor of all the Russias." Likewise they were made to promise that they "would in all matters attempt to further everything which may bring true benefit and service to His Imperial Highness." This oath, which was used regularly until its repeal in 1901,[73] did much to make the Synod an organ of the civil government.

Through the Synod Peter's hand was laid upon the whole church, for in his *Religious Regulation* creating the new body it was granted wide powers: over the dogmatic correctness and the ritual of the church, over its education, over the diocesan administration, over church property, and over the discipline of the monastics and of the parish clergy. Many of the regulations for the governance of the church were such as would be acceptable to anyone who wished it well, for many of Peter's rules were intended to promote education, morality, and benevolent works. There were also provisions that the clergy were to keep the records of vital statistics and that if they found schismatic teachers, monks, "holy men," or the like within their parishes, the priests were to have them seized and sent to the diocesan

[70] Verkhovskoi, *op. cit.*, I, 270–73.

[71] Troitskii, *Tserkov' i Gosudarstvo v Rossii*, p. 46.

[72] Verkhovskoi, *op. cit.*, I, 361–65.

[73] Troitskii, *op. cit.*, p. 46; Verkhovskoi, *op. cit.*, II, 10–11.

authorities. The government's view of the church was most clearly shown by the rule that priests were to inform against persons confessing to them who had had, and had not repented of, evil intent against the state or the sovereign: "And the sanctity of the confessional is not infringed by this disclosure, for the admission of an intended lawlessness which the confessing person is not ready to renounce and does not include in his sins is not a confession or a part of a confession, but a cunning trick to seduce the conscience." Indeed the pastors were required to report not only specific evil intent among their flocks but also general disaffection in the popular mind.[74]

Such was the nature of Peter's great religious measure; thanks to its provisions, the church was now more definitely subordinate to the state than before. The members of the Synod, however, were not entirely satisfied with their position, and at the first meeting they asked Peter that they be granted full power over the church, such as they stated the patriarchs had had; for they claimed that they were actually a church council. This claim Peter did not allow; in the matter of filling each vacant diocese, the Synod was permitted merely to name two (later three) candidates, from whom the Tsar chose the future bishop. To be sure Peter later did grant wider powers to the Synod than those in his original *Regulation*—control of the church lands was given to the Synod in 1724, with the abolition of the Monastery Office, and jurisdiction over religious offenses and over church peasants was placed in their hands—but none the less the Synod continued to be subordinate to the Tsar.[75] In fact after its original protest the Synod did not try to gain power nor to defy the Tsar as Nikon had done in the days of Aleksei, but supported him eagerly and boasted of its loyalty.[76]

While Peter's reform met with little opposition from the hierarchy, it was distasteful to many of the humble folk. To such people the evident subjection of the church to the state and the abolition of the patriarchate seemed proof of what the Old Believers had proclaimed, namely, that Antichrist, the Beast of the Apocalypse, was among them.

[74] Verkhovskoĭ, *op. cit.*, I, 468–86.
[75] *Ibid.*, I, 535–45.
[76] *Ibid.*, I, 572–73.

It is not surprising that the thought that Peter was Antichrist was spread, in different versions, by the priest who was deprived of his bee-hive [by the tax-collector] and of whom taxes unheard of before were demanded, and by the wandering "holy man" whom the police caught, and by the peasant who found himself unable to bear the burden of the new tax, and by the *boiar's* son, bored with his new service duties, and by the widow of the *strelets* [musketeer] who had been broken on the wheel, and by the needy man who was not permitted to ask for alms —by all whom the new system overburdened. . . . They accused the Tsar in the squares, in the streets, and in the churches.[77]

Peter was not the man to overlook such opposition and toward the end of his reign his earlier tolerant attitude changed. He made the Old Believers pay a double tax, their form of worship was not per-mitted, and in other ways they were persecuted; those who proved stubborn opponents of the government were subjected to torture, penal labor, or execution. The number of schismatics continued to grow, however, and although Peter's successors from time to time sent troops into their wilderness refuges and although numbers of them burned themselves alive rather than be caught, their doggedness survived temporary setbacks. Finally with the accession of Peter III in 1762 a more tolerant attitude toward them was adopted.[78]

The death of Peter the Great had little effect in changing the situa-tion of the church. It remained subordinate to the civil power, for although most of Peter's earlier successors were weak, the oligarchic government of this period did not hesitate to interfere with the Synod and to keep it under control.[79] This domination of the Synod was not exercised through the Over Procurator; this official, who was to be an "eye of the Tsar," had no definite rights and powers over the Synod. If he disapproved of the Synod's actions he could only pro-test to the sovereign; and the effectiveness of the protest was often nullified by the right of the bishops to present their own side of the case at court. The other lay officials of the Synod were subject to the clerical members, not to the Over Procurator; likewise the church-men could bring the Over Procurator to heel by withholding his salary.[80] Much depended on the clique in power at court. In the hands

---

[77] Verkhovskoi, *op. cit.*, I, Introduction, p. xvii.

[78] Berdnikov, *op. cit.*, pp. 1007–23.   [79] Verkhovskoi, *op. cit.*, I, 574–86.

[80] N. S. Suvorov, *Uchebnik Tserkovnago Prava*, p. 108.

of the members of the camarilla, rather than in those of the Over
Procurator, lay the power to control the Synod. When Elizabeth became empress in 1741 the Synod hoped to escape from such domination and petitioned the Tsaritsa for a less binding oath and for removal of the civil control over them, but to no avail. The sway of
the court was not relaxed.[81]

When Catherine II became empress in 1762, thanks to the clique
of guardsmen who conveniently deposed and killed her husband,
Peter III, she was welcomed by Metropolitan Sechenov, who said in
his address: "God hath placed the crown on Thy head. He knoweth
how to save the righteous from destruction; he hath seen before
Him Thy pure heart; He hath known Thy sinless ways"—and more
in the same vein.[82] Catherine had won the favor of the ecclesiastics by the enthusiasm which she displayed for her adopted faith.
She was highly respectful to the clergy, fasted regularly, took communion once a year, listened attentively to sermons, and was liberal
with rewards to churchmen.[83] On the other hand she finally solved in
the interest of the state the problem of the landed wealth of the church,
which had troubled the rulers of Russia at least since the days of
Ivan III. Vast areas with their serf populations were taken over by
the state—in all, 991,761 "souls" (males) and approximately the
same number of females, or 13.8 percent of all the peasants of Great
Russia and Siberia.[84] Thus in spite of the small lands left to the
individual monasteries and the larger amount of comparatively worth-
less land in the north retained by the church, it ceased to be a great
landholding institution. This secularization, which was primarily intended to place great resources at the disposal of the state, had also
the indirect effect of making the church even more dependent upon
the state than before.[85] The lands left in the possession of the churches
and monasteries were so unproductive that the monasteries and the
bishops were largely dependent upon the small incomes paid them
from the treasury in compensation for their lost land.

[81] Troitskii, *op. cit.*, p. 54.
[82] S. M. Solov'ev, *Istoriia Rossii s Drevneishikh Vremen*, XXV, 1371.
[83] P. V. Znamenskii, *Rukovodstvo k Russkoi Tserkovnoi Istorii*, p. 403.
[84] D. A. Zharinov, "Krest'iane Tserkovnykh Votchin," in *Velikaia Reforma*,
A. K. Dzhivelegov, *et al.*, editors, I, 147.
[85] Verkhovskoi, *op. cit.*, I, 619.

In dealing with the Old Believers, Catherine broke sharply with the recent past. Although she was pledged to defend Orthodoxy, she, like Peter III, was tolerant in matters of faith, and consequently the Old Believers gradually were freed from active persecution. The laws imposing civil disabilities were repealed and eventually the term *raskol'nik* (schismatic) was dropped from official usage (although it came into use again under Nicholas I). Moreover in Moscow the Old Believers were given two cemeteries—the Rogozhskoe, which was turned into a religious center, with monks, churches, and other buildings of the Old Believers who had their own clergy; and the Preobrazhenskoe Cemetery, which became the gathering place for the "priestless" variety of schismatics.[86] Thanks in part to these mercies vouchsafed by Catherine, the Old Believers flourished, as indeed they did under her successors, Paul and Alexander I.

Although the authorities were thus displaying tolerance toward the church's foes, the Old Believers, those in high places still prized the support of the church, and its anathema continued to be used against enemies of the state. In the seventeenth century Otrep'ev, Akimdov, Stenka Razin, and Mazeppa had been so singled out, and even though the ritual was revised and shortened in 1766, once a year until 1869 the following curse was proclaimed in all Orthodox churches:

> To those who do not believe that the Orthodox monarchs have been raised to the throne by virtue of a special grace of God—and that, at the moment the sacred oil is laid on them, the gifts of the Holy Ghost are infused into them anent the accomplishment of their exalted mission; and to those who dare to rise and rebel against them, such as Grishka Otrep'ev, Ian Mazeppa, and others like them: Anathema! Anathema! Anathema! [87]

Moreover, from 1718 on, the parish church was the official place for the publication of laws and decrees. The clergy supported the state by sermons on state occasions, by their interpretation of the Scriptures, and by their defense of the existing order.[88] Thus the connection between church and state was still firm and strong.

[86] Berdnikov, *op. cit.*, pp. 1024–28.

[87] *Ibid.*, p. 260; A. Leroy-Beaulieu, *The Empire of the Tsars and the Russians*, III, 49, footnote.

[88] Verkhovskoi, *op. cit.*, I, 642–59.

In fact in the nineteenth century the civil control of the church became stronger and even more thorough than before. In 1817 Alexander I created a new ministry, that of Religious Affairs and of Public Education. The Synod, as well as the administration of the non-Orthodox faiths, was under this ministry, and from that time on any shred of independence which the Synod had was gone. The control of this ministry over the Synod lasted only until 1824; but when the ministry was abolished the Over Procurator, formerly an official of little power, was raised to the status of minister, with the Synodal organs as the ministry over which he exercised control. He was admitted to the Council of Ministers; the civilian clerks and officials of the Synod were made subject to him, and he became the sole intermediary between the Tsar and the hierarchy. When Nechaev occupied this office (1833–35) he was held personally responsible for the political trustworthiness of the bishops; he even had some of them followed secretly by gendarmes. His successor, Protasov, took under his own direct control the church's educational institutions and its accounting system.[89] Thus the Synod became a tool in the hands of the Over Procurator, and it became the official usage to refer to his jurisdiction (which embraced the diocesan administration as well as the Synod and the institutions connected with it) as "the Administration for Religious Affairs of the Orthodox Faith."

In this state the Synod remained throughout the reign of Nicholas I. However, in the more liberal regime of Alexander II some of the ecclesiastics dared to hope for the granting of autonomy to the church. Archbishop Agafangel, of Volhynia, dedicated a book to the Tsar, *The Captivity of the Russian Church*—a work filled with complaints against domination by the Over Procurators. In 1869 Metropolitan Innokentii ventured to ask Alexander to have a church council called in order that the administrative system of the church might be changed; but the Tsar merely gave answer, "That is a weighty matter. Some day I shall summon you to discuss it with me." [90] But that day never came. In fact in 1880 a new Over Procurator, Pobedonostsev, entered upon a twenty-five-year domination over the whole life of the church—a period in which conservatism was the guiding principle. The church remained firmly within the toils of civil control.

[89] *Ibid.*, I, 604–5.   [90] Berdnikov, *op. cit.*, pp. 925–28.

One reason for this is not far to seek. The church was used to support the governmental order, and indeed many churchmen did this willingly. When the Decembrists, leaders of a movement for political freedom in 1825, induced some of the troops in St. Petersburg to defy Nicholas I, many of the clergy of the capital, with the metropolitan at their head, went in full vestments, cross in hand, to urge the rebels to submit.[91] The duties of parish priests in supporting the existing order were well outlined in the Imperial Code of Laws of 1832. There was a special obligation for the priest to "warn his parishioners against false and dangerous rumors, to strengthen them in good morals and in submission to their masters, and to try by all means to prevent the disturbance of the peasants. . . ." And if, in spite of this counsel, disorders did occur, the priests had an active part to play in the work of pacification. "When the detachment arrives, . . ." said the law, "then . . . it should immediately gather the people of the neighborhood, and also the priests, and through them [the priests] should admonish the unsubmissive, and should try by all means possible to bring them to proper submission." [92]

In 1839 Metropolitan Filaret of Moscow was asked by Count Benkendorf, Chief of Gendarmes, how the peasants of the provinces of Moscow, Tver, Penza, and Simbirsk could be calmed and their disturbances quieted. The metropolitan suggested that the bishops of the four localities should be urged secretly to inspire the clergy under them

so that they, in their instructions to the people . . . should more frequently remind them how sacred is the duty of submitting to the authorities, and above all to the Highest authority; how necessary is a trusting and united respect for the government, which of course knows better than private persons what is the good of all, and cannot but wish the well-being of its subjects; and how dangerous is credulous acceptance of injudicious or ill-intentioned advice, from which proceed folly and disorders. . . .

As "a more direct means of healing the minds of the people," the bishops were to be instructed to draw up sets of teachings to be used by the priests, "in which, after a brief reminder of past disastrous events, there should be given proper preventive counsel based upon the gen-

[91] Kliuchevskii, *op. cit.*, V, 210.

[92] *Svod Zakonov Rossiiskoi Imperii*, ed. 1832, XIV, "Ustav o Preduprezhdenii i Presechenii Prestuplenii," secs. 299–302.

eral principles of reverence and morality." And further, "As for the possibility of the diffusion of evidently false and wicked rumors among the people, to which it is unwise to refer in sermons, Their Reverences should try to teach to their clergy, and through them to their people, sound and healthy views," by means of personal talks at favorable opportunities which were to be carefully watched for.[93]

Later Filaret was to help in drawing up the Manifesto of 1861, by which the peasants were freed from serfdom. However, as late as 1859 he was still strongly opposed to the liberation of the serfs, for when the periodical issued by the Religious Academy of Kazan was bold enough to print several articles urging emancipation, Filaret showed his disapproval by attempting to have an *ukaz* issued which would have subjected this journal to strict censorship.[94] Filaret's stand in defense of serfdom was not unique among the clergy, for Bishop Ignatii, of Stavropol, in his report on the offending articles coming out of Kazan, stated that "serf-right is a divine institution, supported by the holy fathers of the ruling Church, and confirmed by the reverent Tsars." [95]

Even after the promulgation of the decree abolishing serfdom, Metropolitan Filaret retained his conservative outlook. On September 13, 1861, Count A. P. Tolstoi showed Filaret a proposal for the abolition of flogging as a means of collecting payment from the peasants and, with a hint that this would be an undesirable measure, asked him to show the attitude of the church on this question. Filaret issued a statement against the abolition of flogging, saying firstly that

the question of the use or the abandonment of flogging in the State does not involve Christianity; secondly, there is no basis for saying that "flogging has a harmful effect upon the moral character of the people." It is impossible to think that the Lord God would have legalized the bodily punishment of an offender if this had had a harmful effect upon the moral character of the Hebrew people.[96]

[93] L. Brodskii, ed., *Mneniia, Otzyvy i Pis'ma Filareta, Mitropolita Moskovskago,* pp. 62–63.

[94] S. P. Mel'gunov, "Mitropolit Filaret—Deiatel' Krest'ianskago Reforma," in Dzhivelegov, *Velikaia Reforma,* V, 159.

[95] Mel'gunov, "Epokha Ofitsial'noi Narodnosti i Krepostnoe Pravo," *ibid.,* III, 15.

[96] Mel'gunov, "Mitropolit Filaret," *ibid.,* V, 163.

Thus did the church, through its most authoritative member, serve the government at the time of the Emancipation. Another example of support for the government was given in 1883, at the death of Turgenev. The passing of this renowned enemy of oppression was widely made the occasion for requiem services, largely attended by university students, and sometimes marked by inspiring sermons delivered by young and idealistic priests. So outspoken did some of the orations become that the Synod sent out a circular to the bishops, advising them to caution their priests against too much zeal in delivering funeral eulogies. The priests were to treat the phenomena of social life "only from the Orthodox Christian point of view," and were to "cite . . . only such spiritual traits and actions for the general good as are in conformity with the word of God. . . ." They were told not to judge men or events by mundane standards, as "this violates their duty. . . ." If the bishop had reason to believe that in their sermons there would be "infringements of the proper limits, a lack of restraint and common sense," he was advised to "require them to hand in their sermons for inspection before they were delivered." [97]

These are significant instances, in the second half of the nineteenth century, of the church's efforts to uphold the existing order. However, no one who has studied the relationship between church and state in Russia through the centuries should be surprised at the closeness of the coöperation of the two institutions after the Emancipation. The authorities of the church were pursuing a policy formulated long ago in Byzantium and never forgotten in Russia—a policy which had been of great influence in the Russian land ever since the time when Moscow was first called "the Third Rome." Moreover, as will be shown, the church remained closely linked to the state after 1900; it would stand or fall with the power of the Tsar. The subsequent chapters will attempt to show how completely that communion was maintained and what degree of success attended the efforts of the church to deal with pressing problems in the years that brought two great wars and two great revolutions.

[97] A. A. Zav'ialov, ed., *Tsirkuliarnye Ukazy . . . Sinoda 1867–1895 gg.*, p. 150.

PART II

The Church at the Beginning
Of the Twentieth Century

CHAPTER II

The Russian Church as a State Institution at the Beginning of the Twentieth Century

THE FOREMOST and dominant faith in the Russian Empire is the Christian Orthodox Catholic Eastern Confession.

The Emperor possessing the throne of All Russia may not profess any faith but Orthodoxy.

The Emperor, as Christian Sovereign, is supreme defender and preserver of the dogmas of the ruling faith, and protector of the orthodoxy of belief and the decorum in the holy Church.[1]

With these words the Code of Laws of the Russian Empire indicated the imperial policy. Orthodoxy was officially favored; and the favor here proclaimed did not remain mere empty words. By a number of further provisions the Code of Laws implemented this policy.

Not the least of the aids given to the church were those in the fiscal realm and in the maintenance of its monopoly of propaganda —two subjects that will be discussed in later chapters. Another privilege granted to the Orthodox Church was the right of censorship. All printers were prohibited by law from printing religious books pertaining to the Orthodox religion without the approval of the church's

[1] *Svod Zakonov Rossiiskoi Imperii,* ed. 1857, I, pt. 1, "Svod Osnovnykh Gosudarstvennykh Zakonov," secs. 40–42; *ibid.,* ed. 1906, secs. 62–64. In this chapter many citations have been made from the *Code of Laws (Svod Zakonov)* to show provisions of the law relating to the church as they stood in 1900. In general the procedure has been to cite the law as it stood at some date before 1900, and then to show that the same law was still in effect at some date after 1900, as evidenced by the fact that the provisions cited were found in a later edition of the law.

official censorship committee.[2] The right of the church to censor religious literature could be used with telling effect against opposing denominations, for this privilege covered all religious writings and translations, including works on the services of the church, the lives of the saints, and the Bible and interpretations thereof, as well as works containing expositions of "truths dealing with the fundamentals of the Christian faith or of religion in general." Likewise the ecclesiastical censors were to pass upon works touching Christian morality, upon works of religious instruction, "religious discussions, and other minor productions and translations of religious or Christian content." All works dealing with church history, those touching upon ecclesiastical administration, and those destined for use in courses on religion in the lay schools were also subject to censorship by the church authorities.[3] The law further stipulated:

Above all, works and translations shall not be approved when they contain attacks upon Christian morality, upon the government, and upon religion.

But if there shall be sent or presented to the Censorship Committee a manuscript filled with thoughts and expressions clearly hostile to the spirit of Christianity and destructive of the principles of its moral teachings and the structure and the tranquillity of church and state, then the Committee shall straightway report on this work to the Most Holy Synod, for its consideration.[4]

During the year 1901 the religious censorship committees of St. Petersburg and Moscow examined 3,734 works, of which 3,453 were approved.[5] This relatively small number of rejections, however, does not give a sufficient indication of the importance of the religious censorship; doubtless many works which would otherwise have been published were never written or never submitted because the committees would be sure to reject them. Thus the religious censorship

[2] *Svod Zakonov*, XIV, "Ustav o Tsenzure i Pechati," ed. 1890, sec. 293; *Prodolzhenie Svoda Zakonov*, 1906, XIV, "Ustav o Tsenzure i Pechati," sec. 293.

[3] *Svod Zakonov*, *loc. cit.*, sec. 227; *Prodol. Svoda, loc. cit.*, sec. 227.

[4] *Svod Zakonov*, *loc. cit.*, secs. 262–63; *Prodol. Svoda, loc. cit.*, secs. 262–63.

[5] Sviateishii Sinod, *Vsepoddanneishii Otchet Ober-Prokurora . . . za 1901 g.*, p. 337.

played its part in aiding the Orthodox Church and the state which gave it firm support.

But the governmental support of the church was not limited to these measures, for the church was given representation in several of the political institutions of the realm. The Over Procurator of the Synod was a member of the Committee of Ministers,[6] and, like the ministers, was a member of the highest court in the land, the Senate. He was given the right to attend the meetings of the latter institution when they dealt with matters affecting the church.[7] Similarly each bishop was empowered to appoint a member of the clergy to attend the meetings of the provincial *zemstvo* assembly (a council, mainly elective, having the power to promote public health, education, agriculture, and other local interests) ; and the same right was granted with respect to the county (*uezd*) *zemstvo* assemblies.[8] In like fashion meetings of the town councils might be attended by members of the clergy appointed by the bishops [9] to guard the interests of the church.

All these benefits bestowed on the church by a benevolent government were perhaps less valuable than the care which the provincial governors were required to exercise in behalf of the Orthodox Church. They were instructed

in all cases and with all the powers given to them, to aid the Orthodox spiritual authorities in protecting the rights of the Church and the soundness of its belief, by watching carefully so that heresy, schism,

---

[6] T. V. Barsov, *Sbornik Deistvuiushchikh i Rukovodstvennykh Tserkovnykh i Tserkovno-grazhdanskikh Postanovlenii po Vedomstvu Pravoslavnago Ispovedaniia*, p. 13. This book was published in 1885; in this and subsequent cases in which it has been cited, by investigation in *Polnoe Sobranie Zakonov*, A. A. Zav'ialov, ed., *Tsirkuliarnye Ukazy Sviateishago . . . Sinoda, 1867–1895 gg.*, and *Tserkovnyia Vedomosti* it has been determined that these provisions of the law had not been modified by later legislation, and hence were still effective in 1900.

[7] *Svod Zakonov*, I, pt. 2, "Uchrezhdenie Pravitel'stvuiushchago Senata," ed. 1892, secs. 8 and 35; *Prodol. Svoda*, 1906, I, pt. 2, "Uchrezhdenie Prav. Senata," sec. 8, par. 1; sec. 35.

[8] *Svod Zakonov*, II, "Polozhenie o Gubernskikh i Uezdnykh Zemskikh Uchrezhdeniiakh," ed. 1892, secs. 56–57; *Prodol. Svoda*, 1906, II, "Polozhenie o Gubernskikh i Uezdnykh Zemsk. Uchrezhd.," secs. 56–57.

[9] *Svod Zakonov*, II, "Gorodovoe Polozhenie," ed. 1892, sec. 57; *Prodol. Svoda*, 1906, II, "Gorodovoe Polozhenie," sec. 57.

and other errors born of prejudice and ignorance may not be spread among the inhabitants of the province entrusted to them, and so that (in order to avert this evil and the disaffection caused by it) at the proper moment all those measures enumerated in the general regulations and in the special Imperial commands may be used.

(What these enumerated measures were and what were the results of their application will be shown in greater detail in a later chapter.) Furthermore,

the governors, acting through the city and the county police, shall en- sure that during the conduct of divine service and all other church ceremonies the proper quiet and decorum are not disturbed by anyone, and that for all actions violating this decorum, even though unintentional, the guilty shall be required to answer according to law. The governors shall in this connection provide the necessary protection and assist- ance for the other religious faith practiced freely within the Empire, making sure, however, that no one shall be led astray into these faiths from Orthodoxy; and in general they are not to allow anyone belonging to the sects forbidden by law to attract converts to the said faiths.[10]

Thus the governors, and through them the police, were ordered to limit the missionary work of the non-Orthodox denominations. In- deed by other laws non-Orthodox missionary activity was completely forbidden;[11] the official church, on the other hand, was not only permitted, but was even encouraged to carry on missionary activity —a topic to be treated more fully in a later chapter.

Such, then, was the position granted to the Orthodox Church by the Imperial Russian Government. This church was especially fa- vored and had its interests furthered by political and economic aid and by encouragement to win converts, while the state used its police power to restrict the propaganda of its rivals. In these various ways was the connection between church and state made close. Yet this was not entirely to the benefit of the church, for while the state granted aid and privilege to the official faith, in return it exercised such complete control over the church that the latter could have

[10] *Svod Zakonov*, II, "Obshchee Uchrezhdenie Gubernskoe," ed. 1892, secs. 298–99; *Prodol. Svoda,* 1906, II, "Obshchee Uchrezhd. Gubernskoe," secs. 298–99.

[11] Barsov, *op. cit.*, p. 201. This prohibition did not apply to Finland.

little independence or freedom. The church was thus placed in subjection to the state.

As was stated at the beginning of this chapter, the emperor, as "supreme defender and preserver of the dogmas of the ruling faith," had the right to supervise "the orthodoxy of belief and the decorum in the holy Church." In exercising its control over the church "The autocratic authority acts through the agency of the Most Holy Synod, which was established by it"; [12] however, according to one of the greatest authorities on the history of Russian law, the power of the Tsar did not extend to matters of dogma, for

in defining the competence of the Synod one must keep in mind that the Russian Church, a local church, is part of the Church Universal. Consequently, for the former the dogmas and the rules recognized and confirmed by the Ecumenical Councils [the last one, according to Orthodox teaching, met in 787 A. D.] are binding. Moreover, as a part of the Universal Church, it cannot have a visible head with legislative authority in questions of dogma; in this respect the Orthodox Church differs radically from the Catholic Church, which recognizes a visible head in the person of the Pope.[13]

If the Tsar acted through the Synod, and the Synod was thus limited in power, it follows that the Russian emperor did not possess the power to change the dogma of the Russian Church; according to this definition, his authority extended only to what might be termed administrative control.[14]

Even within these limits, the emperor reserved to himself little direct power over the church. For the most part the Synod was free to perform its functions without the necessity of asking for imperial permission or approval. Only if the Synod desired to supplement the powers originally conferred upon it or "to explain and amplify the existing law or to draw up a new decree" was it required to submit its proposals for imperial consideration.[15] To be sure, if the Synod failed to reach a unanimous decision when considering a matter, the Over Procurator might, at his discretion, submit the question to the

[12] *Svod Zakonov,* ed. 1857, I, pt. 1, "Svod Osnovnykh Gosudarstvennykh Zakonov," sec. 43; *ibid.,* ed. 1906, sec. 65.

[13] A. D. Gradovskii, *Sobranie Sochinenii,* VIII, 388.

[14] N. Suvorov, *Uchebnik Tserkovnago Prava,* ed. 1912, p. 216.

[15] Barsov, *op. cit.,* p. 2.

emperor for final solution; [16] but by far the greater part of the Synod's actions were not submitted for imperial consideration.

In respect to appointments the emperor's power was more extensively used. When a new vicarian or diocesan bishop was to be named, three candidates were selected by the Synod; from these three the emperor chose the one to receive the position.[17] Moreover, the Tsar named the (permanent) members of the Synod, and summoned those bishops who were chosen for temporary attendance at its sessions; the latter were ordered to sit in the Synod "until it is the Imperial will that they should return to their dioceses." [18]

These were the only cases in which the law provided for the personal action of the emperor in the affairs of the church; as a rule his power was exercised only in the administrative field and was not extended to spiritual matters. However, the Russian Empire of 1900 was an autocracy; it is usual for an autocratic monarch to avoid the setting of limits to his power, which might thus smack of constitutional restrictions. Consequently, nowhere did the Russian laws *forbid* the emperor to interfere personally in matters of faith and dogma, and actually in several instances the Tsars did act in cases which touched the sacraments and the beliefs of the church.

It is interesting to note that, while the Synod issued—in addition to its legislation changing the administrative structure of the church, which required the approval of the Tsar—a number of lesser general decrees, orders, and rules, between the years 1884 and 1895, in only six cases was imperial confirmation or consent involved. Four of these concerned purely administrative matters; however, in one instance the Tsar ordered the Synod to decree that in mixed marriages the non-Orthodox spouse must promise not to try to lead astray the Orthodox person.[19] The sixth case involved the naming of the Stundist

[16] Barsov, *op. cit.*, p. 11.   [17] *Ibid.*, p. 101.
[18] *Ibid.*, p. 8.
[19] Zav'ialov, ed., *Tsirkuliarnye Ukazy Sviateishago . . . Sinoda, 1867– 1895 gg.*, pp. 150–56; p. 268. However, a number of enactments affecting the administrative structure of the church were approved by the Tsar after their adoption by the Synod; among such measures were the Codes for the Religious Seminaries and for the Academies, and *Instruktsiia Tserkovnym Starostam (Instructions to Church Elders)*. Legislation of the latter variety was published in *Polnoe Sobranie Zakonov*.

sect as "especially dangerous"; after the Synod had, in 1889, proclaimed that this sect was an extremely dangerous foe of the church, the Committee of Ministers in 1894 decreed, with the Tsar's approval, that the Minister of Internal Affairs and the Over Procurator, acting together, might declare the Stundists an "especially dangerous sect," and might forbid them to have prayer meetings.[20]

Considerable evidence exists to show that on several other occasions the emperors intervened in questions involving faith and morals, which were not included in the cases reserved for their decision. In 1883 Pobedonostsev, Over Procurator of the Synod, wrote to Alexander III concerning a certain woman who had been divorced, and was forbidden by the Synod to remarry. Pobedonostsev urged the Tsar to reject her petition that the ban imposed by the Synod be lifted, not because such an action would be *ultra vires,* but because it would be a bad precedent. Moreover, the Over Procurator suggested that if the petitioner should remarry in defiance of the Synod's edict, it would be permissible for the Tsar to quash a suit before a religious court contesting the legality of the marriage.[21] An interesting example of the intervention of the emperor in a religious question came in 1901. The Synod on February 21 issued an edict excommunicating Tolstoi; this was done without consulting the Tsar, who was angered that he had not been shown the final text of the proclamation; Pobedonostsev wrote an apologetic letter to the emperor, who did not disapprove of the Synod's action, but merely felt that his approval should have been asked.[22]

Perhaps the most significant type of imperial action in purely religious matters was that taken in cases of canonization. In 1903, after an investigation, the Synod decided to canonize the holy man, Serafim of Sarov; but Serafim was raised to the sainthood only after the emperor had noted his approval on the report of the Synod's decision.[23] Nor was this an exceptional instance; studies of canonizations in the nineteenth century show that in each case the approval of the em-

[20] *Ibid.,* pp. 219–22; pp. 261–62.
[21] K. P. Pobedonostsev, *Pis'ma . . . k Aleksandru III,* pt. 2, pp. 34–36.
[22] *Ibid.,* p. 328.
[23] Sviat. Sinod, *Vsepoddanneishii Otchet Ober-Prokurora . . . za 1903–1904 gg.,* pp. 1–5.

peror was obtained,[24] and on at least one occasion the Tsar, Nicholas
I, began the proceedings by ordering the Synod to start the investigation which led to the canonization of a saint.[25] From these facts it appears that the power of the Tsar over the church was not clearly
defined, and that on more than one occasion he intervened in matters
which were in the spiritual sphere.

However, while the Tsar at times did exercise direct control over
the church during the period now under discussion—the first five
years of the twentieth century—the real ruler of the Russian Church
was not the Tsar, but the Over Procurator of the Most Holy Synod,
K. P. Pobedonostsev.

This famous man, who had been the trusted adviser of the ultra-
conservative Alexander III, continued to influence Nicholas II until
1905, and was thoroughly hated by liberal people in Russia because
he used his undoubted ability and intelligence to devote the church
to the cause of conservatism. His cherished dream was to turn the
enlightenment of the young over to the schools of the church—of
which more anon. According to M. Rostovtsev, a member of the
Council of State, Pobedonostsev personally revived the policy of repression in religious matters, after the comparatively mild regime
of Alexander II; the Over Procurator induced a liberally intentioned
Council of State to discard its project for granting extensive legal
rights to schismatics and sectarians, and persuaded it to revive the
old policy of persecution.[26] Moreover Pobedonostsev used all his influence to hinder the introduction of innovations, such as trial by
jury and parliamentary government. "Among the falsest of political
principles," he wrote in 1896, "is the theory of the sovereignty of the
people, . . . the principle that all power issues from the people and
is based upon the popular will." And again, "It is dreadful to think of
our condition if destiny had sent us the fatal gift—an All-Russian
Parliament! May that never be!" [27]

[24] E. Temnikovskii, *K Voprosu o Kanonizatsii Sviatykh*, pp. 13 and 56;
E. E. Golubinskii, *Istoriia Kanonizatsii Sviatykh v Russkoi Tserkvi*, pp. 132–37.
[25] Golubinskii, *op. cit.*, p. 132.
[26] I. V. Preobrazhenskii, *Konstantin Petrovich Pobedonostsev, Ego Lichnost' i Deiatel'nost' v Predstavlenii Sovremennikov Ego Konchiny*, p. 8. The
author was a priest, well known as a supporter of the existing church regime.
[27] K. P. Pobedonostsev, *Moskovskii Sbornik*, pp. 31 and 47.

Pobedonostsev was equally caustic regarding the press; the idea that the judgments of the press are expressions of public opinion was, according to him, an error. "The press is one of the falsest institutions of our time." [28]

Naturally the newspapers paid him back in kind. Upon his death a long line of liberal newspapers agreed with the journal *Nov'* that "the rule, *de mortuis nil nisi bene,* . . . must be laid aside before the bier of such a great governmental figure . . ."; among the organs which so expressed themselves were *Utro, Parus, Birzhevyia Vedomosti, Slovo, Rech, Russkoe Slovo, Russkiia Novosti, Stolichnaia Pochta, Golos Pravdy, Odesskiia Novosti, Kievskii Golos,* and a number of provincial newspapers.[29] *Sovremennaia Rech* wrote, "With unshakeable stubbornness Pobedonostsev crushed all signs of freedom, all glimmerings of new life. He put chains upon the thought of the nation, he built prison cells for those who fought for the rights of the people. He tried to crush in the vise of mere ritualism the quivering conscience of the people." [30]

This judgment could easily be matched with excerpts from other newspapers. Nor was this feeling confined to journalistic circles alone; in an autobiographical sketch presented to Nicholas II in 1902, Pobedonostsev complained that he was viewed by liberals and radicals as "the evil cause of all . . . abuses, violence, and reactionary measures. . . ." [31] This was a misfortune for the Orthodox Church, for the hatred which he aroused could not but embrace to some extent the church which he dominated in his capacity of Over Procurator of the Most Holy Synod.

When Peter the Great created the Synod as the controlling agency for the Russian Church, he also provided for an Over Procurator to represent the Tsar's policies, and to interpose objections and to advise the Tsar if the decisions made by the bishops and the other clergy sitting in the Synod should infringe upon the interests of state. The Procurator, in short, was to be a liaison officer between church and state—"the eye of the Tsar." However, while in the beginning the Over Procurator was merely a check upon the Synod, at the end of

[28] *Ibid.*, p. 57.   [29] Preobrazhenskii, *op. cit.*, pp. 39–52.
[30] *Ibid.*, p. 41.
[31] Pobedonostsev, *Pis'ma . . . k Aleksandru III*, pt. 2, p. 335.

the nineteenth century this official held a position of complete dominance over the administration of the church.

There were several ways in which this control was exercised. First:
the Over Procurator was the intermediary between the Synod and the
emperor. He alone reported to the sovereign concerning the affairs of
the church; he requested the imperial consent and confirmation which
was expressly required for certain general decrees for the church, and
by failure to report them to the emperor, could prevent the confirmation of such decisions of the Synod. Conversely, he interpreted to the
Synod the thought and the will of the emperor, both on the general
trend of church affairs and on individual matters pertaining to the
church.[32] He was "the guardian for the fulfillment of the legal regulations for the Religious Administration."[33] To him was given the
duty of seeing to the "proper, timely, and lawful course and decision
of matters in the Most Holy Synod."[34] He was given "full power to
publish Imperial *ukazes*."[35] Furthermore, at the time of the consideration of business in the Synod "the Over Procurator enjoys the right
to explain the laws and to point to other circumstances which may
have weight in deciding these matters; in the event of disagreement
of the members, . . . either to stop the consideration of the matter,
or to present it to the Highest Authority [the Tsar] for consideration."[36]

It must not be thought that the bishops or metropolitans could
exert influence directly upon the sovereign in such a manner as to
counteract the efforts of the Over Procurator, for these dignitaries
were not allowed audiences with the emperor except in those rare
cases when the Over Procurator arranged for them. This layman was
the church's only spokesman at court.[37]

Even without the sole right of reporting to the emperor, the Over
Procurator would still have been able to hold control over the hierarchs of the Synod, for he was responsible for their presence at its
meetings. The Synod consisted of twelve prelates—four "members"
ex officio (three metropolitans, and the exarch of Georgia, although

[32] M. I. Gorchakov, *Tserkovnoe Pravo*, p. 155.
[33] Barsov, *op. cit.*, p. 11.   [34] *Ibid.*
[35] *Ibid.*   [36] *Ibid.*
[37] *Missionerskoe Obozrenie*, No. 17, 1904, as quoted in *Staroobriadcheskii
Vestnik*, February, 1905, pp. 105–6.

the latter in actuality attended but rarely) and eight or nine bishops, who were summoned by special commands of the Tsar to be present at the meetings of the Synod, and who were known as "those attending." All the prelates who composed the Synod, whether actual "members" or not, attended the Synod only upon receiving special commands from the Tsar. Their attendance was limited in duration to the periods specified in the summons. However, while nominally the summons came from the emperor, the names were proposed to him by the Over Procurator, so that the latter was responsible for their attendance.[38] Moreover the attendance of the bishops was often brief. The Synod's meetings were grouped in three annual sessions, winter, summer, and fall, and usually only six of the twelve hierarchs were asked to attend at a given session. Consequently the bishops and metropolitans were summoned for short periods—for three months, six months, or at most a year. During these brief terms they had little opportunity to exert much influence. Probably prelates who were known to be hostile to the policies of the Over Procurator were rarely summoned to the Synod, for if the summons was not requested by him even the metropolitans remained merely nominal members of the Synod. As a result of their quarrel with the Over Procurator Protasov in 1842, Filaret of Moscow and Filaret of Kiev, two of the most noted metropolitans of the Russian Church, were not summoned to the Synod for many years.[39] Hence the Synod was as a general rule composed of clergy who were attentive to the wishes of the Over Procurator.

It must not be supposed that even an aggressive and independent churchman, if such a one should be named to attend the meetings of the Synod, could accomplish much. The permanent lay officials of the Synod chanceries were much more important. As one bishop wrote in 1905,

The Most Holy Synod is least of all like . . . a holy Church Council. The Synod is a governmental institution: when you enter it, a concierge with a mace greets you; then footmen with gold and silver medals, and

---

[38] Agafangel, Volynskii, *Plenenie Russkoi Tserkvi*, p. 6.
[39] A. M. Ivantsov-Platonov, *O Russkom Tserkovnom Upravlenie*, p. 68. The author, a priest of the rank of dean, was professor of Church History in the University of Moscow.

farther on, officials, officials, officials without end . . . and among them four or five old bishops, who in summer put in an appearance once a week, and in winter, twice a week, for two hours at a time. They are offered various matters to be voted on, sometimes merely the unimportant ones. . . . As long as we have not freed ourselves from the officials, nothing can be said concerning freedom of the Church.[40]

In the hall where the Synod sat, the arrangements all facilitated control by laymen. The ecclesiastics, few in number, sat at a table in the center of the room. Near by sat the Over Procurator with several subordinates, all able to see and to note how the Synod members conducted themselves in the discussion and the voting. Under such close observation there was little opportunity for courageous independent action. Cases were not lacking "where, after zealous canonical consideration in the Synod, members had to leave Petersburg in twenty-four hours, or were sent into retirement, or were subjected to still worse fates. Can they, under the influence of thoughts about all this, consider the affairs of the church with . . . spiritual equanimity?"[41] This passage, to be sure, was written in 1873, but by 1900 the position of the Synod had not changed materially, as far as can be determined.

Moreover, owing to the briefness of the sessions and the great press of business, the members of the Synod had little time for deliberation and consideration. For the most part they were forced simply to pass hastily upon reports and decisions drawn up by the lay officials of the central administration. The actual decisions were so often made by the chancery bureaucrats rather than by the ecclesiastical members of the Synod that Bishop Nikon of Vladimir stated in 1905 that "in the Most Holy Synod a tiny part of the business . . . [is] reported to the Synod meeting, and the great bulk of the cases . . . [are] decided in the chancery and . . . [are] presented to the [ecclesiastical] members in their rooms, merely for signature."[42] According to another bishop who wrote at the same time, most of the decrees of the Synod were formulated by the lay officials in the Synod

[40] Sviat. Sinod, *Otzyvy Eparkhial'nykh Arkhiereev po Voprosu o Tserkovnoi Reforme*, III, 382, Lavrentii of Tula.

[41] Agafangel, *op. cit.*, p. 9.

[42] Sv. Sinod, *Otzyvy*, I, 219, Nikon of Vladimir.

chancery, and the hierarchs of the Synod signed them automatically, with little or no attempt to inquire into the facts in each case.[43] Here was a situation which had called forth the lamentations of Archbishop Agafangel of Volhynia in 1873: "Is it possible to conceive of anything more ill-fitting and harmful for the Holy Church, more disturbing to the feelings of an Orthodox Christian? Laymen control its fate, laymen give direction to it, laymen are in control of the soul and the life of the church!" [44]

So firmly was the real power over the administration of the church in the hands of the lay officials that Professor P. V. Verkhovskoi, of the Imperial University of Warsaw, writing in 1916, stated that the hierarchs of the Synod often knew nothing of Synod business until it was placed before them in reports of the lay officials. After reaching the Synod offices, matters might lie for years without action; moreover, the decision of the Synod might never be carried out.[45] As Bishop Lavrentii of Tula wrote in 1905, "not one decision will be given for signature to the members of the Most Holy Synod if the Over Procurator has not . . . looked at it"; in like fashion, "not one decision signed by all the members of the Synod will be executed if it does not bear the counter-signature of the Over Procurator, 'To be carried out.' " [46] The lay officials serving in the central administration of the church were without exception appointed by him; and from him came their pensions and advancement.[47] Consequently he and not the bishops and the metropolitans possessed the support and the loyalty of the officials. Is it any wonder that when the Synod members made independent suggestions to officials of the chancery, nothing came of it but the response, "We will refer this to His Eminence"? [48]

Thus Professor Verkhovskoi could say quite properly, ". . . it is clear that all the affairs of the Synod are in the hands of the state

[43] *Ibid.,* Supplement, p. 17, Nikodim of Priamur and Blagoveshchensk.
[44] Agafangel, *op. cit.,* p. 7.
[45] P. V. Verkhovskoi, *Uchrezhdenie Dukhovnoi Kollegii i Dukhovnyi Reglament,* I, 600, footnote. A scholarly discussion of the reforms of Peter and their consequences for the church.
[46] Sv. Sinod, *Otzyvy,* III, 385, Lavrentii of Tula.
[47] Barsov, *op. cit.,* pp. 11–12.   [48] Agafangel, *op. cit.,* p. 10.

officials serving in the Administration of the Orthodox Confession [the church administration], who are under the full sway of the Over Procurator." [49] This civil domination over the chief organ of the Russian Church had a far-reaching effect, for the arm of the central administration was long. Many trifling matters which might well have been left to the decision of the diocesan authorities were referred to the Synod, so that a vast amount of formalism and red tape resulted. The evils of delay and administrative complication were all too evident. Often the work of the dioceses was partly paralyzed by the need to wait for approval from St. Petersburg.[50]

The power of the bishops in their dioceses was further restricted by the fact that several important categories of church affairs were put under special committees under the Synod. The findings of these committees, to be sure, had to be approved by the Synod, but none the less the committees could exert strong influence to induce the Synod to approve their decisions, which often restricted the competence of the local bishops. The chief of these committees were the Religious Educational Administration and the Economic Administration; their members were chiefly high lay officials of the Synod chancery, with a few prelates.[51] These special bodies had school inspectors, auditors, and officials on special mission for the Over Procurator, who traveled the length and breadth of Russia and who everywhere were received with fearful politeness by the hierarchs. One hopeful bishop wrote in 1905, "How free the Orthodox bishops will feel when the auditors of the Educational Committee, the missionaries and the Synodal architects cease to travel over the entire breadth of Russia and no longer bring back to the Synod various reports about the bishops." [52] According to a statement quoted from the conservative *Novoe Vremia* (*The New Time*), many hierarchs believed that nothing more than an unfavorable hint from one of these traveling officials was needed to bring a bishop into disfavor with the Over Procurator—with possibly serious consequences for

[49] Verkhovskoi, *op. cit.*, I, 599–600, footnote.

[50] Ivantsov-Platonov, *op. cit.*, p. 67; Sv. Sinod, *Otzyvy*, Supplement, p. 17, Nikodim of Priamur and Blagoveshchensk.

[51] Barsov, *op. cit.*, pp. 11, 21, 22, 27, 50, 55–58.

[52] Sv. Sinod, *Otzyvy*, III, 385, Lavrentii of Tula.

the prelate.[53] Here was an added reason for the bishops to fear and to submit to the Over Procurator.

In general, the prelates of the Russian Church yielded to the wishes of this personage. The men who rose to the rank of princes of the church were for the most part sons of parish priests,[54] without wealth or influence at court. Their only means of obtaining the honor, the material advantages, and the greater power for good that went with the episcopate was to win favor with those in high places. They were advanced in rank by decisions of the Synod, which were really the decisions of the Over Procurator. By these decisions they were advanced through the lower grades on the way to the episcopate and, when a see became vacant, three candidates were named by the Synod, one of whom was granted the bishopric by the emperor. Naturally the successful individuals were chiefly men who had shown a readiness to be guided by the wishes of the Over Procurator.[55]

It must be borne in mind that the episcopal sees were not directly accessible to the secular clergy, who were obliged to marry before ordination. From early times in Russia the bishops had all come from the ranks of the monastics, the so-called "black clergy." No married priest could qualify for the episcopate. Only if a priest's wife had died or was willing to enter a convent was he able to take the monastic vows, and thus to become eligible for the higher positions. Consequently, as most of the monks were of peasant origin and lacked the necessary education, the bishops were often men who, as students, had taken monastic vows and had then gone on to finish the course of one of the religious academies. According to the belief of many of the clergy, when the vows had once been said the student's future history was settled. He no longer had to fear failure in his examinations—he was "dragged from course to course by his ears." [56] Inasmuch as theological students who entered the monastic life were

[53] *Novoe Vremia*, March 27, 1905, as quoted in Preobrazhenskii, ed., *Tserkovnaia Reforma*, p. 94.

[54] *Tserkovnyia Vedomosti*, for 1899, 1900, and 1901. Of the twenty-three whose biographies state their class origins, only four were of the nobility; sixteen, including the metropolitan of Kiev, were sons of parish clergy.

[55] Sv. Sinod, *Otzyvy*, III, 8, Vladimir of Ekaterinburg.

[56] "Letter of an Instructor in a Religious Seminary," *Slovo*, May 3, 1905, as quoted in Preobrazhenskii, ed., *Tserkovnaia Reforma*, p. 472.

scorned by their fellows,[57] they were rare enough to find their way made easy, and for those who won official favor notable careers were opened. For the successful "learned monk" there followed

completion of the course in a halo of official favoritism. Two years as inspector in a seminary, or a supervisor in a church school. Two years of seminary rectorship. Summons into "the body of religious service" [i. e., appointment as abbot of a monastery], prophetically foretelling the nearness of the "naming" [as bishop]. A vicariate with dreams of full standing. An independent diocese, with dreams of transfer to a diocese with greater appurtenances of honor. Transfer to a "noted" diocese, with dreams of an archepiscopate. An archepiscopate.[58]

Such, many priests believed, was the progress of the fortunate and favored monk.

Many of the bishops did not attain their eminence in quite this fashion, however. In 1905 Abbot Nikolai pointed out that in the Synod register for 1897, 78 of the 108 bishops, either active or retired, had been priests. When bereft of their spouses, they had become monks, had entered the academies, and consequently had become eligible for episcopal office.[59] But although their entrance into monasticism came later in life, they like the young "student monks" owed their preliminary appointments as seminary inspectors, school supervisors, or rectors of seminaries, to the Synod,[60] or, as has been said, really to the Over Procurator.

Of course not all of the students in the academies who took the vows, whether former priests or youths fresh from the seminaries, were sure of becoming bishops. But the number of those who took this step was small—there were five of them in 1900 [61]—so that most of them could expect to advance to desirable positions, and those who won favor in the highest spheres might hope for signal honor.

When a man attained the episcopal rank, even if he had the best

---

[57] N. V. Ognev, *Na Poroge Reform Russkoi Tserkvi i Dukhovenstva*, p. 3; N. D. Zhevakhov, *Vospominaniia Tovarishcha Ober-Prokurora Sviateishago Sinoda*, I, 121.

[58] *Birzhevyia Vedomosti*, March 23, 1905, as quoted in Preobrazhenskii, ed., *Tserkovnaia Reforma*, p. 26; also, *Tserkovno-obshchestvennaia Zhizn'*, Oct. 20, 1906, cols. 1448–49.

[59] *Razsvet*, April 10, 1905, as quoted in Preobrazhenskii, *op. cit.*, p. 354.

[60] Gorchakov, *Tserkovnoe Pravo*, pp. 150–51.

[61] *Tserkovnyia Vedomosti*, 1900.

intentions and the sincerest piety in the world, he could do little in his diocese if he opposed the will of the Over Procurator. There were too many weapons in that official's armory. The power to appoint and to remove bishops was reserved for the emperor, after proposals by the Synod. Actually, however, both emperor and Synod were guided by the wishes of Pobedonostsev. As Bishop Vladimir of Ekaterinburg wrote in 1905, "Personally our sovereigns have known few candidates for the episcopal sees, and, while keeping the form of choice by the Most Holy Synod, have handed the actual control over appointments into the keeping of favorites or of the Over Procurators. . . ."[62] Some of the Over Procurators—for instance Chebyshev, Melissino, Protasov, and Count D. A. Tolstoi—were antireligious in nature. These officials treated the bishops as subordinates to be brought into full subjection, and upon the slightest pretext sent bishops into retirement and very frequently transferred them from one diocese to another.[63] The practice of transferring bishops was especially widely used under Pobedonostsev, although he was a very devout man; during his administration the term of service of the greater part of the bishops did not exceed four years in one diocese.[64]

Enlightening examples of these transfers, drawn from an official roster of the Synod for 1905, were given by a St. Petersburg newspaper of that year. "Archbishop Iakov of Iaroslavl and Rostov. On April 29, 1891, made Bishop of Balakhina. On September 29 of the following year, Bishop of Uman. After three and one-half months, Bishop of Chirigin. January 26, 1896, Bishop of Kishinev, and August 12, 1904, Archbishop of Iaroslavl." Thus he held five posts in the course of fourteen years.

"Bishop Khristofor of Ufa and Menzelina. May 25, 1897, Bishop of Volokolamsk. From December 13, 1890, to December 19, 1892, 'in retirement.' In 1892, Bishop of Kovno. June 6, 1897, Bishop of Ekaterinburg. March 29, 1900, Bishop of Podolia, and November 26, 1903, Bishop of Ufa."[65]

That this practice of moving bishops from place to place had, at times, unfortunate results, may well be imagined. Bishop Vladimir

[62] Sv. Sinod, *Otzyvy*, III, 8, Vladimir of Ekaterinburg.
[63] *Ibid.*   [64] *Ibid.*
[65] *Sanktpeterburgskiia Vedomosti*, April 8, 1905, as quoted in Preobrazhenskii, *op. cit.*, p. 330.

of Ekaterinburg clearly showed this in a statement to the Synod. There had been, in the twenty years before 1905, ten changes of bishops in that diocese. This occasioned, he said, a good deal of scoffing at the powerlessness of the bishops, on the part of the local populace, and the factory workers and the educated classes became alienated from their pastors and from the church itself. He wrote:

I remember, that in 1903 there came to me in Orenburg an envoy of His Reverence of Ekaterinburg, now bishop of Grodno, a monk bearing an invitation to the three-hundred-year jubilee of the Verkhoturskii . . . Monastery. . . . As I knew that His Reverence had been sent from Orel to Ekaterinburg against his wishes, and as it was said that he wept when he arrived at his undesired see, in the presence of all the clergy of Ekaterinburg, and openly showed no desire to serve with them for long, I asked the monk, "Will His Lordship live until the jubilee [1904]? I heard that he wept, as did the Most Reverend Irinei, his predecessor?" The monk answered me, "Yes, Their Lordships do not live long with us; they themselves call the Ekaterinburg Diocesan Home their last resting-place. We monks have never seen the faces of some of the bishops." I replied, "Your church is unfortunate; the bridegrooms do not love their bride." [66]

Without doubt the Over Procurator could and did exercise control over the bishops. Those disposed to choose the easier way readily accepted this control; the strong-willed often found themselves out of favor, and were sent to the less desirable dioceses, or worse, into retirement. But if by some chance a bishop was able to stand against this influence, it availed little. For the arm of the Synod—in truth, of the Over Procurator—was long, and many were the matters of diocesan administration which could be settled only after reference to the central authorities. The bishop might not appoint or discharge any of the instructors in the religious seminary in his diocese; he might not remove them, even when they were known to him to be libertines or radicals. Much of the control over the parish schools was in the hands of the many officials of the Synod. Then, too, when churches were to be built in the far-off provinces, the official architects from the capital had to be called in to pass upon the work and to watch it for a day or two. No large-scale repairs might be made in the churches of the provincial towns or in other large centers with-

[66] Sv. Sinod, *Otzyvy*, III, 9–10, Vladimir of Ekaterinburg.

out similar approval. When choosing or changing the printer for the *Diocesan News,* the diocesan authorities had to obtain approval and confirmation from St. Petersburg. No religious brotherhood or trusteeship might be formed, no harsh abbot might be removed, until after correspondence with the Synod and until the bureaucratic machine had ground out its answer.[67]

" 'In everything is the will of God,' the people say about physical forces, but concerning the spiritual and moral realm we must say, 'In everything is the will of the Over Procurator of the Most Holy Synod.' Of course he does not change dogma. But that is because no one is especially interested in that field." [68] These words were printed in *Novoe Vremia (The New Time),* a far from radical newspaper, in March, 1905.

Only part of the diocesan business was left for the bishop to dispose of, and even here he generally counted for little. This was so for several reasons. For one thing, the practice of moving bishops frequently from place to place was a hindrance to any close acquaintance with the affairs of the diocese in which the bishop was more or less temporarily located. Also the dioceses of the Russian Empire were large in area, containing as many as a thousand churches, many of which could be reached only by weary journeys over difficult roads. Hence it was often impossible, if only for physical reasons, for the average bishop to inspect all of the parishes of his diocese during the entire term of his episcopate, to say nothing of complying with the rule requiring a visitation at least every three years.[69] Professor Zaozerskii, of the Moscow Religious Academy, quotes an interesting incident, as reported in one of the Moscow newspapers:

Here is a fact: once I chanced to be at a parish school at lesson time. With the permission of the teacher of religion I asked a bright lad the question, "Do you know what archhierarchs [Russian term for bishops] are?" "I know that they are the officials who condemned Our

[67] *Ibid.,* III, 383–85, Lavrentii of Tula; *ibid.,* Supplement, p. 18, Nikodim of Priamur and Blagoveshchensk; *Novoe Vremia,* March 19, 1905, as quoted in Preobrazhenskii, *op. cit.,* pp. 10–11.

[68] Preobrazhenskii, *loc. cit.*

[69] I. S. Berdnikov, "K Voprosu o Preobrazovanii Eparkhial'nago Upravleniia," *Pravoslavnyi Sobesednik,* Jan., 1906, p. 21; N. Zaozerskii, *O Nuzhdakh Tserkovnoi Zhizni,* p. 16.

Lord." "What were their names?" "One was Annas, the other, Caiaphas." "Do we have archhierarchs now?" "No."

This took place, not in some half-wild province, but in one of the central and more civilized ones, namely, Iaroslavl.[70]

However, more significant than the frequent transfers and the great size of the dioceses as causes for the slight authority of the bishops was the condition of the diocesan administration. In theory the bishop was the supreme figure in the diocese. Actually he had to depend on the religious consistory, composed of four or five priests. But their aid was weak and ineffectual, for, as will be shown, they in turn were dominated by the lay officials of the consistorial chancery. Hence it follows that the real power in the consistory lay with these bureaucrats, and above all with their chief, the secretary of the consistory.

The predominance of the lay officials is another instance of the centralization of religious authority, for the chief of them, the secretary, who ruled the others, was appointed by the Synod "on the nomination of the Over Procurator," and at the suggestion of the latter was removable by the Synod. Nominally the secretary of the consistory was subject to the bishop; however, he was at the same time under the direct orders of the Over Procurator, and "was obliged to fulfil all of his commands." [71] Furthermore, the secretary was required to send to the Over Procurator "periodical information" about the affairs of the diocese [72]—information which might conceivably affect in an unfavorable way the career of a too-independent bishop. The secretary had great power, and as the other officials of the consistory, the bureau heads, the archivist, the registrar, and the rest, were generally appointed at his suggestion and owed their advancement to him and to the Over Procurator, it is not remarkable that they often did not respect the wishes of the bishop when these desires conflicted with those of the secretary.[73]

How strongly the clergy and the leading students of church affairs

[70] Zaozerskii, *loc. cit.*

[71] Sv. Sinod, *Ustav Dukhovnykh Konsistorii*, secs. 283–85. In this and subsequent citations from this source, the sections cited are identical in the 1883 and the 1912 editions, unless otherwise stated.

[72] *Ibid.*, sec. 341.

[73] Sv. Sinod, *Otzyvy*, III, 53, Pitirim of Kursk; Ivantsov-Platonov, *op. cit.*, p. 29.

felt on this subject is easy to determine from the religious literature of the time. Even Metropolitan Vladimir of Moscow, a man noted for his conservatism, voiced his opinion that for the diocesan control to be truly episcopal, proper limits would have to be set to the power and the influence of the lay element in the religious administration; "this can come to pass only when the civil officials, . . . both in their appointment and in the performance of their duties, are subject to the diocesan authorities." [74]

Conceivably the bishop might be able to surmount the various obstacles preventing him from exercising authoritative control and might really make his influence felt throughout the diocese. Conceivably, yes; actually, no. The bishop was the source of formal authority in the diocese; "without the confirmation of the bishop not one recommendation may be put into effect, and his approval is asked for every trifle." [75] Hence the bishop was so overburdened with work that he could not effectively guide his diocese. "In the diocese of Smolensk, ten thousand papers a year on the average come to the bishop for confirmation, in the form of journals, reports, estimates, and requests of different kinds. Of this huge quantity of papers the majority are of such little importance that they could be finally settled in the councils of the district priests, the consistories, or other diocesan institutions. . . ." [76] From the diocese of Olonets came the same report: all the numerous institutions and officials of the diocese presented before the bishop a mass of journals, reports, statements, different sorts of information, accounts, and all sorts of other papers, to say nothing of the documents which he received from private individuals.[77] Consequently the bishop, "who in the main reads only the abstracts of the findings and the decisions on the cases, proceeds . . . in positive darkness, not knowing whether everything is equitable and whether the case has been decided with full impartiality." [78] Under these conditions it would be vain to expect that the bishop, no matter how good his intentions, could wield the real power in the diocese.

[74] Sv. Sinod, *Otzyvy*, III, 237, Vladimir of Moscow.
[75] *Ibid.*, III, 53, Pitirim of Kursk.
[76] *Ibid.*, III, 38, Petr of Smolensk.
[77] *Ibid.*, III, 203, Report of the Religious Consistory of Olonets.
[78] *Ibid.*, Supplement, p. 23, Nikodim of Priamur and Blagoveshchensk.

The bishop, then, burdened by lifeless papers which "shut him off from the living with their sorrows and needs and hamper his spiritual activity," [79] left the decision to the consistory. However, the consistory was as a broken reed. It was usually composed of a few priests of the cathedral town, who could give only part of their time to the work of the diocese. The demands on their energies were great. In 1894 the number of items received by the individual consistories ranged from a minimum of 4,924 to a maximum of 20,317; the outgoing items ran from 6,590 to 24,309.[80] Probably by 1900 the business transacted was even greater, as the population was increasing rapidly. The work of the diocesan administration was supposed to be done by the consistory acting as a body. Even routine matters were required by law to be acted on at the meetings. However, the time available for these proceedings was so limited that the consistory could not spend the proper time on matters that were really important. The consistory of Kherson stated in 1905 that they had a possible working year of 290 days. Their day was five hours, from nine in the morning to two in the afternoon. Some 20,000 papers came before them, so that they had to finish from 70 to 85 items a day, or from 14 to 17 an hour. Thus to each item the consistory could allot only four minutes on the average. Actually, so the consistory of Kherson stated, the consistories did not meet regularly. Instead, the various bureaus of the chanceries or their chief clerks usually drew up the decisions on the various matters as they saw fit, and then the priests who were the members of the consistories signed them as individuals, without the formality of joint consideration [81]—a procedure which was contrary to the Code of Religious Consistories.

Evidently under a system of this sort the real authority and decision rested with the lay officials rather than with the priesthood. In fact the internal organization of the consistory seemed to be expressly arranged with that end in view. There were several bureaus of lay officials, each with its special jurisdiction and each with its ecclesiastical head, the priest who, as member of the consistory, nominally controlled the affairs of the bureau. But these bureaus, whether

[79] Sv. Sinod, *Otzyvy*, III, 203, Olonets Consistory.

[80] Sv. Sinod, *Obzor Deiatel'nosti Vedomstva Pravoslavnago Ispovedaniia za Vremia . . . Aleksandra III*, pp. 110–11.

[81] Sv. Sinod, *Otzyvy*, II, 406–7, Dimitrii of Kherson.

dealing with judicial matters, with parish accounts, with the parish record-books of births, deaths, and marriages, or with other matters, actually were controlled, not by the priests at their heads—they had little time for such supervision—but by the lay bureau heads, the chief clerks, and the like: ". . . the officialdom of the diocese can feel itself almost completely independent of the diocesan authority, and stronger than all the members of the purely religious adminis- tration." [82] One reason for this was the fact that by law "the immedi- ate control over the office force in all respects, and the responsibility for the correctness of the procedure, is entrusted to the secretary." [83]

Every item of the business of the diocese was begun by the receipt of a document of some sort. At once the secretary of the consistory took charge. All responsibility for the order of business was placed upon his shoulders; he had to look into each paper before letting it go further, and to consider each case before it was decided upon.[84] After his preliminary scrutiny, the document was sent to the proper bureau, where a report on the matter was prepared by the officials responsible to the secretary, under the nominal supervision of the priestly member of the consistory who was in charge of this bureau. The report was then presented to the meeting of the consistory by the civilian head of the bureau, with an explanation by the consistory member in charge of the bureau if the latter saw fit to offer one.[85] According to the statement of the consistory of Kherson, the con- sistories gave little consideration to the reports drawn up by the bureaus but, owing to lack of time, signed them without going through the formality of considering them as a body.[86] Moreover, if the con- sistory did discuss a matter at length and then failed to agree on a decision, the secretary, who was always present, was required to ex- plain the essence of the case and to report on the laws which were to be followed in reaching the necessary unanimous decision.[87] The secretary had no vote; but his power of suggestion did much to make up for that lack.

It has been shown that in this series of steps of consistorial pro-

---

[82] Ivantsov-Platonov, *op. cit.*, p. 29.
[83] Sv. Sinod, *Ustav Dukhovnykh Konsistorii*, sec. 296.
[84] *Ibid.*, secs. 298–307.   [85] *Ibid.*, secs. 295 and 304–8.
[86] Sv. Sinod, *Otzyvy*, II, 406–7, Dimitrii of Kherson.
[87] Sv. Sinod, *Ustav Dukhovnykh Konsistorii*, sec. 315.

cedure the secretaries were all-important. "The chief figures in . . . [the diocesan administration] are the secretaries—laymen, officials; there are priests there, but only in the background." [88] " 'Not one paper coming into the consistory may proceed without the approval of the secretary.' This secretary, not named as a member of the consistory, and not a part of it, is in reality the guide and the controller of the meeting. . . ." [89]

One result of this state of affairs was that there were many charges of bribery leveled against the consistories and especially against their chanceries. Mention has been made of the complaint presented by Archbishop Agafangel of Volhynia to Alexander II; in it he stated that the secretaries of the consistories had taken to extorting bribes with great frequency, and that the lesser officials were doing likewise.[90] This complaint was penned in 1873. In 1881 the great church historian and academician, Professor Golubinskii, wrote, "Until quite recently all our official institutions were very corrupt, but none more corrupt than the consistory and its chancery. Other official departments were cleansed either in full or in part, but not the consistory with its chancery." [91] In 1886 and 1887 the Synod found it necessary to send out circulars to the bishops criticizing the financial laxity of the consistorial administrations and ordering reform.[92]

Again in the 1880's the same charges were repeated, with chapter and verse, by the apostle of church reform, the priest and professor, Ivantsov-Platonov. According to him, there was widespread bribetaking in the diocesan administration. Even simple matters involving no special favors were made the occasion for bribery. For example, in some dioceses the routine business of receiving and inspecting the parish financial accounts, record-books, records of confessions, and the like, went through several hands, and in each case money had to

[88] V. Rozanov, *Okolo Tserkovnykh Sten*, I, 356. Rozanov was the writer on church affairs for the influential conservative newspaper *Novoe Vremia* (*The New Time*); at this time he was highly critical of the church administration. Later his views changed, and he became an ardent defender of the church system.

[89] Sv. Sinod, *Otzyvy*, III, 53, Pitirim of Kursk; *ibid.*, Supplement, pp. 22–24, Nikodim of Priamur and Blagoveshchensk.

[90] Agafangel, *op. cit.*, pp. 19–20.

[91] Golubinskii, *O Reforme v Byte Russkoi Tserkvi*, p. 32.

[92] Zav'ialov, ed., *Tsirkuliarnye Ukazy*, pp. 175–76, 183–85.

be paid out. And how complicated a simple parish priest must have found this bribe-giving!

To a man unaccustomed to this scheme of things it is all the more difficult, because for one and the same thing it is necessary to give in several different places—to different persons. It is necessary to give to the district priest; bribes must be given . . . to the consistory members, to the clerk, to the porter; they must be given in the consistory chancery —to the secretary, to the chief clerk, to his assistant, to the protocolist, to the archivist, to the clerks, to the porters—for forwarding the case, for a report, for verification, for the seal—and God knows how much and to whom. Experienced men know this; for each service there is an accepted price, determined by the nature of the service and by the position of the person interested in the case. But for special cases—difficult ones—they charge more than the usual rates; they take several times more, by threats and by violence—money and things; they take as much as they can.[93]

These charges, grave as they were when coming from a respected member of the church, were borne out by further evidence. In 1905 Bishop Filaret of Viatka spoke of the secrecy of the consistorial proceedings, "which offers to the subordinates of these institutions the possibility of permitting abuses—(bribe-taking)."[94] Also the consistory of Kherson, in its report on the need for reform, in the same year spoke of the badly paid diocesan officials, burdened with an impossible amount of work, "which factors give rise to the well-known consistorial red tape and frequently to abuses in respect to bribe-taking."[95]

Proneness to that common disease of bureaucracies, red tape, was a well-known failing of the consistories. All work was transacted through the medium of papers—too numerous and too formal. Many of them involved matters which should not have reached the diocesan authorities at all—for example, they alone might give out the railroad vouchers for the transportation of church bells or provide for the sale of official Synod blanks and marriage crowns.[96] Everything had to be done by "diocesan *ukaz*." Did there arise some simple need —as, for instance, to repair the roof of a church, or its cross and

[93] Ivantsov-Platonov, *op. cit.*, pp. 25 and 32.
[94] Sv. Sinod, *Otzyvy*, II, 511, Filaret of Viatka.
[95] *Ibid.*, II, 407, Dimitrii of Kherson.
[96] *Ibid.*, II, 511–12, Filaret of Viatka.

cupola, damaged by the wind, to mend a sagging church floor, or a fresco which threatened to fall—this could be done only after waiting for an *ukaz*. "Each performance of the marriage service may be done only by *ukaz;* the bells for a vesper service or a liturgy may be rung only by *ukaz;* the baker of communion bread may not bake except by *ukaz.*" [97]

The *ukazes* were forwarded in the form of official packets to the district priests, who then sent them on to the parishes by means of people going thither or by special messengers. Consequently they were often forwarded very slowly. Permission to repair the roof of a church was sometimes received eight months after the sending of the request for this permission, an *ukaz* confirming the election of the elder of a church perhaps six months after his election.[98] "In some churches they keep on praying for the good health of some member of the Ruling House long after his death is everywhere known"—because no *ukaz* is received ordering a change.[99]

The slowness and the formalism of the consistories were troublesome at best, but when the consistory exercised its function as the religious court of the diocese these failings were most marked. As a commission of the clergy of the city of Tver, writing in 1906, stated: "Who does not know how both society and the clergy regard the consistories? The consistorial court and its decrees do not enjoy esteem and trust. People invariably speak and write of the consistories with dislike, with scorn, and even at times with mockery." [100]

In fairness to the members of these organizations, it should be stated that probably the fault lay as much with the procedure as it did with the personnel. The procedure was the antiquated one which the civil courts had discarded in the period of the great reforms of the 1860's. A case started with an investigation, conducted in most instances by a priest of a church near the scene of the dispute. This priest, although very frequently without judicial training, was given the task of collecting all the evidence bearing upon the case. The sheets covered with this testimony were then shown to the two interested parties, who were given the choice of signing them, or, if they

[97] Zaozerskii, *O Nuzhdakh Tserkovnoi Zhizni*, p. 36.
[98] *Ibid.*   [99] Ivantsov-Platonov, *op. cit.*, p. 26.
[100] Sv. Sinod, *Otzyvy*, Supplement, p. 65.

dissented, of indicating in writing their objections.[101] The consistory then received these documents, considered them, and handed down their decision. No witnesses were called to testify in person; the accused and the accuser had no chance to plead their cases before the judges who settled their fate. Everything was decided in formal fashion on the basis of the writings sent in by the investigator.

Of this system of judicial practice there was much criticism, not the least vigorous of which came from the bishops of the Orthodox Church. Bishop Konstantin of Samara pointed out "what opportunities the investigatory method gives for concealing the truth, for slowing up the action of the court, for complicating the case with unnecessary details, and for leading the judges astray"; and he also spoke of the formidable size which the mass of papers assumed.[102] Bishop Afanasii of the Don remarked upon the vast correspondence in these cases, which did not, however, impress him as a valid means of determining the truth.[103]

Not the least of the evils inherent in the consistorial court system was the fact that the consistory exercised both judicial and executive functions. Impartiality must have been difficult under these conditions. Moreover, the real influence and authority was with the officials of the consistory chancery—the lay bureaucrats already discussed. For the ecclesiastical members of the consistory, burdened as they were with duties, could not possibly delve into the mysteries of each case. Instead, they depended upon the summary of the case which had been drawn up in the judicial bureau of the chancery.[104]

In order to eliminate the extraordinary slowness in reviewing and deciding court cases, there is a practice in the consistory of having cases reviewed and the decisions reached by the single member in charge of the "judicial bureau." This is, however, completely illegal. In this connection we must note with regret that among the clergy and in civil society there exists the conviction that the aforesaid illegality is the common thing in the consistory; here, mainly, is the cause for the belief that the consistorial court is an unfair court; there is full opportunity for interested persons to exercise influence by one means or another upon

---

[101] Sv. Sinod, *Ustav Dukhovnykh Konsistorii*, secs. 156–74.
[102] Sv. Sinod, *Otzyvy*, I, 483, Konstantin of Samara.
[103] *Ibid.*, I, 539, Afanasii of the Don.
[104] *Ibid.*, II, 407, Dimitrii of Kherson.

the single member of the consistory, or even upon the secretary who passes upon the finding, in order that the case may have the desired outcome.[105]

More in a similar vein was written by Bishops Kirion of Orel,[106] Serafim of Polotsk,[107] Nikon of Vladimir,[108] and Pitirim of Kursk.[109]

Unfortunately for the church and for the lower clergy, these courts, with all their infirmities, had a weighty influence upon diocesan affairs. They had jurisdiction over the clergy in all "crimes and offenses against their calling, or violations of propriety and good conduct." When a quarrel over church property or moneys arose between two clerics, the local consistory decided the case. It received and judged complaints against the clergy on the grounds of insults or of violations of their obligations. Finally all Orthodox laymen were subject to the consistorial court in all cases involving marriage and divorce.[110]

It was the parish priests especially who had reason to dread the action of the consistory. For a case might be started by any person who had a grudge against a priest, merely by writing a complaint, even anonymously, to the bishop or the consistory. "Cases may start as a result of rumors, on the grounds of accusations, reports, because of communications from official persons or institutions, or on the basis of complaints. . . ." [111] All cases went to the consistory, even the most insignificant, so that it was vitally necessary for the parish priest to keep in the good graces of the diocesan authorities by being properly submissive and by carrying out their wishes to the letter. For no man could be sure that some action of his would not be brought to the attention of the consistory and of the lay officials who dominated it.

Submission to the wishes of their superiors was indeed the rule for the lower clergy, for not only did the diocesan authorities have the means of enforcing control, but the character of the priests was often such as to lead to a minimum of self-assertion. The man who assumed the cassock of a village priest was very apt to have done so not out of zeal for the work of Christ, but because no other course was open to

---

[105] Sv. Sinod, *Otzyvy*, II, 516, Filaret of Viatka.   [106] *Ibid.*, I, 524.
[107] *Ibid.*, I, 150.   [108] *Ibid.*, I, 224.   [109] *Ibid.*, I, 295–96.
[110] Sv. Sinod, *Ustav Dukhovnykh Konsistorii*, sec. 148.
[111] Sv. Sinod, *Otzyvy*, II, 297, Agafangel of Riga; *Ustav*, sec. 153.

him. He usually came from an ecclesiastical family, and his father, who had been a priest before him, had almost certainly lacked the means to give his son a costly university training. Instead the boy had gone to a seminary, where sons of priests received free education. But while this training was free and was almost entirely barred to boys from other walks of life, it was designed to lead only to the priesthood, although a favored few might attain professorships in ecclesiastical institutions through further study in the religious academies. Most seminary students could not transfer to the universities. Religious service was the only career officially intended to be open to them.[112]

The consequences of the restrictions upon the sons of the clergy were serious. Many became dissatisfied with their prospects, and in some manner left the seminaries to go either into the secular schools or into civilian careers for which they had received little training. "The children of the clergy *en masse* have, in recent years, been obsessed by the desire to get a secular education; they flee from the pastoral service. . . ."[113] This dislike of a church career and of the seminary training was also revealed by a "strong fermentation" among the students, "combined with disorders."[114] Strikes, rioting, and personal violence to instructors showed student dissatisfaction.

Such was the atmosphere in which the prospective priests received their training. Those who did enter the ranks of the clergy were sometimes "not only not desirous of" serving in the priesthood, but were "even most undesirable for it."[115]

If even from those seminaries in each of which seven hundred youths are now being educated and from which every year from sixty to ninety

---

[112] Sv. Sinod, *Otzyvy*, I, 525, Kirion of Orel. It should be noted, however, that the Universities of Dorpat, Tomsk, and Warsaw admitted graduates of theological seminaries. The Ministry of Public Education granted this privilege, because these universities had vacancies; seminarists were not admitted by the other universities, as there was an excess of applicants from the secular schools. See: Gosudarstvennaia Duma, *Doklady Biudzhetnoi Komissii,* IV Duma, Session II, No. 4, Stenogram, p. 82. For decree granting seminary graduates the right to enter some departments of the University of Warsaw, see: *Polnoe Sobranie Zakonov,* 1886, No. 3816.

[113] Sv. Sinod, *Otzyvy*, I, 233, Nikon of Vladimir.

[114] *Ibid.,* I, 38, Mikhail of Tomsk.

[115] *Ibid.,* I, 535, Tikhon of the Aleutian Islands and of North America.

graduate, not more than ten a year [from each] go into the priesthood, and these not our best students, but only the unwilling poor ones, then it is clear that our present pastoral school does not fulfil its . . . function. . . . For students with a proper religious attitude, who should be the prevailing type, are the exception, and voluntary pastoral service "by vocation" is entirely unheard of.[116]

So declared Bishop Innokentii of Tambov in 1906. Priests who entered their life work under such conditions might be discontented and rebellious at heart, but as no other livelihood appeared available, and as they had wives to support and perhaps children before long, most of them must have swallowed their discontent and have bowed to the commands of their superiors.

In addition to being often unhappy in their attitude toward their life work, the priests were in an unenviable position with respect to those over them. Of their superiors, probably the bishops disturbed the village clergy least; but some bishops there were who seemed to delight in showing the superiority of their station to those beneath them. The well-known writer on religious matters, Vasilii Rozanov, quotes a priest of a provincial town, who wrote to the newspaper *Grazhdanin* (*Citizen*) as follows:

The bishop receives all the priests in the hall, near the coat rack and the galoshes—receives them all simultaneously and in public; and if anyone is abashed, or presents his petition at all timidly, he holds that priest up to ridicule; so that many lovers of comic scenes take pains to come at the reception hours, to be amused in seeing how this Bishop and Archpastor makes fun of his priests.[117]

The newspaper editor went on to say that this was not an exceptional case. The bishops and likewise the secretaries of the consistories were generally disrespectful, he said, toward their priests. This either cowed the priests or made them angry and defiant, and it usually weakened their authority with the people.[118] Indeed, as another writer pointed out, it is understandable that when a village pastor had journeyed for a hundred *versts* to unburden his soul and to receive encouragement and advice, and then, perhaps because of pressure of

[116] Sv. Sinod, *Otzyvy*, III, 299, Innokentii of Tambov.

[117] *Grazhdanin*, Sept. 9, 1905, as quoted in Rozanov, *Okolo Tserkovnykh Sten*, II, 196.

[118] *Ibid.*

business, had received a cold five-minute reception, he might lose forever his desire to confide in his superior.[119]

Perhaps this superciliousness had only a trifling influence on the parishioners; but other factors of more weight likewise acted to weaken the moral influence of the priest in the village. In the pledge which a candidate for the priesthood gave before his ordination, so Bishop Petr of Smolensk stated, he promised, not so much to serve the church and to obey its canons as "to fulfill the instructions laid down by the civil authorities and, among other things, not to involve himself in the misfortunes of the peasants"—presumably not to support the peasants in their difficulties with the landowners and the civil authorities—under danger of "judgment under the full power of the law, and of deprivation of his status"—unfrocking. This considerably narrowed the activity of the pastor, for the lot of his parishioners was often a bitter one.[120] And indeed the position of the pastor within the church tended to keep him generally submissive, overworked, and cowed.

Directly over the parish priest was the district priest (*blago-chinnyi*), who might be a very menacing figure indeed. This cleric, appointed by the diocesan authorities, supervised the parishes, from ten to thirty, under him. He was instructed to watch the pastors, their lives, their readings, their sermons, and had full opportunity to be the scourge of the priests.[121] In the eyes of the parish clergy the district priest often was a tyrant.

Touching on the matter of sermons, the laws were quite explicit. The parish priests were required to send copies of their sermons and religious teachings to the district priests, who thereupon considered them carefully, and reported to the consistory the erring pastors, "including those priests who do not display proper care" in preparation.[122]

Thus the diocesan authorities retained control over the teachings

---

[119] V. Myshtsyn, *Po Tserkovno-obshchestvennym Voprosam*, p. 7. The author was a regular contributor to the important *Tserkovnyi Vestnik*, published by a group of professors of the Religious Academy of St. Petersburg.

[120] Sv. Sinod, *Otzyvy*, III, 33, Petr of Smolensk.

[121] Sv. Sinod, *Ustav Dukhovnykh Konsistorii*, secs. 63 and 65; Ognev, *Na Poroge Reform*, pp. 5–7.

[122] Sv. Sinod, *Ustav*, secs. 9–12.

offered by the priests to the people. In similar fashion the consistories regulated almost all the details of parish affairs. The appointment of a priest to a parish was decided upon in the diocesan offices.[123] The enlargement or rebuilding of a church, or minor repairs to its roof or *ikonostas*—all these might be done only with the permission of the consistory. The consistory had to be advised on all details of the administration of the landed property of the parish, and full reports on all sums coming in to the church coffers and on the expenditures of the parish had to be made every month. The supply of bridal crowns, of absolutory prayers, and of official record blanks had also to be obtained from the consistory.[124]

Inevitably these reports and requests occasioned the priests a great deal of work, as did the keeping of the records of births, deaths, and marriages. By law each priest had the duty of recording these family events in duplicate books. These entries were legal documents, to which reference was made whenever official papers had to be drawn up. No Orthodox birth was legitimate, no marriage of Orthodox subjects was valid, unless it was entered in the parish books. They were the official sources for evidence needed for passports, conscription lists, police records, and the like. Each time a citation from the record was needed, the priest was obliged to copy the entry, word for word, from the books, to sign the excerpt, and to stamp it with the parish seal.[125] This perhaps seems a trifling matter, but it was not. In 1905 the consistory of the diocese of Kherson stated that about one-third of all its business consisted of forwarding requests for citations from the record-books to the proper parishes, and of hearing charges against priests for improper keeping of the records.[126]

Nor was this all. In addition to the duties laid upon him by the consistory, all sorts of institutions sent demands or requests to the pastor: *zemstvos*, as well as learned and educational, military, sanitary, statistical, agricultural, and archaeological institutions, and others.[127] All this work had to be performed without delay, without objection; otherwise there was the threat of fine and imprisonment

---

[123] Sv. Sinod, *Ustav*, sec. 70.   [124] *Ibid.*, secs. 133, 138, 139, 145.
[125] *Ibid.*, secs. 99 and 101.
[126] Sv. Sinod, *Otzyvy*, II, 408, Dimitrii of Kherson.
[127] *Ibid.*, III, 33, Petr of Smolensk.

for the priest. The *Diocesan News* of Kherson gave a remarkable example of what might be required of the priests. A health officer asked to have the priests of a district send in the following data: the names and birthplaces of the midwives of their parishes, the residences of these women, their domestic status and number of years of obstetrical service, the number of births which they had assisted during certain periods, the number of difficult births which they had aided over a four-year period, what outside help they had called in—whether they had summoned the doctor, the priest, or an obstetrician—and the result in each case! [128]

Naturally the priests complained of being overburdened by this work. One priest listed some nineteen record-books which he was obliged to keep.[129]

Who does not know the type of the shabby, timid "little father" of the village, who is eternally in fear of a visitation of the father *blago-chinnyi* [district priest], of the constable, of the police sergeant; who, together with his psalmist, is eternally writing, by the light of a tiny lamp, tens of "statements" and "reports," which are needed by no one, in order to send them to be numbered and sealed by the consistory? Who does not know the type of "farming" little father, who sows and reaps and journeys to the bazaars and markets in order to buy and sell horses, cattle, sheep, and so on? Who does not know, moreover, the type of little father who is the terror of his parish and of the surrounding district, threatening, at the command of the consistory, "traitors" in the person of teachers of *zemstvo* schools, and writing "reports" to the "province" [the provincial authorities]?

Is this that prophet, pastor, and teacher who can "with his words set aflame the hearts of men," and can teach his parishioners Eternal Truth? Is this that fearless spiritual leader who openly accuses Pilate, who drives the money-changers from the temple, who encourages his flock in disaster, comforts them in sorrow, and for the sake of truth goes to the cross, as did He Whom he names as his Teacher? The answer is clear.[130]

Not all Russian priests fitted into the categories given above. Many doubtless were true shepherds to their flocks, comforting them in distress, and attempting to assuage their sufferings. And yet, as the

[128] *Tserkovnyia Vedomosti,* March 4, 1906, p. 445.
[129] *Ibid.,* Nov. 26, 1905, p. 2089.
[130] *Iuzhnoe Obozrenie,* April 10, 1905, as quoted in Preobrazhenskii, ed., *Tserkovnaia Reforma,* pp. 365–66.

citation suggests, some there were who fell short of the apostolic ideal. May not the reason be found in part in the unfortunate conditions of their service? Overworked, occasionally browbeaten by His Lordship the Bishop, subjected to close supervision that sometimes bordered on spying, hampered by a mass of regulations and interference from above—such were the village priests; and it is not surprising that few of them were noted for defying vested interests or for daring to oppose their superiors. Indeed not a few of them turned their attention, rather, to the rewards given out by those above for faithful service. One such reward was transfer to another parish providing a better income. Of this practice Bishop Stefan of Mogilev stated that these "changes come exceedingly frequently at present, and not by any means always for reputable reasons. . . ."[131] Then there were badges of merit. One Professor Almasov summarizes thus the results of fifteen years of reading the letters sent by parish priests to *Tserkovnyi Vestnik (Church Messenger)*: "As a red thread running through the endless series of questions there is evidence of the attempts of the clergy to obtain the Order of Anne, third class. Those who have no hope of receiving this order at least try for some medal or other."[132] These tokens, incidentally, were bestowed only upon priests who enjoyed the favor of their diocesan authorities.[133]

Under such conditions the clergy were submissive. If some particular priest were too bold a pastor, there was one mighty weapon ready to hand for the authorities to use in quelling him. This was the threat of judicial action.

It was no idle threat. Twelve different punishments might be inflicted by the consistory, ranging from mild penalties, such as unfavorable notations on the service record, fines, and rebukes, to deprivation of the right to perform service for varying periods of time, temporary reduction from priesthood to the rank of deacon or psalmist, imposition of periods of penance in monasteries, and, in extreme cases, unfrocking and permanent reduction in rank, or unfrocking

[131] Sv. Sinod, *Zhurnaly i Protokoly . . . Predsobornago Prisutstviia*, II, 52.

[132] *Ibid.*, II, 498–99.

[133] For investigation of priests before granting awards, see Synod Archives, Chancery of the Over Procurator, 1908, portfolio No. 47.

with the loss of all rights pertaining to the priesthood.[134] In the Consistorial Code the offenses for which these penalties were imposed were grouped, rather illogically, in three categories: violations of priestly duty, of propriety, and of good conduct; offenses arising out of disputes over the use of church property or funds; and affronts to civil or religious persons, and failure to pay incontestable dues and obligations.[135] Permanent unfrocking was to be inflicted only upon priests convicted of major civil crimes which entailed the loss of civil rights, or upon those guilty of heresy, fighting during service time, or reading the service while drunk.[136] But the penalties for less serious offenses were not exactly defined, and it was easy to find a pretext for a weighty punishment if desired. Then, too, trials could be brought about by anonymous accusations and were often accompanied by abuse and injustice, so that even the boldest and most sincere priest must have hesitated to arouse the anger of influential landowners, for he knew that in so doing he exposed himself to the danger of judicial action by the consistory.

Perhaps his superiors might wish to discipline him without a trial. In that case he might be transferred to a different (and poorer) parish, which would "have a very burdensome effect upon . . . his financial position. . . ." [137] There were many reasons why a priest had to be submissive to those in authority.

A Synod circular to the bishops in 1886 seems in part to contradict this statement. The document in question complained that the consistories were too lenient in the exercise of their judicial function. Often a preliminary examination would be made before a case was begun, and sometimes the matter was quietly dropped without a trial. It was said that the accused were frequently permitted to make objections and demurrers, which automatically halted the case for a time. On occasion the consistory let a case lapse completely, and only after repeated urgings was it again taken up. Furthermore, in some cases where parishioners had complained that their priests were guilty of extortion or of drunken habits or of performing service while

---

[134] Sv. Sinod, *Ustav Dukhovnykh Konsistorii*, sec. 176.
[135] *Ibid.*, sec. 148.   [136] *Ibid.*, secs. 177–81.
[137] Berdnikov, *Kratkii Kurs Tserkovnago Prava*, p. 546.

drunk, the contending parties were encouraged to become reconciled, so that the case might be dropped without ever coming to trial as the law required.[138] However, if one may judge by what happened during the Revolution of 1905, these laxly handled cases were probably those in which no state interests were involved and in which the petitioners were humble men without influence in the community. As will be shown in a later chapter, the church could and did deal with its sons who supported principles which were considered to be opposed to its interest and to those of the government.

The rewards and punishments dispensed by the consistories were probably enough to keep all but a very few of the priests in their places, and for those few there was another weapon. This was confinement, by administrative order of the Tsar, in some monastery— and in special cases in the monastery prisons maintained by the Synod —bleak Solovetskii, on an island in the White Sea, and more often the Spaso-Efimevskii Monastery in Suzdal. In these two institutions priests who proved incorrigible, together with "dangerous" sectarian or schismatic leaders, were lodged in small, dark cells, sometimes for life. When, by *ukaz* of the Committee of Ministers of February 11, 1905, imprisonment in monasteries by administrative order of the emperor was ended, seven persons were freed from the solitary cells of Suzdal and Solovetskii.[139]

Father Tsvetkov, a priest imprisoned in Suzdal in 1902, was interviewed in 1904, after his release. An excerpt from his statement shows the uses to which this prison was put:

When they shut me up in the prison cell and I remained alone within four walls, I remembered that they had frequently tried to frighten me with Suzdal. I had for fifteen years written against the consistories, and, after that, for five years against the Synod. As a result, in response to my declarations and accusations, I frequently heard, "Look out, you will land in Suzdal!" and so on. But I never thought that there was such a fortress here, such a prison. I did not know that such coffins were prepared for men.[140]

Of course it must be borne in mind that this was a very rare case. Few Orthodox priests found their way to Suzdal. Moreover, it cannot be

[138] Zav'ialov, ed., *Tsirkuliarnye Ukazy*, pp. 178–83.

[139] *Pravitel'stvennyi Vestnik*, March 5, 1905.

[140] A. Prugavin, *Monastyrskiia Tiur'my*, p. 172.

said that, even in dealing with Father Tsvetkov, the *lettre de cachet* was used precipitately. But while this means of control was seldom used, the threat was there—another reason why most of the white clergy were submissive.

As for the black clergy—the monastics—they also were under firm rule. Seven of the monasteries were of the *stavropigial'nyi* type—that is, under the direct control of the Synod. The others, as well as the convents, were subject to the jurisdiction of the bishop and the consistory of the diocese in which they were located.[141] For immediate control over the monastic institutions there was a supervisor (*blagochinnyi*), who reported to the diocesan authorities.[142] In addition, the individual monks and nuns, besides being under the authority of the heads of their institutions, were also subject to the judicial power of the consistory.[143] Hence the monastics of the lower ranks presented no threat to the authority of the Over Procurator. The bishops also for the most part were docile; the lay officials of the Synod and of the consistories looked to His Eminence the Procurator for guidance, and then saw to it that no member of the clergy opposed his will without penalty. And so strong was the authority of this man over the Orthodox Church that the church's life was controlled by him—a lay official of the Tsar. The Over Procurator of the Most Holy Synod commanded: and in due course, all over Russia, monks and priests did his bidding.

It was no mean domain over which the authority of the Over Procurator extended. In 1900, including cathedrals, monastery and convent churches, institutional churches, and those attached to cemeteries, as well as the many parish churches in cities, towns, and villages all over the country, there were 49,082 churches of the Russian Orthodox faith in the empire. In addition to this there existed 18,946 Orthodox shrines and prayer houses.[144] To serve these places of worship, in the same year, there were 104,446 members of the secular clergy (2,230 cathedral deans, 43,784 priests, 14,945 deacons, and 43,487 psalmists),[145] as well as the monastic clergy, con-

[141] Sv. Sinod, *Ustav Dukhovnykh Konsistorii*, sec. 4.
[142] *Ibid.*, secs. 118–19.   [143] *Ibid.*, sec. 196.
[144] Sv. Sinod, *Vsepoddanneishii Otchet*, 1900, pp. 8–9 of tables.
[145] *Ibid.*, pp. 12–13 of tables.

sisting of 16,668 monks and 41,615 nuns.[146] The ministrations of the clergy were received by the Orthodox inhabitants of the empire, who, according to the official figures, numbered 83,739,659 in 1900. The churchmen christened the 4,833,709 Orthodox children born that year; they married the 835,265 couples of this faith; and they buried the 3,069,776 Orthodox subjects of the Tsar who died in 1900.[147]

The people to whom these churchmen ministered were the folk who composed the Orthodox foundation of imperial Russia. They, together with the clergy, were those whose religious life was dominated by the Tsar's appointed official, the Over Procurator of the Synod. Here were included most of the patient-eyed, broad-faced peasants of the innumerable villages of Holy Russia; only a minority of Russians—the Old Believers and the sectarians—lay without the fold. This was the great Orthodox core of the Russian nation. Truly this numerous group of believers, given religious guidance by priests who obeyed the *ukazes* of the Synod and of its Over Procurator, was a valuable source of support for the Imperial Government of Nicholas II.

Apparently the emperor's government cherished the support which it received from religious authority, for in the Code of Laws it was stated:

To the Emperor of All the Russias belongs the supreme autocratic authority. To submit to his authority, not only from fear, but also from conviction, God Himself commandeth.

Thus to the compelling strength of the civil government and the armed forces of the empire was added the spiritual force of religion. Moreover, this was brought home to each person, for "the loyalty of his [the Tsar's] subjects . . . is confirmed by a universal oath."

[146] Sv. Sinod, *Vsepoddanneishii Otchet*, 1900, pp. 12–13 of tables.

[147] *Ibid.*, p. 6 of tables. According to the census of 1897, of the 125,668,190 inhabitants of the Russian Empire, 87,384,480, or 69.5 percent, were Orthodox; 2,173,738, or 1.7 percent, were Old Believers and sectarians; 11,420,927, or 9 percent, were Catholics; 3,743,204, or 2.3 percent, Protestants; 13,889,-421, or 11 percent, Mohammedans; 5,189,401, or 4.1 percent, Jews; the remainder were unspecified Christians and non-Christians. In the fifty provinces of European Russia, however, the Orthodox formed a larger proportion of the population, with 81.8 percent of the whole. In Siberia the Orthodox formed 86.9 percent of the total. Tsentral'nyi Statisticheskii Komitet, *Raspredelenie Naseleniia Imperii po Glavnym Veroispovedaniiam*, pp. 2–4.

This oath was obligatory for non-Orthodox subjects as well as for adherents of the official church; it was administered to the Orthodox subjects in monasteries, cathedrals, or parish churches, according to convenience.[148]

The coronation of the Tsar took place amid scenes of great pomp and glory in the ancient Uspenskii Cathedral in Holy Moscow, the city of the forty-times-forty churches. Here, as the choir chanted and the fragrant clouds of incense floated up to the dome, the young sovereign was crowned and anointed in the presence of the great folk of the realm. Majestic bearded metropolitans and archbishops in vestments of silk, brocade, and velvet were present in full force, lending a truly Byzantine magnificence to the scene.

The Emperor, before the performance of this sacred ceremony, according to the custom of the ancient Christian Sovereigns and of his God-hallowed ancestors, shall pronounce in the hearing of his loyal subjects the creed of the Orthodox Catholic faith, and then, after donning his robes, upon placing the crown upon his head, and upon taking the scepter and the orb, he shall, with a genuflection, call upon the King of Kings, using the established prayer. . . .[149]

It was in this manner that Nicholas II assumed the crown of the long line of the Orthodox Tsars of Holy Russia. Thus did the church bless his reign—a blessing repeated in all the churches of the empire. Of course only notables were able to see the solemn ritual in the Uspenskii Cathedral. None the less, word of the magnificence of the ceremony penetrated to all corners of Russia, and in time bright lithographed pictures of the coronation were installed in peasant huts in Siberia, in the thatched dwellings of the southern steppes, and in the log houses of the fishing villages of the White Sea coast.

Thus publicly did the Orthodox Church support the Tsar and strengthen his government with its solemn rituals. Likewise it was required by law to support him in secret, for in 1722 Peter the Great had added to the Supplement to his *Religious* Regulation a provision that priests were to disclose to the secret police any information con-

[148] *Svod Zakonov*, ed. 1857, I, pt. 1, "Svod Osnovnykh Gosudarstvennykh Zakonov," secs. 1, 33, 34; *Svod Zakonov*, I, pt. 1, "Svod Osnovnykh Gosudarstvennykh Zakonov," ed. 1906, secs. 4, 55, 56.

[149] *Svod Zakonov*, ed. 1857, *loc. cit.*, sec. 36, note 2; *Svod Zakonov*, I, pt. 1, "Svod Osnovnykh Gosudarstvennykh Zakonov," ed. 1906, sec. 58, note 2.

cerning plots or attempts against the emperor or his government, even when the knowledge had been obtained under seal of the confessional.[150] It is interesting to find Archbishop Iakov of Iaroslavl deploring, as late as 1906, this uncanonical command, although he did not venture to say whether it was still obeyed.[151] No official data are available as to whether Orthodox priests did obey this precept; none the less, this requirement does give some indication of the attitude of the Russian government toward the church. In somewhat similar fashion, the district priests and the diocesan authorities were required by the Code of Laws to supplement the work of the police in seeing that deserters, vagrants, and men without passports were not received or sheltered in the villages under their jurisdiction.[152]

Additional duties of the clergy, as we have seen, were to proclaim imperial manifestoes, *ukazes,* and the like, in their churches; to keep the parish records; [153] and to urge their flocks to submit to vaccination against smallpox.[154] However, these were but minor services; probably the chief and most valuable aid which the church rendered was that of using its authority and influence to silence or weaken opposition to the government, to discredit hostile spokesmen, or to win the rebellious over to submission to the authorities. The following instances of this activity will serve further to clarify the relations between the church and the civil authorities.

In 1902, for example, a circular of the Synod told the bishops that "as in several localities in our dear land ill-intentioned persons, opponents of the lawful authorities, arouse the people," the priests of infected parishes were to be instructed to "take all proper pastoral measures" to prevent peasant uprisings, and "to explain to their flocks all the falseness, according to the Word of God, of the appeals of the evil-minded who urge them to disobey the authorities established by the Tsar and to attack the property of others." The bishops

[150] Verkhovskoi, *op. cit.,* II, 85–86, footnote.

[151] Sv. Sinod, *Otzyvy,* Supplement, p. 255.

[152] *Svod Zakonov,* ed. 1857, XIV, "Ustav o Pasportakh i Beglykh," sec. 586; *Svod Zakonov,* XIV, "Ustav o Pasportakh," ed. 1903, sec. 152, supplement, paragraph 5.

[153] Barsov, *op. cit.,* p. 3; p. 469.

[154] *Svod Zakonov,* ed. 1857, XIII, "Ustav Vrachebnyi," sec. 1009; *Svod Zakonov,* XIII, "Ustav Vrachebnyi," ed. 1906, sec. 790.

were further required to urge priests "who are known for their sound thinking" to give talks in this vein as often as possible.[155]

Following this, the bishop of Poltava, Ilarion, decided to give out circulars to the clergy of his diocese, requiring each priest

to urge his parishioners at service time on Sundays, and holy days, and also when ministering to individuals, to give full obedience to the authorities established by God and the Tsar; to lead peaceful, honorable, and industrious lives; to trust only what is proclaimed in the churches or by the local authorities; to accept no advice from persons not known to them—advice which brings to them harm, and leads to the infringement of order.[156]

Governor Engelhardt, of the province of Saratov, when reporting to the Department of Police on the measures taken by him to deal with revolutionary disorders of the peasants in 1902, stated that, in addition to establishing trustworthy constables at troublesome places, he had requested that the bishop of Saratov "fill any vacant parishes with priests known to him for their energy and zeal in furthering the spiritual and moral enlightenment of the people," and had asked that the bishop should indicate to his priests that "in their pastoral talks with the people they should instill in them respect for the law and should demand from the young respect for their elders and obedience to their parents and to the authorities." [157]

In the same year the famous Father Ioann of Kronstadt, widely regarded as an especially holy person, delivered a sermon on the anniversary of the accession of Nicholas II to the throne. The burden of it was, "The Tsar's authority is a divine institution, necessary and precious for the great social community of man. . . ." [158] And in far-off Tomsk in Siberia, Bishop Makarii preached on the theme, "Whence authority on earth—apropos of the contemporary sedition." He, too, stated that the Tsar was established by God, and that "opposition to the authorities is opposition to God's commandment." [159]

In *Tserkovnyia Vedomosti* (*Church News*) the official organ of the

[155] P. Maslov, *Agrarnyi Vopros v Rossii*, II, 126.

[156] *Revoliutsionnaia Rossiia*, June 25, 1902, pp. 23–24.

[157] M. N. Pokrovskii, ed., *1905—Istoriia Revoliutsionnogo Dvizheniia v Otdel'nykh Ocherkakh*, I, 317.

[158] *Tserkovnyia Vedomosti*, Nov. 2, 1902, pp. 1549–50.

[159] *Ibid.*, Sept. 21, 1902, pp. 1307–11.

Synod, there was printed in 1903 a model sermon to be given before congregations of seasonal workers who were about to go forth in search of employment. In it the workers were cautioned against conversations with schismatics and sectarians, and were especially warned against associating with those evil deceivers who urged the people not to obey the legal authorities, thus

leading simple people into frightful calamities and subjecting them to strict accountability before the Heavenly Tsar—God—as well as before the earthly Tsar.

. . . God protect you, when you meet such folk, from losing your Orthodox faith, your love of the Orthodox Church, of Tsar and Fatherland, and of this your native church and of your spiritual pastors.[160]

In its efforts against subversive influences the church did not pass by the novelist Tolstoi. He was solemnly excommunicated by the Synod in 1901; his teachings, which inspired some of the peasants to dream of a utopia free from poverty and hunger, and in which he condemned oaths, military service, and war, were roundly denounced throughout 235 pages of sermons by Archbishop Nikanor of Kherson, which were published in 1903. ". . . Patriotism," said the archbishop, "[is] the most natural and most holy obligation. Patriotism is love for the Fatherland, loyalty to it, and fealty even unto death. . . ." He continued:

Who of all mortals on earth can be more sacred than the Anointed of God, the God-chosen Tsar? What is more inviolable than his life, with which is so closely linked the life of the whole Fatherland? What is more obligatory than the oath, established and blessed by God, of loyalty to the Tsar, even unto death, unto the shedding of his blood by each of his most loyal subjects? When shedding our blood for the Tsar, we shed it for all that is for us on earth most holy, dear, and beloved—for our faith and sacred things, for our churches and the tombs of our ancestors, for our fathers and brothers, for wives and children, for the family hearth and the family well-being. . . . And the Tsar is the highest, the most holy symbol of all that is dear and beloved and sacred for our hearts in our land.[161]

The oath to which the archbishop referred was an important means of strengthening the loyalty of the imperial armies. In it the soldiers

[160] *Tserkovnyia Vedomosti,* March 29, 1903, pp. 502–3.
[161] Nikanor (Arkhiepiskop), *Besedy i Slova,* pp. 207–8.

promised and swore, "by Almighty God, before His Holy Gospel," to serve loyally and bravely His Imperial Majesty the Emperor and Autocrat, "without sparing my body, to the last drop of blood"; further, "to fight bravely against the enemies of His Imperial Majesty's realm, with my body and blood, on the field and in fortresses, by water and by dry land"; and, "in concluding thus my oath, I kiss the Word and Cross of my Savior. Amen." [162]

In order that the devotion of the men might be strengthened, the armed forces were provided with a complement of chaplains, commanded by the Protopresbyter of the Military and Naval Clergy— a dignitary of episcopal rank, chosen by the Synod, with imperial confirmation, and subject to the jurisdiction of the Synod.[163] The chaplains played an important part in maintaining the morale of the rank and file.

The view of the governmental authorities concerning the military value of the Orthodox faith was admirably expressed in an article in the *Pravitel'stvennyi Vestnik* (*Governmental Messenger*) in 1894. "Faith for long has served . . . as the chief motive force for the most outstanding [martial] exploits," said the article, "and military history . . . furnishes a number of instances of its limitless influence on the soldier." The Orthodox faith, the journal said, equipped the soldier with all the principles necessary for a good warrior—principles which were received by the soldier in simple form over a long period, so that they were "imprinted on his heart," and not merely on his mind and memory. "The Orthodox Church strengthens and imbues in each soldier limitless loyalty and love of Throne and Fatherland, [and] full obedience to his superiors. . . . It likewise teaches him not to fear death, and promises to each one who honorably performs his duty a reward in Heaven."

The Grand Duke who was Commander in Chief of the St. Petersburg Military District, the article continued, was especially appreciative of the value of religion "in respect to the preparation of the troops for war." In addition to seeing to the functioning of the military churches and to encouraging church choirs and the like, the

---

[162] Voennoe Ministerstvo, *Svod Voennykh Postanovlenii*, VI, supplement to sec. 6.
[163] *Ibid.*, secs. 748–62.

Grand Duke required all officers to receive the Eucharist, together with their men, during the Lenten season. " 'The commanders,' said the Grand Duke, 'should constantly implant in their subordinates the conviction that only he who esteems the holy faith and observes the church rules can be a good and loyal servant of Sovereign and Father-land.' " [164]

When actual military operations began, the church proved willing to support them. The expedition against the Boxers was approved by the Synod,[165] and Archbishop Iustin of Kherson told a detachment of embarking soldiers that it was a blessed work to defend fellow Christians from the heathen, and to die courageously for Tsar and fatherland. "Truly, for such brave heroes the door of the Heavenly Kingdom is open, and eternal blessed rest awaits all Christ-loving warriors killed on the field of battle." [166]

In 1904, when war with Japan broke out, the Synod ordered the Tsar's manifesto read in all churches, and prescribed special prayers asking victory over the enemy, with God's all-powerful support.[167] Many telegrams were sent to the Synod by various Orthodox congregations, brotherhoods, and monasteries, enthusiastically expressing loyalty to the Tsar in the hour of battle. The messages were not infrequently accompanied with pledges of money—for the Red Cross, for the wounded, for the use of the army, for strengthening the fleet. Many of the bishops and metropolitans preached sermons supporting the government in the war. Fairly typical was that of Bishop Gurii of Novgorod, who declared: "In the persons of the Japanese, Asia wars against Europe. The Land of the Rising Sun . . . brings to us not the light of truth, which once shone forth upon Europe from Judea in the person of the Savior, but the darkness of heathen-dom. . . ." [168] And after the fortunes of war had turned out to favor the Japanese, the Synod, on August 4, 1904, issued a new edict demanding more prayers "that God may give to our Christ-loving troops the victory over the cruel and crafty enemy." [169]

[164] *Pravitel'stvennyi Vestnik*, Feb. 24, 1894.
[165] *Tserkovnyia Vedomosti*, July 29, 1900, official part, p. 289.
[166] *Ibid.*, July 22, 1900, pp. 1208–9; also, Aug. 5, 1900, p. 1284.
[167] *Ibid.*, Jan. 24, 1904, official part, pp. 42–44.
[168] *Ibid.*, Feb. 7, 1904, p. 206; Feb. 14, 1904, pp. 248–49.
[169] *Ibid.*, Aug. 28, 1904, official part, p. 386.

Thus did the Russian Church assist the imperial authorities in peace and in war. There is reason to feel, however, that in its exhortations the church did not meet with full success. For one thing, by the end of 1904 it was already a commonplace that most of the intelligentsia were lost to the church. "All discussions of the matter lead to one and the same conclusion, . . . that *church and intelligentsia are deeply divided*." [170] Unfortunately, none of the numerous individuals, both ecclesiastics and laymen, who subscribed to this belief, took the trouble to define what was meant by the intelligentsia. The term probably referred chiefly to lawyers, doctors, professors, writers, and others who had received higher educations, but remained outside the service of the government or the church. The testimony on this alienation from the church is quite impressive. At the meetings of the Religious and Philosophical Conference (composed of clerics and laymen) in St. Petersburg in 1902, intellectual leaders of the capital, one after another, declared that "a gulf has been fixed between the church and the intelligentsia"; and most of the speakers hoped for a new morality which would secure for every Russian— "every person living on the Russian land, complete liberation from the nightmare of the Christian State." [171] Among those who testified to the alienation of the intelligentsia were V. Ternavtsev, Father I. O. Al'bov, V. V. Rozanov, V. S. Miroliubov, Professor V. V. Uspenskii, and Bishop Sergii, Rector of the Religious Academy of St. Petersburg. Professor A. V. Kartashev, of the same Academy, declared that "the division between the church and the intelligentsia is such a concrete, evident phenomenon that only a person completely unaware of the Russian life around him could fail to recognize it." [172]

Much more important for the church than the allegiance of the more educated classes was its support from the masses; but even here the Orthodox faith was not entirely secure. Although a Father Gapon could still win a hearing, many of the factory workers were turning from the church to socialism. The process was still far from complete; none the less, in spite of the church's efforts, the events

[170] *Ibid.*, March 30, 1902, p. 445.
[171] *Bogoslovskii Vestnik*, May, 1906, pp. 35–37.
[172] *Novyi Put'*, Jan., 1903, supplement, pp. 5–49.

of 1905 and 1906 were to show that the urban proletariat was becoming estranged.

Both the proletariat and the intelligentsia, however, were relatively few in numbers; and the church could even afford to let many of them go if it could hold the peasantry. That great mass of simple, uneducated folk had for centuries been the mainstay of Orthodoxy, in spite of the schism and the sects; and the doctrines of Marx and of the new science had made much smaller inroads among them than had been the case with the other two groups. The peasantry was the hope of the church—the real heart of "Holy Russia."

None the less, even here the church's supremacy was not uncontested. If the peasants had little to do with the socialism sent to them from the cities, they did have their own varieties of radical organization in the form of the Old Believers and, even more alarming to the church, the rapidly growing sectarian movements, those of the *Molokane*, the *Dukhobortsy*, and especially the Stundists. As will be shown in another chapter, these groups were probably stronger than the church was willing to admit, and were making some way in undermining the influence of the church over the peasantry.

Indeed there seems reason to believe that even without these defections the Orthodox Church would not have been in an impregnable position. Of course the leaders of the church did not admit this. They claimed the Russian peasant as their own and rejoiced at his apparently deeply religious nature. In proof, said they, one had but to see the churches, filled with crowds of reverent worshipers, and the streams of dusty pilgrims who by thousands swarmed to pray before the bones of the saints and the famous wonder-working ikons. None the less, others read the portents differently.

Those who declared that the church did not have a secure hold upon the people stated that the clergy did not enjoy the sympathy and the respect of the masses. The bishops, for example, were said to be far removed from the people. Although most of them had been born into priestly families, when they reached the episcopal rank they became unapproachable, and conducted themselves like spiritual lords.

The bishop may not go anywhere on foot, nor ride with a mere *izvoshchik* [cabman], but must always go in a carriage. The bishop may not receive anyone in his quarters unless he is attired in his silken cassock and regalia. The bishop may not enter a church unless he is supported on both sides by abbots or archpriests, who sometimes are men who, because of advanced years, need support more than he.[173]

Moreover, owing to the huge size of many Russian dioceses and to the burden of administrative detail, the bishop had little opportunity to become acquainted with the mass of the laymen of his diocese. Even the people of the cathedral town were but little known to the bishop. The great majority of them he saw only as members of the reverent crowd which filled the church when he performed service or which pressed close for his blessing. He had little time to talk with them, or if he did engage in conversation, it was only brief and perfunctory. "From appearances he enjoys deep, reverent respect; but he stands on a sort of pedestal, unapproachable by the people, and he does not have vital relations with his flock, or any close religious and moral unity with them." [174]

Actually the bishops knew their dioceses not so much through personal contact as through the thousands of papers which they had to consider each year, as we have seen. A dry, formal attitude toward the problems of their followings was too often the result. Other factors which set them apart from the people were the haughty relations which some of them had with their priests, their adornment with gold orders, glittering stars, and bright ribbons of badges of merit— often symbols of state services—their journeys around their dioceses with full suites of attendants, and their triumphal receptions on arriving in the cities, like those arranged for the highest secular officials. "Why, then, is it remarkable that the Russian bishop . . . appears to the majority only as a high religious official, as a sort of General of Religion, and that he has lost much of his authority as the first of God's servitors?" [175]

Not all of the prelates of the Russian Church were so apart from their flocks. Some of them managed to surmount the obstacles imposed by the duties of their official positions, and to win the love as well as the respect of their people. The touching scenes that some-

[173] Ivantsov-Platonov, *op. cit.*, p. 65.
[174] V. K. Sokolov, "Predstoiashchii Vserossiiskii Tserkovnyi Sobor," *Bogoslovskii Vestnik*, May, 1906, p. 40.
[175] N. D. Kuznetsov, *Preobrazovanie v Russkoi Tserkvi*, p. 114.

times occurred when bishops were moved from their sees to other posts proved that not all of them were out of touch with the hearts of the people. None the less, enough of them were aloof from the populace to affect considerably the views which the people held concerning the hierarchy.

The ordinary monastic clergy also were not always able to command the hearts of the people. Doubtless there were many monks who lived exemplary lives, and who came close to the monastic ideal; but there were so many scandalous reports about monks, not only in the lay newspapers, but also in influential church periodicals, that their reputation in society must have suffered severely. They were accused of amassing very considerable sums of money, in spite of their vows of poverty.[176] Worse still, they were accused of drunkenness and of flagrant immorality. *Tserkovno-obshchestvennaia Zhizn'* (*Church-Social Life*), published by the Religious Academy of Kazan, stated in 1906 that the neighborhoods of all the famous monasteries were populated by women whose children were the offspring of the monks.[177] "If you were to ask all the white clergy at the present time what they want from the monasteries, in the interest of faith and morality, we think . . . they would say . . . 'Improve the life of the monastics, strengthen their discipline.' " [178]

However, whatever the influence of the monastics, high and low, the all-important question was whether the priests of the numerous villages held the allegiance of the peasants. If the peasants followed the counsel of the priests, the church could weather any difficulties. But here too the position of the clergy was not impregnable; near as the parish priests were to the lives of the people, they apparently did not possess the whole-hearted confidence of the masses.

For one thing, the people knew that the priests lived among them, but, unlike the clergy of the Old Believers and the sectarians, were not of them. The priests were not of peasant origin, as we have seen, but were almost always the sons of priests. They had received a seminary education, and their interests and pleasures were different

[176] *Tserkovnyia Vedomosti*, Dec. 23, 1906, p. 3173.
[177] *Tserkovno-obshchestvennaia Zhizn'*, No. 31, 1906, cols. 1040–41, as quoted in A. Palmieri, *La Chiesa Russa*, p. 116.
[178] *Tserkovnyia Vedomosti*, Aug. 12, 1906, p. 2407.

from those of the villagers. The priest's wife wore a hat instead of the kerchief of the peasant woman; his children wore shoes, and went away to school. Only if the spiritual influence of the priest among the peasants were strong would this fact of separate origin be of no moment.

Unfortunately, other things emphasized this lack of close bonds between them. One significant fact was that their economic interests were often opposed. The priest whose church was endowed with a tract of land usually did not try to work it himself, but rented it to peasants, or cultivated it with the aid of hired labor. In either case there were possibilities of friction. Still more important were the fees which the priests charged for their ministrations. When a priest performed a christening or a marriage, blessed the fields of grain or a new well, or buried a corpse, he charged a fee for his services. The priests were most of them quite poor and needed this revenue, but the peasants for the most part were still poorer, and often could ill spare these payments of a few kopecks or a ruble. Not infrequently an unseemly bit of haggling took place before priest and peasant could agree on the amount to be paid. Charges of extortion were heard, and sometimes the angered parishioners started suit before the consistory—occurrences which could not fail to weaken the priests' standing in the villages.[179]

Many observers were also of the opinion that the spiritual side of parish life in Russia was far from satisfactory. The parishioners came when the bells called them to church, the priest performed the rituals, the choir chanted. But much of this was mechanical, without religious feeling.[180] The peasants had no active part in parish life. They did not choose their priest; he was an unknown, sent to them by the diocesan authorities. The villagers had no voice in the affairs of the parish. Once they had elected the elder (*starosta*), they could do nothing about administering the parish funds, about religious discipline within the parish, about repairing or adorning the church. There was, in truth, little parish life.[181]

[179] *Ibid.*, Sept. 7, 1902, p. 1234; *Vera i Razum*, Jan., 1906, pp. 31–32.

[180] *Tserkovnyia Vedomosti*, April 29, 1906, p. 1018; Sv. Sinod, *Otzyvy*, III, 451, report of a commission of the clergy of Enisei Diocese.

[181] Sv. Sinod, *Otzyvy*, III, 581–82, Arkadii of Riazan; *ibid.*, Supplement, pp. 45–46, Nikodim of Priamur and Blagoveshchensk.

Another very real factor in the decline of the church's influence was the personal character of some of the priests. Accusations of drunkenness were all too frequent. The church historian, Golubinskii, writing in 1881, stated: "Not long ago we visited our native hearth, and saw scenes sharply recalling to us our childhood: a drunken priest staggering about the village; a drunken priest returning from a village in a sleigh, embraced in the arms of a deacon." [182] In his *Report* for 1901 the Over Procurator stated that the bishops, in their reports on the condition of their dioceses, noted among their clergy "not a few cases of improper conduct, abuse of spirituous liquors (a vice especially prevalent in all dioceses without exception, particularly among the members of the lower clergy), a careless attitude toward their duties, quarrels between members of the clergy, . . . and so on." Later in his *Report* the Over Procurator weakened the force of this statement by adding that the number of such cases in proportion to the total number of the clergy was very small. [183] None the less, in two dioceses the authorities of the church found it necessary to rule that priests were not to accept vodka from parishioners as payment for the performance of ministrations. [184]

Were most of the priests drunkards? Not at all. Many there must have been who were sincerely religious, leading exemplary lives, performing unheralded their part in helping the people by personal example, and doing much to comfort and console them in their hours of trouble. However, a staggering priest would surely be noticed, whereas ten sober ones would escape notice. Very possibly the number and importance of the cases of intoxication were overstressed. None the less, such cases apparently were frequent enough to lower the prestige of the clergy.

Also important in lessening the influence of the village pastor was the feeling that the priest was acting in the interests of the government and of the wealthy classes which dominated it. During the agrarian disorders in the province of Tula in 1902 the ultraconservative *Moskovskiia Vedomosti* (*Moscow News*) declared, "The local clergy

---

[182] Golubinskii, *O Reforme v Byte Russkoi Tserkvi*, p. 21.
[183] Sv. Sinod, *Vsepoddanneishii Otchet*, 1901, p. 48.
[184] *Tserkovnyia Vedomosti*, Sept. 20, 1903, p. 1459; *ibid.*, Dec. 21, 1902, p. 1812.

have no moral influence at all over their flocks—the priests fear to arouse against themselves the peasants, who have more than once . . . burned their homes." [185] Quite often the priests felt forced to humor the landlords or the government officials. "Have there not been cases where a pastor who has almost completely done away with drunkenness among the people of his parish has been compelled to stop his sermons against drunkenness? It seems that through his sermons he was causing losses to someone." [186] One of the leading journals of the church said it was well known that the sermons of the priests were carefully cleansed of any thoughts that might offend influential persons, so that many of the pastors avoided preaching, whenever they could, or delivered sermons copied out of books. "Not a little harm is done to preaching by the customary view of the authorities that the priest is a person who must be kept in leading strings all his life, and must be strictly watched." [187]

Inevitably some of the public looked on the church and the clergy as on some special department under the control and in the service of the state.[188] "The pastors of the church have lost the confidence of their followers, and whatever the clergy say, even if they disclose the most holy truth, it only appears to the laymen that the pastors of the church are speaking at the orders of the government," [189] said Dean Iankovskii in 1903. Another prominent member of the church said, "The village priest is obliged to fear his district priest, and is also compelled to fear various newly fledged . . . diocesan missionaries and supervisors of parish schools; he must also fear every influential lordling and every rich merchant—in short, he must fear everyone not too lazy to trouble him. . . ." [190] As one noted writer explained,

. . . on the . . . priest they have laid obligations of a purely police nature, forcing him unconditionally to support and to defend the existing state order, to keep watch for persons and manifestations dangerous to it, and to inform the civil authorities about them—which of course deeply undermines the moral authority of the pastor of the church, and

---

[185] Pokrovskii, *op. cit.*, I, 320.
[186] *Bogoslovskii Vestnik*, Oct., 1903, p. 353.
[187] *Ibid.*, p. 356.   [188] *Ibid.*, May, 1906, p. 42.
[189] Protohierarch F. I. Iankovskii, "O Preobrazovanii Russkoi Pravoslavnoi Tserkvi," *Khristianskoe Chtenie*, Nov., 1906, p. 628.
[190] Sv. Sinod, *Zhurnaly i Protokoly*, II, 172.

compels his parish to look upon him as a state official, with whom it does no harm to be more careful.[191]

It may perhaps have been noted that many of the statements quoted here as to the weakness of the influence of the church date from 1905 and 1906, years of great disillusionment for conservative people. Is it not possible, the reader may ask, that the phenomena described were only temporary manifestations which were not characteristic of the years before the Revolution of 1905? To this the answer must be that broad movements in human history rarely develop overnight, and also that much of the evidence predates the Revolution. If the priests proved in 1905 and 1906 to have an uncertain influence upon the people, that condition must have been developing over many years, as increasing numbers of the people of Russia came to feel that the church was a state institution, controlled by officials of the Tsar, and used not so much to uplift the masses as to bolster up the ruling class. To be sure, in 1904 the acceptance of this idea was very far from universal. Nevertheless, as early as the year of the Russo-Japanese war, many of the humble folk of Russia sensed that the connection between church and state was very real and that it did not always work for their benefit.

[191] Sokolov, "Predstoiashchii Vserossiiskii Tserkovnyi Sobor," *Bogoslovskii Vestnik,* May, 1906, p. 42.

CHAPTER III

The Economic Position of
the Church

A NY STUDY of the relations between church and state in the pre-war years in Russia would be incomplete without a study of the economic status of the church—its capital, its income and the sources from which it was derived, as well as the distribution and use of these sums. This is so, not because the state supplied this income directly to the church—most of it, in fact, was received by the church without the intervention of the state—but because the very possession of substantial wealth could not but make the church dependent upon the state for protection. Possibly this fact, in combination with several other influences, played a part in inducing the leading figures of the church, and many lesser ones, to accept state domination and to look upon those opposed to the state as enemies of the church, especially when those opponents of the state order showed a tendency to infringe upon the church's financial interests. Such may well have been the consequences of the material endowment of the church.

That the chief clerics of the Russian Church enjoyed greatly swollen incomes was a favorite allegation of critics of the church. For example, the radical writer Kil'chevskii in 1906 quoted an article from the newspaper *Slovo Pravdy* (*Word of Truth*), with the date not given, in which the following incomes were said to be listed,[1] although without indication of the source of the data:

[1] V. Kil'chevskii, *Bogatstvo i Dokhody Dukhovenstva*, pp. 41–42. Although this chapter deals with the economic condition of the church and of the clergy in the first years of the twentieth century, the materials on church finances during that period are far from complete, so that it has been necessary to draw on evidence which dates as far back as 1870, and also on some pertaining to years just before and during the World War. The evidence from

METROPOLITAN OF MOSCOW

	Rubles
Salary	6,000
Food allowance	4,000
From the Diocesan Home	8,000
From the Chudov Monastery	6,000
From the Troitsko-Sergieva Monastery	12,000
From the Iberian Shrine	45,000
	81,000

METROPOLITAN OF ST. PETERSBURG

Salary	5,000
Food allowance	4,000
From the Aleksandro-Nevskaia Monastery	250,000
	259,000

ARCHBISHOP OF NOVGOROD

Salary	1,500
Food allowance	4,000
From the Diocesan Home	2,000
From the Novgorod *Podvor'e* (a hotel in Moscow)	300,000
	307,500

METROPOLITAN OF KIEV

Salary	5,000
Food allowance	4,000
From the Diocesan Home	10,000
From the Pecherskaia Monastery	65,000
	84,000

the later or the earlier period is included chiefly because it shows the *kind* of income enjoyed by monasteries or churches; presumably the same varieties of income were enjoyed during the years 1900–4. The *amounts* received during the earlier or later periods, however, were doubtless not the same as the receipts from the same sources in 1900–4; the amounts not pertaining to the first five years of the present century have been included merely to give a rough standard for estimating those received during the period under discussion.

These figures, coming from an obviously partisan source and undocumented, are, to say the least, suspect, but they have a certain importance as showing the beliefs that were prevalent in the minds of certain circles. Kil'chevskii's book went through two editions, so that as the church dignitaries were slow to publish their figures it is easy to see that those who wished to believe were readily convinced that the metropolitans and other hierarchs had large incomes. However, it seems highly doubtful that the figures cited above were correct. In 1906 the metropolitans of St. Petersburg, Moscow, and Kiev were the foremost figures in the church, while the archbishop of Novgorod was of lower standing. Yet the latter was credited with having the largest income, 307,500 rubles, while the see of Moscow was said to pay only 81,000 rubles. This alone is enough to cast suspicion on the data furnished by Kil'chevskii.

While his statements are to be regarded with the greatest of caution, it is not wise to jump to the opposite conclusion, namely, that the bishops were struggling in poverty. From the scanty facts which have been found, it appears that the hierarchs of the church in many cases had incomes which were more than ample for men sworn to lead simple and celibate lives and that in some instances they enjoyed actual wealth.

The bishops and metropolitans of the Russian Church received their incomes from several sources. All the bishops of the dioceses received state salaries. According to the schedule in effect in 1900, 12 of them received 4,000 rubles a year; included in this group of state-salaried clergy were the 3 metropolitans whose salaries, according to Kil'chevskii's account, were somewhat larger. One hierarch received 2,750 rubles a year, and the 39 others were granted 1,500 rubles only.[2] However, in 1903, 9 of the most poorly paid group were raised to 4,000 rubles a year each.[3] In addition to the salaries, the state also made allowances of from 3,000 rubles a year upward for the maintenance of each bishop's suite, for repairs to the diocesan home, and the like.[4]

More important for many of the hierarchs was the income which they derived from their positions as head of certain monasteries

[2] *Polnoe Sobranie Zakonov,* 1867, No. 45341.
[3] *Ibid.,* 1903, No. 23559.   [4] *Ibid.,* 1867, No. 45341.

within their dioceses. According to the Synod's *ukaz* of 1897, one-third of the "fraternal" income—that subject to division among the monks of a monastery—was to go to the bishop if he were the head of that monastery.[5] Also, according to law, the *podvor'es* of diocesan homes (if not donated by the state) and the incomes from them were at the full disposition of the bishops of the dioceses.[6] These *podvor'es* were hotels or inns maintained for the accommodation of pilgrims and travelers; often they contained famous shrines. In some cases they were located, not in the diocese of the controlling bishop, but in St. Petersburg or Moscow, on sites which made them very valuable properties, bringing in large incomes.[7] Consequently from the sources listed many of the bishops derived sizable revenues.[8]

Unfortunately the higher clergy in Russia and the central church administration published no periodic figures on the incomes of the clergy; the whole subject seems shrouded in mystery. Consequently it is a very difficult side of the problem to deal with. However, after a great deal of prodding by the Third Duma and with great reluctance, the Synod published its data on the incomes of bishops and metropolitans for 1909. For lack of figures dealing with the period before 1905, the figures for 1909 are given herewith, as probably they offer an approximation of the amounts for the earlier years, although, judging from the accounts of some of the monasteries discussed in succeeding pages, the income before 1905 was probably slightly less.

INCOMES OF BISHOPS AND METROPOLITANS, 1909

(In Rubles and Kopecks)

Diocese	Salary	From the Diocesan Home	From Monasteries Controlled by the Bishop	From Special Funds of the Synod	Total
Archangel	4,000	....	3,583.41	....	7,583.41
Astrakhan	1,500	14,927.13	....	....	16,427.13
Vladimir	1,500	8,000.00	....	....	9,500.00
Volhynia	4,000	....	16,423.14	....	20,423.14
Vologda	4,000	....	....	....	4,000.00
Voronezh	1,500	....	7,366.51	....	8,866.51

[5] Sviateishii Sinod, *Smeta Dokhodov i Raskhodov . . . na 1913 god*, pp. xxxvii–xxxviii.

[6] *Svod Zakonov Rossiiskoi Imperii*, IX, "Zakony o Sostoianiiakh," ed. 1899, sec. 437.

[7] See discussion of *podvor'es*, p. 103.   [8] See the table following.

Diocese	Salary	From the Diocesan Home	From Monasteries Controlled by the Bishop	From Special Funds of the Synod	Total
Viatka	1,500	7,648.13	5,423.36	....	14,571.49
Grodno	4,000	....	2,738.15	....	6,738.15
Don	4,000	1,750.00	....	....	5,750.00
Ekaterinburg	4,000	633.33	600.00	....	5,233.33
Ekaterinoslav	1,500	6,242.61	1,491.04	....	9,233.65
Kazan	1,500	7,908.29	9,222.44	....	18,630.73
Kaluga	4,000	1,300.00	1,500.00	....	6,800.00
Kishinev	1,500	12,965.67	7,522.95	....	21,988.62
Kiev	4,000	....	44,307.34	....	48,307.34
Kostroma	4,000	2,330.00	1,217.28	....	7,547.28
Kursk	1,500	....	7,700.00	....	9,200.00
Lithuania	4,000	2,531.29	18,591.83	....	25,123.12
Minsk	4,000	6,245.00	1,231.15	....	11,476.15
Mogilev	4,000	5,255.54	1,737.00	....	10,992.54
Moscow	4,000	3,000.00	28,599.00	....	35,599.00
Nizhnii Novgorod	1,500	....	6,378.83	....	7,878.83
Novgorod	1,500	9,000.00	....	....	10,500.00
Olonets	4,000	....	2,000.00	....	6,000.00
Orenburg	4,000	516.67	708.83	1,050	6,275.50
Orel	2,500	1,190.75	2,000.00	....	5,690.75
Penza	1,500	2,329.18	....	1,000	4,829.18
Perm	1,500	450.00	....	1,000	2,950.00
Podolia	6,000	....	906.18	....	6,906.18
Polotsk	4,000	900.00	....	....	4,900.00
Poltava	1,500	601.66	3,904.03	....	6,005.69
Pskov	1,500	....	2,000.00	....	3,500.00
Riga	4,000	1,800.00	....	....	5,800.00
Riazan	1,500	2,537.02	1,858.93	....	5,895.95
Samara	1,500	2,983.29	1,500.00	....	5,983.29
St. Petersburg	4,000	5,000.00	15,787.00	....	24,787.00
Saratov	1,500	7,818.27	....	....	9,318.27
Simbirsk	1,500	2,948.41	11,237.79	....	15,686.20
Smolensk	1,500	2,688.00	1,181.20	....	5,369.20
Stavropol	4,000	3,831.60	....	....	7,831.60
Taurida	4,000	3,800.00	3,400.00	....	11,200.00
Tambov	1,500	....	2,603.72	....	4,103.72
Tver	1,500	8,633.28	....	....	10,133.28
Tula	1,500	6,621.24	....	....	8,121.24
Ufa	4,000	2,822.50	....	....	6,822.50
Khar'kov	1,500	16,781.76	....	....	18,281.76
Kherson	1,500	1,916.63	12,000.90	....	15,417.53
Kholm	4,000	....	....	....	4,000.00
Chernigov	1,500	3,000.00	....	....	4,500.00
Iaroslavl	1,500	3,705.55	4,976.85	....	10,182.40

Of the above bishops, all except nine were reported to receive all their meals at their respective diocesan homes; the nine who were not fed at the expense of their diocesan homes received varying allowances for food, which have been included in the above table in the amounts received from the diocesan homes or the monasteries. Many of the dioceses had vicarian bishops, who reported incomes of from 2,000 to 8,683 rubles.[9]

These are the official figures, as submitted by the Synod. It will be noticed that the incomes reported here are very much smaller than those quoted by Kil'chevskii. However, there is some question whether the figures of the Synod are not too low. The metropolitan of St. Petersburg was reported to receive about 25,000 rubles, little more than the archbishops of Volhynia and Kazan, although the metropolitan was head of the Aleksandro-Nevskaia Monastery, one of the richest in Russia. Also, it is worthy of note that Archbishop Savva of Tver, who died in 1896, in his memoirs stated that the metropolitan of Moscow had an income of 68,000 rubles a year.[10] What basis the archbishop had for this statement, and of what year he was speaking, must remain unknown; none the less, his figure is interesting. Unfortunately, while the figures of the Synod are perhaps open to suspicion, and although other statistics submitted by the Synod have been found to be unreliable (those on the numbers of Old Believers and sectarians, discussed in Chapter IV), it is impossible to go behind the data submitted, or to furnish other figures which might be more reliable.

However, even if the figures furnished by the Synod be accepted as correct, there is one fact that seems plain. The bishops of the Russian Church were monastics, sworn to lives of poverty and chastity. They had no family cares, they were provided with free quarters in monasteries or diocesan homes, and in most cases their meals were likewise furnished them by the diocesan homes. Hence their incomes were not required for the necessities of life. Evidently, for monks without family burdens or the need to spend for food and lodging, their incomes, whether of 3,000 or 48,000 rubles a year, were sufficient to permit these ecclesiastics to lead lives of comfort and, in some

[9] Sv. Sinod, Kontrol (Bureau of Comptrol), 1910, portfolio 5a, sheets 31–41.

[10] "Zapiski Preosviashchennago Savvy, Arkhiepiskopa Tverskago," *Bogoslovskii Vestnik*, Sept., 1905, cited in V. Rozanov, *Okolo Tserkovnykh Sten*, II, 188.

cases, of luxury. In 1903 the average annual wage of the factory workers in Russia was 217 rubles; [11] most of the peasants lived on a very low level indeed.[12] Compared to these meager living standards, the incomes of the bishops were comfortable, to say the least. The hierarchs of the church were numbered among those who would lose heavily by any radical change in the existing order.

It has been pointed out that the greater part of the income of the hierarchs came from the monasteries and the diocesan homes (which were also monastic institutions). It was here that most of the wealth of the church was concentrated. These institutions held much of the church's land, the most substantial accumulations of capital, and the most famous treasures of vestments and utensils of precious metals adorned with gems. Yet in spite of the wealth of the monasteries, they had few inmates, and the number of monks and novices actually declined between 1900 and 1905. In 1900 there were 503 monasteries and diocesan homes, with a total of 16,668 monastics; in 1905 there were 487 establishments with 14,953 inmates. In contrast to the monasteries were the convents, numbering 325 in 1900, and 373 in 1905. The number of novices and nuns increased during this period from 41,615 [13] to 48,127.[14] In passing, it is worthy of note that the convents, although they had on the average many more inmates than did the monasteries, were for the most part much less well endowed than the latter, had much smaller sources of income, and, compared with the institutions for men, had little economic significance. For this reason, the pages which follow have but little to say about the Russian convents.

The monasteries, like most of the bishops, derived only a small part of their income from the state. In theory the government subsidies to them were recompense for the confiscation of their lands by Catherine II; consequently those institutions which were established after the confiscation received nothing. In 1905 some 337 monasteries and

[11] Ministerstvo Torgovli i Promyshlennosti, *Svod Otchetov Fabrichnykh Inspektorov*, 1903, p. 171.

[12] G. T. Robinson, *Rural Russia under the Old Regime*, pp. 251–54.

[13] Sv. Sinod, *Vsepoddanneishii Otchet Ober-Prokurora . . . za 1900 god*, pp. 3–6.

[14] *Ibid.*, 1905–7, p. 100.

diocesan homes and 208 convents were favored—about two-thirds of the total of such institutions.[15] Most of the subsidies were quite small—in 1910 most of them ranged between 105 and 5,585 rubles per year. No monasteries, and only five convents, received larger amounts, from 11,950 rubles to the 30,000 rubles of the Krasnostokskii Convent.[16] Hence what wealth the Russian monasteries had was not due in any large measure to support from the treasury.

However, in spite of the secularization of the bulk of the monastery lands in the eighteenth century, the monasteries were far from landless in 1900. According to law, at the time of the secularization or subsequently each diocesan home was to be endowed with 60 *desiatinas* (one *desiatina* equaled 2.7 acres) from the crown lands, while monasteries were to receive from 100 to 150 *desiatinas;* moreover, each diocesan home and monastery was entitled to a mill and a fishing ground.[17] Nor were the monastic institutions limited to these minima; they were permitted to acquire additional uninhabited land, either by purchase or through bequest, with imperial consent.[18] Actually many of the monasteries had lands far in excess of the standard set by law. According to Synod data for 1890, eleven monasteries had more than 2,000 *desiatinas* apiece; of these the Kozheozerskii Monastery had 24,836 *desiatinas*, while the Solovetskii Monastery was endowed with 66,000 *desiatinas.*[19] In 1901 the Grgor'evo-Biziukov Monastery advertised in a St. Petersburg newspaper that it would auction off six-year leases on twenty parcels of land in the diocese of Kherson, with a total area of 21,721 *desiatinas.*[20] In all, in 1905 the monasteries of the Russian Church possessed 739,777 *desiatinas* in European Russia—an amount equal to 0.2 percent of that territory.[21] The province having the greatest amount of monastery land was Bessarabia, followed in order by Archangel, Tambov, Novgorod,

[15] Sv. Sinod, *Vsepoddanneishii Otchet Ober-Prokurora za 1905–7 g.*, p. 100.
[16] Sv. Sinod, *Smeta Dokhodov i Raskhodov*, pp. xliv–xlv.
[17] *Svod Zakonov*, X, pt. II, "Zakony Mezhevye," ed. 1893, sec. 346, notes; *Prodolzhenie Svoda Zakonov*, 1906, X, pt. II, "Zakony Mezhevye," sec. 346, notes.
[18] *Ibid.*, IX, "Zakony o Sostoianiiakh," ed. 1899, sec. 435.
[19] N. A. Liubinetskii, *Zemlevladenie Tserkvei i Monastyrei*, p. 38.
[20] *Sanktpeterburgskiia Vedomosti*, July 12, 1901.
[21] Tsentral'nyi Statisticheskii Komitet, *Statistika Zemlevladeniia 1905 g.; Svod Dannykh po 50-ti Guberniiam Evropeiskoi Rossii*, p. 183.

Kherson, Nizhnii Novgorod, and Vladimir. Much of it was waste land, or far northern forest; but enough of it was usable to bring the estimated value of the church's monastery lands in 1890 to 26,595,690 rubles, according to official figures.[22]

The most far-reaching investigation of the wealth and income of the Russian monasteries was that published anonymously in 1876, but ascribed by writers on church matters to Professor Rostislavov of the St. Petersburg Religious Academy. It was based, according to the author, on the reports of the monasteries themselves and on other official data. He was able to study the reports of 200 monasteries for the years 1870–74. Of these, 59 had less than 150 *desiatinas*; the others had holdings ranging from 150 to 66,666 *desiatinas*; 30 of them had more than 1,000 *desiatinas* apiece. Much of this was forest land. Several of the monasteries reported substantial revenues from the sale of firewood or timber from their holdings; Rostislavov named 4 institutions which reported incomes of more than 1,000 rubles apiece from this source, including the Sarovskaia Monastery (*Pustyn'*), which in 1871 gained 22,666 rubles in this way.[23]

Rostislavov states that the monasteries also profited from their arable land. Of the 10 monasteries of the diocese of Novgorod whose reports he was able to read, all obtained hay from their meadows— from 80 to 200 tons. Most of this was for their own use; but 3 of them reported sales of small amounts of their excess hay to the value of from 132 to 443 rubles. Several of the monasteries reported large harvests of rye, oats, potatoes, and the like, which were presumably used for food for the monks and their livestock—at least 8 horses and 30 cows or more in each institution.[24] Thus the monasteries were often able to produce their own food and even to sell surplus produce and livestock for considerable amounts.

However, while the agricultural operations of the Russian monasteries were productive, the returns were not pure profit. Against them must be charged the expense of hiring labor, for "the work of repairing the monastery buildings and of cultivating the fields is frequently performed by hired labor, and the efforts of the monks commonly are

[22] Liubinetskii, *op. cit.*, p. 34.
[23] *Opyt Izsledovaniia ob Imushchestvakh i Dokhodakh Nashikh Monastyrei*, pp. 77–83. A careful and objective work.
[24] *Ibid.*, pp. 84–87.

confined to caring for the church and the cells." [25] This was written in 1906; in 1870 the Troitsko-Sergieva Monastery spent nearly 20,000 rubles a year for the hire of blacksmiths, locksmiths, agricultural workers, and so on.[26] At the Valaamskii Monastery, in the early twentieth century, much of the farm work in summer was done by the pilgrims who visited the island, and the brick factory, the quarry, the furniture shop, and the monastery steamboats were run by hired labor.[27] At the Tver diocesan home the land directly attached (a garden, an orchard, and a meadow) was worked by hired workers at an annual cost of 1,678 rubles.[28]

Much more often the farm land of the monasteries was rented to peasants of the locality. Thus in 1905 the Tver diocesan home rented more than 81 *desiatinas* of garden, meadow, and plow land, and 3 lakes, for 2,275 rubles.[29] The Simbirsk diocesan home rented out 34 *desiatinas* of its meadow land for 480 rubles a year.[30] The Zhadovskaia Monastery leased plow and meadow land to the extent of 331 *desiatinas* for an annual rental of 1,200 rubles.[31] Its outlying estates were also leased, bringing an annual rental of 5,152 rubles in 1904; only 128 *desiatinas* were kept for the use of the monastery itself.[32]

Many of the monasteries possessed valuable utilities in the form of mills, fishing grounds, and the like. Mention has already been made of the three lakes rented out by the Tver diocesan home. The diocesan home of the diocese of Archangel was even better provided with fisheries. In 1906 one of the near-by villages petitioned the government to give them eleven fishing grounds held by the diocesan home, as they said that these locations had belonged to the village before the Emancipation of 1861. The plea was rejected, however, as the bishop of Archangel declared that the rent of 1,000 rubles per year

[25] *Tserkovno-obshchestvennaia Zhizn'*, Oct. 20, 1906, cols. 1450–51.

[26] Financial statement of the Troitsko-Sergieva Monastery, published by its abbot, *Sanktpeterburgskiia Vedomosti*, Dec. 2, 1871.

[27] M. V. Novorusskii, "Dushespasitel'noe Khoziaistvo," *Sovremennyi Mir*, Sept., 1907, pp. 49–52. An unfavorable, although seemingly accurate, account, based upon observation and study of the monastery's accounts.

[28] Sv. Sinod, Khoziaistvennoe Upravlenie, 1896, portfolio 89, sheets 8–9 and 31.

[29] *Ibid.*, sheets 8–11.

[30] Sv. Sinod, Khoz. Uprav., 1895, portfolio 67, sheet 6.

[31] *Ibid.*, sheet 29.   [32] *Ibid.*, sheet 15.

from these fisheries was very necessary for the support of the home.[33]

The Simbirsk diocesan home and its satellite monasteries were especially well provided with mills. The home itself had a flour mill, rented for 1,200 rubles a year. The Zhadovskaia Monastery owned another, from which it received payments in kind to the amount of 9 tons (500 *puds*) of flour a year. The Syrzanskii Voznesenskii Monastery owned a large mill with 20 hoppers, from which it derived an income of 20,932 rubles in 1904.[34]

The rural possessions of the monasteries were thus productive of wealth, but in respect to cash returns they were in many cases surpassed by the improved urban real estate owned by these establishments. Many of the city monasteries possessed shops and dwellings. In 1904 the diocesan home of Simbirsk received 180 rubles from 3 wooden tenements in the city of Simbirsk. The Zhadovskaia Monastery, connected with the diocesan home, rented its 12 stone shops on the market square for about 2,800 rubles a year.[35] The diocesan home of Tver in 1895 rented a parcel of land to the diocesan taper factory for 115 rubles, leased a blacksmith shop for 80 rubles, and obtained an income of 190 rubles a year from 35 lots in the suburbs of the city of Tver.[36] The Troitsko-Sergieva Monastery declared that in 1872 it received 3,192 rubles from its shops on the market square in Sergiev Posad and a small amount from its other buildings in the same town.[37] However, in 1926 V. D. Derviz published the accounts of this monastery for 1917, in which he listed the income from its real estate in Sergiev Posad—residence property, shops, market squares, and so on—at the figure of 109,440 rubles.[38] But if the statements of Rostislavov be credited, even this sizable figure was surpassed by the income of the Aleksandro-Nevskaia Monastery in St. Petersburg.

A perusal of *Ves' Peterburg*—the city directory—for 1904 shows that this monastery held a large amount of urban property. Exclusive of the grounds of the monastery itself and its large cemetery, and not

[33] Sv. Sinod, Khoz. Uprav., 1906, portfolio 1, sheets 2–7.
[34] *Ibid.*, 1895, portfolio 67, sheets 6, 7, 21.
[35] *Ibid.*, sheets 15 and 32.
[36] *Ibid.*, 1896, portfolio 89, sheets 32–33.
[37] *Sanktpeterburgskiia Vedomosti*, Dec. 2, 1871.
[38] V. D. Derviz, *K Voprosu ob Ekonomicheskom Polozhenii Byvshei Troitse-Sergievoi Lavry*, pp. 9–11.

including its large warehouses, the monastery held title to 64 city plots, almost all of which were occupied by tenements, dwellings, shops, or other income-producing improvements.[39] Its 13 large grain warehouses, which fringed one of St. Petersburg's canals, were also rented for handsome amounts, so that Rostislavov estimated about 1870 that the total rental from the urban property of this monastery was at least 150,000 rubles. Nor was that all; it was entitled to collect 2 kopecks for every sack of grain unloaded at its wharves, which privilege was estimated to produce an additional 50,000 rubles. Thus this great institution was said to enjoy, in 1874, an income which was as great as that of any landlord in St. Petersburg.[40]

The total of the urban real estate held by the Russian monasteries would not be complete without inclusion of the property in Moscow which was owned by them—even in many cases by monasteries which were located in dioceses far from the ancient capital of the Tsars. Thus the Tver diocesan home had a hostelry (*podvor'e*) on the Kuznetskii Most in Moscow, which in 1895 was rented to a private citizen for 35,400 rubles a year.[41] The Valaamskii Monastery, according to one account, enjoyed an income of 35,000 rubles annually from its *podvor'e* in Moscow, and about 50,000 rubles from another in St. Petersburg, to say nothing of an additional 10,000 rubles from other buildings in Moscow, St. Petersburg, and Novgorod.[42] Rostislavov was able to investigate the accounts of 67 monasteries which in 1874 reported incomes from Moscow real estate. Most of them received small amounts, below 10,000 rubles; at the other extreme were the Voskresenskii Monastery, with 40,000 rubles, and the Bogoiavlenskii, with 45,000. He estimated that the Troitsko-Sergieva Monastery received even more from its Moscow property—as much as 100,000 rubles.[43] It is interesting to note that Derviz in his account credits this monastery with 153,561 rubles in 1917 from two *podvor'es* and a number of building plots in Moscow, and with 178,561 rubles from its property in St. Petersburg.[44]

[39] *Ves' Peterburg*, 1904, pt. IV, sections 1–437.
[40] *Opyt Izsledovaniia*, pp. 208 ff.
[41] Sv. Sinod, Khoz. Uprav., 1896, portfolio 89, sheet 33.
[42] Novorusskii, "Dushespasitel'noe Khoziaistvo," pp. 46–47.
[43] *Opyt Izsledovaniia*, pp. 212–21.
[44] Derviz, *op. cit.*, pp. 9–11.

Occasionally the Russian monasteries, instead of renting their urban property, made use of it themselves. Thus the Troitsko-Sergieva Monastery had a lithographing plant, a printing press, blacksmiths' and locksmiths' shops, a brick factory, a taper factory, and a shop for the making of images.[45] The Pecherskaia Monastery in Kiev had an especially fine press in 1874, with a type foundry, photographic equipment, and other paraphernalia equal to that possessed by the largest newspapers.[46] At Valaam there was a wide variety of manufactures—tapers, bricks, rosaries, leather, and pottery.[47] However, although most of the monasteries enjoyed the commercial advantage of freedom from the guild taxation paid by private establishments, their industrial and commercial activity was not great, and what there was for the most part was linked with their function of attending to the religious needs of pilgrims.

The Russian pilgrim was probably the source of the greatest income for the monasteries—income greater than the revenue derived from farm lands and city property, and far exceeding the sums paid by the state. It seems to have been a popular belief that prayers and rituals said or performed in a monastery were much more efficacious than those performed by parish priests. The more renowned monasteries possessed famous ikons which were especially revered by the people, who flocked in great numbers to pay them honor. At Christmas and at Easter, in the summer months, and in lesser measure throughout the year, the monasteries were visited by crowds of the faithful, who came to pray but who contributed not a little to the monastery coffers.

It is impossible to make an accurate estimate of the number of pilgrims annually visiting the Russian monasteries; only the scantiest of statistics are available. But it may safely be said that the total was very large, perhaps running into millions. To Valaam, on an island in Lake Ladoga, came 400 a day throughout the summer, and at the festival of Saints Peter and Paul 4,000 worshipers were present.[48] Various estimates set the number of pilgrims at the Troitsko-Sergieva

[45] *Sanktpeterburgskiia Vedomosti*, Dec. 2, 1871.
[46] *Opyt Izsledovaniia*, pp. 208–10.
[47] Novorusskii, *op. cit.*, pp. 45–46; *Opisanie Valaamskago Monastyria i Skitov Ego*, pp. 83–86.
[48] *Opisanie Valaamskago Monastyria*, p. 28.

Monastery at over 300,000 a year,[49] and the Kievo-Pecherskaia Monastery probably had no less.[50] Other monasteries to which pilgrims came, by train or by boat, as well as in long dusty columns through the forests or over the steppe, were the Solovetskii, Sarovskaia and the Pochaevskaia Monasteries, and a long list of lesser places. Hence it would probably be no exaggeration to set the total number of pilgrims who visited the monasteries in the course of a year at well over 1,000,000.

It would be a mistake to assume that the donations of the visitors represented pure profit for the monastery. By long-established tradition the monastery was obliged to furnish the pilgrims with free meals during their stay—an obligation which Rostislavov estimated cost the Kievo-Pecherskaia and the Troitsko-Sergieva Monasteries some 18,000 rubles a year apiece [51] (perhaps too low a figure). However, there were compensating items which helped to meet this expenditure. While the pilgrims were seated at the long tables, monks held before them bags into which they might drop contributions, and few there were who could not spare a kopeck or two.[52] Thus the cost of the meals was partly defrayed. The monastery could well afford the expense, as the pilgrims contributed sums for tapers, for communion bread, for special prayers and masses, which probably many times exceeded the cost of the food provided by the monastery.

One of the favorite forms of devotion shown by the pilgrims was the placing of candles before ikons in the monastery churches. These tapers were sold by the monks to the visitors at various prices—from a few kopecks to a ruble and more. It was rare that a pilgrim left the monastery without burning at least one taper before an ikon, and many bought several. Consequently the income from this source was great. Among 40 monasteries reporting taper revenue as a separate item, Rostislavov found 13 which received more than 1,000 rubles apiece.[53] As for the great Troitsko-Sergieva Monastery, it reported selling 322,245 tapers in 1870, at the price of 39,528 rubles. However, in the same year it sold twice as many loaves of communion bread,[54]

[49] *Sanktpeterburgskiia Vedomosti*, Dec. 2, 1871; Derviz, *op. cit.*, p. 25; *Opyt Izsledovaniia*, p. 106.

[50] *Opyt Izsledovaniia, loc. cit.*   [51] *Ibid.*, p. 113.

[52] *Ibid.*   [53] *Ibid.*, p. 118.

[54] *Sanktpeterburgskiia Vedomosti*, Dec. 2, 1871.

whereas usually more tapers were sold than loaves. This fact arouses the suspicion that the taper income was incorrectly stated, and that actually it should have been put at 70,000 or 80,000 rubles. Indeed, in 1913 and in 1917, when the annual number of pilgrims probably averaged 350,000, the taper income amounted to 208,000 and 201,275 rubles respectively.[55]

These figures are for the gross income from the sale of candles, and they do not allow for the cost of obtaining them. But as nearly as can be determined, the original cost was not high. The retail price was considerably higher than the wholesale price, and in addition much wax was salvaged from unburned candle ends. One monastery kept on duty a monk who put out tapers which had burned for a time, after which the ends were placed in a box, to be melted down and molded anew. In general the tapers sold for two to three times the original cost. For example, in 1874 one of the convents bought 4.5 *puds* (about 162 pounds) of tapers for 137 rubles, and resold them for 374 rubles.[56]

Much less imposing was the revenue obtained from the various collection boxes and purses which were placed conveniently in the monastery churches to receive the donations of visitors. Of 20 monasteries reporting this item in 1872, only 2 had more than 5,000 rubles.[57]

Another type of revenue—likewise not large—came from the performance of special masses at the request of visitors to the monasteries. To have these ceremonies performed in monasteries seemed most fitting to the pious; poor men who could not afford to pay for individual services often clubbed together for a joint service for the commemoration of all their lost ones, while more wealthy visitors sometimes paid for elaborate rituals performed by three senior monks, at a cost of from 10 to 50 rubles. But none the less, the totals received by the monasteries from this source were not great. In 1872, 9 out of 11 monasteries reporting on this item of revenue received less than 1,500 rubles, while the Ugreshskii Monastery admitted to 3,000, and the Troitsko-Sergieva Monastery reported 12,141 rubles.[58]

The sale of communion loaves was more important from the finan-

[55] Derviz, *op. cit.*, pp. 9–11.
[57] *Ibid.*, pp. 122–24.
[56] *Opyt Izsledovaniia*, pp. 117–18.
[58] *Ibid.*, pp. 124–26.

cial point of view. These were bought by the worshipers, and then were handed to the officiant at the altar for consecration. Sometimes visitors bought several loaves—even as many as 10—of which many were to be consecrated and taken to relatives or friends in the villages at home. Small fees had to be paid to the monks who wrote on them the names of the destined recipients, and larger amounts to the one who consecrated them. As many of the pilgrims showed their piety by buying communion bread, the income which the monasteries received was sometimes large. The Troitsko-Sergieva Monastery in 1871 reported the receipt of 28,709 rubles in this way,[59] while in 1917 the corresponding figure was 58,671 rubles.[60] On the other hand, Rostislavov found that, of 15 other monasteries which listed separately this type of income, 14 received less than 1,000 rubles, while the fifteenth got 2,100 rubles.[61] According to Derviz, who in 1926 investigated the pre-war accounts of the Troitsko-Sergieva Monastery, the sale of communion loaves brought in a rather small surplus over the cost of their preparation.[62]

In a variety of other ways, also, the monasteries of Russia derived money from the reverent pilgrims who entered their gates. Ikons, images, bricks stamped with the monastery seals, religious literature, and other articles of a commemorative nature were sold to them; often scenes suggestive of market day took place at the monastery entrances, as Russian peasants haggled and bargained as they bought their images and ikons. The Troitsko-Sergieva Monastery in 1870 received 3,846 rubles from the sale of olive oil taken from the lamps perpetually burning before the ikons in the monastery churches— oil which the pious Russians regarded as possessing valuable curative properties.[63] Holy water in flasks was sold as well. Then there were fees for minor services performed by the monks—for showing the treasures in the sacristy, or for lowering within reach some of the ikons especially revered by the pilgrims. At the Pecherskaia and Troitsko-Sergieva Monasteries monks collected fees from all who asked for drinks of water from the miraculous wells. At the Pecher-

[59] *Sanktpeterburgskiia Vedomosti,* Dec. 2, 1871.
[60] Derviz, *op. cit.,* pp. 9–11.　　　　　[61] *Opyt Izsledovaniia,* pp. 126–27.
[62] Derviz, *op. cit.,* pp. 23–24.
[63] *Sanktpeterburgskiia Vedomosti,* Dec. 2, 1871.

skaia Monastery, in Kiev, the monks who guided visitors through the catacombs collected fees.[64]

In all these ways pilgrims and visitors contributed to the monastery coffers. From them also came the revenues from the monastery *podvor'es*, the inns or hostelries maintained by most of the monastic institutions close to their walls. Not all of the pilgrims could avail themselves of the inns; great numbers of footsore peasants spent the night under the summer stars. But for the more affluent visitor there was often accommodation like that at the Troitsko-Sergieva Monastery, where a fine, clean hotel offered well-furnished rooms for from 40 to 75 kopecks a night, and more luxurious ones at 2 or 3 rubles. For the poorer pilgrim who dreaded a night in the open, there was a large, unfurnished building where hundreds slept on the bare floor, at the cost of a kopeck or two.[65] At the Valaamskii Monastery was a two-story stone hotel containing 200 well-furnished rooms, as well as a building to shelter wanderers.[66] The monastery received 4,000 rubles in 1904 from its hotel,[67] and the Troitsko-Sergieva Monastery received 23,759 rubles in 1870 from its two hostelries in Sergiev Posad.[68]

Some of the monasteries had additional ways of obtaining income from the pilgrims who visited them. The Valaamskii Monastery, on an island in broad Lake Ladoga, ran two small steamboats to the mainland to transport visitors—a service which in 1904 brought in almost 22,000 rubles.[69] The Nilova Monastery, another island community, also maintained steamer service with the mainland.[70] The Korennoi Monastery, which had no lake, managed to turn even a small stream to good account. Hot and dusty pilgrims were not allowed to bathe in its waters unless they paid the monastery one kopeck apiece for the privilege.[71]

From the dead as well as the living the monasteries of Russia derived income. The Russian of pious ways loved to have commemoration of his dead who were dear to his heart, and turned frequently

[64] *Opyt Izsledovaniia*, pp. 132–41.   [65] *Ibid.*, pp. 196–207.
[66] *Opisanie Valaamskago Monastyria*, pp. 28–30.
[67] Novorusskii, "Dushespasitel'noe Khoziaistvo," p. 46.
[68] *Sanktpeterburgskiia Vedomosti*, Dec. 2, 1871.
[69] Novorusskii, *op. cit.*, p. 46.
[70] *Opyt Izsledovaniia*, p. 206.   [71] *Ibid.*

to the monasteries for this office. But it was rare that the humble peasants could commemorate their dead in this way, as the rates for services were set too high. At the Kievo-Pecherskaia Monastery the rates ran from 60 kopecks for a year's commemoration to 75 rubles for special services said in honor of the deceased, while the Aleksandro-Nevskaia Monastery in St. Petersburg charged 10 rubles for a year's commemoration at the daily service, and from 200 to 1,000 rubles for special services.[72] This schedule of charges surpassed all others, and was designed chiefly for rich landowners or merchants, or dignitaries high in the service of the Tsar. Probably the rates of the Pecherskaia and Troitsko-Sergieva Monasteries were much closer to those of the other monasteries. The second of the two establishments named reported that its income in 1870 "from different persons for burials, services and commemorations" was 5,640 rubles.[73]

In like fashion many of the wealthy desired burial in monastery cemeteries, instead of the usual church burying grounds. Even in the cities, where for sanitary reasons it was undesirable, the interment of members of important families in monastery ground continued. Here again the charges of the Aleksandro-Nevskaia Monastery led all the rest. Burial plots in its large cemetery were grouped, in 1874, in five categories—those sold at 50, 100, 150, 200, and 500 rubles. The monastery made additional charges for putting up markers, headstones, and the like. The funeral expenses, of course, were not included in the cost of the burial plot. To use the monastery's hearses—and no others might be hired—cost from 10 to 50 rubles. Other payments had to be made for the covering for the coffin and for lighting the church in which service was said. As for the service itself, much depended on what was wanted by the mourners. For a solemn requiem in the great church, with the abbot as officiant, and with a full choir, the charge was as high as 150 rubles. Thus for elaborate funerals the total cost often ran from 250 to 500 rubles. And even after interment the monastery continued to receive income from the family of the deceased for requiems, for commemoration, and the like. Wealthy men occasionally donated substantial sums of money for eternal remembrance of their dead.[74]

[72] *Opyt Izsledovaniia*, p. 174.
[73] *Sanktpeterburgskiia Vedomosti*, Dec. 2, 1871.
[74] *Opyt Izsledovaniia*, pp. 181–95.

However, what was true at the Aleksandro-Nevskaia Monastery was not typical of the other Russian monasteries. This establishment was located in aristocratic St. Petersburg, and presumably served the religious needs of men in high places, so that those who gave burial to their dead in its cemetery could pay much more than those who used less prominent monasteries. This was shown by the fact that whereas the Troitsko-Sergieva Monastery, near Moscow, had income from burials and commemorations during 1870 amounting to 5,640 rubles, Rostislavov estimates that the corresponding figure for the institution in the northern capital must have been 28,000 rubles.[75] But while this latter estimate is unique in its size, doubtless there were many of the lesser monasteries which received modest, yet valued, contributions to their funds from commemorations and funerals.

While the monasteries thus ministered to those who sought their services, they were not without other means of contact with the people who lived far from the monastery gates. Often they maintained shrines in different places, not infrequently in the larger cities. Again, on occasion the monks would leave their retreats and go forth into the countryside with banner and ikon, marching in solemn processions to the neighboring villages of their dioceses. And thirdly, individual monks were sent forth from time to time, with the mission of soliciting funds for the benefit of their monasteries. In each case, whether it was the founding of a shrine, a processional, or a journey to solicit funds, the monastery benefited financially.

The shrines maintained by the Russian monasteries were not mere roadside crosses or statues of the Virgin, before which the devout might bow and pray. More nearly they resembled chapels, as they were usually small buildings, lavishly decorated, with one or several monks always in attendance. Sometimes they were equipped with bells, which were rung to attract worshipers. Within the shrines were ikons, before which tapers might be burned by those who stopped to pray, so that, except for the fact that no services were performed, they were churches in miniature. As for their financial value to the parent monasteries, it was largely derived from the sale of tapers, although donations and the vending of ikons, consecrated oil, images,

[75] *Ibid.*, p. 193.

religious literature, and other objects also played a part.[76] Not all of
the shrines, of course, contributed large amounts; of 20 monasteries
listing their revenues from shrines, 11 reported an income of less than
500 rubles in 1874. But on the other hand 3 others had incomes of
this sort ranging from 3,257 to 7,000 rubles, and the very popular
Guslitskii shrine in St. Petersburg was estimated to receive 12,000
rubles annually.[77] This last figure, however, was far exceeded by that
of the famous shrine of the Iberian Virgin at the entrance to the
Red Square in Moscow. According to the official statement published
in 1871, its revenues over the preceding ten-year period amounted to
590,000 rubles, or almost 60,000 rubles a year.[78] This shrine was highly
esteemed by its throng of visitors, and its wonder-working ikon was
so revered that pious families paid liberally to have it transported,
by two monks in a coach-and-four, to christenings, weddings, or other
private ceremonies. The shrine of the Davidova Monastery did likewise with its miraculous ikon, although its popularity was not so
great—as evidenced by the estimated income of this shrine, which
was 40,000 rubles a year.[79]

The processions which set out from the monasteries were somewhat infrequent and, in theory at least, might be organized only with
the consent of the diocesan authorities. Extraordinary events or calamities, such as outbreaks of cholera or typhus, were generally considered fit occasions. When a procession had once left the monastery
gates it proceeded through the countryside, stopping at the villages,
where services were said in the local churches, and the homes of the
pious villagers were blessed by the visiting monks. Often these processions went for long distances, following roundabout courses in
order to visit the populous villages, so that there were cases known
in which the monks were absent from their monasteries for as long
as six or seven months—which did not fail to arouse a certain amount
of criticism. During this period the collections made in the churches
where the monks said service, and the donations given by those whose
homes were blessed by the monks, were added to the funds of the
monastery. Unfortunately, none of the monasteries reported the

---

[76] *Opyt Izsledovaniia*, pp. 142 ff.   [77] *Ibid.*, pp. 145–46.
[78] *Sanktpeterburgskiia Vedomosti*, Dec. 2, 1871.
[79] *Opyt Izsledovaniia*, p. 149.

amounts received in this way, so that there is no way of knowing whether the estimates of as much as 10,000 rubles are correct.[80] It seems likely, however, that the processions were financially productive, for they aroused the parish clergy to make strong protests. An evidence of this was the decree of the authorities of the diocese of Pskov in 1904, wherein the monastic institutions were strictly enjoined from going forth with their ikons in processions without official permission. The reason given for this edict was "the repeated complaints of the local clergy." [81]

The solicitation of funds from well-disposed persons was a widely used means of filling monastery coffers, and those of the convents as well. Monks and nuns were sent forth armed with collection books, in which the donations were to be written down. At times the strength of the appeal was heightened by ikons which the collectors took with them. Sometimes the efforts of the collectors took the form of appeals to passers-by on the streets or in railway stations; sometimes they paid personal visits to wealthy individuals, thus gaining sums of considerable size. The amounts realized by these tours varied greatly. Nine monasteries reported on their collections for 1871, which ranged from 506 rubles to 2,699.[82] In contrast to these amounts were the donations of Countess Orlova, who bestowed 900,000 rubles on the Iur'ev Monastery alone, to say nothing of gifts of 5,000 rubles each to a number of others.[83]

Apparently this means of improving monastery finances was sometimes used too extensively, for in 1901 the Synod felt called upon to issue a decree forbidding many methods of soliciting donations. The edict mentioned the fact that appeals for donations, unauthorized by the diocesan officials, were sometimes sent out by abbots or by mere senior monks. Contributions to pay for memorial services were especially widely solicited. Often the appeals were hectographed, giving in tabular form the scale of prices for requiems. Nor was that all. Often when contributions were received, they were put to personal use by the recipients, who felt free from any fear of apprehension. Further abuses of this kind, the Synod ordered, were to cease.[84]

---

[80] *Ibid.*, pp. 150–61.   [81] *Tserkovnyia Vedomosti*, April 24, 1904, p. 621.
[82] *Opyt Izsledovaniia*, pp. 162–63.   [83] *Ibid.*, pp. 130–31.
[84] *Tserkovnyia Vedomosti*, No. 3, Jan., 1901, official part, p. 20.

One additional source of income for the monasteries was the interest on their invested capital. Some of this capital came from donations; it was increasing, moreover, from the annual surpluses which the monasteries frequently reported. Such surpluses were always added to the capital fund of the monastery at the end of the fiscal year. In 1894 and 1895 the Stefano-Ul'ianovskii Monastery, which had asked for a parcel of state land, was found to have had surpluses of 474 and 276 rubles respectively.[85] The Zhadovskaia Monastery had a balance of 4,290 rubles at the end of 1894.[86] The Tver diocesan home had cash balances as follows: for 1896, 3,316 rubles; for 1905, 3,213 rubles; for 1910, 542 rubles; and for 1914, 127 rubles.[87] The Troitsko-Sergieva Monastery had a cash balance of 18,385 rubles for 1869; its surplus for 1870 was 32,806 rubles.[88] According to the Synod report, for the year 1908 all the Russian monasteries had a total surplus of 1,203,001 rubles. The corresponding figure for 1909 was 1,395,122 rubles.[89]

As for the monastery capital itself, it was quite substantial; as it was obligatory to invest it in government bonds paying 4 or 5 percent interest, it produced a respectable return. Examples of the amounts of monetary capital held by individual monasteries are not wanting. The Stefano-Ul'ianovskii Monastery had a capital of 156,190 rubles in 1895.[90] Valaam had capital to the amount of 300,000 rubles in 1904, which produced an income of 11,500 rubles a year.[91] The diocesan home of Tver had only 5,970 rubles of investments in 1905;[92] the Simbirsk diocesan home had a much larger portfolio of government bonds, to the sum of 32,869 rubles.[93] As for the great Troitsko-Sergieva Monastery, its abbot reported in 1871 that it held notes to the amount of 171,358 rubles;[94] in 1917 it held notes to the value of 928,282 rubles, with an additional 599,102 which belonged to its

[85] Sv. Sinod, Khoz. Uprav., 1895, portfolio 30, sheets 8–9.
[86] Ibid., portfolio 67, sheet 7.
[87] Ibid., 1896, portfolio 89, sheets 4, 15–16, 21–22, and 31.
[88] Sanktpeterburgskiia Vedomosti, Dec. 2, 1871.
[89] Sv. Sinod, Smeta Dokhodov i Raskhodov, 1913, p. xlv.
[90] Sv. Sinod, Khoz. Uprav., 1895, portfolio 30, sheets 8–9.
[91] Novorusskii, "Dushespasitel'noe Khoziaistvo," p. 45.
[92] Sv. Sinod, Khoz. Uprav., 1896, portfolio 89, sheet 4.
[93] Ibid., 1895, portfolio 67, sheet 14.
[94] Sanktpeterburgskiia Vedomosti, Dec. 2, 1871.

ascribed monasteries.[95] The following table is based on the reports of 164 monasteries in 1873:

Number of Monasteries	Investments, in Rubles
18	5,000– 10,000
45	10,000– 20,000
37	20,000– 30,000
24	30,000– 40,000
12	40,000– 50,000
7	50,000– 60,000
4	60,000– 70,000
3	70,000– 80,000
5	80,000–100,000
9	100,000–200,000

In addition to these, the Nilova Monastery had 288,661 rubles' capital, the Solovetskii Monastery had 317,852, and the Iur'ev Monastery 752,618 rubles.[96] Doubtless there were others not included in this list whose investments were as great. According to the Synod's figures for 1909, the monasteries of Russia possessed government securities to the total of 59,920,053 rubles, which bore an annual interest of 2,291,427 rubles.[97]

These, then, were the sources of revenue for the Russian monasteries. Of necessity the data are scanty, and deal chiefly with a few of the larger and more famous establishments. Many there were which were more humble, with incomes which would appear small by comparison. None the less, the famous centers of monasticism in Russia were the pattern for the smaller, less noted institutions. As for the correctness of the figures cited, Rostislavov, whose data have been widely used here, declares, on page after page, that the monastery accounts minimize their receipts. In part this was due, he said, to fear of popular resentment if the true amounts were known, and in part to another reason. The monasteries often found themselves obliged to play hosts to local potentates, to the provincial governors, or to visiting officials from the central administration of the church.

[95] Derviz, *op. cit.*, pp. 11–13.   [96] *Opyt Izsledovaniia*, pp. 240–45.
[97] Sv. Sinod, *Smeta Dokhodov i Raskhodov*, p. xlv.

All of these had to be lavishly entertained; but as it would be unwise to enter in the monastery books that so many rubles were spent
on caviar, champagne, Chateau Lafitte, and other luxuries, there
had developed a practice of creating a secret fund for this purpose
by minimizing the income of the monastery.[98] Hence even free access to all the monastery account books would not have given the
true total of their income—which Rostislavov estimated at 9,000,000
rubles for the year 1875, not including the sums which the monks pock-
eted without reporting them to the treasurers.[99] That this figure was
probably not excessive is shown by the statement of the Synod, prepared for the Finance Committee of the Duma in 1913. In this statement the total income of the monasteries and convents of Russia
for the year 1909 was put at 20,627,286 rubles.[100]

This was a substantial sum, doubtless somewhat larger than the
corresponding figures for the years before 1905; but not solely by
income computed in rubles could the wealth of the monastic institutions be measured. They possessed broad fields and deep forests,
which gave a variety of foodstuffs, such as grain and fruit, mush-
rooms and fish, as well as a whole list of other commodities which
were put to use by the monasteries with only rare mention in the
account books. The purchase of the fir and birch logs used for heating and cooking alone would have required a sizable expenditure if
this wood had not been supplied by the forests of the monasteries.
Hence this income in kind must be borne in mind when forming an
estimate of the economic status of the monastic communities of Russia. Another type of wealth which they possessed in abundance was
in the form of buildings—blocks of cells, together with the structures housing the kitchens and storerooms needed to feed the monks;
ikon and image shops, bookbinderies and bakeries, and other small
establishments in which the monks worked; churches and bell towers
—all surrounded by walls, sometimes both thick and high, and
guarded at the corners or gateways by massive towers, which gave
them the appearance and the security of fortresses. Outside the walls
were the monastery stables, the larger manufacturing establishments

[98] *Opyt Izsledovaniia*, pp. 252–58.
[99] *Ibid.*, p. 304.   [100] Sv. Sinod, *Smeta Dokhodov i Raskhodov*, p. xlv.

of the monasteries, the quarters for the hired workers, the monastery
hostelries, rows of shops on the market square, and other structures; and in distant cities, as we have seen, were located the shrines
and other buildings constructed by the monasteries. Many of these
were productive of revenue, which has been discussed in the preceding pages; but others—the bell towers, and the blocks of cells, which
were built of brick in many of the monasteries, or of logs, as in most
of the convents—paid no cash into the monastery coffers, although
the cells were the dwellings of the monks or nuns, and all, especially
the churches, represented the expenditure of considerable labor and
money.

On their churches and other religious buildings the monasteries
lavished money. In earlier times, when investments in securities were
not known, they had turned their surplus wealth into tangible forms
of property—into land, into chalices, crucifixes, censers, and other
ceremonial articles of precious metals and jewels, and into buildings.
To this heritage of buildings they had continued to add, so that all
but the poorest monasteries and convents were resplendent with gold
or multicolored domes, gleaming crosses, and the white walls of many
buildings. Few were the monasteries which did not have several
hermitages—solitary cells of brick or wood on lonely islands or in
the depths of the forest, where their glittering cupolas and crosses
were seen only by the beasts or by the chance wanderer. Often the
monasteries had within their walls several churches, which in some
cases exceeded the hermitages in number. In 1874 ten monasteries
had five churches each; nine had six, while one had fifteen and another twenty.[101] The Troitsko-Sergieva Monastery had thirteen.[102]
It was even alleged by some churchmen that the superiors of monasteries and convents would often undertake construction not needed
to accommodate either the inmates of the establishments or the pilgrims who visited them.

Everyone knows that abbots and Mothers Superior always gain crosses
and other rewards by putting up buildings for their monasteries or
convents; if there is nothing to be built, they destroy good buildings and

[101] *Opyt Izsledovaniia*, pp. 313–14.
[102] *Sanktpeterburgskiia Vedomosti*, Dec. 2, 1871.

rebuild according to their whims. . . . And all this in order to receive a thousand rubles, or two or three, for their apparent labors, and to show their zeal to the authorities.[103]

This charge the monastics answered by declaring that such construction was undertaken for the greater glory of God; and indeed no proof has come to hand that any other considerations played a part in leading the monastics to build. Whatever the reason, the fact remains that the churches of the monasteries of Russia were numerous, costly, and beautiful. They were roomy and imposing, and for the most part of heavy masonry. As they were built in the various traditional styles of Russian church architecture, they were elaborate in form, being adorned with gilded domes and crosses, and having a profusion of arches and pillars, carved stonework, frescoes, and mosaics, so that the churches of the monastic establishments were by far the most costly of their structures. They, like the cells of the monks, made no direct rental payments to these institutions, but none the less they represented a huge amount of wealth.

The architectural glories of the monastery churches, however, were no greater than those of the wondrous treasures within—the precious articles in their sacristies. Here too were the gifts of bygone centuries, side by side with later acquisitions. Because of their historical value and the workmanship which they represented, it was impossible to compute their current worth, but it was very great.

Even the altars on which stood these precious utensils were in some cases covered with cloth of silver, or with gilded plates of silver. But the communion service—the chalice, the lavabo, the paten, and the monstrance—was far more costly. It was commonly of silver in the larger monasteries, and in some, of gold. Two such gold vessels were of three and four *funts* in weight (one *funt* was 0.9 of a pound). At the Solovetskii Monastery one of gold, enamel, and precious stones weighed more than four *funts,* while the Pskovo-Pecherskii Monastery had a communion service of gold, ornamented with emeralds and rubies, which was over three *funts* in weight. Many monasteries also had Gospels with bindings set with jewels or made of silver or gold. One at Solovetskii had silver covers inlaid with precious stones, which, without the book, weighed 34 *funts;*

---

[103] *Tserkovno-obshchestvennaia Zhizn',* Oct. 20, 1906, cols. 1450–51.

it had been purchased in 1801 for 2,435 rubles. The Kievo-Pecherskaia Monastery had two Gospels bound between covers of solid gold set with gems, one costing 17,773 rubles, and the other 30,000.[104] As for the Troitsko-Sergieva Monastery, which had been a center of Great Russian religious life since Muscovite times, its sacristy was replete with treasures, including donations from the Tsars and the Greek patriarchs, surpassing all others in sheer magnificence. Here was a censer which had belonged to Patriarch Nikon of Russia, of gilded silver, 2 *funts* in weight. Here was a gold cross containing relics, adorned with Burmese pearls and precious stones. There were two sets of altar vessels, one 6 *funts* in weight and adorned with precious stones, the other 12 *funts* in weight and set with diamonds. Ceremonial vestments were there in abundance, made of the most costly fabrics, and often glittering with gems strung on thread of silver or gold; one of the miters was adorned with a ruby worth 20,000 rubles, along with other gems. Other treasures included a jeweled censer, containing 5.5 *funts* of gold, a silver candlestick, 55 *funts* in weight, and a 6.5-*funt* crozier of gold, set with diamonds and other precious stones.[105]

These treasures of the famous monastery near Moscow were the greatest of all those possessed by the Russian monasteries, although the lesser institutions were also repositories of riches. In addition to articles of the types named, many of the monasteries, large and small, had priceless altar crosses—the Voskresenskii Monastery, founded by Patriarch Nikon, had one of solid gold, weighing more than 4 *funts*. There were vestments of brocade, velvet, lace, silk, cloth of silver and of gold—heavily embroidered, and often jeweled. There were miters heavy with precious metals and gems. Many ikons in the monastery churches had frames and pedestals of gold and silver, often studded with precious stones; frequently the paintings themselves, except for the hands and faces, were covered with sheets of precious metal set with stones. The stand for the famous Ikon of the Iberian Virgin was set with 12 large diamonds and 53 small ones, 80 rubies, and 63 amethysts. There were the "Heavenly Gates" in the monastery churches, which separated the chancel from the

[104] *Opyt Izsledovaniia*, pp. 315–43.
[105] *Istoricheskoe Opisanie Sviato-Troitskoi Sergievoi Lavry*, pp. 49–55.

choir; sometimes they were covered with plates of silver, while in one of the churches of the Troitsko-Sergieva Monastery they were of solid silver, more than 160 *funts* in weight. There were arks for the reservation of the Sacrament, reliquaries, censers, lamps, candlesticks, dishes, ladles, containers for holy water [106]—many of them of precious metals, and displaying the best of craftsmanship.

It is interesting to note that when the Soviet authorities confiscated treasures of the church not actually needed for use in religious services, at the time of the famine in 1921, they carefully recorded the amounts of the confiscated riches. In all, they seized 1,078 *funts* of gold, 845,491 *funts* of silver, and 3,290 *funts* of unspecified precious metals. The diamonds taken numbered 33,456—1,313 carats in weight; there were nearly 11 *funts* of pearls, and the other precious stones seized totaled 72,383, and weighed 69 *funts*. In addition, there were a small number of gold and silver coins, and a number of articles containing precious stones not included in the previous categories.[107] Unfortunately the account of the confiscations does not state what proportion of the riches came from monastic institutions; it may be assumed, however, that a very considerable part came from this source.

Here, then, was great wealth; the riches accumulated in the Russian monasteries must have fascinated more than one beholder, perhaps thus giving rise to the belief that the monasteries were fabulously wealthy. The sight of so much treasure and the rumors of lavish monastery incomes played a large part in leading many to urge that the wealth of these institutions was too great and should rather be put to better use.[108] Allied with them were those who declared that for monks to enjoy the large incomes which they were alleged to receive was contrary to the spirit of monasticism.[109] Together these two groups led the attack upon the monasteries—a denunciation which became strong during and after 1905.

The monks, however, did not lack defenders. The hierarchy sup-

[106] *Opyt Izsledovaniia*, pp. 315–43.

[107] B. V. Titlinov, *Tserkov' vo Vremia Revoliutsii*, p. 186.

[108] Novorusskii, "Dushespasitel'noe Khoziaistvo."

[109] *Tserkovno-obshchestvennaia Zhizn'*, Oct. 20, 1906, cols. 1450–51; *Bogoslovskii Vestnik*, Dec., 1905, pp. 801–2.

ported their cause, and the conservative organs of the church—
Tserkovnyia Vedomosti (*Church News*) and *Missionerskoe Obozrenie* (*Missionary Survey*) and the various diocesan publications—
defended them stanchly. The monastic ideal was declared to be the
most perfect form of religious devotion, and the lives of most of the
monks were said to present patterns of piety and sacrifice that might
well be imitated by laymen and priests alike. Moreover, in his *Report* the Over Procurator insisted that the wealth of the monasteries
was justified by the good uses to which it was put. He stated that
the monasteries contributed to the support of the diocesan administrations, and above all carried on extensive educational and charitable
work.[110] As evidence he pointed out that in 1900 there were 172
hospitals maintained by the monastic establishments—chiefly, as his
figures showed, by the convents. Of these, 28 were fully or partially
endowed by private persons, and the others were supported by the
monasteries and by the state. How large the state's contributions
were, was not stated; but the hospital of one convent—a hospital
which the Over Procurator's *Report* held up as a model—received a
subsidy of 80,000 rubles from the treasury.[111] Hence, if this was
typical of the monastic hospitals—which in 1900 provided a total
of 2,027 beds [112]—they may have caused little drain upon the funds of
the monastic institutions.

The monastic institutions also had 123 almshouses; but here too
much the same situation existed. Of these almshouses, 34 were maintained in part by *zemstvo* or by private funds, while state contributions supplemented those of the monasteries.[113] As for the educational work of the monastic institutions, this side of their activities
pleased the liberals even less. As will be shown later, the parish
schools, which the monastics helped to support, were anathema to all
liberals, so that the monasteries and convents received no credit
from them for this expenditure. The contributions made by the monasteries to the diocesan schools were not condemned, but the sums
given for diocesan purposes seemed small to many, as they amounted

---

[110] Sv. Sinod, *Vsepoddanneishii Otchet*, 1900, pp. 41–46.
[111] *Loc. cit.;* also, *ibid.*, pp. 44–47 of tables.
[112] *Ibid.*, pp. 46–47 of tables.   [113] *Ibid.*

to but 473,001 rubles in 1909.[114] Most liberals were convinced that the monasteries gave to the Russian people but little in return for the great sums which they were believed to receive.

Indeed the liberals were not slow to allege that much of the income of the monasteries was spent on the monks themselves, so that their mode of living was far from the monastic poverty advocated by St. Basil. There were some grounds for believing that the monks enjoyed a fair degree of comfort. Most of them received between 100 and 200 rubles a year in cash income, besides free lodging, meals, and, in some cases, clothing.[115] As for the senior monks and the heads of the monasteries, their incomes were much higher, in some instances amounting to thousands of rubles.[116] These personages occasionally left substantial estates. Inasmuch as the monastic code forbade those taking the vows to keep property held before entering monasticism, and as those taking this step lost the right of inheritance,[117] such sums must have been amassed during their lives as monks. At the Troitsko-Sergieva Monastery the senior monk Fotii left an estate of 6,820 rubles in 1870.[118] Especially striking was the case of Abbot Porfirii, of a monastery in the diocese of Smolensk. At his death in 1906 he had in safekeeping, in a Moscow bank, government bonds totaling 56,600 rubles.[119]

Further evidence on this subject was given by the Synod itself in 1892. In a circular message it was stated that the superiors of monasteries often gained full control of the moneys of their institutions, and that the Synod had repeatedly obtained information that they kept the funds in their cells and spent them freely on expensive furniture and rugs, and pictures "frequently of a secular character," or purchased fine horses and carriages. At times they had luxurious dinners on feast days, at which expensive foreign wines were served; costly presents were given to benefactors, and so on. Other superiors

[114] Sv. Sinod, *Smeta Dokhodov i Raskhodov*, p. xlv.
[115] *Sanktpeterburgskiia Vedomosti*, Dec. 2, 1871; Derviz, *op. cit.*, pp. 13–19; *Opyt Izsledovaniia*, pp. 268 ff.
[116] *Opyt Izsledovaniia, loc. cit.*
[117] A. Provolovich, *Sbornik Zakonov o Monashestvuiushchem Dukhovenstve*, secs. 40 and 42.
[118] *Sanktpeterburgskiia Vedomosti*, Dec. 2, 1871.
[119] *Tserkovnyi Vestnik*, Jan. 3, 1907, col. 21.

laid their hands on the trade in ikons and crosses. Another abuse noted was the practice of lodging relatives of the superiors of monasteries in their buildings, as though they were in private summer resorts. Many of the superiors, after their death, were found to have amassed large amounts of money and property, which could have been obtained only through improper use of the monastery funds. The Synod urged that the bishops see that these abuses were ended at once.[120]

It is doubtful, however, whether this situation could have been cleared up by a fiat of the Synod. Indeed it seems that it was not, for in 1906 *Tserkovno-obshchestvennaia Zhizn'* (*Church-Social Life*), a publication devoted to the parish clergy, repeated much the same accusation:

That contemporary monasticism is in a very low moral condition, and even serves as a source of disaffection for the lay world, cannot be doubted. . . . It has even reached the point where monks who have especially large incomes even buy their own carriages. At present many are so fond of money that acquiring it has become their sole aim in life.[121]

Thus the evidence seems to show that some of the monks enjoyed considerable personal incomes. The monasteries, too, possessed comparative riches, including large amounts of capital invested in government securities. Hence the monastics, both individually and collectively, felt that they needed the protection of the state against their critics. Here, then, was a very strong link connecting church and state.

The preceding pages have dealt with the economic condition of the monastic clergy—the metropolitans and bishops, and, following them, the lower ranks of monasticism. It is now time to turn to the "white" clergy—the married priests and the deacons and psalmists. However, as the deacons were few in number, and as the psalmists were peasants who combined a limited religious activity with their peasant life, this study will deal chiefly with the economic condition of the priests.

A traditional and, indeed, official means of supporting the parish clergy was by endowment with land. By law it was established that

[120] A. A. Zav'ialov, ed., *Tsirkuliarnye Ukazy . . . Sinoda*, pp. 248–51.
[121] *Tserkovno-obshchestvennaia Zhizn'*, Oct. 22, 1906, cols. 1450–51.

each parish was to possess at least 33 *desiatinas* of land, which might originally come from the state or from private landowners. In regions where the supply of land was "ample"—a vague term, but the one used in the law—the endowment was to be 99 *desiatinas*.[122] However, in actuality this provision was not everywhere carried out. There were approximately 43,000 Orthodox churches in European Russia in 1900.[123] Those that had lands in this area numbered only 28,675 in 1890; [124] and, as during the years from 1890 to 1900 only 4,463 *desiatinas* of state land were bestowed on the parish churches,[125] the total number of churches with land in 1900 in the same area was probably approximately the same. The area owned by the churches in European Russia in 1890 was quite large, 1,671,198 *desiatinas*. Based on the average values in the different provinces, its worth was estimated at 116,195,118 rubles, and the annual revenue, 9,030,204 rubles.[126] But while this amount was important for the church, it was not enough to maintain all the parishes and their clergy, and represented only a small part of the total land area of the country. In 1905 the churches owned 1,871,858 *desiatinas* in European Russia, which was 0.5 percent of the total of all land in that territory.[127]

Most of the churches which possessed agricultural land had 33 *desiatinas*, except in some of the southern dioceses like Ekaterinoslav, where many of the churches had 99 *desiatinas*.[128] However, for the individual priest the church lands were not an unmixed blessing. Some there were who worked their lands, but when the priest farmed his 22 *desiatinas* (11 went to the psalmist) it is doubtful whether the financial returns were as great as if he had rented the land and devoted his time to meeting the religious requirements of his parishioners. One priest, writing in *Missionerskoe Obozrenie* (*Missionary*

---

[122] *Svod Zakonov*, X, pt. II, "Zakony Mezhevye," ed. 1893, secs. 347–56; *Prodolzhenie Svoda Zakonov*, 1906, X, pt. II, "Zakony Mezhevye," secs. 347–56.

[123] Sv. Sinod, *Vsepoddanneishii Otchet*, 1900, pp. 7–9 of tables.

[124] Liubinetskii, *Zemlevladenie Tserkvei i Monastyrei*, pt. I, pp. 14 ff.

[125] V. Sviatlovskii, *K Voprosu o Sud'bakh Zemlevladeniia v Rossii*, p. 36.

[126] Liubinetskii, *op. cit.*, tables XXIV and XXV.

[127] Tsentral'nyi Statisticheskii Komitet, *Statistika Zemlevladeniia 1905 g.: Svod Dannykh po 50-ti Guberniiam Evropeiskoi Rossii*, p. 183.

[128] Sv. Sinod, Khoz. Uprav., 1909, portfolio 241 (church lands as reported by the parish clergy).

Survey), a very conservative church periodical, stated that to practice agriculture properly a priest must give up about half of his time during the year. Further, he declared that certain features of this work were not fitting for priests. Often there were hard bargains to be driven when selling livestock; to get labor, some priests had to ply the peasants with liquor, or use other unseemly stratagems. Also the breeding of cows and the renting of bulls was too gross for a man of God. "To sum up all that we have said, it must be recognized that the practice of farming and pastoral obligations . . . mutually exclude one another. . . ." [129]

The editor of *Missionerskoe Obozrenie* disagreed with this verdict, stating that the author had painted too black a scene. [130] But other writers corroborated the allegations. [131] Indeed most of the priests in parishes where there was church land apparently found the drawbacks so real, and the obstacles to scientific agriculture created by the three-field system so great, that they did not attempt to work the land themselves, but rented it out to the peasant communes or to individual peasants. [132] Even this solution was far from ideal; there were disputes with the tenants, and a tendency toward exhaustion of the soil through primitive methods. One critic said:

. . . [the priest] does not work the land, he does not love the land, and it has come to pass that he does not love the *muzhik* [peasant]. His land has not made him a farmer, as they doubtless expected when they gave him an allotment. He merely felt like a little *pomeshchik* [landlord], and the better off he was, the farther he moved from the *muzhik*. [133]

Thus in the ranks of the clergy there was developing a good deal of dissatisfaction with the returns from the land allotments, whether the priests cultivated them themselves or rented them to the peasants, and a quest for something more satisfactory was beginning.

[129] Sviashchennik Semeon Popov, "Pravda o Zaniatiiakh Dukhovenstva Sel'skim Khoziaistvom," *Missionerskoe Obozrenie*, June, 1906, pp. 820–29.

[130] *Ibid.*, p. 834.

[131] A. Rozhdestvenskii, *Iuzhno-russkii Stundizm*, p. 29. The author was an Orthodox priest active in missionary work.

[132] *Tserkovnyia Vedomosti*, March 25, 1906, pp. 619–21.

[133] *Kazanskii Telegraf*, April 2, 1905, as quoted in I. V. Preobrazhenskii, *Tserkovnaia Reforma*, p. 241; see also Sv. Sinod, Khoz. Uprav., 1905, portfolio 139, sheets 4–5.

In some localities it was the practice of some of the village communes to devote contributions to the local priests. In the western provinces the governors were instructed, in places where land was not available for the priests, to require the peasants to "grant to the clergy compensation in proper proportion, in the form either of money payments or of products." [134] But the priests who received these contributions found that here too there were difficulties: disputes about the size of the donations, and in bad years, slowness of payment, or even non-payment. In 1892, a year of famine, the Synod issued a circular emphasizing that in cases of non-payment of such legal obligations the police were not to be called in. Instead, the clergy were to use persuasion and other "moral means" of obtaining payment, and were to report continued failure to their bishops. [135] Thus this solution of their financial difficulties did not appear to be the ideal one, and there was little real eagerness for a wider application of this system. Yet in 1905 the peasant communes contributed 6,755,000 rubles for local religious needs, of which 1,575,400 rubles went to maintain the priests and to provide them with homes. [136]

An almost universal means of supporting the priests was by payment for ministrations. Although by canon law it was forbidden to charge for confession or for Holy Communion, for the "optional" services such as marriage, baptism, and burial, contributions might be accepted. Other services for which payments were made were memorial masses, ceremonial processions to bless the homes of parishioners, their wells, their cabbage cellars, their fields, the blessing of ikons, and the giving out of attestations from the record-books. In theory these payments were voluntary contributions, but often they were obligatory in that the priest might refuse to officiate until the money was in hand. There were no rates officially fixed for these services, so that each occasion might involve complicated bargaining. Some priests set low rates for their ministrations, in which case matters went off smoothly with all except unreasonable peasants. For example, the schedule set by the priests of the villages in the province

[134] *Svod Zakonov,* IX, "Zakony o Sostoianiiakh," ed. 1899, supplement to sec. 453, part II, paragraph 10.

[135] Zav'ialov, ed., *Tsirkuliarnye Ukazy,* p. 256.

[136] Ministerstvo Finansov, Departament Okladnykh Sborov, *Mirskie Dokhody i Raskhody za 1905 g.,* p. xxiv.

of Kaluga was two kopecks for the administration of communion (this was illegal, as communion was supposed to be free), one ruble for a liturgy, from one to two rubles for the burial of an adult, three rye cakes for a requiem, from five to eight rubles for a marriage, forty kopecks for a christening, and on holy days payments of from five to ten kopecks.[137] Another priest declared that he charged from three to eight rubles for a marriage, forty kopecks for a christening, ten kopecks for a liturgy, and for a year's remembrance of a relative, from ten to twenty kopecks.[138] These rates were not uncommon.

However, while in some cases the system of payment for ministrations was satisfactory, there were a number of instances where it caused much trouble. As one of the bishops wrote,

The greatest religious evil of the present means of supporting the clergy . . . is that they, in the eyes of the people, become their exploiters, and antagonism develops between the people and the clergy; the clergy try to receive as much as possible, and the people try to give up as little as possible.[139]

Occasionally the cry of exploitation was loudly raised; trials before the consistorial courts were begun, and much hostility to the clergy under accusation was shown.[140] In 1884 the peasants of Gusarevka, in the diocese of Ekaterinoslav, elected a delegate to appeal as follows to the consistory for redress of the high rates set by their priests for their ministrations:

Our clergy have established the payment for christening at sixty kopecks, and propose to raise it to a ruble; and thus they have turned away the peasants from professing their chosen faith, and have prevented parents from acting according to their vows before God. For confession they have set the rate at six kopecks, by means of the sale of tapers; . . . for burial the payment is ten rubles or more; for marriages the payments run up to thirty rubles, and they propose to raise it to fifty rubles.

Consequently we have set the rate for baptizing at fifteen kopecks; for administering extreme unction, five kopecks; for confession, four

---

[137] *Vera i Razum*, May, 1907, p. 550.

[138] *Missionerskoe Obozrenie*, Jan., 1906, p. 105.

[139] Sv. Sinod, *Otzyvy Eparkhial'nykh Arkhiereev po Voprosu o Tserkovnoi Reforme*, I, 446.

[140] *Tserkovnyi Vestnik*, Jan. 3, 1908, col. 9; Rozhdestvenskii, *Iuzhnorusskii Stundizm*, p. 28.

kopecks; for marriages, ten rubles; for writing attestations from the record-books, thirty kopecks; for the burial of an infant, one ruble, and for that of an adult, three rubles; for commemoration of a deceased, for forty days, three rubles, and for a year, ten rubles; for a requiem in a home, one ruble; for a religious procession to bless a field, five rubles; to bless a well, one ruble and fifty kopecks; for blessing a home, two rubles; for a liturgy with canons, fifty kopecks, and without canons, thirty kopecks; and for blessing an ikon, five kopecks.

Unfortunately, there is no way of knowing what would have been the outcome of this petition if it had received consideration. It never came up for decision, because the petitioners had not fortified it with the proper revenue stamps.[141]

Another case of this nature was reported in the religious press in 1912. The *Poltava Diocesan News* told of a parishioner's complaint to the diocesan authorities that his village priest and psalmist had "in extortionate fashion taken eight rubles from him for the burial of his son." The petitioner requested that "the diocesan authorities compel the priest and the psalmist to return the money," and he threatened, in case of refusal, to start a lawsuit.[142] The outcome of this episode, however, was not reported by the journal.

A practice somewhat akin to that of paying for ministrations was that of making periodical donations, either in kind or in money. Sometimes these donations were delivered by the peasants at the priest's house, in the form of pieces of linen, cabbages, butter, eggs, chickens, or geese.[143] In other cases the priests made the rounds of their parishes in order to collect their dues—a practice which consumed much time. Said one bishop:

. . . a great deal of time is spent by the priests in making their fall collections and those of St. Peter's Day, greatly to the detriment of their pastoral activity. In very populous and extensive parishes in several dioceses, as, for example, Viatka, the clergy drive out to make collections or to bless . . . except when the peasants are in the fields or the meadows and during the period of impassable roads. There have been cases where service in the church on holy days has been missed by the clergy, due to their collections and blessings.[144]

---

[141] Sv. Sinod, 1884, portfolio 1192, sheets 2, 3, and 6.

[142] *Tserkovnyi Vestnik*, Jan. 26, 1912, col. 128.

[143] *Pravoslavnyi Sobesednik*, Jan., 1905, p. 159; *Tserkovnyia Vedomosti*, Nov. 26, 1905, p. 2089.

[144] Sv. Sinod, *Otzyvy*, I, 226.

In the city of Moscow the practice of periodic collections flourished also. Some eight or ten times a year the priest, accompanied by the deacon and a few members of the congregation, would go from house to house. At each dwelling all would enter, and a verse of the canticle would be sung; then the priest collected the donation of the parishioner.[145]

Both these methods of paying the clergy had grave disadvantages. Requiring payments for ministrations created bad feeling between priest and parishioners, leading occasionally to charges of extortion and to lawsuits before the consistorial courts, and often stirring up disaffection. Then too receipts from payments for ministrations and from donations were uncertain. The amounts varied greatly, as the clergy had to reckon with the harvest returns and the attitude of the parishioners. Consequently almost all members of the church organization, from the Over Procurator to the parish priest, united in desiring a substitute for these methods of payment. Some of the priests did find a supplement for their normal incomes in serving as religious teachers in *zemstvo* or city schools at sixty rubles a year, or as official administrants of the oaths required in courts of justice. But these expedients were open only to a limited number, and at best they only added to the incomes received by the priests from their other activities, without providing an adequate substitute for them. Moreover, the regularity and certainty of the pay served to call attention to the advantages of state salaries—a form of remuneration long desired by both clergy and Over Procurator.

The movement for state salaries dates back to 1893, when Pobedonostsev appealed to Alexander III, and the desirability of state support for all the Orthodox clergy was formally recognized by the Tsar. To be sure, there had been some salaries paid to the clergy from the treasury before that date, but only in exceptional cases. After 1893, however, the amount of money devoted to this end grew rapidly. In 1900 the treasury assigned to the church 23,559,685 rubles, of which 10,263,396 went to the town and village clergy and to the missionaries.[146] This latter sum was increased by 200,000 rubles in 1901, and by 500,000 rubles in each of the three succeeding years, so that in 1905 there were available nearly 12,000,000 rubles out of

[145] *Missionerskoe Obozrenie,* Oct., 1905, pp. 639–46.
[146] Gosudarstvennyi Kontrol, *Otchet,* 1900, pp. 230–35.

which salaries were to be paid to the clergy. However, not all shared alike in the distribution of this sum. The clergy of the outlying parts of the empire—Poland, the Baltic provinces, Finland, Turkestan, and the Siberian dioceses, as well as the western provinces of the Ukraine and of White Russia, where the competition of Catholicism was strong and payments from Orthodox parishioners none too plentiful—were given much larger state salaries than those of the strongly Russian provinces. The priests of the dioceses of Riga and Warsaw, for example, received state salaries of from 800 to 1,500 rubles a year, while the others in the outlying provinces were paid at the rate of from 300 to 600 rubles. The salaries paid in the regular Russian dioceses, however, were supposed to be 300 rubles a year, with 100 for the psalmist; this rate was adopted as the average norm by the Synod in 1903. Actually, however, many of the priests who received state salaries were still paid at the earlier rate, adopted in 1893, of from 100 to 180 rubles, while many received no state support at all.[147]

No figures are available for the total number of churches which received state support in 1905; but in 1910, out of the 29,946 churches in 39 dioceses of European Russia, 10,153 were given no state salaries whatever, while many of the others received less than the accepted norm. The amount devoted to this purpose in 1910 was about 980,000 rubles larger than the corresponding amount in 1905, so that in the latter year the number of churches whose clergy received state salaries was doubtless somewhat less.[148]

As far as can be ascertained, no statistics were gathered in Russia which might show the average total income of a priest. The size of the parishes, the number of parishioners, the amount of parish land and its productivity, and the amount of state salary paid, if any, all varied so that it is impossible to determine accurately any general average. However, in the religious periodicals of the time some writers gave their estimates of the average priestly income from all sources. In one such estimate in 1906 the amount was given as between 600 and 800 rubles,[149] while another, in 1905, set it at 700 rubles,[150] and a third declared in 1907 that the mean income lay between 400 and

[147] Sv. Sinod, *Smeta Dokhodov i Raskhodov*, pp. lviii–lix.
[148] Sv. Sinod, Khoz. Uprav., 1910, portfolio 33.
[149] *Tserkovnyia Vedomosti*, Dec. 16, 1906, pp. 3125–26.
[150] *Pravoslavnyi Sobesednik*, Jan., 1905, p. 158.

900 rubles.[151] A priest writing in 1908 stated that the average received in rural parishes was not more than 500 or 600 rubles,[152] while in 1915 another went to the opposite extreme, declaring, "We shall scarcely be exaggerating if we say that the average figure for the yearly income now received by a priest is not much less than 1,200 rubles." [153]

The weight of the evidence seems to indicate that the last figure is too high, unless the war or other special factors raised the income of the clergy sharply in the later period. If one may judge by the few estimates cited above, the average income for a village priest in the Russia of 1905 may have been somewhere near 700 rubles. This sum was quite small when compared with the 5,000 and 10,000 rubles and more received by many of the bishops; and certainly numbers of the priests felt that they were very poorly paid. On the other hand, the average priest was well above the economic level of the average peasant or of the average factory worker.

Some of the priests in the cities were decidedly better off in terms of cash income than the village clergy. Especially was this true of the clergy of churches maintained by institutions of the civil government. In 1900 it was provided that the state salaries to the clergy of a church maintained by the Department of Customs Duties of the Ministry of Finance were to be 1,200 and 850 rubles for the first and second priests and 720 for the deacon; [154] in 1905 the state salaries to the clergy of the State Bank were set at 1,500 rubles for the priest, 900 rubles for the deacon, and 600 rubles for the psalmist; all of them were provided with quarters in the building of the bank.[155] Even more generous were the salaries of the clergy of the Church of Christ the Savior in St. Petersburg; the rates of pay, fixed in 1911, were 4,000 rubles for the dean, 3,500 rubles for the canon, 3,000 rubles for the priest, 1,300 for the deacon, and 900 for each of three psalmists.[156] The salaries paid to the cathedral clergy in the provincial towns, on the other hand, were much smaller, although they were larger than those given to many of the village pastors. According to the salary schedule adopted in 1867, most of the cathedral deans were paid 400

[151] *Vera i Razum*, May, 1907, p. 549.
[152] *Bogoslovskii Vestnik*, Nov., 1908, p. 372.
[153] *Missionerskoe Obozrenie*, Jan., 1915, p. 80.
[154] *Sobranie Uzakonenii i Rasporiazhenii Pravitel'stva*, 1900, No. 570.
[155] *Ibid.*, 1905, No. 1080.   [156] *Ibid.*, 1911, No. 939.

rubles a year, the canons 300, and the priests 250 rubles each; in a few dioceses the corresponding salaries ran as high as 700, 550, and 450 rubles each.[157] This schedule remained in force for several decades. In 1895 the salaries decreed for the cathedral of Ekaterinburg were 400 for the dean, 300 for the canon, and 250 for each of the two priests.[158] The schedules of the cathedrals of Omsk and Irkutsk, adopted in 1895 and 1897 respectively, were 650 rubles for the deans, 550 for the canons, and 450 for the priests.[159]

The figures in the preceding paragraph deal only with the state salaries, and do not include other income, such as payment for ministrations and the like. On the other hand, in every town or city there were a number of churches whose clergy were not given the same salaries as those of the cathedral clergy. Hence it is impossible to set with any accuracy the average income of the urban clergy. However, all writers agreed that the priests of the towns received higher total incomes than did the rural clergy.[160]

The parishes of the Russian Church also had their incomes, distinct from those of the clergy and, as shown by sample parish accounts published during later periods, in the great majority of cases not shared by the clergy. In 1900 the parishes collected 6,131,528 rubles in the form of donations, and 10,788,077 rubles from the sale of tapers. Rented property and the interest on investments yielded 3,964,499 rubles; bequests and other miscellaneous sources produced 9,456,597 more, and the parish trusteeships had an income of 4,343,-329 rubles. With these and other lesser items, their total income amounted to 37,492,781 rubles for the year 1900.[161] However, this sum, amounting to nearly 800 rubles per parish, was largely consumed by the cost of repairing and heating the churches, by the purchase of tapers at wholesale, and by the needs of the diocesan authorities, so that little was left for charitable work or education. The Orthodox churches maintained seventy-four hospitals in 1900; but private, community, and state funds, as well as the contribution of

[157] *Polnoe Sobranie Zakonov*, 1867, No. 45341.

[158] *Sobranie Uzakonenii*, 1895, No. 98.

[159] *Ibid.*, 1895, No. 327; 1897, No. 306.

[160] *Tserkovnyia Vedomosti*, Dec. 16, 1906, p. 3216; *Bogoslovskii Vestnik*, Nov., 1908, p. 372.

[161] Sv. Sinod, *Vsepoddanneishii Otchet*, 1900, p. 384.

the churches, played a part in their support.[162] Under parish auspices in 1900 there were 875 almshouses which were supported by private, community, state, and parish funds, with a total accommodation for 11,302 persons.[163] When one bears in mind that there were more than 40,000 churches in the Russian empire, these figures bear out the statements of two of the bishops in 1906: "In rare, very rare, instances does the money raised by the parish trusteeships go to construct and improve educational institutions such as almshouses, hospitals, asylums, and the like"; [164] and, ". . . community benevolent work of the parish is . . . insignificant. . . ." [165]

The reasons for this were not hard to find. Control over the scanty funds of the parish was not in the hands of the parishioners, but was exercised solely by the priest and the parish elder, who were not accountable to the congregation. They themselves were not free agents, for there were exactions made by the diocesan authorities, which had to be met out of the parish funds. There were obligatory imposts for the benefit of the diocesan schools, to help the sick of ecclesiastical families, for the office expenses of the district priests, to increase the pay of the consistories, for the Imperial Palestine Society, and many others. Papkov, a leading authority on parish conditions, stated that the total of these exactions in 1902 was more than 8,000,000 rubles, or more than a fifth of the total income of the parishes.[166] Another writer declared that at one village church in the diocese of Tambov the peasants in the 1880's contributed about 600 rubles a year; in the year 1886 outside obligations took away 296 rubles. In some cases the total of the imposts demanded was twice the size of the income of the parish.[167] As a result, many of the priests and parish elders made a practice of not entering in the parish accounts all the moneys received, so that the demands made of them might be smaller. At the Pre-*Sobor* Conference, a meeting of the leading figures of the church held in 1906, Dean T. I. Butkevich declared, ". . . in . . . [the parish account] books there is not one word of truth." He added that Bishop Amvrosii of Khar'kov fully agreed with him. Nor did the

[162] *Ibid.*, pp. 44–48 of tables.   [163] *Ibid.*
[164] Sv. Sinod, *Otzyvy,* III, 451, Commission of Enisei Diocese.
[165] *Ibid.*, I, 437, Konstantin of Samara.
[166] *Tserkovnyi Vestnik,* July 19, 1907, col. 926.
[167] *Tserkovno-obshchestvennaia Zhizn',* Dec. 1, 1906, cols. 1637–40.

other members of the meeting express disagreement with this statement.[168] Naturally the parishioners tended to become somewhat
cynical in their attitude toward parish affairs, about which they were
able to learn little. Bishop Serafim of Polotsk remarked in 1906:

... the parishioners actually do not know the details concerning the
spending of their moneys, and they cannot be acquainted with them, for,
if the parishioners should learn that almost all of the church income,
in the vast majority of churches, is spent for the maintenance of religious educational institutions [seminaries and diocesan schools] and
for various diocesan purposes, then undoubtedly these disbursements
would evoke from them a justified protest. . . .[169]

This statement seems to be somewhat overdrawn, as the evidence
presented by Papkov tends to show that the diocesan levies were not
much more than a fifth of the total parish income, but coming
from a bishop it does indicate that the levies were burdensome for the
parishes.

Most of the levies drawn from the parish revenues remained in
the diocese, but a small part was drawn into the budget of the central
administrative organs of the church, which were nominally under
the Synod. Their share in the parish income in 1900 was 1,682,484
rubles. The central administration of the church also obtained 828,-
458 rubles from its printing establishments, which enjoyed a monopoly of the sale of books for use in church schools and in the teaching
of the Orthodox religion. Other items of the Synod's income in 1900
were 1,305,026 rubles in interest from invested capital, 528,320 rubles
collected in the eight western dioceses as a building fund, and 2,608,-
679 rubles from the state treasury. The total income of the central
administration of the church in 1900 was 8,870,188 rubles.[170]

It is impossible to determine with any exactness the total income
of the Russian Church and its clergy in any given year. Any estimate
must be a rough approximation. But as the question has real interest
and importance, it seems worth while to attempt an answer, even
though the findings must be regarded with the greatest of caution.

For purposes of convenience the year 1900 has been chosen. In

[168] *Tserkovnyia Vedomosti*, Jan. 13, 1907, p. 326.
[169] Sv. Sinod, *Otzyvy*, I, 164, Serafim of Polotsk.
[170] Sv. Sinod, *Vsepoddanneishii Otchet*, 1900, p. 384.

that year the monasteries and convents may be assumed to have had a cash income of something like 18,000,000 rubles—a figure based upon the fact that they reported revenues of 20,627,286 in 1909.[171] Inasmuch as the statements of the individual monasteries examined by the author showed incomes about 10 percent greater in the years around 1909 than in 1900, the total has been reduced from 20,000,000 of 1909 to 18,000,000 for 1900. As for the parish clergy, their income may perhaps be conservatively set at 49,000,000 rubles. If allowance is made for the fact that many of them were in relatively well-paid urban parishes, and that a number of churches, both urban and rural, had two or three priests apiece and a corresponding number of psalmists and sometimes deacons, it does not seem excessive to allow 1,000 rubles for the clergymen of the average parish. As there were 49,082 parishes in 1900,[172] the figure of 49,000,000 rubles is reached. The other parish income totaled 37,492,781 in 1900; [173] while the special funds of the Synod (after deducting the 1,682,484 drawn from the parishes) amounted to 7,187,704 rubles.[174] The appropriation from the treasury to the church in 1900 was 23,559,685 rubles; but after deducting 10,263,396 rubles, which represents salaries paid to the parish clergy, 2,608,679 rubles included in the special funds of the Synod, and 421,496 rubles paid by the state to the monasteries, the amount becomes 10,266,114 rubles.[175] These items when added together give a total of 121,946,599 rubles.

It will be seen that no figure has been included for the income of the bishops. This is because their income was largely derived from the monasteries and from the treasury, and consequently the figures given for those items include the amounts received by the bishops.

The estimate given for the yearly income of the church is perhaps wrong by a number of millions of rubles; but, even though there may have been some slight duplications in assembling the total, the author believes that any error has been one of conservatism rather than of exaggeration. The income of the parish clergy may well have been larger than the amount estimated, while the figure arrived at for the

---

[171] Sv. Sinod, *Smeta Dokhodov i Raskhodov*, p. xlv.
[172] Sv. Sinod, *Vsepoddanneishii Otchet*, 1900, pp. 8–9 of tables.
[173] *Ibid.*, p. 383.   [174] *Ibid.*, p. 384.
[175] Gosudarstvennyi Kontrol, *Otchet*, 1900, pp. 230–35.

revenues of the monastic institutions, based as it is on the official report, was also perhaps too conservative, since, as has been said, the official figures for these sums were frequently too small. At all events, unless the estimate be very wide of the mark, it serves to show in part why the church as an institution supported the government. The appropriations made by the state to the church were but a trifling part of the total state budget—the church's 23,000,000 were far exceeded by the budget of the Ministry of War, with 324,343,686 rubles, and by that of the Ministry of Means of Communication, with 322,287,968 rubles, and were also surpassed by the budgets for the Navy, and for the Ministries of Internal Affairs, Justice, Agriculture and State Possessions, and of the Ministry of Education [176]—but nevertheless, these state funds made up nearly a fifth part of the church's income, a resource which it could ill afford to lose. As for the rest of the church's revenues, they were raised by the church itself; but none the less the church did not feel entirely secure in the enjoyment of them, so that it valued the protection which the state was able to give to those sources of wealth. Furthermore, the eagerness with which the bishops and the leading church periodicals sought for greater aid from the state argues that most of the leading churchmen were not averse to closer financial relations with the civil power. These circumstances undoubtedly help to explain the fact that when the first test came in the Revolution of 1905, the greater part of the clergy were found among the supporters of the government.

[176] Gosudarstvennyi Kontrol, *Otchet*, 1900, pp. 298, 316, 472, 546, 450, 498, 526.

CHAPTER IV

Religious Education and Indoctrination: Monopolies of the Orthodox Church

WHILE the Imperial government was thus furthering, both directly and indirectly, the economic interests of the church, it was also helping the church to control the realm of ideas. The state gave it full freedom to proselytize, and worked actively to check the propaganda of its enemies; in the field of education also the church was given wide powers and official encouragement. This aid was important for the church. In the following pages an attempt will be made to show in what manner assistance was rendered, and what use the church made of it.

In dealing with the opponents of the Orthodox Church the Russian government had to deal with many groups—among them the Finns and other peoples of the Baltic lands (Esths, Letts, and Baltic Germans) who were Lutherans, and the Catholic Poles. Undoubtedly the latter were troublesome rivals of the Orthodox Church—the centuries of conflict with the Poles in the Ukraine were proof enough of that. Nor did Orthodoxy view with equanimity the possibility of the winning of converts by the Lutherans. But even more than it feared Catholicism and Lutheranism, the Russian Church was perturbed by the inroads made by rival faiths of more recent origin, which were more appealing to the real Russian population than were the "foreign" religions. These domestic foes were sects of various kinds, and especially the Old Believers, or schismatics.

The origins of the Schism have been sketched in the first chapter, as well as the persecutions inflicted upon the Old Believers. Under

Catherine II, Paul, and Alexander I, however, they enjoyed a period of toleration, and many of them, especially those who had grown rich in the manufacture of cloth, in trade, and in money-lending, grew more moderate in their attitude toward the government. So harmonious did the relations become between the Old Believers and the government that in 1800 there was set up a Uniat Church called *Edinoverie*, which used all the forms and rituals which the Synod condemned when used by the Old Believers, but was under the control of the Orthodox bishops and of the Synod. However, most of the Old Believers refused to join *Edinoverie*.[1]

Under Nicholas I, however, the position of the Old Believers changed for the worse. The term *raskol'nik* (schismatic), which had been discarded from official use, was revived and given a derogatory meaning like that of "deserter," and those to whom it was applied lost many of their rights. Their religious property was confiscated, and the formation of monastic institutions by them forbidden. When Orthodox subjects were converted to the Schism, the government took away their children who had been christened in the Orthodox Church, and also closed up many of the prayer houses of the Old Believers. Both the "priestless" Old Believers (*Bezpopovtsy*) and those who had clergy (*Beglopopovtsy*) were harassed by the authorities; the clergy of the latter groups were the special objects of attention. In 1832 there occurred a general round up of the fugitive Orthodox priests who ministered to the *Beglopopovtsy*, based upon the hope that the "priestly" Old Believers, when deprived of their priests, would return to the fold of the official church. But the persecution failed of its purpose. The Old Believers, instead of joining *Edinoverie*, carried on secret worship, and in proportion as the persecution increased, their fanaticism returned, and with it the old prophecies about the end of the world and the legend that the Tsar was Antichrist.[2]

In spite of the severity of the regime of Nicholas, the Old Believers continued to be numerous. The police measures failed—in part be-

[1] N. M. Nikol'skii, "Raskol v Pervoi Polovine XIX Veka," *Istoriia Rossii v XIX Veke*, IV, 50–52; N. Ivanovskii, *Rukovodstvo k Istorii i Oblicheniiu Staroobriadcheskago Raskola*, part 1, pp. 218–29.

[2] Nikol'skii, *op. cit.*, pp. 52–67.

cause the officials of the day were notoriously venal. Count Stenbok, a high official of the period, stated that "priests gladly choose parishes where there are many schismatics, for the schismatics pay them generously not to persecute—in the record [the priests] would inscribe them as Orthodox, and would record them as having been to confession." [3] In 1853 several officials of the Ministry of Internal Affairs made studies of the Schism in different provinces, and their reports, although not tinged with fondness for the Old Believers, told the same story. Sinitsyn, in the province of Iaroslavl,[4] Aksakov, also in Iaroslavl,[5] and Mel'nikov, in the province of Nizhnii Novgorod,[6] all mentioned corrupt bargains between Orthodox parish priests and Old Believers. Arnoldi, in the province of Kostroma, wrote:

> The priests for the most part protect the schismatics, as they get large sums from them. They receive as much as 150 rubles merely for inscribing in the record books marriages of schismatics which they have not performed. . . . In the village of Penka the priest Aliakritskii . . . is a rare exception. . . .[7]

Thus the Old Believers, whether of the priestly or of the priestless (*Bezpopovtsy*) groups, circumvented the government, and never were close to annihilation. In fact it was during the reign of Nicholas I that the *Beglopopovtsy* were able to achieve a regular priesthood. This step, which strengthened them greatly, was made with some difficulty, for the Tsar and the Russian Church used all their influence to prevent it. Nevertheless, after considerable negotiation the Old Believers induced a Bosnian metropolitan, Amvrosii, no longer on active duty, to consecrate three bishops for them at Belaia Krinitsa, in Austria, in the year 1847. The Russian government was furious with the Austrians for their connivance, and made sporadic attempts to arrest the new prelates when they came to Russia. But none the less, in 1859 there were ten of these schismatic bishops in Russia, who, together with some of their priests, formed the council at the head of the priestly church.[8] Thanks to the new bishops, this group of Old Be-

---

[3] V. I. Kel'siev, *Sbornik Pravitel'stvennykh Svedenii o Raskole*, IV, 331.
[4] *Ibid.*, II, 14–15.
[5] I. Aksakov, *Russkii Arkhiv*, 1866, No. 4, cols. 635–36.
[6] P. I. Mel'nikov, *Sochinenie*, VII, 395.
[7] Kel'siev, *op. cit.*, II, 21.   [8] Nikol'skii, *op. cit.*, p. 60.

lievers could now be sure of a constant supply of priests, without having to take in renegade Orthodox clergy.

The acquisition of a hierarchy undoubtedly gave new prestige to the priestly Old Believers; yet it was not an unmixed blessing. One result of the development was that a new split occurred in the ranks of the schismatics. A small part of the priestly Old Believers refused to accept the new priesthood, and clung stubbornly to the use of fugitive Orthodox clergy. However, most of the priestly group accepted the new order with enthusiasm, and the so-called "Austrian denomination" of Old Believers became a formidable adversary for the Orthodox Church. Undoubtedly the possession of a regular hierarchy with the apostolic succession strengthened the movement greatly.

After the death of Nicholas I came a period of comparative peace for the Old Believers. Alexander II was more liberal than his father and, as his attention was turned to more pressing matters, the Old Believers of all groups, both priestly and priestless, enjoyed a period of neglect. There was little persecution; but on the other hand, there was no new legislation for their benefit.

In fact, this very mildness of Alexander caused a split in the ranks of the Austrian denomination. The wealthy leaders of this group living in Moscow were so pleased with the new order of things that in 1861 they induced the council of bishops to send forth a "diocesan message" saying that it was time to discard some of their old beliefs. It was no longer fitting, they said, to believe in the imminent end of the world and the coming of Antichrist. The Tsar was to be recognized as a holy person, protected by God, and worthy of the prayers of true believers. Of course they were not ready to recognize the official church as the true church, but they should no longer regard it as the handiwork of the devil and should admit that the Christ whom it worshiped was the Savior. But alas for the hopes of the Moscow leaders! Many of the rank and file of the Austrian group, especially those living along the Volga and in the forests of the north, were not willing to make their peace with the Tsar and his government, which they had hated for so long. Consequently the ranks of the Austrian group were cleft into two sections—those conservative Old Believers, some of them wealthy, who were concentrated in

Moscow, together with most of their hierarchy; and at odds with them the mass of the peasant Old Believers of this denomination in the provinces.[9] This split continued to plague the Old Believers for decades.

To make matters worse for the Old Believers, a reactionary period set in, in 1881, with the accession of Alexander III, who was guided by Pleve and the Over Procurator of the Synod, Pobedonostsev. Owing to the efforts of the latter official there was issued in 1883 a new law dealing with the legal position of the Old Believers and the sectarians. This new law, while more liberal than the laws actually on the statute books, which were no longer applied, was far less so than had been hoped for by those who sympathized with these denominations.[10] Only in one respect did the law of 1883 satisfy the proponents of full religious toleration: the rights specified therein were granted to "raskol'niks [schismatics] of all sects, with the exception of the Skoptsy" (an immoral sect), and the restrictions had the same scope.[11] Thus sectarians as well as Old Believers were entitled to receive passports, to engage in trade and productive enterprise, and to hold minor office.[12] The law further provided that the raskol'niks might hold group religious services in their homes or in houses of prayer, which were, however, not to resemble Orthodox churches in outward appearance, and were not to have bells visible from outside. Moreover, the raskol'niks were not entitled to build new houses of prayer; in places where they lacked facilities for worship, they might be permitted to remodel buildings already in existence, but only with the permission of the Ministry of Internal Affairs, which permission might not be granted until the Ministry had conferred on the matter with the Over Procurator of the Synod. The raskol'niks were given the right to bury their dead with their own ceremonies, including funeral processions, hymns, and the bearing of ikons; religious vestments were not to be worn, however, even at funerals. In general all other public manifestations of their faith were forbidden, including solemn processions with banners and crosses, and public processions in vest-

---

[9] Ibid., pp. 61–62; Nikol'skii, "Raskol i Sektantstvo vo Vtoroi Polovine XIX Veka," Istoriia Rossii v XIX Veke, V, 228–34.
[10] I. S. Berdnikov, Kratkii Kurs Tserkovnago Prava, pp. 1166 ff.
[11] Polnoe Sobranie Zakonov, May 3, 1883, No. 1545.   [12] Ibid.

ments; the bearing of Old Believer ikons in public, except in the case of funerals; the use of monastic or ecclesiastical garb outside of chapels or prayer buildings; and the singing of *raskol'nik* hymns on the street. The leaders of the denominations in question were not to be subject to persecution so long as they were not guilty of "spreading their errors among the Orthodox" nor of other unlawful actions. They were not recognized as members of the clergy, and possessed no legal rights other than those of subjects of the classes to which they legally belonged. Moreover, very wide discretion in dealing with *raskol'niks* was granted to the Minister of Internal Affairs; he was to issue proper regulations respecting these non-Orthodox subjects, taking into consideration local conditions and the "moral character and other qualities of each sect." [13]

These provisions, which continued in effect until April, 1905,[14] placed burdensome restrictions upon the Old Believers and the sectarians. The Orthodox Church, however, was faced with no such difficulties. Under Alexander III and under Nicholas II many parish schools were established to educate the people in Orthodoxy, and an array of missionaries was sent out to win converts from other faiths. Moreover, until 1905 Pobedonostsev was playing an active part in directing the campaign to strengthen the church, and his ideas underwent no change. The Orthodox missionaries and the police worked actively to convert the Old Believers in the first years of the twentieth century, until the eve of the Revolution of 1905. As these last years of the old regime, untempered by parliamentary forms, show the workings of this system of repression, which had functioned since the death of Alexander II, it seems advisable to make a more detailed study of the numbers and of the tribulations of the Old Believers and of the sectarians during these years.

In 1901 the Central Statistical Committee of the Russian government published a tabulation of the number of Old Believers and sectarians in 1897, "drawn up on the basis of the personal declarations of the persons asked." This statement showed a total of 2,173,-

---

[13] *Polnoe Sobranie Zakonov,* May, 3, 1883, No. 1545.

[14] *Svod Zakonov Rossiiskoi Imperii,* XIV, "Ustav o Preduprezhdenii i Presechenii Prestuplenii," ed. 1890, secs. 45–64; *Prodolzhenie Svoda Zakonov,* 1906, XIV, "Ustav o Preduprezhdenii i Presechenii Prestuplenii," secs. 45–64 (changed April, 1905).

738 Old Believers and sectarians of all kinds, or 2.49 percent of the total population of the empire. This sum was made up of 1,028,437 Old Believers, 176,199 sectarians, and 969,102 persons whose affiliations were not indicated.[15] (These figures did not include the adherents of the Catholic, Lutheran and other religions, which were recognized as lawful only for subjects of non-Russian nationality, such as Poles, Letts, Esths, and Finns.) However, when this total of 2,000,000 is compared with the undocumented claim of some of the Old Believers themselves that they alone numbered 20,000,000,[16] and the statement of the leading lay authority, Prugavin, that the latter figure would be nearer the truth than the former,[17] it becomes evident that further investigation is necessary.

Unfortunately the Imperial government had made few attempts to investigate this subject carefully and had shrouded the matter in secrecy. Prugavin stated that when, in 1880, the Ethnographical Division of the Russian Geographical Society had approved a proposal for a study of the Old Believers, the project was quietly discouraged by the government. Private investigations were forbidden, and the works of foreigners which treated of the subject were either banned or expurgated. Leroy-Beaulieu's book was forbidden; only Volume I of Haxthausen's work was allowed in Russia; Dixon's books were mutilated by the exclusion of several chapters.[18] Aksakov, a state official of the 1850's, wrote that in 1866 all the material on the subject of the Schism was concentrated in the Ministry of Internal Affairs, where cases concerning Old Believers were treated "secretly," "very secretly," or "entirely secretly," and were not available either to the scholar or to the Orthodox clergy themselves.[19]

All estimates contradicting the figures of the tabulation of 1897 go back to an investigation made by the Ministry of Internal Affairs in 1851. Up to that time both police and clergy had taken as correct the official figures of the "registered" Old Believers—those officially inscribed in the record books from birth. These figures were some-

---

[15] Tsentral'nyi Statisticheskii Komitet, *Raspredelenie Staroobriadtsev i Sektantov.*

[16] *Staroobriadcheskii Vestnik,* Nov.–Dec., 1905, p. 696.

[17] A. Prugavin, *Staroobriadchestvo vo Vtoroi Polovine XIX Veka,* p. 17.

[18] Prugavin, "Raskol i Biurokratiia," *Vestnik Evropy,* 1909, V, 655–56.

[19] Aksakov, *op. cit.,* col. 636.

times carried forward without change for forty years, with no account of the excess of births over deaths, to say nothing of possible conversions of the Orthodox to the Schism. Sometimes the police officials arbitrarily reduced the total, year after year, in order to gain credit for zealous efforts in dealing with the Old Believers.

Occasionally a young and zealous official would make an attempt to find out the true state of affairs, which invariably led to the submission to his superiors of a much higher set of figures. But the reception of such revised estimates was discouraging indeed. The enthusiast would be sent a chilly request for further information, with such questions as: "Why had the Schism strengthened its position in such a county and district? Who was responsible for the marked increase in the number of schismatics? What steps were being taken with a view to preventing and destroying schismatic propaganda? Why had the government not been informed earlier of this growth?—and so on." Usually a reprimand would be sent to the hapless underling, who, much wiser in the future, quickly mended his ways, and sent in reports couched in the old hypocritical fashion. But in the 1850's Count Perovskii, Minister of Internal Affairs, reported to the emperor that the official figure of 829,971 was far too low, as there actually were about 9,000,000 Old Believers. As a result, a careful investigation was begun by the ministry.[20]

The reports brought back by the investigating committees were so remarkable—one of them finding nearly forty times as many Old Believers in a certain province as the official figures listed [21]—that new inquiries were made. One and all they told the same story—that the schismatics were vastly more numerous than had been officially stated. Reluctantly the government was forced to admit that in 1859 there were probably about 9,300,000 Old Believers of all varieties in Russia.[22]

With this official figure as a basis, the writer Iuzov, one of the Old Believer bishops, estimated the number of Old Believers and sectarians in 1880 to be about 13,000,000 members: 3,000,000 "priestly," 8,000,000 *Bezpopovtsy*, 1,000,000 members of the Evangelical sects

[20] F. C. Conybeare, *Russian Dissenters*, p. 240; Mel'nikov, *op. cit.*, VII, 397–98.

[21] Mel'nikov, *op. cit.*, p. 400.   [22] *Ibid.*, p. 408.

(*Molokane, Dukhobortsy, Stundisty,* and so on), 65,000 *Khlysty* and *Skoptsy,* and 1,000,000 whose religious faith was unknown.[23] Conybeare, whose recent work, while careful, shows signs of favor for these non-Orthodox groups, judges that by 1900, allowing for the natural growth of the population, there must have been some 20,000,000 of the Old Believers alone.[24]

The discrepancy between the government figures obtained in 1897 and those of Prugavin, Iuzov, and Conybeare is so marked that there is no possibility of reconciling the difference. But if we may take as valid the figure of the Ministry of Internal Affairs for 1859, namely, 9,300,000, then the figures of 1897 seem remarkably low. There had occurred no mass conversions of the Old Believers which could have reduced the number of Old Believers and sectarians from 9,000,000 to 2,000,000. Even the reports of the Over Procurator of the Synod, Pobedonostsev himself, claimed only some 4,000 to 10,000 a year; [25] and when the possibility of winning converts by these denominations from the ranks of the Orthodox is borne in mind—a form of conversion frequently lamented in the Orthodox religious publications —it appears probable that the real figure in 1897 was much larger than 2,000,000. In 1851 there were 58,776,675 people in the empire, not including Finland and Poland; [26] 9,000,000 Old Believers and sectarians amounted to somewhat more than 15 percent of the total. In 1897 there were 117,120,132 people in the empire, without Poland and Finland.[27] If in this somewhat larger area the proportion of Old Believers and sectarians to the rest of the population was the same as in 1851, their number in 1897 must have been about 17,500,000.

The legal position of the Old Believers was not enviable. Mention has already been made of the restrictions upon the building of their houses of prayer, and upon the public profession of their faith. Moreover, the Old Believers were liable to heavy penalties (imprisonment, or exile to Siberia) if they were guilty of "attempting to seduce Ortho-

[23] I. Iuzov, *Russkie Dissidenty*, p. 46.

[24] Conybeare, *op. cit.*, p. 249.

[25] Sv. Sinod, *Obzor Deiatel'nosti . . . Pravoslavnago Ispovedeniia za Vremia . . . Aleksandra III*, p. 310.

[26] P. Koeppen, *Deviataia Reviziia*, p. xii.

[27] Tsentral'nyi Statisticheskii Komitet, *Naselenie Imperii po Perepisi 28-go Ianvaria 1897 goda po Uezdam*, pp. 27–29.

dox persons into . . . [the said] faith."[28] On the other hand, "if professed adherents of another faith wish to join the Orthodox belief, no one may in any manner prevent the fulfillment of this desire."[29] Also there were drastic blasphemy laws, under the terms of which anyone mocking or denouncing the holy things of the Orthodox Church, its rituals, ikons, miracles, clergy, or dogma, might find himself in prison or on the long road to Siberia.[30]

As for the individual Old Believer, his lot might not, at first glance, seem hard. The law promised him freedom of worship, his marriage could be legalized by entry in a police record-book, and his children legitimatized in the same fashion. But this rule applied only to registered Old Believers, and it was very hard to enter this category otherwise than by birth in a family already so registered. Orthodox persons might not lawfully turn to another faith,[31] although there were no penalties inflicted for such a change. Only a person who had never received any sacrament of the official church—beginning with baptism—could be viewed as an Old Believer by the law. A man christened in infancy into the ruling church was legally a member of that church, even though he never received its ministrations again. If a person appeared to be wavering in his belief, the Orthodox clergy were to reason with him and the local police were to be advised.[32] If in the family of an apostate there were children of tender years who had been christened as Orthodox, the Minister of Internal Affairs was to be advised, in order that he might suggest suitable steps to the em-

[28] *Svod Zakonov*, XV, "Ulozhenie o Nakazaniiakh Ugolovnykh i Ispravitel'nykh," ed. 1885, sec. 189; *Prodolzhenie Svoda Zakonov*, 1906, XV, "Ulozhenie o Nakaz. Ugol. i Isprav.," sec. 189 (repealed March 14, 1906).

[29] *Svod Zakonov*, XI, part 1, "Ustavy Dukhovnykh Del Inostrannykh Ispovedanii," ed. 1896, sec. 5; *Prodolzhenie Svoda Zakonov*, 1906, XI, part 1, "Ustavy Dukhov. Del Inostr. Ispoved.," sec. 5.

[30] *Svod Zakonov*, XV, "Ulozhenie o Nakazaniiakh Ugolovnykh i Ispravitel'nykh," ed. 1885, secs. 176–83; *Prodolzhenie Svoda Zakonov*, 1906, XV, "Ulozhenie o Nakaz. Ugol. i Isprav.," secs. 176–83 (repealed March 14, 1906).

[31] *Svod Zakonov*, XIV, "Ustav o Pred. i Pres. Prest.," ed. 1890, sec. 36; *Prodolzhenie Svoda Zakonov*, 1906, "Ustav o Pred. i Pres. Prest.," sec. 36 (repealed March 14, 1906).

[32] *Svod Zakonov, loc. cit.*, sec. 37; *Prodolzhenie Svoda Zakonov*, 1906, *loc. cit.*, sec. 37 (repealed March 14, 1906).

peror.[33] In some cases this led to the separation of children from their parents, in order to "protect their Orthodoxy." Children of apostate parents could not be legitimatized, as such children might be entered in the record-books only if the marriage had been previously entered,[34] and for persons who had once been Orthodox a marriage in the Old Believer faith was equivalent to no marriage at all. Obviously regulations like these seriously restricted the "full religious toleration" enjoyed in Russia, and, if enforced, must have hampered the Old Believers severely. A consideration of the administrative measures of the government will show whether the laws were rigorously applied.

One of the most troublesome questions between the Old Believers and the government was that of opening houses of prayer. In 1898 an official account of the Schism stated that such prayer houses were constantly increasing in number, largely in illegal fashion. For example, in the diocese of Nizhnii Novgorod there were 184 prayer houses of the Old Believers, of which only 12 were authorized. In the diocese of Viatka there were 5 authorized prayer houses, and 60 which were not authorized; in the province of Vologda, where there were officially only 7,841 Old Believers, there were 23 houses of prayer, all opened without permission of the government, and in addition gatherings of Old Believers were being held for group prayers in 19 dwelling houses.[35]

A study of archive documents shows that it was difficult for a group of Old Believers to obtain permission to open a house of prayer. For example, on March 21, 1901, a peasant of the village of Lobaz, in the province of Samara, petitioned to be allowed to turn his house into an Old Believer prayer house. The governor of Samara, reporting on the plea, stated that there were 218 Old Believers in the village, all of them schismatics of long standing, some even from birth. They exercised no evil influence on the Orthodox peasants, and there had been no recent cases of falling away from Orthodoxy. In consequence, he

[33] *Svod Zakonov, loc. cit.,* sec. 39; *Prodolzhenie Svoda Zakonov,* 1906, *loc. cit.,* sec. 39 (repealed March 14, 1906).

[34] *Svod Zakonov,* IX, "Zakony o Sostoianiiakh," ed. 1899, sec. 949; *Prodolzhenie Svoda Zakonov,* 1906, IX, "Zakony o Sostoianiiakh," sec. 949.

[35] Sv. Sinod, *Raskol i Sektantstvo,* p. 5.

favored permitting the Old Believers to have a house of prayer.[36] The Minister of Internal Affairs then took the matter up with Pobedonostsev, stating that apparently there was no reason to refuse.[37]

After consulting the bishop of Samara, Pobedonostsev replied with a lengthy and heated letter, saying that the schismatics had "deliberately lied" in overestimating their numbers; that most of them had been christened as Orthodox and had joined the Schism later in life and hence were still officially Orthodox. To allow the opening of a prayer house, so the local bishop reported, would have a very bad effect upon the Orthodox population, and hence it should not be permitted.[38] The governor of Samara once more reported upon the petition in a favorable vein, now insisting that the Old Believers numbered 217, instead of 141, as Pobedonostsev had stated. He added that even if most of them had been christened as Orthodox, they had never gone to the Orthodox Church since infancy; the younger members had been christened as Old Believers. However, the Minister of Internal Affairs decided that as the Old Believers were not very numerous in the community in question, the petition should not be granted.[39]

Another case of the same sort was that of a group of peasants of the province of Viatka, who petitioned in 1903 to be permitted to open a prayer house in the village of Chernaia Grazna. The governor of the province reported that there were 490 of these Old Believers in that place, and no Orthodox persons, so that he felt it would be proper to permit this prayer house to be established in one of the existing houses, especially as the nearest Old Believer prayer house was seventy *versts* (about forty-five miles) away.[40]

Pobedonostsev, who was asked for his view of the matter, replied with a long and vehement letter in which he denounced these schismatics, and protested against granting them a prayer house. He stated:

1. That many of the petitioners were not born into Schism but into Orthodoxy, and had fallen into Schism twenty, thirty, or forty

[36] Ministerstvo Vnutrennikh Del, Dep. Obshchikh Del, 1901, portfolio 36, sheets 1–3. [Referred to below as M. V. D.]
[37] *Ibid.*, sheets 3-6.   [38] *Ibid.*, sheets 7–8.   [39] *Ibid.*, sheets 9–13.
[40] M. V. D., Dep. Obshchikh Del, 1903, portfolio 58, sheets 1–3.

years before. "None of these persons falling from Orthodoxy into Schism may be considered as completely alienated from the Orthodox Church."

2. That the schismatics already had a prayer house in the village, although it was not sanctioned. The petition under consideration was put forward in order to obtain official approval of their prayer house, so that they might carry on their propaganda more effectively.

3. That the schismatics, by fair means and foul, were carrying on active propaganda to win the Orthodox into Schism.

4. That if the schismatics did obtain this approval, they would not come to the Orthodox missionary meetings.

5. That they wanted to organize a [forbidden] school in their prayer house.[41]

As a result of these arguments, the Minister of Internal Affairs rejected the petition on November 19, 1903.[42]

These were by no means isolated instances. In addition to the two cases already cited, nine similar instances might be adduced. Of these, six turned out unfavorably for the Old Believers, while one was decided in their favor in 1901; the other two, which dragged along for several years, were decided in favor of the Old Believers during the period of revolutionary influence in the last months of 1904 and early 1905.[43] Moreover, of five similar cases which were decided by the Council of Ministers, or by the Minister of Internal Affairs, four went against the Old Believers, and one, in September, 1904, was decided in their favor.[44]

Another sign of the oppression experienced by the Old Believers was given in 1901, when a group of this denomination presented a petition to the Tsar at Livadia, asking that he relieve them of police persecution, of which 25 instances were cited. Some 49,500 names were attached to this appeal.[45] Minister of Internal Affairs Sipiagin soon after reported on 9 of these cases, and stated that reports on the

[41] *Ibid.*, sheets 3–6.   [42] *Ibid.*, sheet 10.

[43] M. V. D., Dep. Obshchikh Del, 1900, portfolios 21 and 133; 1901, portfolios 68 and 85; 1902, portfolios 1 and 49; 1903, portfolios 5 and 26; 1904, portfolio 181.

[44] M. V. D., *Sbornik Postanovlenii po Chasti Raskola (1875–1904 vkliuchitel'no)*, Nos. 107, 116, 119, 120, 127.

[45] M. V. D., Dep. Obshchikh Del, 1901, portfolio 29, sheets 1–5.

others had been asked of the proper governors. The cases verified by the minister included the placing of a priest of the Old Believers under close police supervision, the closing of unauthorized Old Believer prayer houses, the taking away of minor children from Orthodox parents who had joined the ranks of the Old Believers, the seizing of Old Believers' prayer books, ikons, church vessels, and so on. The other abuses, not covered in the minister's report, included the opening of the grave of an Old Believer priest, followed by the exhumation and burning of the corpse; the taking away of children from Old Believer parents; the arrest of priests of this denomination; the seizure of religious articles; and so forth.[46]

In his report to the Tsar, Minister Sipiagin went on to say:

The Orthodox missionaries, without doubt, frequently overstep the bounds established by the law of 1883, and resort to the civil authorities for coöperation in cases where such coöperation is not justified by law. The local civil authorities, and especially the police, in the old way, sometimes entirely arbitrarily, interfere in the religious affairs of the schismatics and take measures which lead the latter to make justified complaints. Moreover, only in rare cases do the religious authorities recognize as proper the petitions of the schismatics for permission to open new prayer houses, on the grounds that each new house of prayer not only helps to strengthen the Schism, but also makes missionary preaching more difficult.

. . .

If the interference of the police in the religious affairs of the schismatics is entirely incorrect, still it is impossible to deny that the clergy in their attempts to protect the fruits of Orthodox missionary teaching very rightly state that the opening of schismatic prayer houses in places where they did not previously exist is not conducive to restoring the schismatics to the bosom of the Orthodox Church. . . . The protests of the bishops against the opening of prayer houses proceed generally from the view that this is dangerous for Orthodoxy and produces disaffection among the believing—but if such protests are recognized to the extent of refusing the petitions of the schismatics, then nowhere and never can new prayer houses be opened. . . .

Sipiagin continued with a proposal for sending instructions to the governors not to interfere with the schismatics unless they actually violated the provisions of the law. This was approved by the Tsar,

[46] M. V. D. Dep. Obshchikh Del, 1901, portfolio 29, sheets 6–13.

and secret circulars were sent out to the governors in March, 1901, urging them to leave the Old Believers alone unless they were actually having a disturbing effect upon the Orthodox population.[47] This probably improved the lot of the Old Believers, but it was far from ending all restrictions on them, and their legal status, as of old, continued to be inferior to that of the Orthodox population.

Other cases serve to show the hindrances, small and great, under which the Old Believers labored. On March 24, 1902, groups of peasants of five villages in the province of Kurland petitioned to be allowed to use steel rails as gongs to call the Old Believers to Sunday service. The police had forbidden the practice in the nineties, even though in neighboring districts rails had been so used. Now the peasants asked again to be allowed to use rails, as there was no Orthodox church near to them to be offended. But the Minister of Internal Affairs informed the governor that, as the privilege was not permitted by existing legislation, the petition should be "considered as not deserving satisfaction."[48]

The law courts were often no more helpful than the Tsar's ministers, for *ex parte* testimony was frequently a factor in deciding questions involving the Old Believers. A number of books, ikons, and other articles pertaining to the cult of this denomination had been taken away from a peasant of the province of Vologda in 1894, although the charges against him—of illegally building a schismatic house of prayer, of forsaking the Orthodox faith, and of leading into Schism a peasant woman of the locality—had been dismissed by the court. The confiscated articles had been turned over to the Orthodox diocesan consistory of Vologda, which thereupon had decided as to the correct disposition of them. The books, "printed at the Uniat Typography with the permission of the proper authorities, and containing no evil-intentioned writings," the ikons, which contained nothing contrary to the teachings of the Orthodox Church, and other articles, including candles, were sent to the Nikolaevskaia Uniat church for church use or for keeping in the church library or the sacristy. Other articles had been sent to the religious seminary of the diocese, to be placed in its library, or to the diocesan home, "as pos-

---

[47] *Ibid.*, sheets 20–32.
[48] M. V. D., Dep. Obshchikh Del, 1902, portfolio 33, sheets 1–3.

sibly being of interest to persons who might study the details of the Russian Old Believers' Schism."

The seizure of these articles had occurred in 1894; in 1900 the owner petitioned for a return of his property. The governor in his report was apparently touched, for he stated that the petitioner was of good conduct, and had belonged to the Schism from infancy, as had his wife. "In the winter of this year," added the governor, "their two grown sons were drowned while crossing a river." However, the ministry in St. Petersburg decided that the petition might not be granted; the ikons and religious books were not returned.[49]

From Tobolsk, in Siberia, came news of religious dissension in 1901. The governor stated that Bishop Antonii had reported that in November, 1900, a village of Old Believers had organized an outdoor procession with cross and ikons, and that the schismatic leaders had worn clerical vestments like those of the Orthodox clergy. When the police had started criminal proceedings the procurator of the court had declared that there were no grounds for action. The governor claimed that as this performance of the schismatics was a public profession of Schism it was dangerous to the Orthodox faith, and hence criminal.[50] However, the Minister of Internal Affairs dampened the governor's ardor by declaring that, as the courts had refused to act, nothing could be done.[51]

In 1902 Pobedonostsev complained to the Minister of Internal Affairs about a similar procession of schismatics in the province of Kherson, in which a "false bishop, a priest, and a false deacon" were in full regalia. He added that this action worked "great damage to the interests of Orthodoxy, which have the greatest state significance," and served to lead astray the Orthodox and to strengthen the Schism.[52] The local governor stated in his report that although the police had been there they were unable to do anything, as the entire village population of three thousand souls, as well as the local officials, were schismatics. However, he rejoiced to say that all three of the "false

[49] M. V. D., Dep. Obshchikh Del, 1900, portfolio 93, sheets 3–6.
[50] M. V. D., Dep. Obshchikh Del, 1901, portfolio 51, sheet 3.
[51] *Ibid.*, sheet 5.
[52] M. V. D., Dep. Obshchikh Del, 1902, portfolio 82, sheets 1–2.

clergy" had been haled into court and ultimately had been fined ten rubles apiece.[53]

Many of the instances of religious interference in Russia were due to zealous civil officials who were rigorous in their support of the official church. But often the initiative came from the Orthodox clergy, and especially from the missionaries, whose task it was to combat the influence of the Old Believers and the sectarians. This fervor on the part of the missionaries led the governor of the province of Ekaterinoslav to make critical remarks about them in his report for 1900. He stated that the missionaries were powerless in the struggle with their opponents, as the measures which they used could not succeed in matters of belief and conscience. The discussions which they organized, and to which the Old Believers were brought, usually by police measures, frequently ended in demands for police charges against the schismatics, as a result of the tactlessness of the missionaries themselves. Many times the government officials were obliged, owing to the incorrect conduct of the missionaries, to take action against the followers of religious bodies tolerated by law. In general the governor raised the question as to whether these missionary activities really did serve to root out false doctrines, and whether they really strengthened Orthodoxy.[54]

The attention of Pobedonostsev and the Tsar was called to these statements, and Governor Keller was asked to justify his remarks. He answered that, although the time allotted to him was short, he would mention a few cases which he remembered.

In recounting the first of these, the governor referred to an Orthodox missionary priest "excelling not in intelligence," who stirred up much trouble in his village, peopled largely with Old Believers. The priest started a flood of correspondence about the alleged facts that the local pastor of the Old Believers wore long hair and beard and dressed in clothes resembling the cassock of an Orthodox priest, and received newspapers addressed to "Priest So-and-so"—acts which were banned as "public manifestations of Schism" by the law of 1883. The missionary asked for special action against the offender, but on

[53] *Ibid.,* sheets 9–10.
[54] M. V. D., Dep. Obshchikh Del, 1901, portfolio 47, sheets 8–9.

investigation the facts appeared to have been greatly exaggerated by the complainant.

Again, a missionary demanded that a cross over a village (*volost*) headquarters be removed by the police, as in the building, which was used largely for secular matters by the local Old Believers, "there might occur conversations and scenes not proper to be under the sign of the Cross." The governor, influenced by the fact that ikons might be displayed everywhere, even in liquor shops, felt that removal of the symbol of Christianity by the police would have a bad effect. Another instance was the case of a missionary who was arguing about fasts at a meeting to which the police had compelled sectarians to come. The missionary could get little satisfaction from his opponents. At length he said that it was not loyal to refuse to observe fasts as long as the emperor strictly observed them; to this a sectarian replied, "Well, indeed the emperor himself doesn't observe all the fasts that you insist on." The missionary had no better answer than to turn to the police and demand the drawing up of criminal charges on the grounds of an insult to His Majesty.

In concluding, Governor Keller remarked that if desired, he could easily furnish many more examples of the incorrect methods of the missionaries.[55]

Examples of a similar attitude on the part of the Orthodox authorities appear frequently in the records. Pobedonostsev, on May 4, 1901, complained to the Minister of Internal Affairs about the propagandist activities of one Bogdanov, of the province of Olonets. The governor of the province reported that this man's activities had ceased to be effective, but none the less the Over Procurator persisted in his denunciations, so that finally the governor was told to keep Bogdanov under strict police supervision [56]—a measure which entailed constant spying on the part of the police and restriction of the subject's freedom of movement.

When, at the time of the Russo-Japanese War, Ivan Usov, "known among Old Believers as Bishop Innokentii of Nizhnii Novgorod and Kostroma," petitioned for release from military service on the grounds that his church forbade a bishop to serve, he received no satisfaction.

[55] M. V. D., Dep. Obshchikh Del, 1901, portfolio 47, sheets 19–21.
[56] *Ibid.*, portfolio 41, sheets 1–6.

To be sure, he stated that he believed in military service for the citizen and said that he could do more service to the fatherland at home than in the army, "by prayer to God for the health of Your Imperial Majesty, and for giving victory to our own Russian Christ-loving army, and also by religious and moral influence over my numerous followers." [57] But the Minister of Internal Affairs, Pleve, stated that as Usov was one of the active false bishops of the dangerous Austrian sect of Old Believers, and as "his removal from Nizhnii Novgorod will end the influence of this teacher of Schism, an influence dangerous throughout the whole region . . ." he would ask that Usov's petition be rejected.[58]

The question of legitimatizing marriages and births was a troublesome one for the Old Believers. The law of 1883 gave to them the right to have these facts recorded in police record-books, without drawing any distinction between recent converts and those who had been born into this faith; actually, however, the enjoyment of this right was at times considerably restricted. In March, 1900, a group of Old Believers petitioned for permission to have their marriages registered. The governor of the province of Vladimir, to whom the petition was referred, declared that actually only two persons had recently applied for the privilege, although the petition bore more than a score of signatures. The first applicant was refused "in view of the fact that in 1850 he was born into Orthodoxy and was recorded in the church record-books on January 3 of that year; his parents were also Orthodox, and at present are still listed as belonging to the Orthodox Church." The second likewise was refused registration of his marriage, "as he and his parents, although they went over from Orthodoxy to Schism, by the church documents are still listed as not having been written off the books." As a result of this testimony the Minister of Internal Affairs denied the petition.[59]

This case suggests that it was difficult for Old Believers who had originally been Orthodox to receive all the rights granted to Old Believers by the law of 1883; further evidence, however, is lacking on this point. An indication of how important this privilege of legal-

[57] M. V. D., Dep. Obshchikh Del, 1904, portfolio 24, sheets 2–3.
[58] *Ibid.*, sheets 4–6.
[59] M. V. D., Dep. Obshchikh Del, 1900, portfolio 39, sheets 1–6.

izing marriages could be is given by the case of Praskova Mamtseva. She had married according to the forms of the Old Believers and at the same time had applied to have the marriage registered by the police. Later her husband was killed by a train. In order to obtain compensation for herself and her children she had to prove that the marriage was legal; but when she asked for a certificate of legality the police refused, as through an oversight the marriage had not been entered on the books and hence could not be regarded as legal, even though it was recognized by the police as having been performed.[60] She now, in 1902, asked to have the marriage validated by the Minister of Internal Affairs, but the minister, upon receiving the petition, decided that, as according to precedent unrecorded marriages could be legalized only by action of the courts, the petition, "as not deserving satisfaction, shall be left without action." [61]

An enlightening piece of evidence on the difficulty of obtaining registration of the marriages of Old Believers and sectarians was produced in the Third Duma in 1909. The Octobrist Kamenskii, spokesman for the Committee on Matters of Religious Belief, found occasion to cite the Minutes of the Committee of Ministers for January 25, 1905, in which reference was made to the manner in which the police performed their duty of keeping record-books for Old Believers and sectarians. Kamenskii read the following excerpt from the Minutes in question: "As a result of the approximate summary made by the Ministry of Internal Affairs for ten provinces and districts for the five-year period of 1899 to 1903, it was shown that out of 29,431 actual marriages 1,840 were entered in the record-books; out of 131,730 births, 1,340; and out of 91,634 deaths, 552." [62]

Occasionally the civil officials displayed a more tolerant attitude toward the Old Believers. For example, when the governor of Ufa in 1903 declared that the local bishop had asked him to protect the Orthodoxy of the minor children of three Orthodox couples who had recently gone over to the Schism, he received little encouragement from the Minister of Internal Affairs. The governor suggested that

[60] M. V. D., Dep. Obshchikh Del, 1902, portfolio 77, sheets 1–2.
[61] Ibid., sheet 5.
[62] Gosudarstvennaia Duma, Stenograficheskie Otchety, III Duma, Session II, part 4, col. 1824.

as the children all had uncles or other relatives who were Orthodox, they should be turned over to these guardians. However, the minister replied that as the Third Missionary Congress in 1898 had voted against such measures, he did not approve of taking the children away from their parents, but instead suggested that the religious authorities be urged to try more active spiritual admonition.[63]

This refusal of the central authorities to interfere in the personal lives of these Old Believers is in sharp contrast to the measures employed in the case of a certain Osip Evgrafov and his wife in 1901. In 1899 the couple had been sentenced by the district court of Ufa to two months' imprisonment for activity as schismatics, this imprisonment to be followed by counsel and admonition by the diocesan authorities. Their two children, Evdokiia, aged four, and Fedosiia, aged two, were to be cared for by Orthodox relatives.[64] However, on April 13, 1901, the governor of the province reported that the relatives were too poor to take the children, and consequently Bishop Antonii of Ufa had had them placed in the Ufa Convent.[65] The Minister of Internal Affairs asked Pobedonostsev if he approved of this measure. The Over Procurator replied, on June 7, 1901, that in general he thought it unwise to send children to convents, but in this case, in view of the exceptional circumstances, he heartily approved. "The decision of the bishop of Ufa to place these children in the Ufa Convent appears to be almost the only means of educating them in the spirit of Orthodoxy." [66] So the children stayed in the convent.

By law the Old Believers were required to bury their dead in a part of the regular Orthodox cemetery. This rule, too, occasionally brought discomfort to the Old Believers, for a group of the priestless sect felt moved in 1904 to request permission to use their own long-established graveyard, which the police had strictly forbidden to them. The petitioners declared that this graveyard had been approved as sanitary, and was so sandy as to be useless for any other purpose. They said, moreover, that they avoided dealings with priests and with the Orthodox, and that they felt it was undesirable to be

[63] M. V. D., Dep. Obshchikh Del, 1903, portfolio 113, sheets 1 and 8.
[64] M. V. D., Dep. Obshchikh Del, 1901, portfolio 39, sheets 4–5.
[65] *Ibid.*, sheet 1.   [66] *Ibid.*, sheet 8.

buried in one and the same graveyard with them. Furthermore, they longed to be buried alongside their fathers and grandfathers in their own cemetery, as the idea of separation from their nearest relatives after death distressed their religious feelings.[67]

The governor of Vladimir reported that these schismatics had petitioned him in similar fashion, but that he had rejected the petition, as the law required them to use a part of the Orthodox cemetery. The original request to close the private Old Believers' cemetery had come from the Vladimir Religious Consistory. Under these circumstances the minister felt that the law must be enforced and he therefore refused to grant the petition of the Old Believers.[68]

In respect to elementary education the Old Believers likewise found themselves at a disadvantage. While various sections of the law on public education provided that schools might be established by city and village communities, and by private individuals, approval had to be obtained from the inspectors of public schools and the county or provincial school boards, which contained representatives of the Orthodox Church. Provision was also made for the closing of schools "in case of disorder and of a harmful tendency of the teaching." [69] Permission from the district school trustee was necessary before the opening of city schools.[70] The Old Believers apparently found it difficult to obtain the necessary permission to found their own schools, for they complained that the law of 1883 gave them no rights in this respect.[71] Evidence of the difficulty which they experienced was given in 1903, when Pobedonostsev wrote to the Minister of Internal Affairs complaining of a school recently opened by schismatics in a village of the province of Viatka. Up to

[67] M. V. D., Dep. Obshchikh Del, 1904, portfolio 145, sheet 1.

[68] *Ibid.*, sheets 2–3.

[69] *Svod Zakonov*, XI, part 1, "Svod Ustavov Uchenykh Uchrezhdenii i Uchebnykh Zavedenii Vedomstva Ministerstva Narodnago Prosveshcheniia," ed. 1893, secs. 3110, 3248, 3478, 3479, 3495, 3513, 3533; *Prodolzhenie Svoda Zakonov*, 1906, XI, part 1, "Svod Ustavov Uchenykh Uchrezhdenii i Uchebnykh Zavedenii," secs. 3110, 3248, 3478, 3479, 3495, 3513, 3533.

[70] *Svod Zakonov, loc. cit.*, sec. 3117; *Prodolzhenie Svoda Zakonov*, 1906, *loc. cit.*, sec. 3117.

[71] Berdnikov, *Kratkii Kurs Tserkovnago Prava*, p. 1190.

that time, he declared, the Orthodox parish school had been very influential in turning the schismatics toward Orthodoxy. Out of forty-five children attending the Orthodox school, only two were of Orthodox origin. But since the opening of the Old Believer school, six children had gone over from the Orthodox school, and eight more were wavering. "And indeed Efrem Korobeinikov [the Old Believer leader] had proudly declared to the missionary that this school was opened with the purpose of serving as a weapon against Orthodoxy." Pobedonostsev accordingly asked that this school be closed at once.

Upon receiving this request the Minister of Internal Affairs communicated with the governor of Viatka, who soon after reported in a secret dispatch that the school had been closed, and that Korobeinikov had been brought to trial for opening it without permission.[72]

Another complaint of the Old Believers was against having to pay taxes for the benefit of the Orthodox Church. The fact that some of their national taxes went for this purpose was bad enough, but when there was a local tax as well it became a real grievance. Thus in 1900 a group of Old Believers in the province of St. Petersburg asked for relief from the persecutions of the local church elder, who wanted them to pay Orthodox church levies.[73] The matter at length was referred to the council of the governor, which ruled that as the decision to impose these taxes had been adopted by a two-thirds vote of the community, it was binding on all. To be sure there had been a decision of the Senate in 1886 on such cases, but it applied only to schismatics inscribed in the official records, who alone were excused from these taxes. The peasants in question were not so inscribed, and so, Old Believers though they were, they were obliged to contribute to the support of the Orthodox Church.[74] A similar case was decided in like fashion against some peasants of the province of Samara, when they protested against the communal decision to support the local Orthodox church.[75]

[72] M. V. D., Dep. Obshchikh Del, 1903, portfolio 194, sheets 1–3 and 7.
[73] M. V. D., Dep. Obshchikh Del, 1900, portfolio 5, sheets 1–2.
[74] *Ibid.*, sheets 9–10.
[75] M. V. D., Dep. Obshchikh Del, 1900, portfolio 111.

The instances which have been cited present actual cases of the oppression of Old Believers, by government and church working hand in hand. The Old Believers were rarely given permission to open prayer houses, although the great number of their unauthorized houses of prayer shows that they enjoyed a precarious form of toleration. To sum up, other difficulties experienced were the occasional harassing of their clergy, at times the seizure of their books and ikons, the impossibility of the registration of their marriages unless they were Old Believers from birth, and the great difficulty of registration, even in such cases, the parallel difficulty of the registration of births and deaths, the closing of their schools and cemeteries, and in some localities the obligation to contribute to the official church. Moreover, it must not be supposed that these were isolated instances of official arbitrariness. These cases, which were taken from the files of the archives of the Ministry of Internal Affairs, could be matched by many similar instances from the portfolios which were placed in the archives at the rate of more than a hundred cases a year. Enough additional samples of this material were examined by the author to demonstrate that the documents cited are typical. Moreover, in view of the difficulties and costs of presenting petitions to the central authorities (a heavy stamp tax was levied upon all such documents), it is probable that there were many such cases which never found their way into the official files. It may be safely stated that the documents here cited present a just picture of the government's dealings with the Old Believers in the years from 1900 to the eve of the Revolution of 1905.

Beside the Old Believers discussed above, there existed in Russia a large variety of sects. The most important of these were the so-called Evangelical sects—the *Molokane,* the *Dukhobortsy,* and the *Stundisty*—and the mystic sects, with a much smaller following— the *Khlysty* and the *Skoptsy.* The *Khlysty* were accused of holding religious orgies marked by sexual promiscuity, while the *Skoptsy* practiced self-sterilization; merely to be a member of either of these sects was an offense punishable by law. On the other hand, the Evangelical sects, with the exception of the Stundists, were given much the same treatment as the Old Believers.

The origins of the *Molokane* and *Dukhobortsy* are veiled in obscurity, although some believe them to be older than the Schism by several centuries.[76] The Stundist faith was probably introduced into the south of Russia by German colonists, and is supposed to derive from the pietism of Philipp Spener. But all three sects had the common feature of resembling the Protestant denominations more than they did the Russian Orthodox Church. They held to belief in the Trinity, but they rejected the sacramental system, the veneration of saints and of the Virgin, the use of ikons and religious vestments, fasting, and the like. They felt no need for a priestly class, but held rather to belief in the efficacy of individual interpretation of the Bible. The adherents of the sects were almost all peasants, with a few townsmen, chiefly of humble origin; their strength was greatest in the southern and eastern provinces of European Russia. One theory advanced is that in the nineteenth century the sects to a considerable extent represented a form of social and economic discontent which found expression in religious forms—in part a disgust with the growing wealth and capitalism of the Old Believers. Certain it is that the *Molokane* and the *Dukhobortsy* in periods of especial fervor during the nineteenth century strongly opposed state obligations such as oaths, taxes, and military service.[77] However, at the opening of the twentieth century the *Molokane* and those *Dukhobortsy* who had not emigrated to Canada seemed to be losing much of their zeal for opposing the obligations imposed by the state; their place in the van of the sectarian movement was taken by the more aggressive Stundists.[78]

In numbers the sects were far inferior to the Old Believers; both the statistics of the government published in 1901 and the estimates of private individuals such as Prugavin and Iuzov, which differed widely from the government's figures for the numbers of the sectarians, agreed that their strength was a mere fraction of that of the Old Believers. The official proportion was one to six,[79] while that

[76] Conybeare, *Russian Dissenters*, pp. 263 ff.

[77] Nikol'skii, "Raskol i Sektantstvo vo Vtoroi Polovine XIX Veka," *Istoriia Rossii v XIX Veke*, V, 265–79. The Orthodox authorities also regarded sectarianism as a form of social radicalism.

[78] *Ibid.*, 280–83.

[79] Tsentral'nyi Statisticheskii Komitet, *Raspredelenie Staroobriadtsev i Sektantov po Tolkam i Sektam.*

given by Iuzov was one to eleven.[80] Certainly the sectarians formed but a small part of the entire Russian population, perhaps one percent in 1900.

It was not until the latter half of the eighteenth century that official notice was first taken of the sects. Even then they were regarded as unimportant. Under Catherine II and the first Alexander they enjoyed for the most part the benefits of noninterference. But under Nicholas I a rigorous campaign of repression ensued. By article 197 of the Criminal Code the Old Believers and the sectarians were divided into "less harmful," "more harmful," and "especially harmful" groups. The last rubric included the *Molokane*, the *Dukhobortsy*, and some minor denominations, all of whom were forbidden to have group prayer meetings. As for the *Khlysty* and the *Skoptsy*, the government put them into a special criminal category, and persons adhering to them automatically became liable to exile to Siberia.[81]

Under Alexander II there was little attempt to enforce this law, and under Alexander III it was replaced by the law of 1883. By the latter statute, as has been stated, the same rights were given to "schismatics of all groups," including all sects except the *Skoptsy*. Thus there were now no "less harmful" or "more harmful" denominations, although the new law did provide that, in all cases where permission or confirmation of the Minister of Internal Affairs was required, he was to take into consideration the local circumstances and conditions as well as "the moral nature of the teaching and of the other characteristics of each denomination." This latter provision received important application only in respect to one sect, the rising group of Stundists, which in 1894 was designated as "especially dangerous" by the Minister of Internal Affairs and the Over Procurator, with the permission of the Committee of Ministers [82]—a matter that will be discussed later.

Let no one believe, however, that in 1883 restrictive measures against the other sectarians ceased. As was true of the Old Believers, the sectarians, including those who enjoyed the full measure of toleration granted by the statute, met with difficulty in the in-

---

[80] Iuzov, *op. cit.*, p. 46.   [81] Berdnikov, *op. cit.*, pp. 1127–29.
[82] A. A. Zav'ialov, ed., *Tsirkuliarnye Ukazy . . . Sinoda*, pp. 261–62.

terpretation of the law and occasionally in administrative action. Their troubles were not entirely over.

One of the measures of last resort used by the government and the church was the imprisonment of sectarian leaders in the prisons of the bleak Solovetskii Monastery on an island in the White Sea, inside the Arctic Circle, or in those of the no less forbidding Spaso-Evfimevskii Monastery at Suzdal. Here sectarian leaders, and for that matter a few Old Believers and even an occasional refractory Orthodox priest, were lodged in solitary confinement under guard of armed soldiers. Several writers have testified to this practice. Dixon, an Englishman who visited the Solovetskii Monastery in 1868, saw there two men in solitary confinement under military guard—both of them sectarians sent thither by the Synod and the civil power.[83] Arsen'ev, writing in 1905, quoted a recent article from the newspaper *Rossiia* about a certain priest, Petr Zolotnitskii, who espoused the Schism and in consequence was imprisoned in the Suzdal Monastery in a solitary cell for thirty-one years.[84] The fullest discussions of this subject, however, are in the works of A. S. Prugavin, an authority on the Schism and the sectarians. Prugavin has based his statements upon official documents, and, in the cases which have admitted of verification by the author, his data have proved to be thoroughly accurate.

According to Prugavin, in 1902 there were twelve persons confined in the prison of the Suzdal Monastery, some of whom had been there for as long as ten or even twenty years. One Nikolai Dobroliubov, for example, had been there for twenty-three years. Others had come there more recently ; the peasant Fedoseev and the priest Tsvetkov were both imprisoned there in the year 1900.[85] The words of the diocesan authorities of Samara concerning Fedoseev are very enlightening, as showing the view of at least some of the rulers of the church regarding this means of discipline:

With respect to unrepentant and dangerously evil heretics and propagandists, the diocesan authorities have proceeded to extreme measures,

---

[83] W. H. Dixon, *Free Russia*, I, 224–50.

[84] K. K. Arsen'ev, *Svoboda Sovesti i Veroterpimost'*, p. 183; A. Titov, *Odin iz Zakliuchennykh v Suzdal'skoi Kreposti (Delo O. Zolotnitskago)*.

[85] Prugavin, *Monastyrskiia Tiur'my*, p. 28.

through petitions to the Most Holy Synod concerning removing them from the midst of the Orthodox flock by means of imprisonment in the Spaso-Evfimevskii Monastery [in Suzdal]. They were compelled to act in this fashion with a certain Ermolai Fedoseev, who lived in a cave and by his own personal righteousness attracted to himself a crowd of simple people.[86]

Another sectarian from Samara, Ivan Chuchikov, was imprisoned in Suzdal because "he proclaimed himself a healer and miracle-worker, and thus exploited the religious feelings of the simple." But fortunately for Chuchikov, he had influential friends and protectors who obtained his speedy release, much to the disgust of the religious authorities of Samara.[87]

Another case of monastery imprisonment was that of V. A. Rakhov. This man was lodged in the prison of the Suzdal Monastery for carrying on work much like that now performed in America by the Salvation Army. Prugavin declares that Rakhov gave up a business career in Archangel to do charitable work among the poor. In the winter of 1893 he rented rooms in that city and fed more than one hundred persons every day. When these rooms were closed, owing to his failure to secure official permission for his work, he continued to help the needy, the homeless, and the orphaned. Because he held prayer services and sang hymns at his gatherings, his quarters were searched and he was brought into court, but the charges against him were dismissed. The civil authorities were satisfied, but the ecclesiastical authorities were not. The bishop of Archangel urged the Synod to imprison Rakhov in Suzdal as a preacher of Stundism.[88]

As a result of the insistence of the Orthodox hierarchy, Rakhov was placed in solitary confinement in the monastery prison. Here, according to the report of the Abbot Dosifei, he conducted himself well, disclosed no religious errors, and was zealous in attending the church services. In 1895 he humbly petitioned for a hearing, a chance to justify himself; but no action was taken. His father's appeal to the Tsar fared no better.[89]

The young man's excellent conduct won the favor of the Abbot Dosifei, who in 1898, and again in 1899, urged that Rakhov deserved

---

[86] *Samarskiia Eparkhial'nyia Vedomosti*, Aug. 15, 1901, p. 886.
[87] *Ibid.*, p. 887.   [88] Prugavin, *Vopiiushchee Delo*, pp. 6–12.
[89] *Ibid.*, pp. 14–18.

freedom. A new abbot, Serafim, came to Suzdal and soon became convinced of Rakhov's innocence. He petitioned for the young man's release in 1899, twice in 1900, and again in 1902. Finally in July, 1902, Rakhov was released, "to live in Archangel under special supervision of the religious authorities."[90]

The Imperial government itself corroborated some of the reports about the use of monastery prisons by issuing a reassuring statement in 1905. In announcing the end of this form of punishment, it stated that, instead of the 900 persons who were rumored to have been released, in 1905 there had been only 7 persons in confinement, all of whom had been liberated. (This figure does not, however, include a number of persons released at this time, who had been sent to do penance in the ordinary monasteries for brief periods, by order of local bishops.) Five of these 7 persons had been placed in the Suzdal Monastery as a result of the petition of the Minister of Internal Affairs, for spreading sectarian doctrines; one, Fedoseev, mentioned above, had been imprisoned there, by imperial decree, "for spreading among the people superstitious and false statements touching the holy relics and the miracle-working ikons," while a certain Leont'ev had been incarcerated in the Solovetskii Monastery by "Most August" decree (i. e., of the emperor) "for spreading among the peasants false doctrines which aroused them against the Supreme Authority and the Orthodox clergy." The release of these prisoners, according to the statement of the government, ended confinement in the monastery prisons.[91]

Of course it must be borne in mind that these seven were exceptional cases, only a few individuals out of the hundreds of thousands of sectarians. Probably most of the dissenters suffered no individual hardship. But even in the case of the most humble followers of the sects there was uncertainty and danger, for there was always the possibility that the heavy hand of the police might descend. As will be shown, the sectarians had few rights guaranteed to them, so that ample opportunity existed for trouble between the sectarians and the authorities.

In considering the treatment accorded to the individual Russian sects, the *Molokane* and the *Dukhobortsy* come first. These de-

[90] *Ibid.,* pp. 19–36. [91] *Pravitel'stvennyi Vestnik,* March 5, 1905.

nominations, which were somewhat alike in principle, were the most numerous of all the sects and in their teachings represented a typically Russian brand of pietism.

The *Molokane,* so called because, unlike the Orthodox, they drank milk during Lent, resembled the Quakers more than they did the followers of John Calvin. By the beginning of the twentieth century, however, they had largely abandoned their refusal to bear the obligations imposed by the state.[92] None the less, they continued to be subject to the restrictions placed upon the dissenters by the law of 1883. Persons who had been enrolled in the Orthodox Church were refused permission to leave the ranks of the church and to obtain official recognition as *Molokane* [93]—although there was no penalty provided by law for the mere act of leaving the church. In attempting to open houses of prayer the *Molokane* faced the same obstacles that hampered the Old Believers. Not even the plea that they had most faithfully performed their military service could relieve them of this restriction.[94]

Sometimes official measures against the *Molokane* took more active forms, as in the case of a woman of the sect in the province of Astrakhan, who petitioned the Minister of Internal Affairs for protection against persecution by the police. The governor of Astrakhan in his report said that the police official against whom complaint had been made had actually gone to prayer meetings of the *Molokane* for observation, and had twice compelled the woman Sirova to go with him to the house of the priest—on the second occasion at the command of the local district priest—in order that attempts might be made to convert her to Orthodoxy. His excellency added that this action of the constable was unwarranted; he should not have gone into the meeting, as it only aroused the anger of those present. The governor, in consequence, had advised the constable to stop the practice.[95]

Occasionally the *Molokane* were deprived of their children by

---

[92] Conybeare, *op. cit.,* pp. 289–317.
[93] M. V. D., Dep. Obshchikh Del, 1900, portfolio 25; 1901, portfolio 75; 1904, portfolio 133.
[94] M. V. D., Dep. Obshchikh Del, 1900, portfolio 52.
[95] M. V. D., Dep. Obshchikh Del, 1903, portfolio 14, sheets 1 and 3.

police and clergy, "in order to protect their Orthodoxy." In the province of Taurida four families were deprived of their young in 1892 and in 1895. In answer to the resulting outcry in the newspapers, the Orthodox diocesan missionary wrote an apologia:

Why is there usually no such uproar in all other instances when the laws are enforced? Why do the private protectors of state interests keep silent at the numerous cases of enforcing the laws against thieves, murderers, and other ill-doers? Do they then think that harming the interests of the church does less harm to the fundamental principles of state life than, for example, horse-stealing? [96]

Prugavin told of another case of the taking away of children in the province of Samara in 1897. The parents could obtain no satisfaction from either bishop or governor, while the police and the missionaries told them that the children would be returned only when the parents embraced Orthodoxy. In despair, the *Molokane* appealed to the capital but, until Tolstoi took up the matter, nothing was done for their relief. Tolstoi's letter, widely printed in Russia and abroad, created such a furor that the children were quickly released, and Pobedonostsev stated that the whole episode had been a mistake upon the part of the local officials.[97]

In 1903 one of the diocesan journals printed the recollections of an Orthodox priest, an article which serves to show the attitude taken by some of the clergy respecting the seizure of children from dissenters. The narrator told how, a number of years before, he and other parish priests had led the lay and religious authorities in carrying off sixty children *en masse* from the village of Prishiba. At the appointed hour the police chief and the constables went to the village with Orthodox people from other districts, who wanted to take the children for bringing up—"of course as unpaid workers." The houses were occupied by the police in order to prevent concealment of the children, who were seized and delivered to their new keepers. Naturally there were distressing scenes—the fathers for the most part implored, while the mothers "met the police like lionesses."

[96] Arsen'ev, *op. cit.*, pp. 195–6.
[97] Prugavin, "Raskol i Biurokratiia," *Vestnik Evropy*, 1909, Vol. 6, pp. 162–66.

Some seized any weapon which came to hand; but to no avail. "These warlike unfortunates were carried off in chains to jail. . . . The great cry of Rachel was heard afar off." [98]

Of course the taking of the sixty had happened before the twentieth century began, and represents a policy which had largely been abandoned before the year 1900. But even in the twentieth century this practice had not entirely disappeared. In 1901 the governor of Astrakhan, in reporting on the petition of a *Molokan* peasant woman, stated that in 1895 the two children of this woman had been forcibly handed over to their Orthodox uncle for upbringing. However, Ignatiia, aged sixteen, had escaped, and her mother had hurriedly married her to a man of her sect. The other daughter, said the governor, had just returned home, and as she was now fourteen years of age, he proposed to let her stay there. [99]

Even as late as 1903 some of the authorities of the church still wished to employ the old measures, for on January 30 of that year Pobedonostsev wrote to the Minister of Internal Affairs asking him to take steps to protect the Orthodoxy of the children (aged eight, six, and two) of Anna Proskuriakova, who had recently joined the *Molokane*. The minister, however, declared that, although approving in principle, he did not think it wise to take the children away from their mother. Instead, he suggested a trusteeship of the leading villagers and the priest to watch over the religious upbringing of the children. [100] As a result, the governor of Tambov reported in June that the children were being watched over by their grandfather, by the headman of the village, and by the local priest. [101]

The most famous of all persecutions of sectarians in Russia was that of the *Dukhobortsy*, many of whom later emigrated to Canada. In this case the motive of the government was apparently political, with the religious element much less potent. A revival of hatred for militarism among the *Dukhobortsy* led them to refuse military service, and what followed was largely the result of that refusal. [102]

[98] *Saratovskiia Eparkhial'nyia Vedomosti*, 1903, No. 23, pp. 1209–11.

[99] M. V. D., Dep. Obshchikh Del, 1901, portfolio 64, sheets 1–3.

[100] M. V. D., Dep. Obshchikh Del, 1903, portfolio 10, sheets 1–3.

[101] *Ibid.*, sheet 6.

[102] Sv. Sinod, *Raskol i Sektantstvo*, p. 37; A. Maude, *A Peculiar People*, pp. 167–74.

The *Dukhobortsy* suddenly came to official notice in the second half of the eighteenth century. For a period after 1792 they were persecuted by the local officials of the province of Ekaterinoslav, where the governor feared them because their religion seemed strange to him. Under Alexander I, however, they were tolerated and even granted land at Molochnaia in the Taurida, on which to plant their settlements. Here they practiced a primitive form of Christianity and had a communal economic system which seemed to flourish. Their doctrine seemed to be that Christ is within us, being born, suffering, and rising again as the spirit is reborn from sin; instead of believing in the Heaven of the Orthodox they believed in the transmigration of souls, with a Heaven as the ultimate goal. Marriage they did not consider necessary—instead they practiced free cohabitation; the other sacraments were likewise dispensed with. Also, like the *Molokane,* they were opposed to bearing arms and taking oaths.[103] At times they did satisfy the authorities by hiring substitutes or by serving in the military supply trains; but those who were forcibly enrolled in line regiments on at least one occasion threw down their arms in battle.[104]

In 1841, under Nicholas I, they were moved to the Caucasus. Here they became prosperous and contented, in large measure owing to advantageous supply contracts during the Crimean War. Their former fanaticism died down, they made no objection to conscription, and were in good repute with the authorities.[105] However, trouble began again in 1881, when Petr Verigin became the most influential leader of the sect; after dissension within the group, he was exiled by the government, first to the north, and then to Siberia. In 1894 Verigin was greatly influenced by the teachings of Tolstoi; at once the *Dukhobor* leader sent word to his followers to abstain from oaths, to refuse military service, and to burn their arms. Many *Dukhobortsy* thereupon deserted from the army or refused to serve, and in 1895 they publicly burned their weapons. Distressing scenes followed. The sectarians were disrespectful to the officials, refused to pay taxes, and were generally hostile to the government. In retaliation,

---

[103] O. M. Novitskii, *O Dukhobortsakh,* pp. 25–55; Conybeare, *op. cit.,* pp. 270 ff.
[104] Conybeare, *op. cit.,* p. 284.   [105] Maude, *op. cit.,* p. 155.

the authorities exiled more than a hundred of them to Iakutsk in Siberia, some for eighteen years, but more for an indefinite period.[106] Cossacks were sent among the others, many were flogged, and troops were quartered in their homes. Not long after this the entire group were deported to the high Caucasus, where the climate and the lack of economic security began to decimate them. But owing to the interest of Tolstoi and of sympathetic foreigners, they were soon allowed to emigrate.[107]

The troubles of the *Dukhobortsy* were not yet over. They settled first in Cyprus, but soon found it to be unhealthful. Then in 1899 they were moved to Canada, where they were given extensive lands on the western prairies. But owing to the advice of Tolstoi they set up a communal system and soon were at odds with the Dominion government over road taxes, land payments, and the registration of marriages, births, and deaths. In 1903 Verigin arrived from Siberia and succeeded in restoring harmony for a time, but the trouble broke out again. The fanaticism of the sectarians was shown by their nude parades and their refusal to use horses for hauling wagons and for plowing.[108] Thus the *Dukhobortsy* seem to have been a difficult problem for the authorities, both in Russia and in Canada.

As for the *Dukhobortsy* who remained in Russia—a minority group of the more conservative wing, who did not revere Verigin—they apparently lived at peace with the government, although they were hostile to the Orthodox Church, and were reported to be poor soil for missionary work.[109]

Although probably not the most numerous, the most important of the sects, at least in rapidity of growth and in the hostility which it aroused in official circles, was the Stundist. The theology of this denomination was German in origin, perhaps going back to the pietist Philipp Spener. In the early nineteenth century German settlers carried their teachings to the Black Sea region, where these ideas soon gained a strong moral influence over the surrounding peasantry. Up to 1870 the Stundists remained within the Orthodox Church,

[106] Maude, *op. cit.*, p. 155; *Missionerskoe Obozrenie*, June, 1905, pp. 1423–24.
[107] Maude, *op. cit.*, pp. 34–38; A. Palmieri, "The Russian Dukhobors," *Harvard Theological Review*, VIII (1915), 66–70.
[108] Maude, *op. cit.*, pp. 199 ff.; Palmieri, *loc. cit.*
[109] Sv. Sinod, *Raskol i Sektantstvo*, pp. 44–45.

much as the early Methodists remained for a time within the Anglican communion; after that date they began to break away and to establish a separate identity. Their creed was similar to that of the Baptists. They practiced adult baptism by immersion, believed in salvation through faith, and rejected the sacramental system, the hierarchy, the ritual, the fasts, the crosses, and the ikons of the Orthodox Church.[110] The Stundists taught that all government and all oppression were created by man, for God had created the blessings of this world for the equal enjoyment of all. Hence to please God and to end evil men should try to abolish the exploitation of the weak by the strong, and to establish by peaceful means a communal system under which all would live only by the sweat of their brow.[111]

A very potent influence which helped the rise of Stundism in Russia was a longing on the part of some sections of the peasantry for a faith that insisted on the puritan virtues. The Orthodox priest Rozhdestvenskii in his study of the Stundists declared that this movement appeared to be a reaction against the drunkenness, theft, and immorality prevalent in the south of Russia. Many Stundists declared that before being converted they had led dissolute lives. One Riaboshapka averred that before he became a Stundist he had "known vice in all its forms." "I worked at farming," said the Stundist Umskii to the village teacher, "and I was then just as sinful as all the Orthodox now are. I loved to get drunk and to sin with strange women, and I so ruined my farm that there was almost nothing to eat. . . ." A police official of the province of Kherson, in a report concerning a village of Stundists in 1882, stated that the latter declared that the chief cause of their joining the sect was a wish to separate themselves from the society in which they were living, and in which there flourished such demoralizing vices as drunkenness, quarreling, theft, and lechery. "On entering the sect they broke their bonds with their former society, and began to lead new lives." [112]

Another significant bit of testimony came from the very conservative Bishop Makarii of Tomsk in 1905:

[110] Nikol'skii, "Raskol i Sektantstvo vo Vtoroi Polovine XIX Veka," *Istoriia Rossii v XIX Veke*, V, 283.
[111] A. Rozhdestvenskii, *Iuzhno-russkii Stundizm*, pp. 187–208.
[112] *Ibid.*, pp. 33–34.

We must state the fact, sad as it is for the Orthodox person, that the Old Believers and the sectarians, both with us in far-off Siberia, and everywhere, in literacy and in knowledge of matters of faith stand far higher than the Orthodox. The Old Believer knows how his denomination differs from others, the sectarian knows the Gospel and is everywhere prepared to read it and to explain it, and both know how to dispute according to their teachings with the Orthodox, who in the overwhelming majority are without reply and are even astonishingly ignorant.[113]

Coming from such a source, this is favorable testimony indeed; but none the less it availed not. The state authorities, apparently disturbed by the rapid growth of the sect and its hostility to the political and social order, took drastic action. In 1894, in response to an earlier appeal by the Synod, the Committee of Ministers, on the grounds that the prayer meetings of the Stundists were "bringing disorder into the life of the local parishes" and served "as a very useful means of extending the false doctrines of the Stundists among the Orthodox," decreed that the Minister of Internal Affairs, acting together with the Over Procurator of the Most Holy Synod, might declare this whole sect to be "especially dangerous," and might forbid the Stundists to hold group prayer meetings. This was duly done.[114]

The accusations against the Stundists became more serious later, for Skvortsov, the chief Orthodox missionary, declared that by casting aside the Orthodox Church, "which is the support of our state and social life, the Stundists cast aside all forms of social life"—i. e., tend toward anarchism. They were, he added, very hostile to military service and to war, and believed that "he that taketh the sword shall perish by the sword." But, said Skvortsov, if the Stundists had their way and the existing state order were abolished, their wish was to replace it by "nothing other than socialism and communism."[115] In 1901 the governor of the province of Khar'kov reported that in the village of Pavlovka some Stundists, "being in a condition of religious frenzy, began to behave violently," broke the windows of the church and the sacred vessels, ripped the hangings from the altar,

[113] Sv. Sinod, *Otzyvy Eparkhial'nykh Arkhiereev po Voprosu o Tserkovnoi Reforme*, III, 377.
[114] Zav'ialov, ed., *Tsirkuliarnye Ukazy . . . Sinoda*, pp. 261–62.
[115] D. I. Skvortsov, *Sovremennoe Russkoe Sektantstvo*, pp. 33–34.

tore apart the Gospel, and broke and destroyed in wild abandon. Several even trampled on the altar in order to break the boards, and the women tore off the ceremonial coverings with their teeth. When the mounted constable appeared, they attempted to pull him from his horse, so that he had to seek safety in flight.[116] Many of the offenders were taken to court as a result of this affair; according to the report of the governor, forty-five of the sixty-six accused were sentenced to hard labor for from four to fifteen years, and four others to imprisonment for from three to eight months.[117] The bishop of Khar'kov declared that the cause of this affair was the incitement of a sectarian leader, Feodosienko, who claimed to be the prophet Moses and stated that he had been sent to wreak vengeance on the *pans* (lords) and on all those wishing unrighteousness. As the Stundists were already longing, according to the bishop, for the day when "the earth will be common to all, when the *pans* will be overturned, and there will be no authorities, no army, no courts, no prisons," it did not prove difficult for the agitator to spur them on against the Orthodox Church, "which does not approve such senseless dreams. . . ."[118]

Other less specific accusations of dangerous beliefs on the part of the Stundists were made. The Over Procurator accused them of "a socialist and nihilist tendency," and of preaching a false doctrine which was anti-Christian in its dogmas and antigovernmental in its point of view.[119] Some of the Stundists of the province of Khar'kov were even said to have ceased to take an interest in religion. Instead of praying or singing at their meetings, it was alleged by the Over Procurator that they read books of antireligious and antigovernmental character, and carried on discussions which dealt exclusively with social and political questions.[120] According to the bishop of Kherson, some Stundists went even further. He stated that it had been proved that the sectarians had taken part in the secret movement among the workers of the city of Nikolaev, namely, the formation of the so-called "Union of Russian Social Democrats."[121]

[116] M. N. Pokrovskii, ed., *1905—Istoriia Revoliutsionnogo Dvizheniia v Otdel'nykh Ocherkakh*, I, 322.
[117] *Ibid.*, p. 324.   [118] *Ibid.*, p. 323.
[119] Sv. Sinod, *Raskol i Sektantstvo*, pp. 15–16.
[120] *Ibid.*, p. 25.   [121] *Ibid.*

This accusation and others made against the Stundists were given as justification for the active campaign against these sectarians. How thorough the central authorities were in this campaign may be gathered from several communications of Pobedonostsev. On March 15, 1900, he wrote to the Minister of Internal Affairs that while the law of 1879 recognized the sect of Baptists as a "permitted" sect, it referred only to Baptists of German ancestry—i. e., those whose forbears had never had any connection with the Orthodox Church. The law did not apply to anyone of Russian ancestry who might claim to be a Baptist; "there are and must be no Russian Baptists." He went on to say that the Stundists, who were officially an "especially dangerous sect," and who were forbidden to hold group prayer meetings, insisted on identifying themselves with the Baptists. These attempts of the Stundists to gain the privileges granted to the Baptists were illegal, for such attempts "separate them [the Stundists] from their native Orthodoxy, introduce confusion into the conscience of the Russian people, and are attacks upon the unity of the Orthodox Church and of the Russian nation." He asked that the police be sure not to give to the Stundists any legal document identifying them as Baptists.[122] Inasmuch as the documents referred to were the passports, residence permits, birth and marriage certificates, and the like, which were obligatory for all Russian subjects, the measure urged by Pobedonostsev had considerable significance.

The Minister of Justice was also appealed to by Pobedonostsev, and as a result the minister sent a circular to the criminal courts, instructing them to punish the Stundists according to law, and in cases involving punishment for holding public prayer meetings not to let them escape by calling themselves Baptists.[123]

The Over Procurator of the Synod was not yet satisfied. Again he wrote to the Minister of Justice, urging him in a secret letter to amplify the wording of his circular. He suggested that after the words *public prayer meetings* there be added the following: "i. e., those which are not confined to the close family circle, but are visited by outside persons," so that all these illegal gatherings should be punished as such. Also, to explain the phrase, "consisting of the

[122] M. V. D., Dep. Obshchikh Del, 1900, portfolio 28, sheets 1–3.
[123] *Ibid.*, sheet 4.

prayers and rituals proper to Stundism," he proposed the addition of the following: "such as the group singing of special verses from the Bible and of hymns from the service books of the sect, *The Voice of Belief—Religious Verses,* or *A Christian's Petition;* the reading, by anyone of the gathering, of chosen parts of Holy Scriptures, with explanation thereof in the spirit of the false doctrines of the sect; also, kneeling devotions with improvised 'inspired' prayers, without the sign of the cross." Further, he urged that the following words be added after the name *Baptist:* "recognized by our legislation as legal only for followers of the German Protestant sect." [124]

As a result of these efforts of Pobedonostsev, the Minister of Internal Affairs sent a secret circular to the governors, telling them not to allow Russian Stundists to masquerade as Baptists. This applied particularly to their applications for documents such as passports, residence permits, and the like.[125] This new rule soon began to bring hardships to the Stundists. A petty bourgeois of the Caucasus asked for a new passport, declaring himself to be a Baptist; but as he was of Russian ancestry this was not officially possible, and so he was refused both passport and residence permit, although for years these had been granted to him regularly. Without these documents, he lost his employment and his livelihood.[126]

The Stundists do not seem to have been deprived of their children as the *Molokane* sometimes were. Only one case directly involving the children of Stundists is contained in the archives of the bureau of the Ministry of Internal Affairs which dealt with sectarian matters for the early years of the twentieth century, and in this case, although Pobedonostsev wrote urgent complaints concerning the mother, Natalia Shumilo, the only result was that the governor of the province of Volhynia reported that the children, although still with their mother, had been placed under the religious and moral guidance of the leading Orthodox persons of the village.[127] But in applying other persuasions to Stundists, the authorities, lay and ecclesiastical, were not so reluctant.

In February, 1900, for example, the governor of Vitebsk reported

[124] *Ibid.,* sheets 5–6.   [125] *Ibid.,* sheets 8–9.
[126] *Ibid.,* sheets 14–15.
[127] M. V. D., Dep. Obshchikh Del, 1902, portfolio 32, sheets 1–5.

that in a certain farmhouse the local police had discovered a secret meeting of thirteen persons engaged in religious discussion. On the window sills were found books of a religious nature, and in the ikon corner of the room, instead of ikons, there hung two pieces of cardboard covered with illustrations and texts from the Holy Scriptures. In spite of the lateness of the hour a lively discussion was going on.

Upon being questioned, those present declared that they had all gathered at the home of one Gavrilov, their very close friend, before going on to the market in the city of Liutsin the next day. They had been occupying themselves with the reading of the Bible. The host and several of the others called themselves "Baptists," adding that members of their denomination always had Bibles with them. Upon investigation, it was disclosed that two of the men, Ian Geide and Nikolai Semenov, had previously been convicted of spreading Stundism. The charges based upon this meeting, together with the books and the cardboards used, were sent to the religious consistory of Polotsk, and police surveillance was established over Vasilii Gavrilov.[128]

The governor sent in a later report in October of that year, in which he stated that the religious consistory of Polotsk had referred the matter to the Procurator of the Vitebsk district court, "in order to start court proceedings against them [the Stundists] and to bring them to a strict legal accountability." [129]

In this case the police had apparently initiated the action independently, but in some instances the first step was taken by the authorities of the church. For example, in 1901 Pobedonostsev wrote to the Minister of Internal Affairs to complain of the activities of Ivan Roslavlev, who, he said, was spreading Stundism. Pobedonostsev said that this man was steward on a large estate, and that he refused to rent land or to give employment to Orthodox peasants, while he helped his own people greatly.[130]

The governor of Khar'kov reported that this was true—Roslavlev did refuse land, work, and loans to Orthodox peasants, while he readily helped his coreligionists. "Roslavlev, for his own ends, acts

---

[128] M. V. D., Dep. Obshchikh Del, 1900, portfolio 18, sheets 1–2.
[129] *Ibid.*, sheet 4.
[130] M. V. D., Dep. Obshchikh Del, 1901, portfolio 44, sheet 1.

very slyly and carefully, and at the services of the Orthodox clergy follows all the rites in order to avoid all suspicion of belonging to the Stundist sect." He was successful, too, in his propaganda, for instead of the formerly solid Orthodox population in the village, there were now twenty-two families out of the fifty-four that had embraced Stundism. They held their meetings openly by day, instead of in furtive fashion by night, "which bears exceedingly hard upon the spirit of the Orthodox population that is not yet shaken in its faith." The matter ended with an order from the minister for a strict police watch over Roslavlev, for one year.[131]

Occasionally the civil authorities showed themselves to be more tolerant than the church. In 1902 Pobedonostsev wrote to the Minister of Internal Affairs to ask punishment for a peasant of Volhynia who had buried his son with Stundist rites in the Orthodox cemetery; but the minister gave him no satisfaction. Again the Over Procurator took the initiative, with the statement that the peasant meeting of this Volhynian village had voted to expel eight Stundist families from the village. He urged that these families be sent out of the province by administrative order, as they were very troublesome and irritated the Orthodox villagers.[132] However, the minister found that a decision of the senate established a precedent against such action, as the Stundists had not actually committed any crimes.[133]

It was now the turn of the Stundists mentioned to complain, which they did in a petition to the governor general of the district, enumerating beatings, deprivation of freedom, and other abuses. The governor of Volhynia was asked to report on the case. He declared that he thought that the best way to stop the trouble would be by administrative exile of the chief offenders for a period of from three to five years.[134] But the governor general of the district of Kiev in his report declared against exiling the Stundists from Volhynia, saying that their success in proselyting was due to "the unpreparedness of our village clergy and the darkness of the peasants." He proposed that the trouble be settled by quartering a constable in the village, by increasing the pay of the priest, "which should make him more

[131] *Ibid.*, sheets 3 and 5.
[132] M. V. D., Dep. Obshchikh Del, 1902, portfolio 29, sheets 8–12.
[133] *Ibid.*, sheets 13–14.   [134] *Ibid.*, sheets 15–21.

zealous," and by appointing to the village church a psalmist with seminary training, with a suggestion that he should "read in church so that all can understand every one of his words." [135]

The refusal of the civil authorities to take drastic action did not, however, mean that the Stundists were no longer to be restricted, for when a group of peasants of the province of Kiev, who declared themselves to be not Stundists, but Baptists, asked to be permitted to worship without restraint, the answer was in the negative. Governor Trepov of Kiev reported to the minister that these peasants were Stundists, as the local Orthodox pastor and the district priest had said so. Hence they had no right to call themselves Baptists, and the petition should not be granted. And it was not,[136] for the officials took the testimony of the Orthodox clergy rather than that of the sectarians themselves.

The question about the nature of Stundism was continually cropping up, and almost invariably the declarations of the dissenters had no validity in the eyes of officialdom. Thus a group of peasants of the "Evangelistic Faith," of the province of Khar'kov, vainly petitioned in 1903 to be relieved of police persecution. They were not permitted to have prayer meetings in their homes; the police took away their religious books, even when they had been approved by the censors, and haled the owners into court. "And all these persecutions and abuses by the local authorities are directed against us, as we must state, at the hostile suggestion of the diocesan missionary and of the Orthodox clergy," for, said the petitioners, the authorities of the church had wrongfully dubbed them Stundists and had applied to them the legal penalties proper for that sect. Both the rural and the city courts, they added, on the basis of the law of 1894, which applied exclusively to Stundists, had "at various times condemned several of our number, because of our group prayer meetings and because of the burial of our dead, to fines of twenty-five rubles or imprisonment for as much as ten days."

They went on to complain that their marriages were not recognized as legal, and they were nowhere recorded; their children, born of marriages solemnized according to their faith, also remained un-

[135] M. V. D. Dep. Obshchikh Del, 1902, portfolio 29, sheets 29–39.
[136] M. V. D., Dep. Obshchikh Del, 1901, portfolio 13, sheets 1–2 and 4–5.

recorded, or were recorded under their mothers' names as illegitimate, and thus had no legal right to the property of their fathers. Moreover, when it came to military duty, they had no means of presenting the proper family records or of obtaining any authorized legal exemptions from service. Hence the petitioners asked that they be assured against interference with their religious services, and that they be permitted to record their births, marriages, and deaths.[137]

This petition, which was signed by 285 persons, was accompanied by a printed statement of their beliefs. They believed in the Trinity and in salvation through faith; baptism and communion were regarded as symbols; marriage was looked upon as a holy union, with divorce only for adultery. They also recognized the civil authority as established by the law of God, and declared it proper to pray for the Tsar. They proclaimed their willingness to perform military service, although they prayed devoutly for peace; also they were ready to take oaths and to perform the necessary civic duties.[138] Nothing in this creed specified their attitude toward economic matters; however, their professed willingness to be submissive to the authorities was an indication that they apparently contemplated no revolutionary economic action.

Certainly this creed would have been regarded as loyal in western Europe, and its adherents welcomed as good citizens, but not so in the Russia of 1903. The governor of Khar'kov was able to demonstrate to his own satisfaction that by their creed these people had proved themselves to be Stundists; for they admitted belief in salvation through faith and rejected the sacramental system. Furthermore, they had shown their "clearly Stundist, antigovernmental convictions."

For their belief taught them to subject themselves to the civil authorities in everything not clearly contrary to the law of God; but as each man was to interpret the law of God for himself, or under the guidance of one of the self-chosen leaders of the sect, actually this nullifies the authority of the state. Thus there is opened a wide range for all sorts of illegal and anarchistic attitudes among the mass of the sectarians. Thus the creed of the petitioners, which does not allow them to hate

---

[137] M. V. D., Dep. Obshchikh Del, 1903, portfolio 97, sheets 1–3.
[138] *Ibid.*, sheet 5.

their enemies, and which preaches that all oaths are condemned by God, regards war and military service as contrary to the law of God, and rejects the oaths established by law as blasphemous promises.[139]

Thus the governor of Khar'kov. And although the sectarians had expressly stated their willingness to take oaths and to perform military service, the Minister of Internal Affairs accepted the governor's argument and designated the petitioners as Stundists. They might have no prayer meetings; their marriages might be recorded only if the persons involved had never, from birth, been listed as Orthodox, while Stundist children were recognized as legitimate only if the marriages of their parents were recorded.[140]

How the close alliance between missionaries and police operated may be seen in yet another instance. Six peasants of the province of Kiev complained to the Senate at St. Petersburg that their religious books had been seized, and that when they had protested, no notice had been taken of their complaint. The governor testified that these persons were Stundists, and that the police had stopped prayer meetings in their quarters. At these gatherings the police had seized religious books: two copies of the New Testament with psalters, several books and brochures by Count Tolstoi, a volume entitled *Discussion of the Holy Teachings of the Christian Church*, and another called *Favorite Verses*. These were turned over to the local missionary and to the religious consistory of the diocese of Kiev.[141]

The governor, in a later report, declared that books and manuscripts were very important in the efforts of the Stundists to spread their faith. Many of these books, "although passed by the religious censor, were still considered by the diocesan authorities to be not in conformity with the spirit of Orthodoxy," and these authorities wanted them sent to the religious consistory to be placed in the library of the Sofiiskii Cathedral in Kiev. Moreover, the police did not have a complete list of the dangerous books and hence seized all books in the possession of known Stundist propagandists and sent them to the religious authorities for inspection. The religious consistory looked over the books and brochures and decided which, if any, should be returned to their owners. Beside the sectarian hymn

[139] M. V. D., Dep. Obshchikh Del, 1903, portfolio 97, sheets 6–8.
[140] *Ibid.*, sheet 9.
[141] M. V. D., Dep. Obshchikh Del, 1901, portfolio 68, sheet 4.

book, *Favorite Verses,* the following were indicated by the diocesan authorities as among the books subject to removal from circulation: *The Holy Book of the Old and New Testaments,* printed at Vienna, a publication of the British Bible Society, and *The Old and New Testaments* in five volumes, published by the same society and printed in St. Petersburg in 1882 at the Synod Typography.[142]

It is curious to find the police and the religious authorities confiscating religious books which had already been passed by the official censors. However, the missionary leaders of the church were finding it increasingly difficult to punish the Stundists through the ordinary legal channels, for the courts were reported by *Missionerskoe Obozrenie (Missionary Survey)* to be averse to reaching convictions, under the laws of 1883 and 1894, against prayer meetings of the Stundists, and in 1904 all Stundists brought to trial under these laws were freed by order of the courts.[143] Indeed the church often found that even in dealing with the so-called "mystical sects" it was far easier to resort to administrative action than to obtain convictions in the courts.

While there were many other religious denominations in Russia in the early twentieth century, only the "mystical sects"—the *Skoptsy* and the *Khlysty*—will be treated in these pages, for the other groups were so much like the denominations already discussed and so much smaller than the *Molokane,* the *Dukhobortsy,* and the Stundists that it is unnecessary. The two mystical sects had one thing in common: they both held that marriage and sexual relations were sinful, and hence they attempted to mortify the flesh. The *Skoptsy* were so extreme in their belief that they resorted to mutilation of both men and women, in order to destroy the carnal principle. They were severely punished, the penalties meted out to the adherents and propagators of the sect being exile to Siberia, in some cases with forced labor for fifteen years.[144]

The *Khlysty* were a sect which held a somewhat less radical faith. They believed in the reincarnation of Christ, and termed their leaders

[142] *Ibid.,* sheet 5.   [143] *Missionerskoe Obozrenie,* Jan., 1905, pp. 174–77.
[144] Svod Zakonov, XV, "Ulozhenie o Nakazaniiakh Ugolovnykh i Ispravitel'nykh," ed. 1885, secs. 197–202; *Prodolzhenie Svoda Zakonov,* 1906, XV, "Ulozh. o Nakaz. Ugol. i Isprav.," secs. 197–202 (repealed March 14, 1906).

"Christs," or in the case of their female leaders, "Mothers of God." Marriage they regarded as sinful, and they often spoke of their children as "little sins," and of their wives as "gifts of the Devil." Their religious meetings took place at night and were often accompanied by flagellation; hence the name of the sect (from *khlyst*, a whip). At these ceremonies hymns were sung, and generally there occurred a frenzied sort of dance about the hut, often accompanied by leaping, shrieking, foaming at the mouth, utterance of strange words and phrases [145]—phenomena much like the manifestations reported at some of the revivals and camp meetings of the American backwoods. But, perhaps because of the secrecy of these meetings, persistent accusations were made that on these occasions the *Khlysty* performed grossly immoral acts of sexual promiscuity.

The most fantastic of these charges was that at various times at their night meetings the *Khlysty* groups cut off the left breast of one of their "Virgins" or "Mothers of God" and then used the flesh in rites of communion. Another charge was infanticide, which had so often been made against the early Christians in Rome. One of the leading Orthodox missionaries, however, declared in 1896 that the sole evidence for the first accusation was testimony extracted under torture in 1721 and that there was no basis for either of these imputations.[146]

Much more widely held was the belief that the religious rites of the *Khlysty* terminated with the sudden extinguishing of the light in the hut, whereupon the frenzied participants threw themselves upon the floor and gave themselves over to promiscuous sexual intercourse. Several reputable historians in Russia have given credence to this idea, among them Professor Paul Miliukov. However, the evidence available seems to show that while the *Khlysty* were not wholly consistent in their asceticism, their rites were rarely if ever the orgies imagined. Professor Karl Grass, of the University of Dorpat, in his monumental book examines each piece of evidence with truly Teutonic thoroughness, and concludes that although there may have been some individual cases of sexual indulgence after these rites, there was apparently no religious sanction for such actions. In fact he declares

[145] Conybeare, *op. cit.*, pp. 350–51.

[146] Ivanovskii, "Sudebnaia Ekspertiza o Sekte Khlystov," *Zhurnal Ministerstva Iustitsii*, 1896, No. 1, pp. 86–95.

that the testimony which had been cited is all against the probability of such promiscuity among the *Khlysty;* the testimony is all second- or third-hand, most of it self-contradictory, or only hearsay evidence. Grass's conclusion is that the *Khlysty* were probably more continent than the mass of the Russian peasantry, even though there doubtless did occur isolated cases of intercourse during the period when most of those present were sleeping the sleep of exhaustion on the floor of the darkened hut.[147]

The Orthodox missionary Ivanovskii also believed that the *Khlysty* were not so bad as they had been painted. He stated that promiscuity on the part of the *Khlysty* did occasionally occur, although "no one has seen it." But according to him it was a comparatively rare phenomenon and one unknown to many congregations of *Khlysty.* Ivanovskii thought that probably their vices were less significant than those of some of the other denominations, notably the priestless Old Believers, who were not punished except for propaganda. Hence he urged that the *Khlysty* should be regarded merely as one of the "especially dangerous" sects, and should be punished only as propagators of dangerous teachings.[148]

Apparently the actions of the government with respect to the *Khlysty* were chiefly directed against those who extended the teachings of the sect. In 1900 four leaders of the *Khlysty* appealed to be permitted to return from Transcaucasia, whither they had been exiled for their religious teachings. Three of them were permitted to go back, for they had joined the Orthodox Church.[149] Moreover, Pobedonostsev's lengthy complaint respecting the activities of one Mikhail Riabov was an attempt to check the efforts of a leader of the *Khlysty.* The letter stated that in 1900 the Synod, warned by Metropolitan Antonii, had asked for imperial permission to place Riabov "in the arrest division of the Suzdal Spaso-Evfimevskii Monastery until he recants and repents," but that it had been necessary to give up this idea. The Over Procurator added that since that time the *Khlysty* community organized by Riabov had increased its activity, and that he and his followers were guilty of sexual excesses, superstitious acts,

[147] K. K. Grass, *Die russischen Sekten,* I, 434–47.
[148] Ivanovskii, *op. cit.,* pp. 98 ff.
[149] M. V. D., Dep. Obshchikh Del, 1900, portfolios 43, 46, 71.

178 Education and Indoctrination

and so on.[150] The evidence against Riabov was not strong enough to warrant taking the case to court, in spite of the explicitness of the law; if it had been, probably this appeal of Pobedonostsev to the Minister of Internal Affairs need not have been made. The Minister of Internal Affairs was open to reason, however; on July 5, 1904, by administrative order, he forbade Riabov to live in the province of St. Petersburg for two years.[151]

Another difficult problem which faced the Russian Church was that of the Uniats, descendants of Orthodox Russians who had lived chiefly in the eastern provinces of the medieval Polish-Lithuanian state. In the late sixteenth and early seventeenth centuries, while still under Polish rule, most of them were induced to recognize the authority of the pope, although they retained their Orthodox liturgy and customs. This compromise remained in force until the nineteenth century, when Russia dominated this part of Poland. In 1839, under Nicholas I, the Russian authorities forced the Uniats of the Ukrainian and White Russian provinces to renounce their connections with Rome and to become Orthodox. The results of this action, however, proved unfortunate. In the words of the *Report* of the Over Procurator for 1905–7, "The haste of the civil authorities in the matter of reuniting the Uniats, and their use of administrative measures— . . . this is what formed the contingent of the so-called determined resisters. . . ." Many of the latter never accepted their changed position, or ceased their efforts to return to their former allegiance to the papacy.[152] In 1875, after the Polish uprising of 1863, it was decided to apply this treatment to the other Uniats of the former Kingdom of Poland, especially in the provinces of Sedlets and Lublin. They might have been won over by patient efforts, as many of them were Ukrainian in language and descent, but once more the Russian authorities were not patient. The local governor and one of the Uniat bishops apparently hoped to win official favor, and "hastened unnecessarily, acted rashly and forcibly and thus very much aggravated matters." ". . . As energetic forms of administra-

[150] M. V. D., Dep. Obshchikh Del, 1904, portfolio 11, sheets 1–9.
[151] *Ibid.*, sheet 10.
[152] Sv. Sinod, *Vsepoddanneishii Otchet Ober-Prokurora . . . za 1905–1907 gg.*, pp. 124–25.

tive pressure were brought to bear, there occurred a number of shocking incidents, disturbances and pacifications; hussars and Cossacks were ordered to assist the 'voluntary' conversion to Orthodoxy, and thus the question of reuniting these Uniats acquired the character of a real scandal."[153]

After this beginning, the new religious life of the Uniats did not proceed smoothly. Even in the Ukrainian and White Russian provinces, where the conversion first took place, the gains of the church were far from secure. The church authorities claimed that the mass of the Uniats accepted their religious status with enthusiasm, but in the next sentence added that the Polish landowners and the Catholic clergy were dangerous foes of Orthodoxy, often stirring up the peasants against the Russian Church.[154] In some instances Catholic priests induced Uniat mothers to permit the christening of their children according to the Roman rite, and acted as teachers of the Polish language.[155] As for the predominantly Polish provinces, here Orthodoxy maintained itself with difficulty. The number of the "determined" Uniats was great, and both they and those who nominally accepted Orthodoxy openly sought to return to Catholicism.[156] In the latter provinces in 1899 there were about 440,000 Orthodox and 81,000 of the "determined resisters." In addition there were 7,749 known to be wavering in their religious allegiance. Rather than have them christened as Orthodox, their parents kept 27,910 children unchristened, and 10,585 marital unions were not sanctified.[157] Of course in these provinces the number of the Catholics was vastly greater than that of the Orthodox, and even in several of the White Russian and the Ukrainian provinces the Orthodox were in the minority. They were outnumbered by the Catholics in the dioceses of Lithuania, Grodno, Polotsk, Volhynia, Mogilev, and Podolia.[158] In the province of Vilna the Orthodox were but one-fifth of the total population, and in that of Kovno one thirty-eighth.[159]

[153] A. A. Kornilov, *Kurs Istorii Rossii XIX Veka,* III, 196–97.
[154] Sv. Sinod, *Vsepoddanneishii Otchet . . . za 1883 g.,* pp. 80–87.
[155] Sv. Sinod, *Obzor Deiatel'nosti . . . za Vremia . . . Aleksandra III,* p. 192.
[156] *Ibid.,* p. 186.
[157] Sv. Sinod, *Vsepoddanneishii Otchet . . .za 1899 g.,* pp. 85–86.
[158] *Ibid.,* 1903–1904, p. 144.   [159] *Ibid.,* 1900, pp. 187–88.

With this difficult situation in mind, the Synod drafted a series of rules to regularize the status of the Uniats. They were approved by the Emperor Nicholas in 1898 in the following form:

1. On the strength of the act uniting them with the Orthodox Church in 1875, all former Greco-Uniats are considered Orthodox.
2. Persons descended from former Greco-Uniat parents are recognized as Orthodox, even though they may have been christened before 1875 in a Catholic church.
3. Persons born to parents of Roman Catholic belief, but christened in Greco-Uniat churches before 1875, need not be numbered with the former Greco-Uniats.
4. Persons born before 1875 from mixed marriages of former Greco-Uniats with Catholics are listed: persons of the male sex—in the faith of the father, and persons of the female sex—in the faith of the mother.[160]

In spite of these measures and of other efforts of the Russian Church and the Imperial government, the position of Orthodoxy remained insecure in the provinces where Polish influence was strong. The Over Procurator's *Report* for 1901 spoke of the "alienation of a considerable part of the former Greco-Uniats from the Orthodox Church and their desire to go over to Catholicism," and mentioned that the younger far outdid the older generation in their hostility to Orthodoxy.[161] The *Report* for 1902 stated that in the Ukrainian and White Russian provinces the Catholics, far from losing ground, were actively pushing their cause, especially with the building of large churches. In the Kholm-Warsaw diocese the opposition of the "determined," who in places outnumbered the Orthodox, was so effective that the Orthodox clergy were often greatly discouraged.[162] Thus the efforts of the Russian government and of the Orthodox hierarchy were not sufficient to overcome the opposition of the Uniats.

Thus the Imperial government helped the Orthodox Church in its attempts to retain complete control over the religious life of the Tsar's Russian subjects. When the church's missionary activities in the form of preaching and example failed to achieve success, the help of the police was sometimes invoked in order to convert stubborn sectarians or Old Believers, or at least to prevent them from converting the Orthodox. However, as 1905 drew nearer, there was

---

[160] Sv. Sinod, *Vsepoddanneishii Otchet . . . za 1898 g.*, pp. 32–33.
[161] *Ibid.*, 1901, pp. 143 ff.   [162] *Ibid.*, 1902, pp. 100–2.

evident a tendency to abandon the more stringent of the measures, although neither church nor state gave up the principle that for the Tsar's subjects of Russian ancestry there should be only one religion, the Orthodox.

In other ways as well, the state extended its assistance to the church. As was shown in a preceding chapter, the church enjoyed the right of religious censorship, useful in checking antireligious propaganda, and helpful in stopping the flow of printed matter which might win converts for the other denominations. And while propaganda objectionable to the church was restrained, the church and its adherents had full opportunity and encouragement to publish a quantity of material favoring its cause.

Missionary work also was a field reserved for the Russian Church: "Within the borders of the state only the official Orthodox Church has the right to convert the followers of other Christian religions and other believers [non-Christians] to receive its teachings concerning belief." The laymen and the clergy of other religions, Christian and non-Christian, were most strictly enjoined "not to try to convince the minds of persons not belonging to their religions," and if they contravened this rule, they were to be "subject to the penalty provided in the criminal law." No penalties, however, were provided in the Code of Laws for laymen who converted non-Orthodox persons to non-Orthodox Christian faiths; but the non-Orthodox clergy, "for receiving into their faith, without special permission in each case, any of the other-believing Russian subjects," were to be subject to penalties ranging from a severe reprimand for the first offense to suspension from or deprivation of ecclesiastical rank for repeated offenses.[163] On the other hand, "if professed adherents of other faiths wish to join the Orthodox belief, no one may in any way prevent the fulfillment of this wish." While even the tolerated religions like the Catholic and the Lutheran Churches were forbidden to win converts, even from the heathen tribes of Siberia, the Orthodox missionaries

[163] *Svod Zakonov*, XI, part 1, "Ustavy Dukhovnykh Del Inostrannykh Ispovedanii," ed. 1896, sec. 4; *Prodolzhenie Svoda Zakonov*, 1906, XI, part 1, "Ustavy Dukhovnykh Del Inostrannykh Ispovedanii," sec. 4 (changed March 14, 1906). *Svod Zakonov*, XV, "Ulozh. o Nakaz. Ugol. i Isprav.," ed. 1885, sec. 195; *Prodolzhenie Svoda Zakonov*, 1906, XV, "Ulozh. o Nakaz. Ugol. i Isprav.," sec. 195 (repealed March 14, 1906).

were encouraged to go up and down the land, winning converts from the ranks of Catholic Poles and Protestant Letts as well as from the Old Believers and the sectarians and from the heathen of the East. This was no small mark of favor.

In the field of education also, the Orthodox Church occupied an especially favored place. According to the ideas of the ruling circles of imperial Russia in the days of Alexander III, it was safe to impart to the populace only that knowledge which harmonized with the accepted principles of Orthodoxy, autocracy, and nationality. Consequently Pobedonostsev found it possible in 1884 to convince the Tsar that the educational problem of the empire could best be entrusted to the Orthodox Church, which had so many times proved its loyalty to the autocratic principle. The rising *zemstvos* were urged to turn over their new schools to the ecclesiastical administration; funds were solicited from rich and poor alike to build up the church's schools, and appropriations from the treasury were added to the resources of these institutions. Up to that time the church's schools had been moribund; however, the subvention from the treasury increased from 17,000 rubles in 1881 [164] to nearly 7,000,000 in 1900 [165] and, thanks to this and to the energy of the Over Procurator, the elementary schools of the church began to play an important part in the educational work of the country.

At the same time, however, the elementary schools under the jurisdiction of the Ministry of Education—the schools of the *zemstvos* and of the municipal *dumas* or councils, as well as a number of county, technical, and handicraft schools of various types which were managed by the political units which founded them, subject to the supervision of school trustees and inspectors representing the ministry —these schools were also developing with great rapidity and managed to compete most successfully with the parish schools. By 1898 the number of Orthodox church schools of all types had reached the figure of 40,028, which was considerably more than that for the ministerial schools, which numbered 37,046. However, if the number of pupils is considered, a different situation will be noted. The

[164] Solov'ev, "Trudy i Zaslugi K. P. Pobedonostseva na Blago Very Pravoslavnoi Tserkvi," *Vera i Tserkov'*, 1905, VII, pp. 745–46, cited in Palmieri, *La Chiesa Russa*, p. 217.

[165] Sv. Sinod, *Vsepoddanneishii Otchet*, 1900, pp. 339–42.

ministerial schools had 2,650,058 pupils, or 63 percent of the total, while the church schools accommodated only 1,476,124, or 35.1 percent.[166] By 1904 the numerical superiority of the schools of the Ministry of Education had become more marked. In that year, of the 12,400,000 children between the ages of eight and eleven, 5,237,-000, or 42 percent, were in school; 3,273,500 were in the schools under the Ministry of Education, while 1,888,600 were in those of the church.[167] Thus it appears that the secular schools had a considerable advantage in the number of pupils over the schools of the Orthodox Church.

From a qualitative point of view also, the Synod's schools were inferior. In 1900, of the 42,604 church schools, 21,711—over half—were "schools of literacy."[168] These, which existed only in the church's educational system, were makeshifts similar to the Lancastrian schools of early nineteenth-century England. In them the instruction was given to small groups of children by teachers little older than their charges, miserably paid, and with little, if any, pedagogical training. There must have been many pupils who got only an exceedingly small amount of knowledge from the "schools of literacy."[169]

Even in standard elementary schools of the Synod—the "one-class schools," with a single teacher, giving a two-year course—where the teachers were better qualified, the curriculum seemed poorly suited to the actual needs of the peasant children. First place was given to the teaching of "Law of God"—i. e., instruction in the Bible, catechism, and prayers, given by the Orthodox parish priest or the deacon. Seven hours a week were devoted to this subject. Training in church singing was allotted four hours; four hours a week were given over to the study of church Slavonic, the liturgical language of the church. Seven hours went to the study of the Russian language and literature, six to arithmetic, and three to handwriting. In 1903

---

[166] Ministerstvo Narodnago Prosveshcheniia, *Statisticheskiia Svedeniia po Nachal'nomu Obrazovaniiu v Rossiiskoi Imperii*, p. iii.

[167] *Tserkovnyia Vedomosti*, Oct. 18, 1908, p. 2092.

[168] Sv. Sinod, *Vsepoddanneishii Otchet*, 1900, p. 337.

[169] *Svod Zakonov*, XI, part 1, "Svod Ustavov Uchen. Uchrezhd. i Ucheb. Zaved.," ed. 1893, secs. 3435–45; *Prodolzhenie Svoda Zakonov*, 1906, XI, part 1, "Svod Ust. Uchen. Uchrezhd. i Ucheb. Zaved.," secs. 3435–45.

a third year was added to the curriculum of the one-class school; in it the other subjects were supplemented with three hours of elementary Russian history and three lessons a week in geography. The "two-class schools," which had two teachers, gave a fourth year of instruction in the same subjects as those taught in the third year of the one-class school.[170] Some of the church's schools also added some training in such practical subjects as agriculture, carpentry, and domestic science; but in general it will be seen that the church schools did not stress practical subjects in their training of the young.

In respect to the teaching staff, the parish schools had little in their favor, for their salary conditions were so poor that most of them could not get well-trained teachers, but had to depend on those who were too young and too poorly trained to find places in the better-paid schools of the *zemstvos* and the towns. Not even the increasing subsidies from the imperial treasury were sufficient to give salaries to the parish schoolteachers equal to those received by the teachers in the ministerial schools. In 1902 at least 41 percent of the parish schoolteachers were below twenty-one years of age, and another 30.5 percent were between twenty-one and twenty-five. Out of the 41,-861 lay teachers in the schools of the church throughout the empire in that year, 8,722 had less than one year's experience; 7,577 had served one year; 6,631 for two years; 4,923 for three years; 3,659 for four; and only the 10,349 remaining had served for five years or more.[171] Undoubtedly the low salary schedule had a great deal to do with the large turnover of the teaching personnel which was remarked by the Over Procurator in his *Report* for 1900. In that year 911 teachers gave their services free; 18,969 received less than 100 rubles; 6,680 received less than 150 rubles; 5,740, less than 200 rubles; and 3,960 less than 250 rubles. The 2,421 remaining received the 300 rubles a year which was the usual salary of the teacher in the *zemstvo* or the town school. It must be added that more than half of the parish schoolteachers who received less than 200 rubles a year were given free rooms; but, as Pobedonostsev himself remarked, their pay was

[170] *Sobranie Uzakonenii i Rasporiazhenii Pravitel'stva*, 1889, No. 442; Sv. Sinod, *Pravila i Programmy dlia Tserkovno-prikhodskikh Shkol i Shkol Gramoty*, pp. 65–112.

[171] Sv. Sinod, *Tserkovnyia Shkoly Rossiiskoi Imperii, 13 Iiunia 1894–1903 g.*, p. 9.

pitifully small,[172] even though out of the 38,774 lay teachers in the fifty provinces of European Russia in 1905, 16,982 had no teaching certificates of any kind.[173]

The parish schools had to depend for their support upon a variety of sources, lay as well as ecclesiastical. In 1900 the treasury furnished 6,821,150 rubles; 826,947 were contributed from local taxes for the church's schools; local sources—churches, monasteries, parish trusteeships, and the peasant communes—gave the sum of 6,335,358 rubles more, while the Synod contributed 569,320, making the total 14,552,775 rubles.[174] Thus these schools leaned heavily upon the treasury and upon secular organizations for their support.

But the church's efforts to bring up the children of Russian nationality in the spirit of Orthodoxy were not limited to those who entered the doors of its own schools. All public schools were required by law to give their pupils the proper number of lessons per week in "the Law of God"—i. e., religion. Not only did this apply to the elementary schools, but to the secondary schools as well.[175] Religious instruction was given by Orthodox priests or by other teachers approved by the diocesan authorities. However, in the regions inhabited by persons of other faiths, such as the Polish and the Baltic provinces, the Crimea, the Caucasus, and similar non-Orthodox areas, confessional schools were permitted for the non-Orthodox who were not of Russian nationality,[176] and even in the Russian provinces special Jewish schools might be established where the Jewish population was large enough to warrant this.[177] Moreover, in the schools in the cities, Orthodox religious instruction was required to be given only to the Orthodox children; only if the others requested it were they to be

[172] Sv. Sinod, *Vsepoddanneishii Otchet*, 1900, pp. 348–49.

[173] Tsentral'nyi Statisticheskii Komitet, *Ezhegodnik Rossii za 1905 god*, pp. 504–5.

[174] Sv. Sinod, *Vsepoddanneishii Otchet*, 1900, pp. 339–42.

[175] *Svod Zakonov*, XI, part 1, "Svod Ust. Uchen. Uchrezhd. i Ucheb. Zaved.," ed. 1893, secs. 1476 (supplement), 1699 (supplement), 1823 (supplement), 3124, 3471; *Prodolzhenie Svoda Zakonov*, 1906, "Svod Ust. Uchen. Uchrezhd. i Ucheb. Zaved.," secs. 1476 (supplement), 1699 (supplement), 1823 (supplement), 3124, 3471.

[176] *Svod Zakonov*, loc. cit., secs. 3534, 3566, 3569; *Prodolzhenie Svoda Zakonov*, 1906, loc. cit., secs. 3534, 3566, 3569.

[177] *Svod Zakonov*, loc. cit., sec. 3423, note 2; *Prodolzhenie Svoda Zakonov*, 1906, loc. cit., sec. 3423, note 2.

given this teaching. For the non-Orthodox children the teaching of their own form of religion was permitted, in the Russian language, and only for those pupils whose parents requested it.[178] However, no such provision applied to the rural schools of the Russian provinces; there the religious instruction was under the supervision of the Orthodox bishops, and the law said nothing concerning instruction in other creeds.[179]

The religious instruction of the Orthodox Church in the schools gave the clergy opportunity to exert moral and religious suasion over the school children; it was also advantageous for the state, for inculcation of loyalty to the Tsar went hand in hand with instruction concerning the beliefs and the ceremonies of the Orthodox Church. This fact is clearly shown by the following passage from a catechism prepared for school use in 1895 by the School Committee of the Synod:

Q. What says the Fifth Commandment?
A. Honor thy father and thy mother. . . .
Q. Should we honor only our parents?
A. Beside our parents, we should respect all those who in any way fill their places for us.
Q. Whom, then, should we honor?
A. 1. First and most of all, the Tsar.
2. Pastors and spiritual teachers.
3. Kindly persons, our superiors, and teachers.
4. Our elders.
Q. Why should we especially respect the Tsar above all others?
A. Because he is the father of the whole people and the anointed of God.
Q. What does the Word of God teach concerning respect for the Sovereign?
A. "Fear God. Honor the king" [in the Russian version, Tsar] (Pet. 2: 17). "My son, fear thou the Lord and the king; and meddle not with them" (Prov. 24: 21). "Render therefore unto Caesar the things which are Caesar's; and unto God the things that are God's" (Matt. 22: 21).

[178] *Svod Zakonov, loc. cit.*, sec. 3124, notes 1 and 2; *Prodolzhenie Svoda Zakonov*, 1906, *loc. cit.*, sec. 3124, notes 1 and 2.

[179] *Svod Zakonov, loc. cit.*, secs. 3469–3511; *Prodolzhenie Svoda Zakonov*, 1906, *loc. cit.*, secs. 3469–3511.

Q. How should we show our respect for the Tsar?
A. 1. We should feel complete loyalty to the Tsar and be prepared to lay down our lives for him.
2. We should without objection fulfill his commands and be obedient to the authorities appointed by him.
3. We should pray for his health and salvation, and also for that of all the Ruling House.
Q. With what spiritual feelings should we fulfill these commands?
A. According to the words of the apostle Paul, "Not only for wrath, but also for conscience sake" (Rom. 13: 5), with sincere esteem and love toward the father of our land.
Q. What should we think of those who violate their duty toward their Sovereign?
A. They are guilty not only before the Sovereign, but also before God. The Word of God says, "Whosoever therefor resisteth the power, resisteth the ordinance of God" (Rom. 13: 2).[180]

Here, obviously, was instruction of a type suitable to be of great service to the government of Russia. As this catechism was prepared by the School Committee under the Synod, which had complete power to approve all books used in the instruction carried on in the church schools, this or a similar catechism was used in all of the parish schools, and probably by the teachers of the Orthodox "Law of God" in the secular schools. Such precepts, if well taught, must have exercised a powerful influence upon the minds of the young.

The church also had a number of schools used to impart special training to persons destined to serve the church in one capacity or another. There were the "second-class schools," which received children who had finished the course of the elementary schools and gave them three years of additional work in religious subjects and in geography, mathematics, natural science, and didactics. This qualified them to become teachers in the church's "schools of literacy."[181] For further educational training there were the teachers' schools where, in separate institutions, men and women were given training sufficient to qualify them for licenses as elementary teachers. Here, too, much of the time was spent on religious subjects—catechism, church singing, religious history, church Slavonic—along with Rus-

[180] P. Smirnov, *Nastavlenie v Zakone Bozhiem*, pp. 133–35.
[181] *Sobranie Uzakonenii*, 1902, No. 644, secs. 34–38.

sian literature, geography, history, natural science, mathematics, and pedagogy.[182] From the second-class schools and from the teachers' schools came most of the new teachers for the parish schools of the church.

For the daughters of the parish clergy the church maintained a special type of diocesan school, usually with a six-year course, where no tuition fees were paid. The subjects studied were much the same as those in the teachers' schools, but the purpose of the diocesan women's schools was not that of preparing teachers. It was to educate the girls "in the rules of propriety and righteousness, in the teachings of the Holy Church, in order that they may be good wives for ecclesiastics, good mothers, and skillful housewives." [183]

The Russian dioceses also maintained special schools for the sons of the clergy. After obtaining an elementary education, they entered the four-year religious schools, and then for the most part went to the religious seminaries. Here they found few boys from secular families. By law only 10 percent of the student body might come from non-ecclesiastical circles and, although this rule was not rigidly enforced, the Over Procurator was desirous of keeping out students from other walks of life, as few of them completed the course and entered the priesthood. Hence the seminaries were filled largely with sons of the parish clergy.[184]

At first glance it would seem that the priest's son enjoyed exceptional advantages. He passed from the elementary school into the diocesan school, where he paid no tuition. From there he went to the seminary, also a free school. If he were fortunate, he was able to obtain one of the numerous government or privately endowed stipends, which provided him with an allowance for his food in the seminary dining room and for his clothing. On graduating, he was almost sure to obtain a parish, where he could at once settle down to married life in reasonable security. But in spite of these advantages, a number of articles in the religious press and other evidence indicate that the seminary students were far from satisfied.

One reason for this was that the food provided them by their

[182] *Sobranie Uzakonenii*, 1902, No. 644, secs. 46–56.
[183] *Polnoe Sobranie Zakonov*, 1901, No. 20565, paragraph 3.
[184] Sv. Sinod, *Vsepoddanneishii Otchet*, 1900, pp. 320–21.

stipend of 105 rubles was said to be both scanty and unappetizing. A certain Dean Iurashkevich in 1910 wrote an article for *Tserkovnyia Vedomosti (Church News)*, analyzing his experiences as rector of a seminary. He stated that seminary riots over the herring or the gruel were an old story, well known before the Revolution of 1905. Often, he said, trouble would flare up, occasioned by a cockroach which had fallen into the *borshch*, or a mouse's tail in the soup. The real cause, however, according to him, was "angry dissatisfaction with the scantiness of the state maintenance." After careful study, he had found that for each person the total sum available was twenty or twenty-one kopecks for a day's meal.[185] Thus it would seem difficult for the students to get enough to appease their hunger.

Another sore point in seminary life was the disciplinary system. Articles in noted church periodicals declared that the proctors and instructors had largely given up any thought of developing Christian attitudes in their charges and kept them in order by harshness. Courtesy, these articles stated, was completely lacking in the instructors' treatment of the youths: "the favorite names which they call the students are fool, jackass, good-for-nothing, imbecile." The students used all their ingenuity to retaliate. "In the seminary there prevails a reign of terror." Seminary instructors used to say that their duty was a regular martyrdom.[186] For the students, who were subject to punishments such as deprivation of meals and imprisonment in seminary jails,[187] it could have been little better.

But the basic cause for the dissatisfaction of the students was that, as has been said in an earlier chapter, few of them wanted the life of a priest, the career for which they were destined. Over and over again the religious periodicals of the time stated that the priests who could possibly afford to do so sent their sons to the secular schools rather than to the seminaries; those who did go to the seminaries did so chiefly because they had no other chance for an education. "From

185 *Tserkovnyia Vedomosti*, Sept. 25, 1910, pp. 1652–1653.
186 *Tserkovno-obshchestvennaia Zhizn'*, No. 31, 1906, pp. 1032–34; No. 34, pp. 1131–33; and No. 38, pp. 1270–72, as quoted in Palmieri, *La Chiesa Russa*, pp. 235–36; P. Krasin, "Vospitanie v Dukhovnoi Seminarii," *Trudy Kievskoi Dukhovnoi Akademii*, Aug.–Sept., 1906, p. 715.
187 Sv. Sinod, *Zhurnaly i Protokoly . . . Predsobornago Prisutstviia*, IV, 32, Division V.

students dissatisfied with their positions come bad priests, . . . who sullenly abuse the school which nurtured them, and in their eyes, enslaved them, and who with pathological eagerness try to obtain any civil employment"—so complained an author in the *Vladimir Diocesan News,* early in 1905.[188] Dean Panormov, Rector of the seminary of Tomsk, declared, "The fact is, that the better students, with the blessing of their fathers, try to avoid the religious life; only their mothers, perhaps, are saddened by the change." [189]

One result of the reported lack of zeal for the service of the church was that there were frequent disorders in the seminaries. In 1886 the Synod found it advisable to issue a decree that seminary students were not to have firearms or other weapons in their rooms, and to order the proctors to search their baggage when they returned from vacations and to make occasional inspections of their belongings during the year.[190] In *Tserkovnyia Vedomosti (Church News)* a writer stated that "disorders and unrest in . . . our religious educational institutions began to appear quite early, even in the middle 1890's." [191] Archbishop Antonii of Volhynia declared in 1906, "There were disorders . . . in the seminaries when this movement [the revolutionary movement] had not even been noticed. Big disturbances, several every year, began in the seminaries in 1898. . . ." [192] "The seminary 'riots' began, not with last year, but long before the beginning of the liberative movement [the Revolution of 1905] ; the history of the seminaries for the last ten years has been full of them, and they arose even earlier; at the present time they have merely taken on a mass character, and openly display the dislocation of the seminaries which has been in preparation for decades." [193]

Quite as serious was the allegation that the students lacked religious feeling. Here is the observation of one witness:

By chance I went as a mere observer to service in one of the largest seminaries. Before me stood a huge crowd of youths, jammed tightly in a not very roomy church. In that crowd I saw some talking, laughing,

---

[188] *Tserkovnyi Vestnik,* Feb. 3, 1905, col. 132.   [189] *Ibid.,* col. 143.
[190] Sv. Sinod, *Obzor Deiatel'nosti . . . za Vremia . . . Aleksandra III,* p. 606.
[191] *Tserkovnyia Vedomosti,* Jan. 27, 1907, p. 137.
[192] Sv. Sinod, *Zhurnaly i Protokoly,* II, 539.   [193] Krasin, *op. cit.,* p. 714.

reading papers and booklets, but I did not see any praying; many students left the church and there in the vestibule smoked cigarettes; the proctors, doubtless, saw all this, but evidently they felt their complete powerlessness to deal with this huge crowd, undoubtedly infected with a frightful religious indifference by those numerous elements who entered only for the sake of a free education. . . , and who remained entirely strange to the idea of serving the Church of Christ. . . .[194]

From the evidence presented the conclusion is inevitable that the religious seminaries were in an unfortunate condition. The Revolution of 1905 was to disclose, lurking in the institutions which were to prepare pastors for the church, still more serious dangers for both church and state. When we turn, however, to the four religious academies of St. Petersburg, Moscow, Kiev, and Kazan, a less troubled scene is met. The academy students were the pick of the seminaries; good marks in conduct as well as in studies were required for admission to the higher institutions. Thus the more stormy spirits among the seminary students did not enter the academies, and a quieter atmosphere prevailed. Moreover, the academy students were on the highroad to success; they had ahead of them promising futures in the field of teaching or in other well-paid posts. Consequently it is not surprising that the academies were much more peaceful than the seminaries.

But while the highest educational institutions of the church did their work with little disturbance, it is impossible not to feel that the other attempts of the church to maintain an empire over men's minds were not achieving the success hoped for by those who directed the policies of Russian Orthodoxy. The Old Believers and the sectarians still remained outside the church, and the educational efforts of the parish schools were being vigorously challenged by the secular schools of the *zemstvos* and the towns. Moreover, the habit of leaning upon the state in times of difficulty could not but affect the church's ability to cope with a crisis, and must have caused it to lose prestige in the eyes of many. The stormy days of the Revolution of 1905 were to unleash powerful forces which would certainly affect the church, and would force it to show to what extent it was linked with the civil government of the Tsar.

[194] Sv. Sinod, *Zhurnaly i Protokoly*, II, 547.

PART III

Liberalism and Conservatism
During the Revolution
of 1905

CHAPTER V

A Free Church in a Free State?

THE STORM which had long been threatening the autocratic regime broke early in 1905. Even before this, there had been increasing signs of discontent. The year 1903 had been troubled with peasant disorders, some of which required the use of the troops before a sullen peace could be restored. There followed the war with Japan, which was never popular, in spite of the efforts of the conservative press and the church to arouse patriotic sentiment. The news from the theater of war did little to make the adventure more appealing; defeat followed defeat in Korea and on the plains of Manchuria, and the fall of Port Arthur in January, 1905, brought to the attention of all the sorry fact that the Russian armies were suffering humiliation at the hands of their Asiatic foes. Under these circumstances popular indignation mounted, and found expression in a variety of ways. The reactionary Minister of Internal Affairs, Pleve, was assassinated on July 15, 1904; at a meeting in November the *zemstvos* demanded constitutional government; and although in December the emperor issued some vague promises of reform, the strike of the factory workers in St. Petersburg grew in intensity as 1904 drew to a close. Nor did 1905 open more auspiciously. On January 9, "Bloody Sunday," great bands of the strikers, men, women, and children, carrying ikons and led by a priest, Father Gapon, marched to lay their petitions at the feet of the Tsar in the Winter Palace. They were met by a deadly fire from the rifles of the troops who barred the way, and scores were killed. With that bath of blood there began the active period of the Revolution of 1905.

During the mad months that followed—months filled with strikes and riots, assassinations and armed uprisings, floggings and executions, punitive expeditions and summary courts-martial, to say nothing of the wave of bloody pogroms which aided the forces of reaction to regain control—the Orthodox Church was inevitably involved. As might have been expected, the close bond between the autocratic government and the Synod caused the latter to take a stand of active opposition to the revolution and to liberalism in general. It was not astonishing to their contemporaries to find the hierarchs of the Russian Church almost uniformly supporting the government; it was, however, with some surprise as well as pleasure that liberals noted that substantial elements within the church openly sympathized with the "liberative movement," and that some few churchmen actually took part therein. These progressive elements were some of the "white clergy" (the parish priests), and the church periodicals which voiced their views.

Among these journals one of the most noteworthy was *Tserkovnyi Vestnik* (*The Church Messenger*) of St. Petersburg. This periodical, which was published by professors of the religious academy of the capital, had a wide circulation and a long tradition of support of the interests of the parish clergy. Sometimes the *Messenger* had even gone so far as to be severely critical of and even hostile to the monastics. The liberalism of this journal was repeatedly shown during the revolutionary years. Not long after the horrors of Bloody Sunday, its editor wrote a leading article in which he discussed the "Cause of These Sad Events." Although he blamed the movement of the workers on "a strange fire set burning in their minds by enemies of Russia," he went on to deplore "the innocent victims . . . —the sad corpses of children, youths, and women and casual passers-by." Moreover, the editor was realistic enough to see as a significant factor the lives of the workers "herded in damp cellars, cold garrets, and the corners rented out by those who exploit the needs of the working people. . . . They live miserably, in filth, with impossible sanitary arrangements." [1] Here was displayed a social consciousness, a humanitarianism, which much exceeded that to be found in the messages of the Most Holy Synod.

Nor was this an isolated instance. Again in October, 1906, the periodical gave space to a long article on the poverty and the misery

[1] *Tserkovnyi Vestnik*, Jan. 20, 1905, cols. 65–67.

of the city working people, in which the author urged the churchmen to defend the workers against the capitalists, to help arbitrate
industrial disputes, and to work for the organization of Christian
labor unions, as had been done in Germany and Austria.[2] In similar
fashion, the journal's regular commentator, Myshtsyn, had written
in the issue of November 26, 1905, "In our opinion the only solution
for our clergy is this—to support the interests of the peasants, and to
speak out in defense of their political and economic rights." Even
though Myshtsyn based his opinion on very practical grounds, rather
than on the justice of the demands of the peasants—he referred to
the threats to withhold support for the parish clergy, which were
voiced at the Peasant Congress in Moscow [3]—still this was a more
liberal position than that taken by most of the representatives of the
higher clergy. Other indications of the progressive tendencies of this
periodical were given in an editorial published in 1906 in praise of
the recently dismissed First Duma,[4] in a sharp attack on the counter-
revolutionary policies of the government,[5] and in a series of denunciations of the reactionary parties. In general, then, *Tserkovnyi Vestnik*
expressed liberal views, and showed itself decidedly critical of the
official policies of the Synod.

In following this course *Tserkovnyi Vestnik* was not alone. The
publication of the Moscow Religious Academy, *Bogoslovskii Vestnik* (*The Theological Messenger*), occasionally suspended its con-
templation of matters philosophical and historical long enough to
print an article decidedly hostile to the reactionary members of the
higher clergy and sympathetic with the liberal bloc. Other church
publications which from time to time contained liberal articles were
Vera i Razum (*Faith and Reason*), *Khristianskoe Chtenie* (*Christian
Reading*), and the *Trudy* (*Works*) of the Religious Academy of
Kiev. The most outspoken of all the religious periodicals, however,
was *Tserkovno-obshchestvennaia Zhizn'* (*Church-Social Life*), which
was published by the Religious Academy of Kazan. In a series of
articles in 1906 the editors of this periodical, which first appeared in

---

[2] *Ibid.*, Oct. 5, 1906, cols. 1285–89.
[3] V. Myshtsyn, *Po Tserkovno-obshchestvennym Voprosam*, part 2, p. 36.
[4] *Tserkovnyi Vestnik*, July 20, 1906, cols. 933–35.
[5] *Ibid.*, Oct. 12, 1906, col. 1317.

December, 1905, attacked the policies of the heads of the church and deplored their sympathy with the extreme nationalist-reactionary movement of the "Union of the Russian People." On April 21 an editorial denounced the ultra-conservative views of Archbishop Antonii of Volhynia and boldly praised the liberal Cadet (Constitutional Democratic) party.[6] In the next issue "the contemporary liberative movement," which "has come to protect the laboring and possessionless masses," [7] was approved. In June the government became the subject of heated denunciation for having permitted the horrors of the Belostok pogrom against the Jews, "the mass killings of persons frequently entirely inoffensive—feeble old men, women, and children." [8] Furthermore, space was given in the issue of December 1, 1906, to an answer to the warning of the Union of the Russian People that a Jew might become Over Procurator of the Orthodox Church if this race were given equal rights with subjects of Russian blood. In his reply the priest Mikhail Levitov stated that even this would not be as calamitous for the church as had been the sway of some of the former Orthodox Over Procurators.[9]

Such, then, were the leading liberal publications of the church world. Obviously they were not revolutionary in character and did not endorse the forceful tactics of the parties of the Left. But for the Russia of 1905 and 1906 the sentiments which they voiced were decidedly advanced, and quite different from those held in the higher circles of the church. Moreover, their liberalism was highly significant, for next to *Tserkovnyia Vedomosti* (*Church News*), which voiced the official views of the Synod, these were the best known of the church periodicals and those most widely read by the Orthodox pastors. The fact that such publications existed and flourished argues that there must have been a numerous group of priests who were liberal in their political and economic views.

Unfortunately it is quite impossible to tell how numerous were the liberals among the Russian clergy, or to ascertain how radical were their views. In 1905 and 1906 there were repeated accounts of priests who were punished for their rashness by the authorities, and even a few cases in which meetings of the clergy expressed views that were

[6] *Tserkovno-obshchestvennaia Zhizn'*, April 21, 1906.
[7] *Ibid.*, April 28, 1906, cols. 645–46.
[8] *Ibid.*, June 9, 1906, col. 865.   [9] *Ibid.*, Dec. 1, 1906, cols. 1651–52.

decidedly advanced. In the fall of 1905 a group (number unknown) of village priests of the diocese of Ekaterinoslav proposed that the priests as leaders of the people should ". . . explain the real condition of our political life in spite of the prohibition of the authorities," and went on to demand that the priests and the psalmists, whether provided with land or not, should have a share in the elections to the Duma—which elections should be by direct equal suffrage, and by means of secret voting.[10] Quarrels occurred between the diocesan congresses and the bishops in Tver, Kaluga, and Kazan.[11] In Voronezh the diocesan congress of the clergy, early in 1906, heard with approval orators who protested against the contemporary violence (of the government) and declared it to be the duty of the clergy to join the "liberative movement." "The congress was very critical of the proposal to increase martial control, finding that it not only oppressed social life in general, but in particular made difficult the work of the pastor. The attitude of the congress toward control [of the lower clergy] by the church authorities was *exceedingly* hostile." [12]

Even more outspoken were certain declarations published by other groups of liberal clergy. In 1906 a number of priests of St. Petersburg stated that the clergy had long been the servants of the autocracy —"in the name of God they once approved slavery, serfdom, and so on"—and had opposed all liberal ideas. However, they averred, Christianity required the clergy to guide the people toward a Christian civilization, to protect labor from capital by striving to win fair wages and leisure time for the workers. The clergy should especially love and sympathize with the suffering peasantry, who needed a speedy solution of the land problem.[13] When the radical Father Petrov was exiled to a monastery because of his liberal writings, "A Group of Moscow Clergy" issued a condemnation of this punishment and declared that it did not have the support of the majority of the clergy of Moscow.[14]

Not all of the clergy were satisfied with anonymous opposition to

[10] *Pravo*, Nov. 27, 1905, cols. 3821–23.
[11] *Tserkovnyi Vestnik*, June 1, 1906, cols. 729–930; *ibid.*, Feb. 23, 1906, col. 242.
[12] *Pravo*, Feb. 26, 1906, col. 738; *Moskovskiia Tserkovnyia Vedomosti*, May 21, 1906, p. 61.
[13] *Tserkovnyi Vestnik*, March 16, 1906, cols. 321–31.
[14] *Ibid.*, Jan. 25, 1907, cols. 114–15.

the conservative forces; some resorted to open denunciation of reaction, and a few went from words to deeds. In August, 1906, the governor of the province of Kazan telegraphed to the Minister of Internal Affairs as follows:

> In the village of Mamykovo . . . on the evening of August 17 a drunken crowd, . . . at the head of which were the local priest, Paul Anastasev, and the psalmist, . . . made an armed attack on the police sergeant and ten constables . . . in the tea shop; after many warnings, . . . fire was opened on the crowd; the priest Anastasev was seriously wounded in the left shoulder and the right thigh, and the psalmist . . . and a peasant . . . were killed. . . . The wounded priest was sent to a hospital, and his life is in danger. [He died a few days later.] [15]

In October, 1906, newspaper accounts appeared of the exiling of three priests of Shusha, in whose churches stores of bombs had been found.[16] After the Moscow uprising in December, 1905, a priest, Kazanskii by name, was arrested, and in his rooms was found the treasury of a strike committee, from which he gave out aid to the strikers. It was further alleged that this priest had even collected and distributed weapons to the insurgents, and had performed special prayers for "the fallen fighters for freedom." [17]

This readiness to share in violent action was, however, very exceptional. Much less rare was oratory like that of a priest of the province of Archangel, Father Popov. The local gendarme headquarters reported that he, in his capacity of president of a peasant congress, "astonished the majority of the assembled peasants by his passionate attacks on the government, and by bold remarks about the Sovereign Emperor, calling His Majesty a drinker of blood and a tyrant over the people, and also talked of the necessity of having an elected ruler." In answer to his speech one of the peasants is reported to have said, "This father should be dragged out by the hair and thrown through a hole in the ice." [18] Several other agitators in priestly cassocks were mentioned by the police, in the provinces of Perm, Tula, Voronezh, Kazan, Penza, and Samara.[19] In 1905 Adjutant

---

[15] M. N. Pokrovskii, ed., *1905—Materialy i Dokumenty*, Vol. 5-i, pp. 480–81.

[16] *Pravo*, Oct. 15, 1906, col. 3185.   [17] *Kolokol*, Jan. 3, 1906.

[18] Pokrovskii, *op. cit.*, Vol. 5-i, pp. 5–6.

[19] *Ibid.*, pp. 48, 139, 271, 482, 581, 607, 667.

General Maksimovich, who was sent on a special mission into the provinces of Saratov and Penza, said, "Unfortunately it must be said that there are priests attracted by extreme ideas, who . . . have an exceedingly bad effect upon the peasants."[20]

Another indication of liberal or radical views among the priesthood is given by the appearance in the newspapers of the revolutionary period of occasional items concerning the arrest or imprisonment of members of the clergy. At times, however, the offense appeared to be no greater than in the following instance: "On February 27 the priest of the village of Uspensk, . . . in the province of Vladimir, Father Preobrazhenskii, was arrested. The pretext for the arrest was a chat with parishioners about the significance of the Manifesto of October 17. . . . Father Preobrazhenskii is in the Aleksandrovskii Prison. The arrested priest is sixty years old. He has served thirty-seven years."[21] Another newspaper article spoke of a Father Meretskii, of the province of Voronezh, who was lodged in prison:

. . . there came into Valuiki a crowd of peasants from two neighboring settlements, numbering about two thousand persons, who, . . . singing "Spasi Gospodi" ["Save us, Lord"], freed their pastor from the prison, and likewise the other prisoners. The priest and the peasants wept. Following this the priest held prayers in the town square in the presence of a numerous crowd, after which a meeting was held. Cossacks who soon appeared in the town broke up the crowd and re-arrested the priest.[22]

In addition to the relatively small number of priests who learned to know the interiors of prisons, there were many more who suffered milder punishment at the hands of the ecclesiastical authorities. Such penalties took the form of suspension from office, periods of required penance in monasteries, removal to parishes which provided scanty livings, even excommunication. "In Kazan three priests, one deacon, and one psalmist were removed from office by the diocesan authorities for spreading disturbing ideas, and were deprived of the right of performing service."[23] "Twenty priests of the diocese of Kursk have

[20] N. Karpov, ed., *Krest'ianskoe Dvizhenie v Revoliutsii 1905 Goda v Dokumentakh*, p. 259.

[21] *Pravo*, March 12, 1906, col. 961. This reference and the subsequent ones are taken from *Pravo's* quotations from the leading newspapers of the day.

[22] *Ibid.*, Jan. 22, 1906, col. 264.   [23] *Ibid.*, Jan. 29, 1906, col. 375.

been brought up on charges of carrying on political propaganda. Bishop Pitirim deprived them of the right of performing service and then ordered an investigation."[24] In Khar'kov "the priests Shapovalov, Voznesenskii, Kuplenskii, [and] Grigorovich . . . declared against the death penalty and were removed from service by the consistory."[25] In the words of *Tserkovnyi Vestnik*, "One cannot say that the birth into new life was accomplished without suffering among the clergy. The telegraph every day brings reports of searches in the rooms of village priests, of arrests, administrative exiles, and the like. . . . *Kolokol* [*The Bell*, the unofficial organ of the Over Procurator] rightly states that the church 'will deal with them.' "[26]

For the student it is disappointing to find that there are no available statistics as to the number of priests who felt the heavy hand of their lay and temporal rulers because they professed liberal views. They were doubtless only a small fraction of the more than forty thousand Orthodox priests in Russia, but they were numerous enough to draw attention. After the dissolution of the First Duma, one of the church periodicals said, "In the lists sent in to the Synod by the bishops of the dioceses of Kazan, Smolensk, and Nizhnii Novgorod alone, there are noted as many as four hundred politically untrustworthy priests." The writer continued, "Truly there is no diocese where there are not priests who have suffered from the reactionary zeal of Their Lordships."[27]

Even the punishment of the clergy for this cause is not reliable proof that these priests were liberal. During the revolutionary period some of the bishops were prone to punish priests on the basis of only slight knowledge of the circumstances,[28] so that it is quite possible that not all of those so dealt with were guilty. All that can be said is that a significant fraction of the clergy was tinged with liberalism, and that a few adhered to the radical ideas of the Left.

In the First Duma, in 1906, the liberal element among the priests was in evidence. There were only six Orthodox priests among the deputies; only two showed vaguely conservative sympathies, while

[24] *Tserkovnyi Vestnik*, Oct. 1, 1906, col. 3027.
[25] *Ibid.*, Jan. 29, 1906, col. 374.
[26] *Tserkovnyi Vestnik*, March 16, 1906, col. 333.
[27] *Tserkovno-obshchestvennaia Zhizn'*, July 28, 1906, col. 1061.
[28] *Tserkovnyi Vestnik*, Jan. 18, 1907, col. 91; *Kolokol*, March 29, 1906.

the others were outspoken in their progressive beliefs. Father Po-
iarkov urged that all private, state, and crown lands be distributed
among the peasants, and expressed willingness to have the lands of the
church and the monasteries treated in the same way.[29] He also proposed that the Duma rebuke the reactionary press for its pogrom
propaganda, and denounced the government for continuing to use the
death penalty.[30] Father Ognev likewise demanded the abolition of
the death penalty; he even praised the ideals and sincerity of many
of the political prisoners, and took to task those churchmen who upheld sentences of death.[31] Still more daring were the words of Father
Afanasiev: he declared that because the government continued to
use the death penalty, God would brand it as he had marked Cain.[32]
He attacked the use of Cossacks in repressing the people, and assailed
those who declared that the Don Cossacks were ready to rise up
against the Duma because of its lack of patriotism. Such "patriotism,"
he added, had led to the defeats of Tsushima and Mukden.[33] At another session of the Duma he denounced the Tsar's ministers for
oppressing the people, and especially for plotting and organizing the
terrible pogrom at Belostok. In indignant tones he prophesied, "A
frightful Judgment Day awaits you." [34]

After the dissolution of the First Duma, the government made
great efforts to secure the election of conservatives to the next. As
will be shown later, the Synod instructed the clergy to attend the election meetings, and by preaching timely sermons and by performing
the prescribed prayers to work for the naming of candidates who
sympathized with the government. Great numbers of priests seem to
have obeyed these commands, but the results of the preliminary elections were quite disappointing to the leaders of the church. In county
after county priests were chosen as electors—but priests known for
their progressive tendencies. In Orlovskii County, in the province of
Viatka, five priests, all of them progressives, were chosen at the meeting of the large landowners; in the county of Tula four electors were
chosen, all priests, and all "noted for their progressive activity."

[29] Gosudarstvennaia Duma, *Stenograficheskie Otchety*, I Duma, pp. 130–31.
[30] *Ibid.*, pp. 429–30; pp. 959–60.
[31] *Ibid.*, pp. 1495–97.   [32] *Ibid.*, pp. 906–7.
[33] *Ibid.*, p. 1318.   [34] *Ibid.*, p. 1645.

Somewhat similar results were seen in several counties of the provinces of Orel, Saratov, and Tambov.[35] Furthermore, while two bishops and eleven of the lower clergy were elected to the Second Duma, only the bishops and two priests were conservative enough to be supporters of the government, while the remaining priests included among their number three Cadets (Constitutional Democrats) and four members of the more extreme Leftist parties, one of them a Socialist Revolutionary.[36]

For the Synod this result was disappointing enough; but worse was to follow. Instead of exerting a quieting influence in the Duma, most of the priests who spoke from the rostrum proved to be strong critics of the government and its counter-revolutionary activities. Such a one was Father Brilliantov, who spoke on the torture of political prisoners. He declared that many political prisoners were persons of high ideals and character, not deserving of harsh treatment, and that his calling required him to be on the side of the oppressed.[37] A ministry responsible to the Duma was demanded by Father Grinevich, another of the liberals, who also asked for a commission to frame a new agrarian law to give land to the peasants.[38] Father Kolokol'nikov likewise wanted a generous solution of the land question. The land, he said, was a gift from God to all and should not be bought and sold, but should be freely given to those who would till it with their own hands.[39] Father Vladimirskii condemned the field courts-martial as not in keeping with the teachings of the Gospel, and asked that the government cease ordering executions, as the first step toward ending political killings by both the revolutionaries and the government. He also strongly deplored the pogroms, which had cast such a blight upon Russia.[40] But the most outspoken of the priests in the Duma proved to be Father Tikhvinskii. He spoke against the field courts-martial and the death penalty as being contrary to the teachings of Christ, and called on the government and the bishops of the church to renounce them.[41] In a speech in behalf of agrarian legislation, he declared that the

[35] A. Smirnov, *Kak Proshli Vybory vo 2-uiu Gosudarstvennuiu Dumu,* pp. 138–39.

[36] Gosudarstvennaia Duma, *Stenograficheskie Otchety,* II Duma, preface, pp. 27–33.

[37] *Ibid.,* Section II, cols. 271–72.

[38] *Ibid.,* Section I, cols. 189–90; col. 545.   [39] *Ibid.,* cols. 782–83.

[40] *Ibid.,* cols. 486–90.   [41] *Ibid.,* cols. 430–32.

progressive clergy were willing to give up their land, as they were close to the peasants at heart. All land, he said, should be common property, like the water and the air, for peace would come to Russia only when the peasants had the land. On another occasion he praised Herzenstein, a Jewish member of the First Duma and a Cadet, who was anathema to all supporters of the government. And again he declared that while St. Paul had said that all authority is from God, the unjust authority of the ministers did not derive from a divine source. "How I wish I could fly on a magic carpet and with the cap of invisibility to the foot of the throne and say, . . . 'Sire, Thy foremost enemy, the foremost foe of the people, is this irresponsible ministry.' " [42] Here were statements that were sure to anger the princes of the church.

These defiant priests annoyed the Synod authorities by their speeches. They were soon to give greater offense. On May 7, 1907, there was an interpellation from the Right concerning an attempt to kill the Tsar. The members of the Left ostentatiously stayed away from the chamber, among them the priests Grinevich, Brilliantov, Arkhipov, Kolokol'nikov, and Tikhvinskii. This was regarded by the Synod as an insult to His Imperial Majesty, on the grounds that "esteem for the existing state authority and the state order, and even more, esteem and non-hypocritical loyalty to the Sovereign Emperor as the Anointed of God, has been inseparably connected with the religious calling by the principle of pastoral service"; and the Synod decided that it was incompatible with priestly duty to belong to political parties which "have forgotten the obligation of the oath and strive to overthrow the state and the social order and even the Tsar's authority." The culprits were called upon to give explanation of their absence from the session in question and to resign publicly from their respective parties.[43] Father Grinevich made his peace with Metropolitan Antonii of St. Petersburg; but the three who belonged to the Labor group, and Father Brilliantov, a Socialist Revolutionary, refused to obey the dictates of the Synod, and consequently orders that they be brought to trial were sent to their several dioceses.[44]

The prelates of the Orthodox Church could and doubtless did

[42] *Ibid.*, cols. 786–89.
[43] *Tserkovnyia Vedomosti*, May 12, 1907, official part, p. 200.
[44] *Ibid.*, June 2, 1907, official part, pp. 220–21.

console themselves with the thought that these troublesome priests were isolated examples of a spirit which seemed rare among the great mass of the clergy. No such comforting explanation was possible in accounting for the disorders among the theological students during the years of the Revolution. In some cases the disorders took the form of personal violence against the instructors and the administrative staffs. In the seminary of Smolensk a student attacked the rector with a *nagaika* (a Cossack whip); acid was thrown into the face of the rector of the Khar'kov seminary.[45] Several members of the school staffs were shot and killed by their students.[46] The rector of the Odessa institution was beaten by the students before the eyes of his faculty. In the seminary of Voronezh a bomb was set off in a stove near the teachers' room.[47] Other explosions occurred in the seminaries of Moscow and Nizhnii Novgorod.[48] In one institution the presence of armed forces was necessary to restore order; in another the administrative staff had to escape from the seminarists with the help of a rope ladder.[49] Such were the happenings during 1905, 1906, and 1907. Much of the violence was probably due to local grievances— harsh discipline, bad food, and the like—but the disturbances were so widespread and so much more frequent than they had been before the Revolution that it is hard to believe that there was not some revolutionary spirit back of the outbreaks. And indeed there were other incidents in the seminaries which could not be charged to local circumstances nor to personal spite.

One very serious manifestation was the occurrence of sacrilegious or antireligious deeds. In the University of Kiev the students, many of them perhaps Jewish, when on strike were more respectful toward an ikon than were the students of the seminary of Taurida in their treatment of sacred things.[50] The seminarists of Simbirsk caused a "chemical obstruction"—i. e., created a highly obnoxious odor—in church while the service was in progress. The St. Petersburg students printed an open letter to the "council of professors of St. Petersburg

[45] *Tserkovnyi Vestnik,* March 16, 1906, col. 336.
[46] *Tserkovnyia Vedomosti,* Oct. 13, 1907, p. 1755.
[47] *Tserkovnyi Vestnik,* June 8, 1906, cols. 742–43.
[48] *Ibid.,* May 17, 1907, cols. 656–57.
[49] *Ibid.,* May 5, 1905, cols. 552–53.
[50] Sv. Sinod, *Zhurnaly i Protokoly . . . Predsobornago Prisutstviia,* IV, Division V, p. 250.

University," in which the young men declared that they had "neither the calling nor the desire to enter the priesthood or the religious academy," while a group of seminarists of Tobolsk proclaimed, "we do not know of one graduate of our seminary who has entered the priesthood out of sincere conviction." [51]

Doubtless the fact that the students were dissatisfied with school life inclined them favorably toward the radical ideas which were being circulated. Forty-eight of the fifty-eight seminaries experienced strikes in the autumn of 1905, and a congress of seminarists was held not long after.[52] A second congress of seminary students took place in December, 1906, after a fresh wave of strikes. Representatives of thirteen of the schools were present. Their meetings were held on Christmas Eve and on Christmas Day, when most people were in church. The demands of these seminary students, however, were far from devout. They declared that they had absolutely no religious belief at all, and sent messages to all the seminaries, urging opposition to the "sorry servants of the autocratic police regime," and recommending that their fellows join one or the other of the parties of the extreme Left.[53] More specifically they demanded the liberalizing of study and instruction in the seminaries, freedom to hold meetings and to organize, and the right to enter the universities without burdensome restrictions. These points in the program were followed by a declaration that a free school such as had been described would be possible only in a state that was really free. For this reason the seminary delegates urged their fellow students to resort to political action in such parties as the Socialist Revolutionary and the Social Democratic.[54]

It is difficult to say how well this program represented the sentiment of the majority of the seminarists. There is reason, however, to believe that socialist ideas had made their way into the seminaries on a fairly large scale. The students, according to one observer, read cheap leaflets on socialism, which infected them with a desire to save the proletariat.[55] On the other hand, another clerical commentator said that the students in his seminary read no theology, and were

[51] *Ibid.*   [52] *Tserkovnyi Vestnik,* Aug. 10, 1906, cols. 1031–33.
[53] *Tserkovnyia Vedomosti,* Oct. 13, 1907, p. 1756.
[54] *Ibid.,* Sept. 22, 1907, pp. 1621–23.
[55] *Tserkovnyi Vestnik,* Aug. 10, 1906, cols. 1031–33.

entirely ignorant concerning current theological periodicals, but when
an instructor asked if they knew the works of Kautsky and Bebel, all
had read them.[56] On May 1, 1906, many of the seminary students went
on strike, although some of their chief grievances had been remedied
and in spite of the knowledge that a strike was sure to mean the loss
of a full year's scholastic standing, if not permanent expulsion.[57] At
the seminary of Orel students held a solemn requiem, accompanied
by revolutionary orations, in honor of their fellows "who had fallen
in the fatal struggle for freedom"; in the Iaroslavl institution, even
the monks who served as instructors made fiery speeches to the students.[58] The seminarists of St. Petersburg also showed their radical
sympathies by welcoming Father Tikhvinskii,[59] whose outspoken remarks in the Second Duma have already been mentioned. Even as
late as August, 1908, after the revolutionary movement had spent its
force, the Synod urged the seminary staffs to make strenuous efforts
to inculcate the necessary patriotism and loyalty to the government in
the minds of their charges, as well as to ferret out materialistic literature and to eliminate it from the schools.[60] These facts seem to be in
harmony with the statement of a professor of the Religious Academy of Kiev, that in many instances the seminary students, when
beginning strikes, admitted that they had no local grievances.[61] Indeed the religious seminaries must have thoroughly discouraged the
heads of the church, for the same professor stated, "Such hostility,
hatred, and fierceness toward the heads of the schools, such violent
ways of showing dissatisfaction, such 'riots,' such extensive, long-
lasting strikes, of such an elemental character as those which take
place in the seminaries, are unknown in the secular secondary
school." [62]

The potency of the revolutionary ferment was further shown by
the academies, where the students were usually moderate. These

[56] *Tserkovnyia Vedomosti,* Oct. 13, 1907, p. 1760.
[57] *Tserkovnyi Vestnik,* Aug. 10, 1906, cols. 1031–33.
[58] Sv. Sinod, *Zhurnaly i Protokoly,* IV, Division V, p. 260.
[59] *Ibid.,* p. 250.
[60] *Tserkovnyia Vedomosti,* Aug. 16, 1908, official part, pp. 259–64.
[61] P. Krasin, "Vospitanie v Dukhovnoi Seminarii," *Trudy Kievskoi Dukhovnoi Akademii,* Aug.–Sept., 1906, p. 715.
[62] *Ibid.*

institutions experienced strikes and boycotts, and in the St. Petersburg Academy a solemn requiem was held for Lieutenant Schmidt of revolutionary fame—"for a murderer, a person guilty of many killings, who declared his unbelief before he died," as one indignant professor described him.[63] On another occasion, students of one of the academies printed a "bold and saddening letter to the archpastors of the Russian Church," which, the commentator said, filled all readers with astonishment "at seeing such insolence from students of one of the highest religious educational institutions. . . ."[64] One of the leading Russian theologians of the period stated that the disturbances in the academies were due not to internal conditions of discipline or food, but to sympathy with the radical ideas of the times. "The evil influence spoiling the academic atmosphere came to the academies from without."[65]

The evidence presented in the preceding pages points clearly to the fact that among the priests of Russia's towns and villages there was a small but significant minority who were willing to defy the civil and the religious authorities by displaying sympathy for the disturbed populace. Similar sentiments, in more extreme form, were more widely held by the students of the seminaries and of the religious academies. Quite a different state of affairs is noted among the bishops and the other higher clergy. Although, as will be shown later, there is an abundance of evidence that the hierarchy as a whole strongly disapproved of the upheaval of the people, it has proved exceedingly difficult to gather information about any bishops who sympathized with the "liberative movement." The newspapers and the other periodicals of the liberal camp, most of which would have been glad to note sympathetic views held by the upper clergy, failed to mention such manifestations. The only mention of liberalism on the part of any of the hierarchs which has come to light is found in the pages of *The Russian Banner,* an organ of the thoroughly reactionary Union of the Russian People.

An individual was not necessarily a radical because he incurred the dislike of this party; many persons of the mildest liberal sympathies were anathema to the Union of the Russian People. None the less,

[63] Sv. Sinod, *Zhurnaly i Protokoly,* IV, Division V, pp. 62–63.
[64] *Ibid.*   [65] *Ibid.*

the letter of Dubrovin, reactionary of note, to Metropolitan Antonii of St. Petersburg is important, if only because it shows how unusual liberalism was in the higher circles of the church. Dubrovin denounced the metropolitan because the latter had flatly refused to officiate at ceremonies of the Union of the Russian People, an organization which the metropolitan had repudiated with the words, "I do not sympathize with your parties of the Right, and I consider you to be terrorists; the terrorists of the Left throw bombs, while the Right parties, instead of throwing bombs, stone all those not in agreement with them." [66] Further, Dubrovin accused the metropolitan of fostering liberal vicarian bishops in his diocese and of protecting a group of thirty-two liberal priests of St. Petersburg who had printed several outspoken manifestoes; Fathers Gapon and Petrov, alleged radicals, were harbored by him, and he was said to have turned *The Church Messenger* and *The Church Voice* into "revolutionary organs." Within the Religious Academy of St. Petersburg, which Dubrovin alleged had become "a nest of revolutionaries," Metropolitan Antonii retained Abbot Mikhail even when that professor had proclaimed himself a socialist. Antonin, another liberal monastic, was also harbored, even after he had declared that autocracy was a heathen system, and had compared its defenders with the worshipers of the Dalai Lama. Finally, the catalogue of the metropolitan's sins included such offenses as failure to support the war with Japan with proper zeal, the ousting of several conservative churchmen, and the proposing of a reprimand for Metropolitan Vladimir of Moscow, who had issued a noted proclamation against the liberals.[67]

If this indictment were true *in toto*, then Metropolitan Antonii belonged in the liberal camp. The editor of *The Russian Banner*, like many extremists, was notoriously unreliable, but there is undoubtedly some truth in these statements. The northern capital did contain a number of liberal clergymen, and while eventually the St. Petersburg metropolitan moved against some of the more outspoken liberals, he did not stand out prominently as a leader of reaction. As far as can be determined, Metropolitan Antonii was for a time an isolated upholder of mild liberalism among an exceedingly conservative upper clergy.

[66] *Russkoe Znamia*, Supplement, Dec. 5, 1906.   [67] *Ibid*.

However, while the struggle for *political* innovations and reforms seems to have attracted comparatively few of the clergy, the movement for *ecclesiastical* reform was enthusiastically endorsed by many churchmen, both high and low. From time to time in the past there had arisen critics of the bureaucratic control of the church, which had been instituted by Peter, and an unsuccessful appeal had been made to Alexander II for the calling of a Church Council, or *Sobor*. During much of the long era of Pobedonostsev, such aspirations had to be forgotten, but by 1905 the social atmosphere had changed sufficiently to lend strong encouragement to hopes of reform.

Even as far back as 1902 the idea of a change in the control of the church had begun to revive: *Moskovskiia Vedomosti* (*The Moscow News*), politically a very conservative paper, printed an editorial urging that the head of the church should be the metropolitan of St. Petersburg, who should bear *ex officio* the title of patriarch. The Religious and Philosophical Conferences in St. Petersburg in 1903 voiced a belief that a council of the church should be called to make the needed reforms. *Novoe Vremia* (*The New Time*), a leading conservative newspaper of St. Petersburg, and *Bogoslovskii Vestnik* (*The Theological Messenger*) of the Religious Academy of Moscow, also urged that a council or *Sobor* be convened to give the church self-government.[68] But it was not until 1905 that the first steps were taken.

On December 12, 1904, the Tsar issued an *ukaz* promising a number of reforms, including the granting of religious toleration. The task of framing the necessary legislation was left to Count Witte and the Council of Ministers. However, it was not long before it became evident that to grant religious freedom, as had been promised, would greatly improve the position of the Old Believers and the sectarians and that the Orthodox Church would then be at a disadvantage in its competition with its rivals. Hence a special conference of the ministers was held, to which Metropolitan Antonii of St. Petersburg was summoned, in the absence of Pobedonostsev, who was ill at the time. It was contrary to precedent for the ecclesiastics to express their views except when urged to do so by the Over Procurator, but the

[68] F. V. Blagovidov, *K Rabote Obshchestvennoi Mysli po Voprosu o Tserkovnoi Reforme,* pp. 13–14.

metropolitan did so, in the form of questions. He asked whether the relations between church and state should not be subject to revision, so that the church might win more favor in the eyes of the people. Should not the state control over the church be lessened, as this control deprived the church of real influence? Would it not be better to allow the church to manage its own affairs entirely independently? Should not the clergy be given a share in the political institutions of the empire? and lastly—as parish autonomy and decentralization of control were necessary, and as these changes could be brought about only through a general reform of the administration of the church— should there not be a general gathering, or *Sobor,* of higher clergy, lower clergy, and laymen, to settle these several problems? [69]

These cautious suggestions were in harmony with the ideas of Witte, but he was not satisfied with the hesitant tone of the memorandum of the metropolitan. Witte consequently hastened to incorporate these ideas in a note which was presented to the emperor. In it he stated that to give religious freedom to the Old Believers and to the sects would hurt the Orthodox Church unless it, too, were given freedom. As evidence of this he pointed to the decline of the religious spirit among the educated classes, and even among the masses—a decline due to the formalism of the Orthodox Church, the lack of popular participation in its affairs, the absence of stimulating preaching, and the red tape of the consistorial bureaucracies. To remedy these failings a *Sobor* was needed—an institution characteristic both of early Rus and of the Orthodox Church. Witte declared that the church reforms of Peter were not canonical, and had perverted the Russian Church into a dry, official state institution with no real life. The Russian parish, instead of being a vigorous, popular organism, as it was of old, had lost its vitality, because the priest had been burdened with functions which made him an ally of the police, namely, the duty of violating the confessional, of helping to levy taxes, and the like; because the priests were a closed caste; and because the priests had to ask payment for their ministrations, which caused disaffection on the part of the peasants, who considered them to be *kulaks* (exploiters). To correct the weakness of the parish, the priest should be given a salary, either from the *zemstvo* or from the state.

[69] N. D. Kuznetsov, *Preobrazovanie v Russkoi Tserkvi,* pp. 7–10.

The parishioners should receive the right to elect their priest and to control the general affairs of the parish. Furthermore, religious education needed revision, as it was too formal and theoretical. Because of the restrictions upon the libraries of the seminaries, the seminary students received little training in meeting the arguments of their adversaries. All these failings, Witte said, were basic weaknesses of the church, which could be corrected only by a *Sobor* composed of laymen and of churchmen of all ranks.[70]

Soon after the presentation of Witte's memorandum, Pobedonostsev learned what was taking place and hastened to combat the move for a liberal church administration. He sturdily defended the reforms of Peter, and declared that there was no need for sweeping changes, since the bond between church and state was necessary for both, and brought no oppression of the clergy.[71] Witte soon replied to this, and an acrimonious interchange followed, which stopped only when the emperor, at the request of Pobedonostsev, took the matter out of the hands of the ministers and referred it to the Synod, on March 13, 1905.[72]

This apparent victory for the Over Procurator soon turned out to be a step in the direction of reform, however, for the Synod proceeded to draw up a report to the emperor, urging the calling of a *Sobor* and the naming of a patriarch, as well as most of the other changes advocated by Witte: reform of the diocesan administration and courts, and especially limitation of the power of the civil officials of the dioceses; reform of the religious seminaries; the granting of more autonomy to the parish; and the like.[73] Strong support for these proposals was given in an open letter of a group of thirty-two priests of St. Petersburg, who declared that the weaknesses of the Orthodox Church could be remedied only by a *Sobor* (March 17, 1905). Several of the moderate and liberal secular and ecclesiastical periodicals and newspapers also declared in favor of this proposal, notably *Tserkovnyi Vestnik* (*The Church Messenger*), *Rus'*, a moderate newspaper of St. Petersburg, *Birzhevyia Vedomosti* (*Bourse News*), the

---

[70] *Ibid.*, pp. 26–36.

[71] I. V. Preobrazhenskii, *Tserkovnaia Reforma: Sbornik Statei Dukhovnoi i Svetskoi Periodicheskoi Pechati po Voprosu o Reforme*, pp. 87–88.

[72] Kuznetsov, *op. cit.*, pp. 48–58.   [73] *Ibid.*, pp. 59–61.

organ of the financial interests, and *Slovo* (*The Word*), and *Svet* (*The World*), two liberal newspapers of the northern capital, as well as the conservative *Novoe Vremia* (*The New Time*).[74] Many letters were received by the editors of the liberal religious periodicals, *Tserkovnyi Vestnik, Bogoslovskii Vestnik* (*The Theological Messenger*), *Pravoslavnyi Sobesednik* (*The Orthodox Companion*), from the urban and the provincial clergy; almost all of them supported the idea of a *Sobor* which would include the parish or "white" clergy as well as the bishops.[75] The reactionary newspapers like *Moskovskiia Vedomosti* (*Moscow News*) were moderately disapproving of the proposal for a *Sobor*, or even, like *Den'* (*The Day*), denounced the idea as an attempt of the Jews to weaken the Orthodox Church; [76] but with an overwhelming sentiment in favor of the *Sobor*, the Synod felt emboldened to disregard this opposition. So strict was the rule that all official communications between the Synod and the Tsar must go through the Over Procurator, that the metropolitans and bishops of the Synod were obliged to transmit their proposals to the emperor through a subterfuge. Several of the churchmen went to him with an ikon for presentation and used the occasion to give him their petition.[77] Partial success attended this stratagem, for the emperor soon made this response to their resolution:

I feel that during the troubled time we are passing through it is impossible to accomplish so great a work as the calling of a Russian *Sobor*, which demands quiet and consideration. I propose, when a favorable time shall come, to set this great work in motion, after the ancient example of the Orthodox Emperors, and to call the *Sobor* of the All-Russian Church for canonical consideration of subjects of faith and church administration.[78]

In this fashion the obstacle of Pobedonostsev's disapproval was surmounted, and the proposal for the *Sobor* was placed in the hands of Nicholas II. Many of the parish clergy and their sympathizers were, however, far from pleased with the action of the bishops, for the latter in their petition to the emperor had asked for a church council

[74] Preobrazhenskii, *op. cit.*, pp. 1–47.
[75] *Ibid.*, p. 492.   [76] *Ibid.*, pp. 73–119.
[77] P. V. Verkhovskoi, *Uchrezhdenie Dukhovnoi Kollegii i Dukhovnyi Reglament*, I, clvii–clviii.
[78] *Tserkovnyia Vedomosti*, April 2, 1905, official part, p. 99.

which should be composed of the higher clergy only.[79] The moderate and liberal press came out strongly against such a narrow application of the conciliar principle,[80] and church periodicals and noted theologians added their voices to the chorus.[81] A typical comment was that of *Tserkovnyi Golos* (*The Voice of the Church*), which said, "We believe in the *infallibility of the church,* but do not believe in the *infallibility of the episcopate.* . . . The episcopate is not the church, but rather a part of it. . . . Its desire to usurp in the *Sobor* the place of the whole church . . . is sinful because it is egotistical." [82]

It is significant that the proposal to elect a patriarch to replace the Over Procurator as administrative head of the church likewise called forth a large amount of comment, both favorable and unfavorable. For the most part it was the ecclesiastical journals representing the liberal part of the white clergy which were critical of the restoration of the patriarchate. The most outspoken was *Tserkovno-obshchestvennaia Zhizn'* (*Church-Social Life*), which declared that the bishops were supporting the return of the patriarchal regime in order to increase the prerogatives of the hierarchy and the monks. The secular absolutism of the Over Procurator would be replaced by the absolutism of a bishop. Instead of a secular pope—the Over Procurator of the Synod—there would be a spiritual pope who would hold the church in his hands and would not break the chains. While this control would be more canonical, it would be no more desirable than the former variety.[83] *Bogoslovskii Vestnik* and the *Tserkovnaia Gazeta* (*The Church Gazette*) also opposed a restoration of the patriarchate. The latter journal declared that the patriarchate was a product of the development of the monarchical principle in the state. The original establishment of the patriarchate had marked the defeat of the conciliar principle and had contained the germs of papal supremacy and of clericalism.[84] If one may judge by these articles and by the letters which appeared in such important newspapers as *Novoe Vremia, Russkoe Slovo* (*The Russian Word*), a widely read Moscow newspaper, *Syn Otechestva* (*Son of the Fatherland*), a liberal news-

---

[79] Kuznetsov, *op. cit.,* pp. 62–63.   [80] Preobrazhenskii, *op. cit.,* pp. 533 ff.

[81] *Tserkovnyi Vestnik,* April 14, 1905, cols. 462–67; Myshtsyn, *Po Tserkovno-obshchestvennym Voprosam,* p. 24.

[82] A. Palmieri, *La Chiesa Russa,* p. 18, footnote.

[83] *Ibid.,* pp. 70–71, footnote.   [84] *Ibid.,* p. 76.

paper of St. Petersburg, and many others, many of the parish clergy and their supporters felt that it would be little better to have as head of the church a powerful patriarch instead of the Over Procurator.[85] Distrust of the upper clergy by the parish priests was spread on these pages for all to read.

Another important phase of the movement for ecclesiastical reform was the effort to renovate the diocesan administrative system. Much has been said in an earlier chapter about the weaknesses of the dioceses as administrative units. In 1905 and 1906 these failings were thoroughly aired. Count Witte's original proposals had included the reform of the diocese and of the parish and, although the summoning of a *Sobor* and the abolition of the Over Procurator's dominance over the church received greater attention from those desirous of change, reform of the local units of the church was not lost sight of. Embraced in this reform movement was an attempt to have the ranks of the episcopate open to married priests—the white clergy—through election by the clergy and the laymen of the dioceses.[86] Hopes were expressed that under this condition the bishops might be less domineering:

> We must cure our bishops of the disease of highhandedness, with which almost all of them are afflicted—a disease which often comes close to being despotism, and sometimes is nothing else; we must end the possibility of the selection of bishops who are flighty and headstrong, or shameful bribe-takers (we have known both kinds in our time); we must, finally, make peace between the monk-bishops and the white clergy. . . . We do not know and cannot say to what extent hostility to the monk-bishops has spread among the white clergy, but it is certain that in a very considerable part of our clergy it exists, and is very strong; we ourselves have several times witnessed how white priests froth at the mouth when discussing the bishops.[87]

So wrote Professor Golubinskii, author of a four-volume history of the church which was commended by Pobedonostsev, and holder of a chair at the Theological Academy of Moscow. Others felt that the gulf between the bishops and the lower clergy would be less deep and wide if the bishops were not so burdened with office work. They were

[85] A. Palmieri, *La Chiesa Russa*, pp. 74–76.

[86] V. Vvedenskii, in *Tserkovnyi Vestnik*, July 14, 1905, cols. 866–69; *Missionerskoe Obozrenie*, June, 1905, pp. 1452–54.

[87] E. E. Golubinskii, *O Reforme v Byte Russkoi Tserkvi*, pp. 116–17.

believed to know little of the life of the dioceses, so overwhelmed were they by the mountains of papers from the consistories. "The consistory kills the bishop." [88] Professor Butkevich illustrated the pettiness of the routine matters with which the bishops were burdened by stating that as president of the board of a diocesan women's school he had found it necessary to get the confirmation of the bishop before paying the teachers' salaries, and even before a copper could be spent to shoe a horse.[89] Others reformers turned their attention to the scantiness of the diocesan social work—the rarity of diocesan almshouses, night lodging houses, homes for wanderers.[90] But above all, the proponents of diocesan reform voiced urgent demands for sweeping changes, or even the abolition of the control of diocesan affairs by the consistory.

Mention has already been made of the failings of the consistorial administration which had been noticed in the years before the Revolution. During 1905 and 1906 the same facts were presented, the same criticisms reworded; the red tape, the inefficient procedure were again described by critics and investigators.[91] The bureaucratic and inequitable nature of consistorial trials was again criticized.[92] Above all, however, those who urged diocesan reform disapproved of the well-known fact that the priests who were the actual members of the consistories made little attempt to formulate policies and to make decisions, but rather left them to the lay staffs of officials in the consistory chanceries.[93] Nor did these critics fail to point out that the power placed in the hands of these poorly paid officials led, in many cases, to bribe-taking and extortion. In fact, these charges were supported in striking fashion by a secretary of one of the consistories, who sent in to *Tserkovnyi Vestnik* an explanation of the causes of the failings of the diocesan administrations. He stated that the average

[88] Arkhimandrite Mikhail, in *Tserkovnyi Vestnik,* July 21, 1905, cols. 897–901.
[89] Sv. Sinod, *Zhurnaly i Protokoly,* I, 430.
[90] *Tserkovnyi Vestnik,* April 5, 1907, col. 461.
[91] *Ibid.,* July 21, 1905, cols. 897–901; June 15, 1906, col. 793; Sv. Sinod, *Zhurnaly i Protokoly,* I, 428, 509, 512.
[92] Sv. Sinod, *Otzyvy Eparkhial'nykh Arkhiereev po Voprosu o Tserkovnoi Reforme,* I, 150, 224, 295–96, 524.
[93] *Tserkovnyia Vedomosti,* March 12, 1905, p. 466; Sv. Sinod, *Zhurnaly i Protokoly,* I, 510.

consistory of a diocese had to handle nearly forty thousand documents a year—that is, nearly ten thousand for each of the departments of the chancery. This quantity of work, he stated, was much greater than that required of the chanceries of civil institutions of comparable standing. He added: "The consistories are denounced for slowness, but a worse evil is that of bribe-taking. If we continue the comparison [with offices of the civil government], then we will not wonder that, in spite of all the measures taken, no one has succeeded in stamping it out." The cause of this evil, he stated, was the scanty pay of the consistorial officials, which forced them to resort to corruption.[94]

According to many earnest supporters of the church, one of the fundamental causes of its weakness lay in this unsatisfactory condition of the diocesan administration. Such persons believed that it would be useless to talk of establishing the conciliar principle in the church unless the uncanonical control by the lay bureaucrats of the consistorial chanceries, and especially by their secretaries, could be done away with, and unless in place of this irresponsible lay control there could be instituted a new system of diocesan control, subject to the wishes of elected councils of laymen and clergy. The church could not be truly conciliar at the top, if its local subdivisions remained centers of petty despotism.[95]

In the opinion of many noted reformers, another part of the church which stood in urgent need of the introduction of the conciliar principle was the parish. These reformers pointed to the many evidences of absolute control of the parish from above. The priests were appointed by the bishops and the consistories, in most cases without the formality of consulting the wishes of the parishioners.[96] The pastors were subject to transfer from one parish to another at the whim of the diocesan authorities; such transfers were often made for reasons of politics or favoritism or grudges.[97] The priests were overburdened with office work, which made it difficult for them to find time for the proper performance of their pastoral duties. Another complaint was

[94] Secretary of a Consistory N. N., in *Tserkovnyi Vestnik,* March 10, 1905, cols. 300–4.
[95] N. V. Ognev, *Na Poroge Reform Russkoi Tserkvi i Dukhovenstva,* pp. 15–16; *Missionerskoe Obozrenie,* June, 1905, p. 1453.
[96] Preobrazhenskii, *Tserkovnaia Reforma,* p. 422.
[97] *Tserkovnyi Vestnik,* Aug. 31, 1906, col. 1146.

that the constant supervision from above, with the threat of punishment if the displeasure of their superiors were incurred, hindered a bold exercise of spiritual functions.[98] As for the parishioners, they had no share in the parish activities or in the control of the property and the funds of the churches. This often led to the burdening of the parish churches with diocesan dues and imposts, which the congregation knew little about or were unable to prevent if they did know.[99] Many students of the question ascribed to this non-participation of the congregation in parish affairs the decline that was so evident in the religious feeling of the people.[100]

The parish clergy and their partisans were not entirely consistent, however, for while they wanted to grant a measure of self-government to the various parts of the church, they were very eager to provide the priests with a source of income other than the fees exacted from the people. Dependence upon payment for ministrations was felt by the priests to be too fertile a source of conflict with the peasants, who were prone to bargain with the clergy over the fees for baptisms, weddings, or funerals, and often regarded the priests as extortioners and at times made complaints to the consistory if they felt that the charges were too high.[101] Hence the white clergy and their friends were eager that the priests be given state salaries in place of the collections for ministrations and of other payments by the parishioners. Some of the priests were even willing to surrender the parish lands to the peasants, if the state would pay pastoral salaries;[102] others clung to their plots of ground, but with one accord they sought for state support.

There was disagreement on other details of parish reform. Some reformers wanted to have the parish priests chosen by the parishioners, with the confirmation of the bishop;[103] this proposal, however, was frequently omitted from the lists of desiderata drawn up by the

[98] "Pastyrskoe Oskudenie," *Tserkovno-obshchestvennaia Zhizn'*, No. 23, 1906, p. 778, as quoted in Palmieri, *La Chiesa Russa*, p. 320.

[99] A. Boldovskii, *Vozrozhdenie Tserkovnago Prikhoda* (*Obzor Mnenii Pechati*), pp. 59–60; *Tserkovnyi Vestnik*, June 30, 1905, cols. 816–18.

[100] *Bogoslovskii Vestnik*, Oct., 1902, quoted in Boldovskii, *op. cit.*, p. 26.

[101] *Vera i Razum*, Jan. 1, 1906, pp. 31–32; *ibid.*, March 1, 1906, p. 232.

[102] *Tserkovnyia Vedomosti*, March 25, 1906, pp. 619–21.

[103] Ognev, *Na Poroge Reform*, p. 16; "Golos Sel'skago Sviashchennika," *Tserkovnyi Vestnik*, quoted in Preobrazhenskii, *Tserkovnaia Reforma*, p. 421.

priests themselves. Another suggestion was that the parishioners might be permitted to meet for the purpose of discussing the affairs of the parish and to elect a parish council—a vestry—to share in the control of the property and the funds of the parish; [104] under the existing conditions, the control was in the hands of the priest and the *starosta,* or elder; the latter, while elected for three years by the congregation, could not be removed or disciplined during his term of office by the parishioners.[105] The Synod showed willingness to make concessions on this point without waiting for the calling of the *Sobor,* for in a decree of October 18, 1905, it declared that where the people desired they might hold parish meetings, at which they might elect vestries of twelve men. "The members of the vestry may be asked by the clergy and the parish elder to participate in the handling of the church finances." However, the powers of these vestries and of the parish meetings were not defined, and their decisions were to be subject to the approval of the diocesan authorities, who were to have the power to decide all cases in which misunderstandings arose.[106] Not even partial success met the proposal to give the parish the rights of a corporation, including the power to acquire and to sell property,[107] but the demand for this reform was never very strong. Likewise the suggestion that in place of the district priests councils of priests should be elected to act as courts of first instance for the clergy, was not acted on by the Synod, but remained one of the many questions postponed for consideration by the *Sobor.*

Discussion of the proposals for ecclesiastical reform would not be complete without mention of the demands for a remedy of the abuses of the monasteries. *Tserkovnyi Vestnik* took the lead against them, advancing to the attack with the help of ammunition supplied by several of the diocesan publications. The bishop of Orel, it said, had criticized the wandering and the immorality of the novices, and the hiring of too many outside workers. ". . . Monasteries must not resemble lords' estates, or asylums for healthy men." From Novgorod came criticism of the nuns for their too-active quest for donations, which

---

[104] Boldovskii, *op. cit.,* pp. 12–16; Ognev, *op. cit.,* p. 30.
[105] Sv. Sinod, *Ustav Dukhovnykh Konsistorii,* secs. 94–96.
[106] *Tserkovnyia Vedomosti,* Nov. 26, 1905, official part, pp. 523–25.
[107] *Ibid.*

took them into shops, railroad stations, liquor stores, restaurants, and the like. At an official congress of the clergy of the diocese of Perm, some of the delegates decided that the monasteries were an evil influence and that most of them should be closed.[108] The consistory of Kazan found that the monasteries of that diocese were violating rules when taking ikons out on processions to the villages; the monks failed to observe properly the precepts of decorum, and displayed a careless attitude when performing ceremonies.[109] And finally *Tserkovnyi Vestnik*, which cited these instances, declared that the inmates of most of the monasteries were chiefly interested in obtaining donations from the public, and that true religious feeling was not in them.[110] From reading this periodical, one gathers the impression that it was so hostile to the control of the church by the monastic hierarchy that it hoped to discredit the higher clergy by attacking monasticism in general.

However, *Tserkovnyi Vestnik* was not the only church journal to call attention to failings of the monasteries. *Tserkovnyia Vedomosti*, the official publication of the Synod, to which all parishes were required to subscribe, also printed some unfavorable comment. In 1906 it stated that Bishop Arsenii of Pskov had found it necessary to take in hand the work of straightening out the affairs of the monastic institutions in his diocese. In order that the monks—for the most part expelled seminary students or simple peasants—might overcome their weaknesses, he ruled that strict control must be established over them: all must labor; all must eat at the common table; no women were to be allowed within the cells of the monks; and all must perform their worship properly.[111] This periodical reprinted a sermon of Antonii, of the Kirillo-Belozerskii Monastery, to his fellow monks, which contained the following salient phrases:

From the pulpit we . . . say that God loves labor, that he commanded man to gain his bread by the sweat of his brow; and nevertheless we do nothing, we amass capital, we forget the slightest self-restraint, and on love of our neighbor we look as on an obligation which does not apply to us who are monks. . . .

If in the West, monasticism is dying from political causes, with us,

[108] *Tserkovnyi Vestnik*, Sept. 7, 1906, cols. 1178–80.
[109] *Ibid.*, July 14, 1905, col. 888. [110] *Ibid.*, Oct. 4, 1907, cols. 1284–86.
[111] *Tserkovnyia Vedomosti*, March 18, 1906, p. 596.

although unaffected by politics, it is dying as a result of the fact that in spirituality and morality it is continually sinking lower and lower.[112]

Reform of monasticism was the final point in the schedule for the reform of the church. Monastic reform, however, did not involve the reintroduction of the conciliar principle, which was the heart and substance of the other phases of the reform movement. Most of the hopes of those who wanted important changes in the church centered in the introduction of a more representative form of control. It was expected that not only would democratization of the church be applied to its central administration, but also that it would be the guiding principle in establishing better conditions for diocesan and parish life. Almost all reformers believed that the authority of a general council of the Russian Church would be necessary in taking the first steps toward abolishing time-hallowed abuses. The calling of the *Sobor,* to be sure, had been deferred until the occasion might be more propitious; but the *Sobor* was not to be entirely forgotten. In July, 1905, the Synod asked the bishops to send in their opinions on the questions of church reform: on the *Sobor,* on the proper form for the higher administration of the church, on diocesan and parish reorganization. It was hoped by many who were desirous of reconstructing the church that the reports of the bishops would lead directly to the longed-for assembly.

Sixty-two bishops sent in their views to the Synod before the end of January, 1906. They were almost unanimous in their desire to have the control of the church in their own hands. An overwhelming majority wanted the voting in the *Sobor* to be by the higher clergy only, although many were willing to have members of the lower clergy and the laymen, elected by their fellows or appointed by the bishops, present in a consultative capacity. Twenty-three bishops expressed a desire to have a patriarch who should be head of the church and should act as its spokesman before the emperor, but they wished him to be merely *primus inter pares.* The bishops had no wish to grant to the patriarch powers which would lead him to follow the path of papal absolutism.[113] Furthermore, distrust of the attitude of the

[112] *Tserkovnyia Vedomosti,* Dec. 21, 1906, p. 3173.
[113] Sv. Sinod, *Otzyvy Eparkhial'nykh Arkhiereev,* three vols. and supplement.

lower clergy was shown by the fact that only five of the prelates voted in favor of the election of bishops or their selection from the ranks of the parish priests.[114]

On the other hand, the recommendations of the bishops gave strong support to the principle of conciliar action; often these recommendations showed a liberal trend which did not harmonize readily with the contemporary actions and the public utterances of some of the more reactionary hierarchs. Nearly all of the bishops favored the creation of metropolitanates, where councils would be held from time to time to dispose of some of the business hitherto handled by the Synod. The diocesan congresses of the clergy, which had been strictly limited in competence, should be permitted to discuss pertinent matters of all sorts; their recommendations, however, should be carried out only with the approval of the bishops of the respective dioceses.[115] Thirty-nine of the bishops were of the opinion that the consistory must be replaced by a council of presbyters, composed in whole or in part of members elected by the clergy of the diocese. The judicial functions of the consistory should be placed in the hands of judges, elected by the clergy, who should use the procedure employed in the contemporary civil courts (except that there was to be no jury). Even the bishops who wanted to retain the consistories felt that they needed thorough renovation, and almost all of the hierarchs were determined to have the staffs of the diocesan administrations appointed and removable by the clergy or the bishops of the dioceses, rather than by the central administration of the church.[116] The bishops also believed that the interests of the dioceses would be furthered if the practice of transferring bishops from place to place were stopped, or at least greatly curtailed.[117] In their opposition to the election of bishops they took a stand which was opposed to the democratization of the church, but in general their proposals showed a realization that the diocesan administration stood in need of broad reforms.

The suggestions of the bishops for improving the parish administration displayed a readiness to permit much more freedom than hitherto. The parishioners, through their meetings and elected vestries, should exercise a great deal of control over the affairs of the

[114] *Ibid.*   [115] *Ibid.*   [116] *Ibid.*   [117] *Ibid.*

parish. The people should have the right either to elect their own priests or, as most of the bishops advised, to express preferences which, when possible, should be considered by the bishops when making appointments. Very considerable sentiment was shown in favor of turning over the disciplinary and supervisory powers exercised by the district priests to councils elected by the clergy themselves.[118] Also the morale of the future priesthood would presumably be raised by the more liberal conditions of seminary education advocated by the bishops. They urged that in the seminaries the sons of priests be given training equivalent to that offered by the secular gymnasia, and that those who completed the course should have full freedom to enter the universities if their means permitted. For students who had completed the equivalent of the gymnasium course and who desired to become priests, whether they came from priestly families or not, a three-year course in theology should be offered. Thus it was hoped to end the dissatisfaction of the priests—who disliked having their sons, who often yearned for a career in civil life, enter the priesthood—as well as to bring into the ranks of the clergy a group of more zealous and sincere men. Finally, almost all of the bishops spoke in favor of having the lower clergy take part in political life, even to the extent of accepting election to the Duma.[119]

While these opinions were still being collected, a further step was taken in the direction of a church council. On January 14, 1906, the emperor appointed a Pre-*Sobor* Conference, to be made up of ten bishops and metropolitans and twenty-one of the leading professors of the religious academies and the universities; Prince Obolenskii, who had replaced Pobedonostsev as Over Procurator on October 20, 1905, and his assistant were also ordered to attend. The purpose of this conference was to prepare the agenda for the coming *Sobor* and to reach preliminary conclusions for its guidance.[120] This step was not, however, entirely welcome to those who placed most hope in the results of the expected *Sobor*. The members of this conference had been appointed entirely too secretly and in too autocratic a fashion for the taste of the liberals of the church. Many of the latter also voiced disappointment because no representatives of the lower clergy

[118] Sv. Sinod, *Otzyvy Eparkhial'nykh Arkhiereev.*
[119] *Ibid.*
[120] *Tserkovnyia Vedomosti*, Jan. 21, 1906, official part.

were included.[121] On the other hand, the conservative members of the church expected little good from the conference. Archbishop Antonii of Volhynia wrote:

There are some real atheists in it (Kliuchevskii, Mashanov) and some Protestantizers (Golubinskii, Svetlov, Rozhdestvenskii), many fools, very many sad drunkards (Kliuchevskii, Mashanov, Ivanov, Chistiakov, Zaozerskii, Glubokovskii, Golubev, Butkevich), but the chief thing is . . . all of them, whether liberals or conservatives, are *priestlings* [i. e., sons of priests].[122]

The use of the term "priestlings" suggests that perhaps these professors might be disposed to support the claims of the parish priests in the Pre-*Sobor* Conference. However, the findings of the conference were not entirely satisfactory to the liberals among the lower clergy. For the most part the recommendations of the bishops were closely followed. The conference proposed the election of a patriarch to preside at the *Sobors* and at the meetings of the Synod; he should act as the church's representative in its dealings with the civil power, and supervise the enforcement of the decrees of the Synod, but should have no other special powers. *Sobors* should be held at regular intervals to elect the patriarchs and the Synod, and to decide questions important to the church. The conference urged that the *Sobors* should include one layman and one priest from each diocese, who should be appointed by the bishop from candidates named by the diocesan congress. The voting power, however, should be reserved solely to the bishops. During the interval between the sessions of the *Sobors*, the Synod was to act as the ruling body for the church. The conference wished the Over Procurator to be merely an observer of the actions of the *Sobor* and of the Synod, with the right to raise objections if he considered that the interests of the state were in danger.[123]

In its proposals for the selection of bishops, the conference failed to urge the abolition of the old rule that only monastics could become bishops. On the other hand, it introduced a decided novelty by proposing that the bishops should be chosen by local *sobors*, to be held in the seven metropolitanates (the creation of three new metropolitans

---

[121] *Tserkovnyi Golos*, quoted in *Tserkovnyi Vestnik*, Feb. 16, 1906, col. 202.
[122] *Krasnyi Arkhiv*, 1928, No. 31, p. 209.
[123] Sv. Sinod, *Zhurnaly i Protokoly*, II, 670–73.

was suggested). The bishops should be named from candidates proposed by the congresses of the clergy and the laymen of the several dioceses. The diocesan administration should be in the hands of the bishop and the diocesan board (*pravlenie*) ; unlike the old consistory, the diocesan board was to consist of three members elected by the diocesan congress and approved by the bishop, as well as three appointees of the bishop. The secretary should be named by the bishop and approved by the Synod.[124] The proposals of the conference assigned to the diocesan board no new powers in the diocesan administration. In general it should take the place of the consistory, except that it should not exercise judicial functions.[125]

The proposals which the conference adopted for the reform of the diocesan judicial system provided extensive changes. Not only should there be local courts to handle minor cases; special diocesan courts should be instituted, consisting of an equal number of appointed and elected members, the latter to be chosen by the diocesan clergy; all members were to receive confirmation by the Synod. That both complainants and defendants should appear in person before the court was a significant feature of the new judicial system. The power to confirm or disapprove the decisions of the court was, however, as before granted to the bishop. Moreover, a trial should be undertaken only after an investigation, and then only with the approval of the bishop.[126]

With respect to the parish, the conference adopted a general formula which affirmed the right of the clergy and the congregation to administer the parish property, subject to the control of the bishop.[127] Finally by a close vote it was decided to settle the problem of the religious seminaries by continuing the combination of a general educational course with theological training, the proposal for separating the theological and the general courses being rejected.[128]

When these decisions of the Pre-*Sobor* Conference were published, they occasioned a number of highly critical articles in the liberal organs of the ecclesiastical press. An especially sharp fire was directed at the proposal that the members of the *Sobor* from the white clergy

[124] Sv. Sinod, *Zhurnaly i Protokoly*, III, 384–85.   [125] *Ibid.*
[126] *Ibid.*, III, 385–86.   [127] *Ibid.*, III, 386.
[128] *Ibid.*, II, 671.

and from the ranks of the laymen should have merely a consultative voice. Moreover, the system by which they were to be chosen seemed designed to limit the influence of these two groups in the *Sobor*.[129] Thus *Tserkovnyi Vestnik* quoted with approval the words of *Novoe Vremia* (*The New Time*) that "there is a struggle going on between the partisans of episcopal domination and the representatives of the conciliar principle." [130] On another occasion the ecclesiastical journal stated, "*Novoe Vremia* is disturbed by the fact that under the name *Sobor* something else is being fabricated—a congress of bishops." [131] A note of disillusionment crept into the comments of some of the ecclesiastical editors: "Hitherto, expectations have centered in the nation-wide *Sobor*. Now, after the work of the Pre-*Sobor* Conference, some among the clergy are beginning to speak of 'crushed hopes.' " [132] However, there were still those who remained confident that the *Sobor* would meet in the near future, and that it would be able to do much toward improving the condition of the Russian Church.

When Count Witte had urged reform of the church, the chief reason which he had given was that the new privileges and rights granted to the Old Believers and the sectarians would give them the advantage in their struggle with the Orthodox Church. The process of extending the rights of the non-Orthodox had begun in December, 1904, when the emperor issued an *ukaz* in which he promised several reforms, among them religious liberty.[133] This set of promises was to be the basis for later legislation. A temporary enactment on religious liberty came on April 17, 1905. One of its provisions enabled anyone to leave the Orthodox Church in order to enter any other Christian faith, with no loss of rights and no other penalties. The law provided that if parents changed from one belief to another, their children under fourteen years of age would take the new faith of the parents; however, if one of the latter remained in the original belief, the younger children were likewise to stay in that faith. Children of fourteen years or more were not to leave the church, even if their parents did, until they

[129] *Tserkovnyi Vestnik*, Aug. 31, 1906, cols. 1130–31; *Tserkovno-obshchest-vennaia Zhizn'*, May 19, 1906, cols. 742–46.
[130] *Tserkovnyi Vestnik*, May 18, 1906, col. 640.
[131] *Ibid.*, June 1, 1906, cols. 716–17.
[132] *Ibid.*, Aug. 17, 1906, col. 1071.
[133] *Polnoe Sobranie Zakonov*, 1904, No. 25495.

reached the age of twenty-one. These provisions applied not only to the Old Believers and the sects, but also to the other non-Orthodox faiths; [134] hence it is not surprising that after the publication of the law of April 17 many who had found it politic to adhere to the official church moved to make a formal change of religious profession.

The serious nature of the defections from the Orthodox Church was indicated by the *Report* of the Over Procurator for 1905, 1906, and 1907. During these years numerous reversions from Orthodoxy to the Catholic Church took place in the western dioceses. The total ran as high as 119, 278 in the diocese of Kholm, with many also in the dioceses of Lithuania, Minsk, Warsaw, and Grodno, and other districts. [135] *Tserkovnyia Vedomosti* admitted that 233,000 persons in all left the Orthodox Church to join the Catholic faith in the years from 1905 to 1909; [136] and although the Over Procurator's *Report* attempted to gloss over the defections by saying that most of these people had been only nominally Orthodox, as their ancestors had accepted the Orthodox faith because of police pressure, [137] still the losses were not pleasant for the official church. Moreover, 14,500 were lost to the Lutheran Church, and some 50,000 reverted to Mohammedanism during these years, in addition to smaller groups who went back to their native Buddhism or heathenism, and those Jews who returned to the faith of their fathers. In all, the number of persons who deserted the ranks of the Orthodox to join the above denominations from April 17, 1905, to May 1, 1909, was officially set at 301,450. [138] How many others changed their religions without the formality of public registration of the change cannot here be determined.

The Orthodox Church published no statistics on the number of people who left the Orthodox communion to join the Old Believers and the sectarians during this period. There is reason to believe that their number was large. For one thing, the law of April 17, 1905, granted these denominations rights which they had not previously legally enjoyed. Their religious congregations were permitted to own property; their clergy were freed from military service and were to

---

[134] *Sobranie Uzakonenii i Rasporiazhenii Pravitel'stva*, 1905, No. 526.
[135] Sv. Sinod, *Vsepoddanneishii Otchet*, 1905–7, p. 29.
[136] *Tserkovnyia Vedomosti*, March 6, 1910, p. 475.
[137] Sv. Sinod, *Vsepoddanneishii Otchet*, 1905–7, pp. 33–34.
[138] *Tserkovnyia Vedomosti*, March 6, 1910, p. 475.

be entitled to use ecclesiastical titles. All of their houses of prayer which had been sealed up were to be opened, and a general permission to build new ones was granted. The Old Believers and the sectarians were no longer to be required to bury their dead in the Orthodox cemeteries, but were entitled to have their own. And it would now be possible to legitimatize their marriages and births, since their clergy were given the right to keep parish record-books. Other important rights conferred on the Old Believers and the sectarians by the decree of April 17 were eligibility for public office and that of organizing schools, subject to the jurisdiction of the Ministry of Public Education. Moreover, their children in the public schools might be given religious instruction by properly qualified persons of their own religious denominations.[139]

Under these favorable circumstances the Old Believers started a wide movement to open houses of prayer, considerably aided by a circular in harmony with the new law, which was sent by the Minister of Internal Affairs to the governors of the provinces on April 21, 1905. The governors were ordered "to unseal all houses of prayer which have been closed both by administrative order and as a result of the decisions of courts of law. . . . The unsealing of all houses of prayer is to be done without any ceremony, and without permitting any external manifestation which might lead to the disaffection of Orthodox persons." [140] However, for the Old Believers it was not enough merely to open their old houses of prayer; even before this they had begun to seek the construction of new ones. On January 2, 1905, a group of Cossacks of the province of Orenburg petitioned the Minister of Internal Affairs for permission to construct a new house of prayer in place of their old tumble-down building. This petition had previously been rejected by the governor of the province; but none the less, on April 27 he reversed himself, saying "at present, in view of the freedom given to the Old Believers, I, for my part, would propose to grant the above petition." This was done by the Minister of Internal Affairs soon after.[141] Nor was this an exceptional instance, for Old

[139] *Sobranie Uzakonenii*, 1905, No. 526.
[140] Ministerstvo Vnutrennyih Del, Department Obshchikh Del, 1905, portfolio 5. [Referred to below as M. V. D.]
[141] M. V. D., Dep. Obshchikh Del, 1905, portfolio 7.

Believers in the provinces of Perm and Viatka met with the same success.[142] In the province of Minsk a group of schismatics even received permission to hang a bell upon their house of prayer, and to place a cross over the door [143]—privileges unheard of a year earlier.

An indication of the activity of the Old Believers is given by the great increase in 1905 in the number of petitions which they presented asking for permission to open houses of prayer. The number of such requests was 40 in 1902. By 1904 it had risen to 74, and in 1905, 135 petitions were sent in to the Ministry of Internal Affairs.[144] And as these petitions were almost invariably granted in 1905,[145] instead of being rejected as in years past, the opportunities for schismatics to attend services of their cults must have increased considerably.

In other important ways the changed attitude of the government aided the Old Believers. In December, 1905, a group of schismatics in Siberia asked that their religious leader be excused from military service. It was decided that, in view of the new legislation, all religious ministers of the Old Believers would be exempted from military duty.[146] On other occasions several congregations of Old Believers in different provinces asked permission to organize religious processions around their houses of prayer at Easter or on other festival days. These petitions, too, were granted.[147] The Minister of Internal Affairs was ready also to satisfy two requests of the Old Believers in 1905 for the legitimatizing of their marriages.[148]

The treatment accorded to sectarians in 1905 also indicated a new spirit, although full evidence is lacking. A group of *Molokane* living in Erivan petitioned that they be permitted to have a house of prayer. The Ministry of Internal Affairs was not called upon to make a decision, however, for on April 30 the governor of Erivan announced that he had already given permission to hold services in a specially built

[142] M. V. D., Dep. Obshchikh Del, 1905, portfolios 58 and 105.

[143] M. V. D., Dep. Obshchikh Del, 1905, portfolio 191.

[144] M. V. D., Dep. Obshchikh Del, *Opis' Del I-ago Stola (po chasti raskola) III Otdeleniia, 1890–1905.*

[145] Eight portfolios dealing with such requests were examined for the year 1905; all were granted, and no case of refusal was found.

[146] M. V. D., Dep. Obshchikh Del, 1905, portfolio 221.

[147] M. V. D., Dep. Obshchikh Del, 1905, portfolio 44.

[148] M. V. D., Dep. Obshchikh Del, 1905, portfolios 104 and 197.

prayer house.[149] Again, when a group of sectarians in Odessa complained that the local police had broken up their prayer meeting and had beaten, insulted, and flogged them, their complaints were not disregarded as once would have been the case. Instead, the Minister of Internal Affairs took up the matter with the governor of Kherson, who reported that the offending police had already been dismissed and brought to trial for their unlawful actions.[150]

Thus after the decree of April 17, 1905, both the Old Believers and the sectarians enjoyed a more tolerant attitude on the part of the Imperial government. There were, moreover, some later laws and favorable administrative decisions. The decree of June 25, 1905, provided for the pardoning of persons convicted of the less serious religious offenses; for those punished for serious offenses—those of the *Skoptsy*, for example—the sentences were commuted to one-half or one-third of the original penalties.[151] Less favorable to these denominations were the new rules governing changes from the Orthodox faith to another Christian belief. These rules, issued in a circular of the Minister of Internal Affairs to governors on August 18, 1905, supplemented the decree of April 17. The person wishing to leave the official church was to inform the police, who would then notify the governor of the province of this declaration. The governor was required to approve the change before a month had elapsed, but in the meantime the Orthodox clergy, who had at once been notified of the impending defection,[152] would have ample time to attempt to persuade the person concerned not to leave the Orthodox faith. However, the law of October 17, 1906, providing for the organization of the Old Believers and the sectarians into "congregations" with self-government and the right to own property, was liberal enough to cause mild rejoicing among the members of these religious groups. Even the provision of this law that only the Orthodox Church was permitted to carry on propaganda among the members of other faiths [153] did not obscure the fact that the legal position of these two groups had improved greatly since 1904.

[149] M. V. D., Dep. Obshchikh Del, 1905, portfolio 35.
[150] M. V. D., Dep. Obshchikh Del, 1905, portfolio 32.
[151] *Sobranie Uzakonenii*, 1905, No. 1035.
[152] I. S. Berdnikov, *Kratkii Kurs Tserkovnago Prava*, p. 1323.
[153] *Pravo*, Oct. 22, 1906, cols. 3217–21.

Undoubtedly the effect of this more favorable official attitude was to promote the growth of the Old Believers and the sects. To the missionaries of the Orthodox Church, however, this official toleration of their rivals was very dispiriting. The head of the church's internal missions, Skvortsov, declared that never had this form of missionary work been so unsuccessful as in 1906, because the government had taken away "its hand of authority and law, which had suppressed the free, unpunished sowing of the tares of false teaching in Christ's field." He stated that the Old Believers and the sectarians were active, while the Orthodox clergy were discouraged and had almost given up their efforts against their exultant rivals.[154] Another reason for the success of these faiths was that many of their internal theological differences were done away with in 1906. In July of that year the largest denomination of Old Believers—the so-called Austrian group—which for decades had been split over the question of the correct attitude toward the government and the official church, composed their differences. According to the agreement reached, the Old Believers should pray for the Tsar, but should resist all overtures from, and compromises with, the state church.[155] There had already been a coalition of the chief sectarian groups. On May 31, 1906, at Rostov-on-the-Don, the Stundists, the Baptists, the *Pashkovtsy* (a small sect in St. Petersburg), and the Evangelical Christians (the *Dukhobortsy* and the *Molokane*), had united under the name of "Evangelical Christian Baptists." [156] These groups merged by compromising their theological differences, although they retained their separate organizations. Thus both the sectarians and the Old Believers, by closing their ranks, strengthened themselves for the fray.

The government was not long in disclosing a leading motive for its new policy toward the Old Believers. In April, 1905, the Tsar sent a telegram to the governor general of Moscow, ordering him to unseal the altar of the Rogozhskoe Cemetery, that great center of the priestly Old Believers in Moscow. To the official command the emperor added, "May God bless them and make them wise so that they may, in all sincerity, coöperate with the desires and the attempts of the Orthodox

[154] *Missionerskoe Obozrenie*, Jan., 1907, pp. 126–27.
[155] *Ibid.*, June, 1907, pp. 964–65.   [156] Berdnikov, *op. cit.*, p. 1324.

Church to unite them with it, and to end the burdensome historic church Schism, which only the church can end, by a decision of the *Sobor.*"[157] The Old Believers were delighted with the opening of their religious center, and during the solemn ceremony when the altar was unsealed many of them wept for joy, the choir sang "long life" to the emperor, and several noted members of the cult expressed heart-felt gratitude to him for this concession. It is significant, however, that no mention was then made of reuniting with the Orthodox Church.[158] In fact, although several members of the Pre-*Sobor* Conference spoke in favor of recognizing the authority of the Old Believer bishops if they should make their peace with the official church,[159] the Austrian sect of the Old Believers moved away from union with this body. When the two wings of this important Old Believer group merged, the more moderate fraction agreed to accept a resolution condemning "the Nikonian Church"[160]—a development which did not promise the early reconciliation for which the Tsar had hoped.

The attempts of the government to gain the political support of the Old Believers met with no better success. When, in December, 1905, representatives of the *Bezpopovtsy* (priestless) for the first time attended the sixth annual congress of the Austrian following, the president of the congress, at the request of the local governor (who probably feared unfavorable action on the part of the gathering), refused to let the assembly discuss the question of a vote of thanks to the emperor for the concessions granted to them. However, this dis-creet policy was not satisfactory to some of the younger members of the congress: they held a rump meeting and spoke bitterly against the government. They declared that the concessions made to them were merely a trick—that they had existed as a faith for 250 years without favors from the ruling powers, and could still do so. What Russia really needed, they said, was a constituent assembly. On the other hand, during the regular sessions of the congress, Kartushin, Old Believer Bishop of Moscow, took a very conservative attitude, declaring that the Manifesto of October 17 was a forced surrender by the

[157] *Missionerskoe Obozrenie*, May, 1905, pp. 1200–1.
[158] *Ibid.*, 1202–4. [159] *Ibid.*, April, 1910, p. 702.
[160] *Ibid.*, June, 1907, pp. 964–65.

emperor and urging his coreligionists to try to prevent limitation of the imperial will.[161] According to an observer who reported the meeting, most of the Old Believers probably held political views which were between these two extremes. The older members seemed to accept the program of the Cadet party, except for a few capitalists who were Octobrists, somewhat to the right of the Cadets. The younger element among the Old Believers, however, was evidently in sympathy with the parties of the Left.[162]

In November, 1905, there was an attempt to win some of the Old Believers over to support the ultra-conservative parties. In one of its issues of that month, *Moskovskiia Vedomosti* (*The Moscow News*) printed an anonymous appeal purporting to come from a union of Old Believers, and urging their coreligionists to enter "the ranks of [the organization called] Truly Russian Men and to lend comradely support against the enemies of the Fatherland—the traitors and rebels who are stirring up dissension in Russia."[163] However, several well-known Old Believers of Moscow hastened to deny that the supposed union had ever existed, and an unofficial meeting of many Old Believers of that city was held to denounce this alleged fraud. In their speeches the orators at this meeting declared that the Old Believers as a group sympathized with the "liberative movement." One declared:

> The present government does not wish freedom; it has always fiercely persecuted the "schismatics" for their religious convictions, and if it now has given some freedom to the Old Believers it is with the purpose of attracting them to its side during the present difficult period. But who can guarantee that the rights given to the Old Believers will not once more be taken away at the first favorable opportunity . . . ? . . . Once more they will be enslaved, if the liberative movement is not crystallized in definite form.

Another speaker said:

> The world lies steeped in evil, and we should work for the accomplishment of the Kingdom of God here upon earth. . . . The contemporary political movement, which is directed toward the freeing of our land from irresponsible authority, does not urge vengeance for former violence;

---

[161] S. P. Mel'gunov, *Iz Istorii Religiozno-obshchestvennykh Dvizhenii v Rossii*, pp. 27–30; *Missionerskoe Obozrenie*, April, 1910, pp. 701–9.

[162] Mel'gunov, *op. cit.*, pp. 34–35.   [163] *Ibid.*, pp. 21–22.

it strives for truth. The liberative movement is holy work, the work of Christ.[164]

After a number of speeches in this vein, the meeting adopted a resolution condemning the allegedly false proclamation in *Moskovskiia Vedomosti* and declaring that the members of the meeting "expressed a zealous wish that the Duma might be called in the very near future, in order to realize the principles proclaimed by the Manifesto of October 17." [165]

The gathering which adopted this resolution was, as has been said, an unofficial assemblage of some of the Old Believers in a single city only; however, it was soon followed by a congress of plenipotentiary representatives of all the chief denominations of Old Believers, which met in Moscow in January, 1906. They voted that the Old Believers should work for the election of a liberal Duma and should actively participate in the elections. On the other hand, they were in favor of retaining the monarchy, and their agrarian policy was not extreme for the Russia of early 1906, in that they favored the selling of private land by the government to the peasants, with fair compensation to the dispossessed owners.[166]

Thus the government's overtures to the Old Believers failed to win their support and to induce them to approve the idea of uniting with the official Orthodox Church. Possibly it was strictly religious differences that prevented reconciliation, or it may be that the Old Believers were not satisfied with the concessions which had been made to them. Perhaps, too, some of them felt that the official policy of moderation was only temporary, and that as soon as it felt strong enough the government would revert to its former attitude and would sweep aside all those who advocated conciliation. If the Old Believers foresaw such a change, they were not alone in their expectations. By the early months of 1906 many Orthodox churchmen of liberal ideas were noting the rising forces of reaction which were contending against liberalism in the church, and were becoming increasingly fearful that a revival of the policy of rigorous control would undo the good that had been done and deliver the church again into the firm grip of those who had formerly held it in subjection.

[164] *Ibid.*, pp. 23–25.   [165] *Ibid.*, p. 26.   [166] *Ibid.*, pp. 27–28.

CHAPTER VI

"God Is High Above and the Tsar Is Far Away"

AFTER THE rifles of the troops on Bloody Sunday had turned the march of Father Gapon's followers into a massacre, the Synod soon made clear its attitude toward the revolutionary movement by issuing two special messages to be read from the pulpits of all the Orthodox churches in Russia. The first of these laid the blame for the shooting, not upon the authorities who ordered the volleys, but largely upon foreign foes. It read:

By the Grace of God, the Most Holy Ruling Synod to its beloved sons of the Holy Orthodox All-Russian Church:

God has visited our dear Fatherland with a great calamity. Now for nearly a year Russia has been waging a bloody war with the heathen over her historic mission as the founder of Christian enlightenment in the Far East, for honor and righteousness, which were outraged by the unexpectedly bold onslaught of the enemy. No matter how much our Most Reverend Sovereign, filled with love of peace, sought to avoid this war, the conflict was forced upon Russia. . . .

. . . But now a new trial from God—a sorrow sadder than the first—has visited our beloved Fatherland.

In the capital and in the other cities of Russia strikes of workers, and street disorders, have begun. Russian men, deeply Orthodox, from years of old accustomed to stand for Faith, Tsar, and Fatherland, but now led on by . . . the enemies, domestic and foreign, of our Land, . . . have thrown aside their peaceful occupations, have decided through force and violence to obtain their rights, alleged to have been trampled on, have caused a multitude of disorders and disturbances to afflict the peaceful inhabitants, have left many without a piece of bread, and have brought some of their brethren to needless death. . . . Saddest of all is the fact that the disorders were organized with bribes from the enemies of Russia and of the whole social order. Considerable sums were sent by them in order to produce civil strife among us, so that, by drawing the workers from their labor, they might prevent the timely dispatch of naval and land forces to the Far East. . . . Our enemies must tear asunder our strongholds—the Orthodox Faith and the autocratic authority of the Tsar. By the help of these, Russia lives and has grown great and strong, and without them she will fall. . . .

The remainder of the communication of the Synod was a vigorous attempt to bring an aroused people back to submission. It read:

The Most Holy Synod, sorrowing over the fatal disorders in the contemporary life of the Russian people, in the name of the Holy Mother and of the Orthodox Church beseeches all her sons: *Fear God. Honor the Tsar* (I Pet. 2: 17), and *Let every soul be subject unto the higher powers; for there is no power but of God* (Rom. 13: 1).

Pastors of the Holy Orthodox Church! *Preach the word, be instant in season, reprove, rebuke, exhort with all long suffering and doctrine* (II Tim. 4: 2), and *Be thou an example of the believers in word, in conversation, in charity, in spirit, in faith, in purity* (I Tim. 4: 12). . . .

These appeals were accompanied with directions that special prayers be offered, that God should save the land from treasonable attack, and that He should protect the Tsar.[1]

Not long after this the Synod ordered that all priests be required to read in the churches on the next Sunday or feast day "the most gracious words of His Imperial Majesty to the deputation of workingmen from the capital and the suburbs," and ordered the bishops of the dioceses to have copies of the Tsar's speech printed for distribution to the people.[2] The speech, which was delivered on January 19, blamed the disaster of January 9 on "betrayers and enemies of the Fatherland" who had led the workers astray. The Tsar asked the workingmen to be patient, and to have confidence in his efforts and those of the employers to better the lot of the working classes. Again, on February 4, 1905, the Synod voted to print in its official publication, *Tserkovnyia Vedomosti (Church News)*, another article which it hoped would spur the clergy on to energetic efforts to win the

[1] *Tserkovnyia Vedomosti*, Jan. 15, 1905, official part, supplement.
[2] *Ibid.*, Jan. 29, 1905, official part, p. 42.

loyalty of the people to the government. This article was an excerpt from the report for 1903 of the commandant of the city of Nikolaev, stating that many of the local workers "were tending, under the influence of evil-intentioned persons, to accept false economic doctrines and antigovernmental ideas." At the suggestion of this commandant "and with the energetic coöperation of the local clergy," talks on religious and moral questions were arranged for the benefit of the workers in the chief factories and also in the admiralty shipyards, with the purpose of "strengthening a sound understanding concerning faith, morality, and the necessity for order in social life." The materials used as the basis for the talks were "the Word of God, the history of the Orthodox Church, and the history of the Russian state, with indication of the chief examples testifying to the limitless love and loyalty of the Russian subject to Throne and Fatherland." [3] Clearly, here was an example which the Synod wished its priests to follow.

No further moves were made by the Synod against liberalism and radicalism until its meeting of October 28, 1905, at which time the Synod listened sympathetically to the reading of a proclamation which one of the bishops had sent to the parishes of his diocese. In it he said: "A whole series of calamities has been sent upon our land by the Lord, for our sins—disastrous war accompanied by internal difficulties—calamities which are now turning into complete anarchy. In many places in our land there is hunger, as well as all kinds of disorder. What more we must expect for our transgressions, only our God knows." The bishop went on to direct that the priests of all the churches of his diocese should include a special petition in the liturgy at all services "until the Lord shall send peace and an end to rebellion in our land." The wording of the required petition was: "And we pray that Thou wilt protect our imperial city and all our land from hunger, destruction, hail, flood, fire, the sword, invasion by foreign enemies, and from internal strife; and we pray that it may be pleasing to our kindly and loving God to turn aside His wrath from His servants and to spare us His just and righteous anger." [4] The Synod

[3] Sv. Sinod, 1905, portfolio 592; *Tserkovnyia Vedomosti*, March 5, 1905, official part, pp. 72–73.

[4] Sv. Sinod, 1905, portfolio 3175.

voted approval of this prayer, and it was printed in the official church notices for the attention of the Russian clergy.[5]

However, while the general trend of the Synod's messages dealing with the problems of the day was conservative, it showed that it was not ready to endorse the more extreme measures to which some of the higher clergy had begun to resort. On October 29, 1905, *Tserkovnyia Vedomosti*, the official publication of the Synod, contained an article entitled "A Propos of the Saddening Events of October 16 in Several of the Churches of Moscow." The article stated that the message sent by Metropolitan Vladimir of Moscow to the churches of his diocese, "What we should do in these our troubled days," could, in the opinion of the Synod, be interpreted as a summons to violence. The *Vedomosti* said that the bishops should advise their priests to calm the people "in a spirit of universally fraternal Christian love." [6]

This rebuke to the metropolitan of Moscow was a blow to the reactionaries; nevertheless the Synod continued to be imbued with conservatism. Its members visited the emperor on November 4, at which time he expressed a hope that "all the clergy, and especially the village clergy, will make sincere and truly Christian efforts to restore peace and quiet among their flocks, and to fulfill every one of the duties placed upon them; for without this . . . there cannot possibly be any fruitful development of the vital forces of the land." [7]

Another indication of the continued conservatism of the Synod was given on December 20, when it deliberated "concerning the prejudicial conduct of several priests at the time of popular disturbance in their localities"—a deliberation that took a direction which gave liberals no cause for rejoicing. According to the official reports of this discussion, the Synod had learned that in several dioceses there were isolated instances where priests in their talks with parishioners "without sufficient thought, or in some cases even deliberately, gave false interpretation to the decisions and actions of the government, thereby stirring up the people to oppose the lawful authorities." The Synod regarded these cases as unfortunate exceptions to the general rule that the Orthodox clergy had been "truly loyal to the state order," and hoped that most of the clergy would "not cease to summon the

---

[5] *Tserkovnyia Vedomosti*, Oct. 29, 1905, official part, p. 498.
[6] *Ibid.*, p. 499.   [7] *Ibid.*, Dec. 3, 1905, p. 2110.

Orthodox people to steadfast observance of the established laws and to submission to the lawful authorities." In order to prevent the recurrence of "the aforesaid most sad happenings," the Synod commanded the bishops to restrain the priests under their jurisdiction by advice and exhortation; when information should be received concerning improper activities of any of the clergy, especially in instances of "insubordination to the lawful authorities and violation of the state order," the bishops were ordered first "to take decisive measures against the guilty persons, immediately removing them from the place of their criminal activity and prohibiting them from performing holy services until the cases are settled"; and secondly "to begin, without fail, investigation of the activities of such persons. . . ." [8]

Likewise, in the month of December, 1905—the month of the Moscow uprising, and of mutinies, martial law, and general strikes —the Synod adopted, printed, and distributed a lengthy prayer service "for peace at the time of internecine strife, and for the assuaging and ending of internal dissension and disorders." This service included appropriate psalms and readings from the New Testament, as well as prayers to "save us from our enemies" and to "abate all the conflicts now taking place, and the bloodshed and the internecine strife, and give peace and quiet." [9] Clearly this was an attempt to preserve the *status quo* in the face of angry revolutionaries.

On the other hand, in February, 1906, the Synod again showed itself unwilling to countenance the extreme actions of some of the reactionary clergy. At this time the notorious Abbot Arsenii, a monk who was famed for his preaching of anti-Semitic violence and who "from the pulpit in Iaroslavl had proclaimed anathema to all members of the intelligentsia," was sent into exile in the Solovetskii Monastery on an island in the White Sea, and the appeal of the reactionary Union of the Russian People for pardon for Arsenii's offense was rejected. [10]

With respect to the Duma, the Synod's policy was at first somewhat indecisive. The priests were told to vote and to use their influence upon the electors, and were advised that they might accept election as

[8] *Tserkovnyia Vedomosti*, Jan. 7, 1906, official part, pp. 6–7.
[9] Sv. Sinod, 1905, portfolio 3204.   [10] *Pravo*, Feb. 26, 1906, col. 735.

deputies, but they were forbidden to join any of the political parties: "his [the pastor's] one union is with Christ in the Church of God." The Synod also instructed the priests to warn their flocks not to be led astray by "the promises of men who do not believe in God and who place material well-being above all else," and not to be snared "by hopes of much freedom in civil affairs. . . ." The Synod approved of "all who proceed along the path of peace, love, and order, all who stand for the true faith, for the Orthodox Tsar, and for the indivisibility of our Fatherland. . . ." [11] Moreover, while the Synod, late in 1906, decreed a celebration in the churches in honor of the anniversary of "the gift of October 17"—the imperial Manifesto of 1905 which had promised the Duma—the ruling churchmen appended an explanation that the freedom granted did not warrant headstrong action, and warned all church members to avoid strife and to be guided by love toward all Orthodox brethren, as well as toward "those strange to our holy faith." [12]

While the Synod was still moderate in its pronouncements in October, 1906, signs were soon observed that its policies were becoming more conservative. In January, 1907, Archbishop Iakov of Iaroslavl was transferred from his archepiscopal see to the comparatively humble diocese of Simbirsk, in the trans-Volga region. Many of his clergy were sorry to see him go and even telegraphed to the emperor and to the Synod asking for reconsideration of the decision, but to no avail. "Rumor ascribes the transfer of the archbishop to the efforts of politicians belonging to the 'Union of Truly Russian Men' [an ultra-conservative group], toward whom the archbishop manifested 'an attitude not sufficiently friendly,' " [13] stated the *Tserkovnyi Vestnik* (*The Church Messenger*).

In May, 1907, the government announced that it had discovered a plot to assassinate the emperor. The Synod thereupon hastened to send him the following telegram of rejoicing:

Great Lord,
Thy Tsar's Throne is the basis of Russian statehood, the stronghold of the unity and the stability of the Russian power. Thy life is the

---

[11] *Tserkovnyi Vestnik*, Feb. 23, 1906, cols. 227–28.
[12] *Tserkovnyia Vedomosti*, Oct. 7, 1906, official part, p. 426.
[13] *Tserkovnyi Vestnik*, March 8, 1907, cols. 323–25.

guarantee of our well-being and happiness, and its inviolability is sacred to the heart of each of us, the subject of our heartfelt prayers to God to protect Thee, His Anointed, under the shelter of His blessing.

Always imbued with this consciousness, we, members of the Most Holy Synod, and other bishops temporarily in the capital, gathered to consecrate our Brother the Bishop of Baku, on learning of the treasonable plot against Thy precious life, now zealously give thankful prayers to the All Highest that He did not allow a sacrilegious hand to touch Thee, and we offer, together with our strong love and loyalty to Thee, Lord and Protector of the Orthodox Church, our most loyal sentiments and joyous greetings on Thy escape from threatening danger.

The Synod also ordered that special prayers of thanksgiving be said in all Orthodox churches in Russia.[14]

As a sequel to this plot there followed the disciplining of the five priests in the Duma who, as members of radical parties, had absented themselves while the Duma was voting congratulations to the Tsar on his escape. The offending priests were summoned before Metropolitan Antonii of St. Petersburg, who, acting at the request of the Synod, ordered them to resign publicly from the parties to which they belonged. "Metropolitan Antonii likewise declared to them that they must not adhere to the unorganized Left, but only to the Monarchists, the Octobrists, or the unorganized Right. . . ."[15]

The attitude of the Synod on political questions did not become more liberal, even when the Revolution no longer presented much danger to the established regime. In 1908 the Synod ordered the distribution and use of copies of a new prayer, to be said because of continuing disorder and fratricide in Russia.[16] Inasmuch as the Synod had refused to condemn the use of violence by the government, and as by 1908 the ruling body of the church, as will be shown later, had displayed sympathy with the groups involved in unofficial counter-revolutionary violence, the prayer mentioned above was probably issued in the hope that the rebellious peasantry and other restless elements might be induced to accept their lot in life. When the eightieth anniversary of the birth of Lev Tolstoi drew near in August of the same year, the Synod published a message appealing to all true

[14] *Tserkovnyia Vedomosti*, May 12, 1907, official part, inclosure.

[15] Gosudarstvennaia Duma, *Stenograficheskie Otchety*, II Duma, Part 2, col. 595.

[16] *Tserkovnyia Vedomosti*, Feb. 23, 1908, official part, inclosure.

sons of the Orthodox Church not to participate in the celebration, as the Count was a heretic and a dangerous innovator, in that he was opposed to war, to the paying of taxes, to the institution of private property, and the like [17]—charges which were well-founded. And in 1909, when an unspecified diocese asked that it be permitted to be lenient with a young priest guilty of antigovernmental activity, the diocesan authorities were told that the offender must not be spared, but must be expelled from the body of the church through judicial proceedings.[18] Thus the Synod throughout the revolutionary period showed a tendency to use its powers to repress liberalism and radicalism and to inculcate loyalty to the Tsar and his officials.

During the years of revolutionary upheaval the upper clergy also displayed their conservatism. Even Metropolitan Antonii of St. Petersburg, who was attacked for his "liberalism" by the reactionaries, turned out to be no liberal at all, but a pillar of conservatism, as was shown by several of his sermons in February and October, 1905.[19] Metropolitans Vladimir of Moscow [20] and Flavian of Kiev [21] were strong in their denunciations of everything that smacked of the Left. Several of the archbishops were stanch supporters of autocracy, among them Agafangel of Riga,[22] Dimitrii of Kazan,[23] and Arsenii of Khar'kov.[24] A number of other hierarchs proved to be equally firm defenders of the autocratic regime, urging the clergy of their dioceses "to take part in the struggle against disorder, treason, the development of socialist ideas, and the like." Especially noted in this respect were Archbishops Antonii of Volhynia [25] and Aleksii of Taurida [26]— the latter being so hated by revolutionaries that three attempts were

[17] *Ibid.*, Aug. 23, 1908, official part, pp. 270–72.
[18] *Ibid.*, Feb. 21, 1909, official part, p. 54.
[19] *Ibid.*, March 12, 1905, pp. 451–52; Nov. 19, 1905, pp. 1991–92.
[20] *Ibid.*, Feb. 11, 1906, pp. 253–58.
[21] *Pravo*, Nov. 26, 1906, cols. 3698–99.
[22] *Tserkovnyia Vedomosti*, Feb. 18, 1906, p. 334. Archbishop Agafangel did, however, urge the protection of innocent persons involuntarily drawn into the revolutionary movement.
[23] *Ibid.*, Aug. 13, 1905, p. 1407.
[24] *Vera i Razum*, Oct., 1908, pp. 137–38.
[25] *Tserkovnyia Vedomosti*, June 25, 1905, pp. 1074–77; *Tserkovnyi Vestnik*, June 22, 1906, cols. 805–9.
[26] *Tserkovnyia Vedomosti*, Oct. 14, 1906, p. 2721; *Moskovskiia Tserkovnyia Vedomosti*, June 25, 1906, p. 172.

made upon his life.[27] Saratov became a center of counter-revolutionary activity, doubtless in part owing to the zealous efforts of Bishop Hermogen;[28] while Makarii of Tomsk, by his articles and by his sermons, won the reputation of being an outstanding conservative or even a reactionary.[29] In addition to these prelates who surpassed all other bishops in their firm opposition to the demand for change, there were many others among the higher clergy whose utterances and actions showed a variety of political views ranging from extreme reaction to mild conservatism, but almost never attaining to liberalism. Only rare exceptions, such as Archbishop Iakov of Iaroslavl who was supposed to have suffered demotion because of too mild views, showed any leanings toward the liberal position, while the bishops of Simbirsk, Perm, Voronezh, Tambov, Podolia, Lithuania, Smolensk, Orel, Vologda, Grodno, Nizhnii Novgorod, Viatka, Stavropol, Kholm, Mogilev, Polotsk, Pskov, Orenburg, Kishinev, Minsk, Kursk, Kaluga, and Tver showed themselves to be conservatives or reactionaries. In their sermons and articles these bishops strongly favored the autocracy, denounced those who desired change, and urged the people not to be led astray by those who promised them fine things if they would but defy the officials of the Tsar.[30] As an article in the ultra-conservative *Moskovskiia Vedomosti* (*Moscow News*) stated, the higher clergy were "in the majority noted for their extreme conservatism. . . ."[31]

The bishops then, almost without exception, were conservative or even reactionary. Among the lower clergy, however, there was considerable diversity of political opinion. While the passage quoted above added, ". . . the representatives of the white clergy evidently try to avoid extremes, either of the Right or of the Left, . . ." there were some priests who were forced by their convictions to join the radical parties of the Left, and others who were equally determined

[27] *Tserkovnyia Vedomosti*, Jan. 6, 1907, p. 29.

[28] *Pravo*, Jan. 30, 1905, col. 282.

[29] *Tserkovnyia Vedomosti*, Jan. 8, 1905, pp. 51–54; Sept. 24, 1905, pp. 1641–44; Aug. 27, 1905, pp. 1476–79.

[30] *Tserkovnyia Vedomosti*, 1905–7; *Missionerskoe Obozrenie*, 1905–7; *Tserkovnyi Vestnik*, 1905–7.

[31] Quoted in *Tserkovnyi Vestnik*, March 20, 1908, cols. 362–64; see also V. K. Sokolov, "Nashi Episkopy i Samoderzhavie," *Vestnik Prava*, 1906, No. 3, pp. 15–16.

adherents of the extreme Right. By their prayers and their sermons and through the distribution of printed material published by the Synod or by other organizations favorable to the policies of the government, the conservative and the reactionary priests tried to restrain the people and attempted to discredit the liberal parties and the Duma. In some cases they even attempted to stimulate violence against those whom they regarded as enemies of the autocracy.

"The revolutionary movement in Russia met obstacles and opposition from the clergy in general and from the missionaries in particular. Many cases could be cited . . . where popular disturbance, all ready to break out, or even already active, was stopped by the preaching of priests and especially of missionaries," [32] wrote *Missionerskoe Obozrenie*, the strongly conservative journal of domestic missions. At times this preaching proved a handicap even to those who were merely striving for peaceful reforms. In March, 1905, a special committee of the City Duma of Nizhnii Novgorod found that "many priests preach sermons against the intelligentsia who are working for reforms, articles against them are printed in the official . . . diocesan journals, and so on." [33] In Kherson a meeting of the provincial *zemstvo* (an elected assembly enjoying considerable powers in local matters) found it necessary to give consideration to slanderous attacks upon the intelligentsia which were being made "by various 'dark forces'—(even from the local pulpits). . . ." [34] Sometimes, if the contemporary newspapers can be believed, this dislike of the intelligentsia was directed against the teachers in the *zemstvo* schools. In one village of the province of Orel a priest explained that the official phrases of an imperial manifesto which he had just read meant, "Do not listen to the teachers, who eat forbidden food during the fasts." [35] Another priest in a village of Poltava was incensed when a teacher started to leave the church on Sunday, and shouted, "Police! Hold the *zemstvo* teacher, as I have still to read the speech of the Sovereign to the workers of St. Petersburg!" And he was reported to have followed this outburst with a sermon which consisted almost entirely of assaults upon the teachers and the schools of the *zemstvos*. "Why do you send your children to . . . [these] schools? Can the

---

[32] *Missionerskoe Obozrenie*, April, 1909, pp. 689–90.
[33] *Pravo*, April 10, 1905, col. 1143.
[34] *Ibid.*, July 10, 1905, col. 2264.   [35] *Ibid.*, March 20, 1905, col. 853.

zemstvo teachers impart anything good to your children?"[36] And in still another village the priest, after reading the Synod's message of January 15, 1905, concerning the current sedition and the hired agents of treason, preached a sermon to the effect that the disorders were caused by the women teachers, "who do not believe in God and do not respect the rules of morality."[37]

Some of the other messages delivered from the pulpits, as reported in the newspapers, were also rather demagogic in character. One such sermon explained to the congregation that the workers' movement in St. Petersburg and other disorders of the period were due to "the trickery of Germans, Jews, and Poles."[38] Similarly a priest in Voronezh thundered from the pulpit that the "trouble" then prevalent was caused by persons in the pay of the Japanese. He also begged his parishioners not to read any newspapers, as they were printed "by the enemies of the government and of the Orthodox Church."[39]

Not infrequently the counter-revolutionary efforts of the clergy were more systematic in character. At one of their district meetings the clergy of Riazan discussed the question of combating the propaganda of the Socialist Revolutionaries among the peasants. It was decided: (1) that the clergy should study the propaganda of the Socialist Revolutionaries and also the doctrines of the church on social questions, so that they might better defeat the arguments of their adversaries; (2) that a special printing press should be set up in Riazan, to produce counter-propaganda; (3) that the priests should attend the meetings of the Socialist Revolutionaries for the purpose of heckling the speakers; (4) that opposition meetings should be organized.[40] A certain Father Kremlevskii, writing in *Tserkovnyia Vedomosti*, urged that the priests do their part in fighting the evil developments of the times, and advised that special brotherhoods be formed to print leaflets, proclamations, and the like, and that the priests distribute them. Also he declared that frequent talks with the peasants would help to calm them.[41] The decisions of the diocesan

---

[36] *Pravo*, April 10, 1905, col. 1144.
[37] *Ibid.*, March 20, 1905, col. 853.   [38] *Ibid.*, Feb. 20, 1905, col. 534.
[39] *Ibid.*, April 24, 1905, col. 1313.   [40] *Kolokol*, Jan. 26, 1906.
[41] *Tserkovnyia Vedomosti*, Dec. 3, 1905, pp. 2116 ff.

congress of the clergy of Podolia were of a similar tenor. The pastors were advised to work energetically among their people, and to quiet them by means of heart-to-heart talks. They were to try to restrain the young, and also to use every opportunity to distribute literature of a suitable nature.[42]

The use of printed propaganda to sway the people was an important part of the counter-revolutionary activity of the clergy. A congress of clergy in the diocese of Perm voted unanimously to edit and send throughout the diocese numbers of pamphlets intended to calm the people, as well as leaflets on the agrarian question. One hundred rubles were appropriated for this purpose, and two editing committees formed, one to issue leaflets on the agrarian question, the other to publish material on "the liberative movement" in general.[43] Work of this kind was highly organized in the diocese of Moscow, where the religious authorities, as will be shown later, were reactionary. A series of special talks with the masses was formally organized, and the speakers were provided with leaflets from the Moscow diocesan home, for distribution.[44] Nor was this proceeding unknown elsewhere. In 1907 a priest writing in *Vera i Razum* (*Faith and Reason*) stated: "For three years I have been practicing in my parish the free distribution of pamphlets, using for this purpose especially *Troitskii Listok* (*The Troitskii Leaflet*) and *Pochaevskii Listok* (*The Pochaev Leaflet*), the publications of *Missionerskoe Obozrenie* [which was decidedly conservative in tone], and leaflets from the printing house of Fesenko in Odessa."[45] The first two periodicals were published at the Troitsko-Sergieva and the Pochaevskaia Monasteries respectively, and the latter of these two publications, which will be discussed later, was reactionary.

Apparently considerable success attended the pacifying efforts of some of the priests. In the province of Penza a village pastor succeeded in restoring discipline in a trainload of rebellious soldiers returning from Manchuria; when he fell on his knees on the station platform his prayers and his exhortations sufficed to check the mutiny. Another priest in the diocese of Pskov "by his useful pastoral activity helped

[42] *Ibid.*, pp. 2128–29.   [43] *Ibid.*, Dec. 2, 1906, p. 3057.
[44] *Moskovskiia Tserkovnyia Vedomosti*, Sept. 25, 1905, p. 407.
[45] *Vera i Razum*, Jan., 1907, p. 267.

greatly to quiet the aroused peasant population at the time of the agrarian disorders occurring in 1905." The dean of a cathedral in the Caucasus preached so earnestly against the revolutionary movement that he succeeded in weaning his flock away from those who were arousing them and induced them to remain loyal. The revolutionaries were so incensed at this that shots were fired into his bedroom at night, and later his house was burned. The chaplain of a disciplinary battalion at the risk of his life urged and besought the rebellious convicts to return to order. In the diocese of St. Petersburg a police officer was in grave danger at the hands of angry peasants; the priest of the village rescued him from the crowd and sheltered him in his home.[46] At the time of the mutiny of Kronstadt in October, 1905, when a crowd of rioters was surging through the streets and burning buildings, three priests of a garrison church put on their vestments, took ikons and a crucifix, and knelt in the street singing a hymn. The mutineers stopped, took off their caps, and began to cross themselves. After this the mutiny came to a speedy end.[47] Again when mutiny broke out in Sevastopol, the chaplains of two of the regiments succeeded in keeping their troops loyal, and thus these troops could be used later to help put down the disorder.[48]

In various agrarian disturbances the priests also played a part. In the provinces of Khar'kov,[49] Poltava, and Tambov,[50] village pastors were able to keep their parishioners from attacking the estates of neighboring landlords. A priest in Livonia tried to quiet a rebellious group of peasants and was nearly killed as a result.[51] In Tambov a priest not only succeeded in restraining his own peasants, but was even able to get them to protect the estate against others.[52] When the manager of an estate in the province of Khar'kov was threatened, the priest received the endangered man in his home and sheltered him. In strikes, also, the priests proved to be influential. When, during a strike in a factory in Vladimir, conflict loomed between strikers and police, a priest intervened with marked success.[53] A priest of

---

[46] Sv. Sinod, *Vsepoddanneishii Otchet*, 1905–7, pp. 5–8.

[47] *Tserkovnyia Vedomosti*, Dec. 10, 1905, official part, p. 545.

[48] *Ibid.*, March 11, 1906, pp. 518–20.   [49] *Ibid.*

[50] *Ibid.*, Aug. 12, 1906, pp. 2418–20.   [51] *Ibid.*

[52] *Ibid.*   [53] *Ibid.*, March 11, 1906, pp. 519–20.

Samara preached to his people against attacking a neighboring factory, only to have his home assaulted as a result. Nothing daunted, he gathered his parishioners together and led them, with cross and ikons, to bar the path of the younger men who were determined to join in the fray at the factory.[54]

Of course not all of these priests acted thus because they wished to aid the government; many doubtless wished to avert fratricidal strife or to save the people from the inevitable consequences of illegal deeds. None the less, the result was to support the government and to weaken the revolutionary movement.

While these pastors were thus openly upholding the cause of law and order, there doubtless were others who were working unheralded in the same cause. Julius Hecker, who became a professor in the Religious Academy of Moscow after the Bolshevik revolution, writes:

Some went so far as to abuse the most sacred institution of the church, the confessional, for spying purposes, and the blood of many innocent victims may be charged to this heinous espionage. One priest, who had his parish in a district where there were many revolutionaries, confessed to me some time ago his guilt of this black crime. . . .[55]

On the other hand, Pobedonostsev, in his answer to Witte's appeal for reform of the church in 1905, declared that Peter the Great's demand that the clergy violate the secrecy of the confessional in this way had long been a dead letter.[56] No documents have come to hand regarding this important point, but there is evidence that at least one priest was in close touch with the police during this period. This pastor of Khar'kov wrote to the local commandant of gendarmes that he had obtained the confidence of several of his parishioners and consequently had been able to discover copies of a secret leaflet of the Social Democratic party. He added:

Thanks to this trust, I know what is going on around me in the village, and can firmly protect autocracy and the social order; indeed, to deprive me of this trust among my parishioners would automatically destroy a protection for Throne and Fatherland, which support, although not great, is far from insignificant. . . . After all this has been said, I can

---

[54] *Moskovskiia Tserkovnyia Vedomosti*, Sept. 3, 1906, pp. 417–19.
[55] J. Hecker, *Religion under the Soviets*, p. 26.
[56] N. D. Kuznetsov, *Preobrazovaniia v Russkoi Tserkvi*, p. 46.

now inform your highly well-born Excellency that the leaflet was received from. . . .

The names and the circumstantial details followed.[57]

What the reward might be for valuable service to the government may be learned from a petition sent to the Synod by the school board of a parish school in the province of Pskov. The petition asked that their priest, Father Tsvetkov, be awarded a cross for "his exceedingly zealous and useful pastoral activity, which aided in quieting the disturbed peasant population at the time of the agrarian disorders which occurred during the past year." His activity had consisted of "preaching timely and countless sermons" and of talks in the homes of the people, "inspiring the peasants with true sentiments conforming to the Word of God: about true freedom and the sin of arbitrary action; about the rights and the duties of citizens in general and of the peasant in particular; about the illegality and sinfulness of burning and violence, by means of which the peasants were thinking to obtain land from the landlords." The pastor had also discussed the future Duma, which alone, he said, could fully consider the needs and satisfy all the lawful wishes of the peasant population. Thus he had "checked in time the agrarian disorders which were already beginning in his parish, and the parishioners, hearing his pastoral voice, had ceased to go to the meetings held by traitors in November and December of 1905." [58]

The documents dealing with this case fail to say whether Father Tsvetkov received the cross which had been asked for him; but other documents show that a number of priests were given recognition of this sort for activity similar to his. In 1908 Stolypin, Minister of Internal Affairs, wrote to Izvolskii, Over Procurator of the Synod, stating that the governors of the provinces of Kazan, Vitebsk, and Vologda had petitioned for the suitable recognition of several priests of their provinces "for especially zealous labors in pacifying the population and in strengthening the legal order, which appears particularly important under the exceptional conditions of contemporary state life." There followed a list of thirty-six persons, mostly priests

[57] M. N. Pokrovskii, ed., *1905—Istoriia Revoliutsionnogo Dvizheniia v Otdel'nykh Ocherkakh*, I, 319–20.
[58] Sv. Sinod, 1906, portfolio 89.

and deans of cathedrals, but including some missionaries, heads of monasteries, and the like. A similar list of five was sent in soon after by the governor of Podolia. However, the diocesan authorities refused to recommend some of the candidates for honors, while four of the original group had already been rewarded, so that the list was reduced to thirty-three. Of this group nine received the Order of St. Anne, while the other twenty-four received crosses or formal thanks from the emperor.[59]

Another example of the same method of rewarding loyal servants was given when "the Sovereign Emperor . . . augustly decided to reward Dean Aleksii Kilinov, for his outstanding activity in diverting the local parishioners from participation in the disorders occurring in 1905, with the Order of St. Anne, second class." Father Kilinov served in the diocese of Kursk; he was granted his honors on January 9, 1906.[60]

In this fashion the Imperial government showed that it realized the importance of the services of the priests to the existing order. Their significance was fully appreciated, too, in a quite different quarter. The active revolutionaries on several occasions thought the priests sufficiently important enemies to make attempts on their lives. Mention has already been made of reports concerning priests in Livonia, the Caucasus, and Samara who suffered attack, and more striking testimony was given by Archbishop Aleksii of Taurida in his message to his clergy in September, 1906. First on his list of victims from the ranks of the clergy was Father Troepolskii, "well remembered because he always acted upon a high plane of pastoral duty, and by his blessed words restrained his parishioners from joining in anarchism." Another priest, Father Maksorov, was wounded in the head by a bullet from a revolver fired by a revolutionary "because he always held back his flock from agrarian disorders." Father Aleinikov suffered a similar attack and later, during his absence from home, all his possessions were plundered "by a crowd of evil-doers, led by revolutionaries"; his family barely escaped destruction. Another priest received a threatening letter, apparently from Socialist Revolution-

[59] Sv. Sinod, Chancery of the Over Procurator, 1908, portfolio 47, sheets 1–5, 42, 50–52.
[60] *Ibid.*, 1906, portfolio 191.

aries, in which he was called vile names, and was warned that he would be killed unless he resigned his parish; an attack was actually made upon his home, but he escaped. In the city of Theodosia the dean of the cathedral buried a police officer who had been killed by revolutionaries and preached a sermon over his grave. Not long after he received an anonymous letter which said, "You are next, you leader of the Black Hundreds [counter-revolutionary bands], you inspirer of pogroms, you Jesuit, covering yourself with the name of God. Prepare, Black Hundred priest, for your inevitable destruction. . . ." Lastly Bishop Aleksii mentioned a priest who was attacked in his home by a trio who inflicted three knife wounds in his back and shoulders, struck him in the abdomen, and finally took his money.[61] It is impossible to say whether the priests in the diocese of Taurida suffered more severely at the hands of revolutionaries than did those of other dioceses, but it seems probable that several others could provide similar lists.

Mention has been made several times of the distribution of printed propaganda by churchmen, in the hope of calming the disturbed populace or of diverting their attention. In view of the importance which this reading matter assumed in the campaigns of the clergy against the revolutionary movement, it is not amiss to consider the content of these publications.

One important type of conservative printed material available to the priest was the official church periodicals. First among these was the official journal of the Synod, *Tserkovnyia Vedomosti* (*Church News*). Its pages contained not only the official notices of the Synod, but also articles, editorials, excerpts from the diocesan press, reprints of sermons of noted churchmen, and the like. One has only to glance at a few numbers of this journal, for one of the revolutionary years, to realize that it stood for the program of the conservative parties, though it did not advocate the violence which they sometimes practiced. For conservative and reactionary priests and also for those who were uncertain what course to take, it must have been a veritable treasure house of encouragement, inspiration, and ideas. Its reprinted sermons could of course be drawn upon by the conservative pastor. Very similar in tone to this official weekly was the daily newspaper

[61] *Moskovskiia Tserkovnyia Vedomosti*, Oct. 8, 1906, pp. 544–45.

Kolokol (*The Bell*), which devoted much space to the affairs of the church. It was edited by Skvortsov, a leading missionary, and according to the *Tserkovnyi Vestnik* it was subsidized by "the Administration of the Orthodox Faith," [62] i. e., by the central administration of the church. Indications of the attitude of this newspaper were given in an editorial of July 11, 1906, which enthusiastically approved the dismissal of the Duma,[63] and by the favorable reports of the reactionary Monarchist Congress at Kiev in its issues of October 6 and 7, 1906.[64]

Another source of conservative inspiration for the priests was the various official diocesan journals. Many of these publications, which reflected the opinion of the diocesan authorities, were strongly conservative in character. An outstanding exponent of this attitude was the *Moskovskiia Tserkovnyia Vedomosti* (*Moscow Church News*). An article published in its pages in July, 1905, sharply criticizing the noted liberal, Father Petrov, was typical of its viewpoint.[65] A fair sample of its conservative tone was the editorial entitled "What the clergy should do in view of the socialist and revolutionary ideas current among the people." [66] The diocesan publication of the Taurida was of the same character. A prominent place in its pages was given to such articles as the description of a meeting of the clergy of the town of Kerch, which resolved: "To turn serious attention to the possibility of the appearance of agrarian disorders, and to take pastoral measures against them. . . . It is necessary to explain in sermons how contrary to the Christian Faith is violence, and how sacred is the right of property." [67] The *Ekaterinoslav Diocesan News* printed the opinion of a priest that only enemies of the state order, fishers of men in troubled waters, desired reforms.[68] It was editorially proclaimed by the *Mogilev Diocesan News* that those who wished freedom of speech and of the press were "heralds of sham freedom, or, more truly, of license, who are prepared to overthrow the laws of

[62] *Tserkovnyi Vestnik*, Sept. 7, 1906, cols. 1157–61.
[63] *Kolokol*, July 11, 1906.   [64] *Ibid.*, Oct. 6 and 7, 1906.
[65] *Moskovskiia Tserkovnyia Vedomosti*, July 31, 1905, p. 326.
[66] *Ibid.*, June 11, 1906, pp. 122–24.
[67] Quoted in *Moskovskiia Tserkovnyia Vedomosti*, June 25, 1906, p. 172.
[68] Quoted in *Sanktpeterburgskiia Vedomosti*, May 28, 1905, cited in I. V. Preobrazhenskii, *Tserkovnaia Reforma*, p. 544,

God and man." [69] According to the *Orel Diocesan News*, "The inspirers of this disorder are almost all talkers of nonsense. . . . The voice of the church with respect to these men is as follows: 'O cast out from us all the violent treachery of our enemies.'" [70]

Another conservative publication was the *Diocesan News* of Saratov, the organ of the counter-revolutionary Bishop Hermogen. In the summer of 1905, according to a newspaper report, the employees of the provincial *zemstvo* of Saratov voted to stop printing this periodical on the *zemstvo* press. After investigation, the *zemstvo* board concurred in this decision, "as they realized that the *Diocesan News* . . . was sowing disorder and hatred among the population. At the same time, the provincial *zemstvo* administration forbade the printers to accept any orders whatever from the editors of the *Diocesan News*." [71] This decision of the *zemstvo* officials had an interesting sequel. A private printing house, that of a certain Tobias, declared its readiness to print the *Saratov Diocesan News*, and was immediately boycotted by local commercial and manufacturing firms: ". . . one large commercial and manufacturing house issued instructions to its office not to order anything from . . . Tobias, and likewise not to make any purchases from his stationery store." [72]

These periodicals were chiefly of value as a source of inspiration for the priests themselves, rather than as providing materials for wide distribution, though the *Moscow Church News* did give this advice to its subscribers: "When a priest is a subscriber, he should not throw away his copies, but should give them to the parish. . . . The priest at all favorable times should read to his parishioners articles which throw light on current events, or even give [his periodicals] to the literate parishioners for reading to the peasants in their homes, in private gatherings, or in tea rooms." [73] But this method of influencing the people had obvious limitations, so that it was necessary for the clergy to have an additional type of material for distribution.

Much of the counter-revolutionary material intended for wide popular consumption was directed specifically against the Socialists.

[69] Quoted in *Sanktpeterburgskiia Vedomosti*, May 28, 1905.   [70] *Ibid.*
[71] Quoted in *Pravo*, July 17, 1905, col. 2345.
[72] *Ibid.*, Aug. 2, 1905, col. 2478.
[73] *Moskovskiia Tserkovnyia Vedomosti*, June 11, 1906, p. 124.

In his *Report* for 1905–7 the Over Procurator listed titles of works of anti-Socialist propaganda which were distributed by church agencies during these years. Three of them were by Metropolitan Vladimir of Moscow: *To Rich and Poor, On Labor and Property,* and *The Social Problems of the Family.* Bishop Platon contributed *Christianity and Socialism;* other works were entitled *On the Christian Attitude toward Property, An Exposition and Analysis of Socialism, In Defense of Patriotism,*[74] *Beware of Deceiving Speeches,* and *May a Christian Be a Socialist?* [75]

There was also available a great deal of printed material, strongly counter-revolutionary in character, which attempted to arouse popular passions against those who wanted change, and especially the Jews. In works of this type the Jews were pictured as plotters who were attempting to weaken the Russian state so that the great Jewish international financiers might enslave the Russian people. The facts that many of the revolutionaries were of Russian or of other non-Jewish origin and that among the international bankers there could be found many who were not Jews, were disregarded, and almost all of Russia's ills were blamed on this race. Thus there is reason to suspect that the anti-Semitic propaganda was intended, by at least some of the propagators, to divert the attention of the Russian masses from their grievances against their Russian masters by turning their wrath against the Jewish population.

Much of the counter-revolutionary propaganda was of an ephemeral character and never found its way into libraries or archives; however, some samples have been preserved. One strongly reactionary publication was the *Pochaevskii Listok* (*Pochaev Leaflet*), a weekly periodical published as an organ of the local branch of the "Union of the Russian People" by the monk Iliodor in the Pochaevskaia Monastery in Volhynia. It contained bitter anti-Semitic propaganda, together with flings at the Duma and at radicals and liberals in general, as well as occasional attacks upon the Poles. A publication of this kind must have had a very disturbing effect upon the ignorant peasants of the locality.

Pochaevskii Listok was not only edited by the monk Iliodor, but

[74] Sv. Sinod, *Vsepoddanneishii Otchet,* 1905–7, p. 122.
[75] Izdatel'stvo "Vernost'," *Spisok Izdanii.*

was approved by the abbot of the monastery, as censor, so it cannot be regarded as a surreptitious sheet. Its pages contained articles and cartoons savage in tone. After the frightful pogrom at Belostok in June, 1906, *Pochaevskii Listok* printed an editorial entitled "The Hebrew Campaign," the burden of which was that the Jews themselves had arranged this pogrom in order that during the resulting outcry they might obtain equal rights with the Russians.[76] The issue of August, 1906, contained an account of the alleged finding of five large bombs beneath the pavement of a street in Poltava over which a religious procession was about to pass.[77] In another issue, in an article boasting of the strength of the Union of the Russian People, the statement was made that "In the Black Hundred ranks there are now about six million enrolled members."[78] This was a remarkable statement, for the Black Hundreds were widely believed to be the perpetrators of the pogroms and other outrages. What these Black Hundreds were to accomplish was indicated by this appeal, which appeared in the columns of the *Listok:*

True Sons of Russia!

The Lord has visited our Russian Land with grievous torments. It is painful to think of the riots, destruction, and murder which are now being caused in Rus, as our internal foes, the revolutionaries, try to crush our dear land. . . . Now our enemies want to abolish Autocracy in Russia, and to introduce a republic. Shall we exchange our Orthodox Russian Sovereign for a president—some Jew or Pole? Will the Jewish yoke rest easily upon us?[79]

Of similar caliber was the daily paper *Pochaevskiia Izvestiia* (*Pochaev News*), edited and censored by the same monks as *Pochaevskii Listok* and printed on the press of the monastery. Its first issue, on September 1, 1906, set the tone for the future numbers with an article, "How to Save Yourselves from the Jews."[80] Others followed—"The Jews Are Talking Slander,"[81] "O God, Protect Us from the Jews,"[82] "The Jews, Our Enslavers and Our Despoilers."[83] There

[76] *Pochaevskii Listok,* June, 1906, No. 26, p. 202.
[77] *Ibid.,* Aug., 1906, No. 32, pp. 358–59.
[78] *Ibid.,* Dec., 1906, No. 52, pp. 519–20.
[79] *Ibid.,* Oct., 1906, No. 40, pp. 421–22.
[80] *Pochaevskiia Izvestiia,* Sept. 1, 1906.   [81] *Ibid.,* Jan. 12, 1907.
[82] *Ibid.,* Jan. 28, 1907.   [83] *Ibid.,* Jan. 30, 1907.

were cartoons of Jews insulting Christ in the Temple, and of mocking Jews selling ikons to peasants.[84] In the issue of June 19, 1907, was printed a large cross with an inscription set in its angles, "Lord, Save Us from the Jews!"[85]

Here was material well calculated to inflame an ignorant populace. Similar material was produced by the monarchist organizations— such ultra-patriotic secular groups as the Union of Russian Men and especially the Union of the Russian People. These organizations, whose relationship with the church will be studied later, posed, unrebuked by the Synod, as the most faithful defenders of the Orthodox faith, while actively engaged in propaganda which was evidently intended to stir the people to hate the Jews, as well as the radicals and even the liberals. Samples of this propaganda were the following brochures: *The Russian Revolution and Hebrew Social Democracy*, which advanced the theory that both Social Democracy and "its vociferous Jewish gods: *Marx, Lassalle, Engels, Bebel, Liebknecht,* and others," and international capitalism, also dominated by the Jews, were forms of the great Jewish movement to enslave the world;[86] and *The Enemies of the Human Race*, which proclaimed that the Jews, with the aid of Freemasonry, were seeking world dominance through the employment of secrecy, trickery, lying, hypocrisy, and treason.[87] *The Plot against Russia,* printed by the Union of the Russian People, used the same arguments. All of Russia's defeats and failures in the Japanese war and in the Revolution were due to Jews and Masons, and Russia with her true Christianity was the only obstacle in the way of their march to world domination. The lesson derived from these alleged facts was that the Russians should stand firm against anarchists, socialists, and other alleged allies of the Jews, and should protect Orthodoxy and Autocracy from enslavement by this race.[88]

These pamphlets were attempts to inflame the masses against the Jews and the radicals with whom they were supposedly allied. A similar production was the brochure issued by the Union of Russian Men, entitled *The Orthodox Brotherhood in Struggle for the Ortho-*

[84] *Ibid.*, April 20, 1907.   [85] *Ibid.*, June 19, 1907.
[86] Iakovlevin, *Russkaia Revoliutsiia i Evreiskaia Sotsial-Demokratiia.*
[87] G. V. Butmi, *Vragi Roda Chelovecheskago.*
[88] Soiuz Russkago Naroda, *Zagovor Protiv Rossii.*

dox Faith and the Russian Nationality. This work preached that Russia was being attacked by outlandish races and beliefs, not in open combat, but by deceit and treason. "The enemies of Russia are attacking the Tsar's Autocracy, they are killing the Tsar's servants, they wish to deprive the Russian People of their God-given leader; they attack the favored Orthodox belief . . . in order to topple over and to uproot the true Russian Orthodox faith." And at the end, in heavy type, this pamphlet proclaimed: "The Life-giving Cross of our Lord is our strength; with this we shall conquer. God is with us— be wise, ye heathen, and submit—for truly God is with us!" [89]

As has been stated, these monarchist organizations were secular in character and had no official connection with the church at this time. However, they posed as most devoted protectors of the Orthodox faith, a pose which the Synod did nothing to repudiate. Moreover, as will be shown later, the church eventually placed the seal of its official approval upon the Union of the Russian People, and several highly placed churchmen showed their sympathy with it in divers ways. Indeed some of them went so far as to perform acts which were in part responsible for stirring up the people to the point of pogroms against the Jews and others whom the mobs felt to be enemies of the autocratic regime.

One of the more extreme of the prelates was Archbishop Antonii of Volhynia. His reactionary sermons have been mentioned earlier. It was in his diocese that the noted *Pochaevskii Listok* and *Pochaevskiia Izvestiia* were printed. In his letters to his friend Metropolitan Flavian of Kiev, he revealed a strongly counter-revolutionary attitude. On October 20, 1905, after the issuing of the October Manifesto granting the Duma, he wrote:

Today before the requiem for Alexander III, I delivered an ultra-reactionary sermon, and in the evening at vespers, for the first time in three years, I did not preach; my service was more like a requiem for Russia. In place of the ten prescribed verses of the Gospel, I read John 8: 31–42, and as a prayer I read, not the thanksgiving, but the prayer for the Tsar which is in the liturgy.

Here they say that in Kiev the Russians have killed fifteen hundred Jews, and have thrown them into the Dnepr and burned their homes.

---

[89] Soiuz Russkikh Liudei, *Pravoslavnoe Bratstvo v Bor'be za Veru Pravoslavnuiu i Russkuiu Narodnost'.*

Woe to us if the people do not arise for themselves and the Tsar; otherwise Witte will bring him to the scaffold. For everything is happening as I prophesied in my sermon of February 20.[90]

Another who seems to have held views of the same sort was Metropolitan Vladimir of Moscow. If he left any such revealing letters as did Antonii of Volhynia, they are not available; but he won renown by virtue of the special message which, "by command of the higher diocesan authorities," was ordered read in all the churches of the diocese of Moscow on October 15, 1905:

What We Should Do in These Our Troubled Days.

Your hearts will empty of blood when you see what is being done around us—already not the Poles, not foreign enemies, but our own Russian people, who have lost the fear of God and believe in traitors, hold our first capital, as it were, in siege. . . . At the order of hidden traitors, strikes are beginning everywhere, in factories and mills, in schools, and on the railroads. And now it has come to this, that the supply of necessities of life has stopped. . . .

Oh, if our unfortunate workers knew who they are who lead them, who control them, who send to them these trouble-makers and instigators, they would turn from them as from poisonous serpents, as from rabid animals! Here is the truth—these so-called "Social Democrats" are revolutionaries who have long denied God by their acts; they have renounced, or perhaps never knew, the Christian faith; they attack its servants, its laws, and mock its holy things. Their chief nest is abroad; they dream of enslaving all the world; in their secret writings they call Christians cattle, to whom God gave, they say, the form of man in order that they, the chosen, might enjoy our services. . . . With satanic cunning they catch in their nets light-minded persons. . . .

Protect yourselves, beloved brethren, protect yourselves and your children from these deceivers; for the sake of God, for the sake of your own eternal salvation, protect yourselves! Woe to the world from deceit—says the Savior—but still more, woe to him from whom cometh deceit.

What is to be done? We must recognize the danger. . . . And then —each one of us is a son of our native land, a true subject of his Tsar. Can a son be indifferent to the groans of his suffering mother? Yet now she, our native land, once holy, and now so sinful before God—she groans, tormented, rent by her children, our unfortunate brothers. What would you do, a loving son, if your younger brother began to strike, to torment, your mother, to abuse her and dishonor her? Oh, of course, nature it-

[90] *Krasnyi Arkhiv*, 1928, No. 31, pp. 207–8.

self would call upon you in the words of God's commandment: Honor,
love, protect thy mother. . . .

But look! Her unfortunate, maddened children are tormenting your
dear Mother, your native Rus, they are trying to tear her to pieces, they
wish to take away her hallowed treasure—the Orthodox Faith. . . .
They defame your Father-Tsar, they destroy His pictures, they disparage
His Imperial decrees, and mock Him. Can your heart be calm before
this, O *Russian* man? Does not your heart burn with rage, does not your
whole being shake with indignation, righteous indignation? What should
you do?

Again ask of your conscience. It will remind you of your truly loyal
oath. It will say to you—be a loving son of your native land, be an ar-
dently loyal servant of your Tsar. Perform the tasks which the Tsar's
servants ask of you. Be prepared to die for the Tsar and for Rus. Remember how your forefathers untrembling died for Him. . . .[91]

This message created a great stir in Moscow. On October 16 the
City Duma heard reports from its members on the effect of the reading of this communication. One member stated that in the church
which he had attended, a student in the congregation shouted to the
priest that he had no right to utter such sentiments. The student was
ejected from the church and thereupon was attacked by a mob. It
was reported that at another church "hostile cries burst forth from
the congregation; it was proposed to petition the Over Procurator of
the Synod to decree that the Synod Printing House be forbidden to
print such sheets, so that Orthodoxy should not be made a tool in
the conflict between different sections of the population." The City
Duma, after hearing these reports, voted to request Metropolitan
Vladimir to take proper measures against stirring up the people to
violence through the teaching of the church.[92]

Another reputed instigator of violence was Bishop Nikon of
Serpukhov, vicar of the diocese of Moscow. One of the Moscow newspapers printed a letter from the head of a county *zemstvo*, who declared that when the bishop made a journey about the diocese in the
summer of 1905 one of his suite gave out appeals "to fellow sons of
the Fatherland," the contents of which were "so disturbing, bare-
faced, false, and harsh that it is impossible to understand how a

[91] *Moskovskiia Vedomosti*, Oct. 16, 1905.
[92] *Russkii Vestnik*, Oct. 16, 1905, quoted in Myshtsyn, *Po Tserkovno-
obshchestvennym Voprosam*, Part 2, p. 18.

minister of the altar could take . . . [them] under his protection." [93]
Another journal reported that Bishop Nikon was active in forming
a fighting band disguised as a religious brotherhood in the Chudov
Monastery; the alleged founders were noted reactionaries of Moscow.[94]

These reports concerning the activity of Bishop Nikon were not
supported by direct evidence, although the well-known counter-
revolutionary attitude of his superior, Metropolitan Vladimir, lends
credibility to the accounts. The evidence cited on the attitude of
Metropolitan Vladimir and Archbishop Antonii, however, is not subject to question. In view of these facts, it is not surprising that some
members of the lower clergy and of the monastic groups acted in
similar fashion. A number of reports of reactionary agitation by members of the clergy were printed in contemporary newspapers. It is
impossible to determine the accuracy of such items or the frequency
of such actions, but a few instances will suffice to show what the
liberal press was reporting concerning some of the clergy. In February, 1905, it was stated that in the village of Lopatin, in Saratov,
"there is being organized a band for combating treason. Father
Smirnov is acting as organizer of the band, with the assistance of the
police chief and the commandant of the fire department. There have
already been two meetings of persons wishing to join the band." [95] In
another village of the same province, the peasants, under the influence of a sermon delivered on the theme of "Treason and Domestic
Enemies," attacked the *zemstvo* school. "The teacher, who was warned
by his pupils, . . . escaped in time from the school, thus saving his
life. The crowd also intended to attack the *zemstvo* doctor." [96] In the
village of Bogodukhov (province not specified) there was "opened a
religious brotherhood with the purpose of uniting the 'intelligentsia'
with the clergy, for combating treason." [97] "In the Odessa diocesan
school the priestly teachers are zealously distributing proclamations
calling for the beating of the Jews." [98] A priest of the Taurida was
reported by a newspaper to have preached a sermon attacking the
"so-called best men" in the Duma. He ridiculed the proposals of the

[93] *Pravo,* July 24, 1905, col. 2404. [94] *Ibid.,* April 3, 1905, col. 1023.
[95] *Ibid.,* Feb. 2, 1905, col. 535. [96] *Ibid.,* March 6, 1905, cols. 699–700.
[97] *Ibid.,* Aug. 14, 1905, col. 2622. [98] *Ibid.,* June 11, 1906, col. 2077.

Duma parties on the agrarian question and added, "They do not mention the holy Orthodox Faith; they have decreed the Jewish Sabbath a holiday, and they wish to do away with our holy Sunday." [99]

There were other reports of priestly activity of a similar character. At the request of a priest of the village of Mastinovka, in the province of Penza, "who is a well-known Black Hundredist," the mounted police were called out several times, and the priest plied them with vodka. "The policemen cruelly beat innocent inhabitants who are disliked by the priest. The peasants have sent a complaint to the bishop." [100] And in St. Petersburg, *Birzhevyia Vedomosti* (*The Bourse News*) reported that the famous Father Ioann of Kronstadt had preached a sermon to a selected gathering "On the Jews in General, and in Particular on the Pogroms." The group present, composed chiefly of his devoted followers, became more and more excited as his sermon progressed. The lesson of the message was that "the Jews bring the pogroms upon themselves, and in this is seen the hand of God, punishing them for their grievous sins against the government." [101]

Even more active in their incitement, according to the secular press, were some of the monks. Mention has already been made of the Abbot Arsenii, who for a time was exiled to the Solovetskii Monastery for his extreme counter-revolutionary agitation. He does not seem to have moderated his tone after his return, for in December, 1906, according to a newspaper report, he called a meeting in the church in the village of Afimovka, in one of the southern provinces, "and from the pulpit he and his fellows in sharply inflammatory terms called the people to struggle against the Jews, the sellers of Christ." [102] In the village of Valuia, in the province of Khar'kov, the monk Ignatii, of a local monastery, read from the pulpit, apparently as a supposed imperial manifesto, a "Black Hundred leaflet from the Pochaevskaia Monastery, which ended with the words, 'The people's sentence upon democrats is beating and the gallows. God grant that it may be so forever.'" [103] A more detailed story was told in a monthly periodical in 1908; it described a large monastery near the boundary of the

---

[99] *Tserkovnyi Vestnik,* July 13, 1906, col. 912.
[100] *Pravo,* Dec. 10, 1906, col. 3891.   [101] *Ibid.,* Dec. 17, 1906, col. 3991.
[102] *Ibid.,* cols. 3992–93.   [103] *Ibid.,* Dec. 31, 1906, col. 4169.

provinces of Kursk and Chernigov, where it had been found necessary to turn some twenty of the five hundred monks into mounted guards in order to protect the lands and forests of the monastery from the hostile peasants. An outstanding feature of the monastery's conservatism was said to be the activity of the monk Agafodor, who frequently traveled around the countryside to organize local branches of the Union of the Russian People, often harangued the passengers in railroad cars, and distributed pamphlets supporting "the sacred right of private property" and blaming all of Russia's troubles on the Jews.[104]

A direct connection with the pogrom at Kursk on October 19, 1905, was assigned, in a report published by the journal *Obrazovanie* (*Education*), to one of the monasteries. An eyewitness is alleged to have stated that a procession, authorized by the police, in honor of the October Manifesto, was broken up by an assault of the Black Hundred, while the police and the Cossacks stood idly by. "After this the Black Hundreds were summoned to a monastery for a ceremonial Te Deum in the presence of the governor, followed by a patriotic manifestation with a military band, a portrait of the Tsar, and national flags, under escort of the Cossacks." This led finally to plundering the shops and houses of the Jews, which lasted all night.[105]

The same account stated that a few days later a certain Father Psarev discussed these happenings while commenting on an official message of the Synod. He said: "Honorable Christians! A certain Over Procurator of the Most Holy Synod has proposed to the bishops, and they . . . to the priests, that we pacify the people; but I shall not pacify you; let them pacify you who began it. . . ." He went on to list the difficulties of the times, the rioting, the high prices due to strikes, and the like. He concluded his sermon with a reference to a

handful of men whom we have here in Kursk; recently they went along Moscow Street with red flags; the red flag, I must tell you, means blood; but another group, of honorable men, broke up that band. It is untrue that they [the latter group] were summoned [by agitators]; no, God himself inspired them to stand for the right. And two of them have been

---

[104] S. Lisenko, "Chernaia Sotnia v Provintsii," *Russkaia Mysl'*, 1908, No. 2, pp. 20–28.

[105] I. P. Belokonskii, "Chernosotennoe Dvizhenie," *Obrazovanie*, Jan., 1906, pp. 60–62.

buried, killed by the revolver of a lawyer. Who compose the party of unclean men? *This party consists of Jews, the good-for-nothing mayor of this town, his assistant, and various doctors and lawyers.* Thus, Christians, I shall not pacify you. . . . I shall not tell you what you should do; I have only told you whence all this came.[106]

Most noted of the monks who carried on reactionary agitation was Iliodor, already named in these pages as the editor of *Pochaevskii Listok* and *Pochaevskiia Izvestiia*. Not only did he publish these periodicals and work actively to form branches of the Union of the Russian People in the diocese of Volhynia, but he also wrote inflammatory pamphlets, of which a few samples have been preserved. His *Lament over the Destruction of the Dear Fatherland* apostrophizes Holy Mother Rus. "Hand and foot thou art fettered in Jewish chains; Jewish capitalists have bound thee." He went on to claim that almost all of the Tsar's ministers were betrayers, bought by the gold of the Jews; here lay the cause of Russia's low estate.[107] *When Will There Be an End?*—another of his works—held the same message: "Save us from the race accursed of God—the Jews; for they are the ones chiefly to blame for our disasters." The pamphlet went on to list the evils to be blamed upon this race, accusing them of causing the death of Russian soldiers on the plains of Manchuria, and of responsibility for the corpses floating in the waves of Tsushima, as well as for the "seas of blood" which had "drowned the unity of Russia." [108]

A most striking specimen of Iliodor's propaganda was entitled *The Vision of a Monk*. In his vision the monastic saw on one side "the holy Black Hundred," which was ready to fight "for Faith, Tsar, and Fatherland." "But where were their enemies? Where were these blasphemers of God and of everything holy? . . . He turned his head to the left and saw these enemies." Those whom he saw upon the left were decidedly less numerous than those on the right, and among them there were but few simple peasants; their ranks were filled chiefly with petty bourgeois, students, factory workers. The monk noticed that among the enemy stood representatives of many races; "and especially noticeable were the Jews; they almost all stood in front." Finally the pamphlet told how God appeared, to confound his

---

[106] I. P. Belokonskii, in *Obrazovanie*, Jan., 1906, p. 66.
[107] S. M. Trufanov [Iliodor], *Plach na Pogibel Dorogogo Otchestva*, pp. 6–10.
[108] Trufanov, *Kogda-zhe Konets?*

enemies and their leader, Satan, and how God's followers, the Black Hundred, with the aid of the angels and the saints, and with the Tsar as their leader, fell upon Satan's band and killed them or forced them to flee.[109] So ended the monk's vision.

The more extreme of Iliodor's publications made his name noted throughout Russia—so much so that the Synod, which was generally conservative in its actions, rebuked him. In its decree of February 14, 1907, it declared that

the inclusion of articles which summon the Russian people to undertake bloody self-help against the violators of the social order, and [which urge] the representatives of the church to bless such self-help—especially in journals printed in the Pochaevskaia Monastery, so deeply esteemed by the Orthodox population, and edited by persons of religious rank who should be preachers of the love of Christ—is exceedingly regrettable and unworthy of the Orthodox Church.

Consequently the Synod decreed that Archbishop Antonii of Volhynia should dismiss Iliodor from his post as editor of *Pochaevskiia Izvestiia* and *Pochaevskii Listok*.[110] But in spite of this rebuke, Iliodor was heard from again.

Certainly not all of the Orthodox clergy preached pogroms or distributed anti-Semitic propaganda. Many were completely passive; others, a much smaller group, actively worked to prevent pogroms. An example of the anti-pogrom spirit among the clergy was supplied by Dean Nadezhdin. In an article in the *Olonets Diocesan News* he mentioned the distressing events that were happening in the cities of Russia—in one, the beating of the entirely peaceful intelligentsia; in another, a Jewish pogrom of unprecedented violence; in a third, attacks on students; and in a fourth, "a frightful mass action of the mob which gives to the fire more than six hundred persons, while the bloodthirsty, bestial crowd watches this frightful hecatomb." His remedy for this was the instilling of true Christian love by pastors of the church.[111]

Another message calculated to calm the populace was printed in the Moscow newspapers, at the request of the "Society of the Friends of Religious Enlightenment," soon after the publication of the

[109] Trufanov, *Videnie Monakha.*
[110] *Tserkovnyi Vestnik*, March 1, 1907, col. 302.
[111] Quoted in *Missionerskoe Obozrenie*, Nov., 1905, p. 111.

counter-revolutionary message of Metropolitan Vladimir, "What We Should Do in These Our Troubled Days." The Moscow priests who were members of the society mentioned the appeal issued by the so-called "Holy Union of National Defense" to Orthodox Christians to gather for the protection of the faith of Christ, the Tsar, and the Fatherland. The priests declared that this union had no reason to term itself holy and repeated the earlier messages sent by the Synod, to the effect that "The heart of the Tsar is in the hand of God." Hence all should subject themselves to the ruler's will, for *"he who thinks by violence and disorder to render a service to the Sovereign lays on his soul a heavy burden. He serves only the secret and the open enemies of his Tsar. The Russian Orthodox Sovereign is himself great and strong enough to punish the violators of the law through the legally appointed authorities."* [112]

Some of the clergy were not content merely to give pacifying counsel to their people, but were personally active in stopping pogroms or in lessening the horrors of counter-revolutionary violence. According to an Odessa newspaper, a Jew of the city of Voznesensk sent a letter to the archbishop of Kherson, praising the action of several Orthodox priests who had sheltered Jewish women and children during a pogrom, and especially of the two priests who had forced their way into the mob of men who were wrecking the bazaar, tried to stop the plunderers, and come very near to being beaten by them.[113] Again, a Jew of Mariupol wrote a letter to Bishop Simeon of Ekaterinoslav, praising the deeds of several priests of the county of Mariupol during the local pogroms.[114] From the tribune of the Duma was proclaimed the action of a monk during the terrific pogrom in Tomsk. Seeing a mob beating a student in front of the seminary, before which a student had just been killed, the young monk in charge ran out to the pogromists, raised his crucifix, and said loudly, "Why do you beat my brother?" The crowd actually turned aside, so that other students had a chance to drag the victim into the building. Thanks to this, his life was saved.[115]

[112] *Russkiia Vedomosti,* Nov. 5, 1905.
[113] *Tserkovnyia Vedomosti,* Feb. 18, 1906, p. 341.
[114] *Ibid.,* Feb. 25, 1906, pp. 391–92.
[115] Gosudarstvennaia Duma, *Stenograficheskie Otchety,* I Duma, section I, p. 1811.

There were also instances in which bishops acted to stop pogroms. On the second day of the Kiev pogrom of October, 1905, "when outrage and licentiousness reached their height," Bishop Platon, one of the vicars of the diocese, appealed to the mob to stop beating and robbing the Jews. In order to heighten the force of his appeal, he organized a solemn procession through the streets of the Jewish quarter and begged the mob to spare the lives and the property of the Jews, even falling on his knees before the ruffians. On one occasion a member of the mob dashed up to him with a threat, shouting "So you're for the Jews!" The rest of the crowd appeared more respectful, but continued their looting.[116]

While there is available no evidence to show that other bishops emulated Bishop Platon's personal example, Bishop Innokentii of Tambov did send a proclamation to the residents of his diocese, telling them that appeals for pogroms against the Jews were sinful and that Christianity was a religion of peace.[117] Likewise, Bishop Parfenii of Podolia told his priests to array themselves in their vestments and with their crucifixes to go before mobs engaged in pogroms against the Jews, in order to calm their angry passions.[118] Other instances of this sort there may have been, for in February, 1906, a priest wrote to *Missionerskoe Obozrenie*, ". . . many pastors of the church went before the people, in order to recall their sons to peace and quiet. Some of the pastors performed services for the gathering crowds, hoping to give a prayerful trend to the manifestation of popular feeling, while others went to the raging crowds and summoned them to gentleness and sanity." [119] Unfortunately the citation does not indicate whether the mobs in question were intent on attacking the Jews of the ghetto or the estates of Russian landlords.

Indeed while some of the clergy were striving to prevent violence and to calm the mobs, their restraining influence was undone by the increasing encouragement given by noted churchmen and even by the Synod to the reactionary counter-revolutionary organizations, which frequently practiced violence. On August 20, 1906, for example, in the hall of the diocesan home in Moscow there was held a joint

[116] *Materialy k Istorii Russkoi Kontr-revoliutsii*, I, 235, Report of Senator Turau on the Kiev pogrom.

[117] *Tserkovnyia Vedomosti*, Nov. 19, 1905, p. 1996.

[118] *Ibid.*, p. 1997.   [119] *Missionerskoe Obozrenie*, Feb., 1906, p. 260.

meeting of the Society of Russian Patriots and the Union of the Russian People, at which Dean I. Vostorgov, a noted reactionary, performed a ceremonial requiem for the victims killed in the attempted assassination of Prime Minister Stolypin.[120] Approval on the part of the highest Orthodox clergy was more clearly manifested at the time of the "All-Russian Congress of Russian Men" at Kiev on October 1, 1906. "The Congress opened . . . with a Te Deum performed by Metropolitan Flavian of Kiev together with vicarian bishops Platon and Agapit, and many other clergy. After the service, His Lordship preached a sermon in which he called on the Russian men to unite." [121]

This congress closed on the same note. After the last session, all the members went to the Kievo-Pecherskaia Monastery, with Dean Vostorgov at their head; there Metropolitan Flavian and the vicarian bishops "performed a solemn service of thanksgiving, with the singing of 'long life' to the Sovereign Emperor and to all the Ruling House. . . . All those attending were blessed with small ikons sprinkled with holy water." Afterward there was a requiem for those who had given up their lives at the hands of traitors "in behalf of Faith, Tsar, and Fatherland." [122]

The metropolitan of Kiev was not the only highly placed churchman to set the seal of his approval on this congress, for the following telegram was received by the president of the gathering:

Deeply touched by the attention of the Congress of Russian Men. It would be sinful for a servant of the Church not to respond to the prayers of those in whose hearts God "hath proclaimed the good tidings of His Church." I earnestly pray to the All-Highest that He may help the Congress of Russian Men to attain the blessed desires which inspire them.

Vladimir, Metropolitan of Moscow.[123]

The desires of the congress to which the metropolitan had reference in large part consisted of hopes that the enemies of Orthodoxy, Autocracy, and Nationality might be confounded.[124] Among its leading members were Abbot Arsenii, Gringmut, Prince Shakhovskoi, Dubrovin, and other noted reactionaries including the editors of the most extreme counter-revolutionary newspapers, such as *Moskovskiia*

[120] *Veche*, Aug. 25, 1906.   [121] *Ibid.*, Oct. 5, 1906.
[122] *Ibid.*, Oct. 12, 1906.   [123] *Ibid.*, Oct. 10, 1906.
[124] *Ibid.*, Oct. 5, 1906.

Vedomosti (*The Moscow News*), *Den'* (*The Day*), and *Russkoe Znamia* (*The Russian Banner*).[125] In the minds of the liberal section of Russian society these men were responsible for the spreading of anti-Semitic and counter-revolutionary propaganda, and thus in part for the wave of pogroms.

Nor, according to newspaper reports, were these the only instances of ecclesiastical favor for the reactionary groups. In Vilna, on December 10, 1906, the opening of a branch of the Union of the Russian People was attended by the priest Golubev. "Before the opening, a Te Deum was said, at which the diocesan choir sang. The priest Golubev, Davydov, and others spoke in the Black Hundred spirit." [126] "In Sevastopol Bishop Aleksii of Taurida has urged the priests to attend the meetings of the Union of the Russian People." [127] "In Minsk in the diocesan home, closed meetings of the Union of the Russian People are being held. Only those summoned are admitted." [128] "Pastors and congregations of churches of the Taurida, of Perm, of Tambov, and of several other dioceses were strongly urged by their bishops to join 'the Union of Truly Russian Men.' " [129] At the monarchist congress in Moscow in April, 1907, Metropolitan Vladimir performed a liturgy for the members in the Uspenskii Cathedral, and he and many other members of the clergy took part in their procession through the streets.[130] And in the autumn of 1907 the diocesan authorities of Kazan declared that to keep the emblems and banners of the Union of the Russian People in the churches was not only "permissible, but even desirable, so that to everyone it will be clear that the Holy Orthodox Church fully approves and blesses the high patriotic holy cause of the Union of the Russian People and takes this work under its prayerful protection." [131]

As was stated earlier in this chapter, the Synod, during 1905 and 1906, by its rebukes to Abbot Arsenii and to Metropolitan Vladimir, showed itself unwilling to countenance the extremes of the counter-revolutionaries, even though its general policy was conservative. Indeed even in 1907 it administered reproof to the agitator Iliodor.

---

[125] *Ibid.*
[126] *Pravo,* Dec. 17, 1906, col. 3992.
[127] *Ibid.,* Dec. 10, 1906, col. 3885.
[128] *Ibid.,* Dec. 23, 1906, col. 4087.
[129] *Tserkovno-obshchestvennaia Zhizn',* Dec. 15, 1906, cols. 1714–15.
[130] *Vera i Razum,* May, 1907, pp. 565–66.
[131] *Ibid.,* Dec., 1907, p. 859.

Nevertheless, by 1907 the policy of the Synod was becoming more favorable to the parties of the extreme Right. On January 20, 1906, Bishop Vladimir of Kishinev sent an inquiry to the Synod: "May the clergy become members of the Union of the Seventeenth of October [a mildly liberal party]?" The question was answered by Metropolitan Antonii of St. Petersburg, who replied that the clergy should not attach themselves to political parties, "but should bear in mind above all their service to the church, which stands above and outside all parties. A Synodal explanation of the proper attitude of the clergy in this respect will follow." [132] However, this neutral stand was not satisfactory to some members of the reactionary parties. On October 13, 1906, the Elizavetgrad branch of the Union of the Russian People telegraphed to the Over Procurator, "Kindly permit the clergy of Elizavetgrad County, Diocese of Kherson, to take part in the meetings of right-thinking men, called by the Union of the Russian People in November. . . ." [133] The Synod now replied, "The Most Holy Synod does not forbid the clergy to take part in lawful gatherings." [134] When the Ufa branch of this party sent a similar request to the Synod early in 1907, the same reply was made.[135] Thus the Synod withdrew from its former position of disapproval of priestly participation in all parties, and in veiled form gave the clergy the right to take part in the moderate and conservative parties as well as in the most reactionary of them all. Indeed this permission to join "lawful gatherings" in actuality allowed the clergy to join all parties from the Right to the Progressives of the Left Center and even the Cadets. Several priests of the Third Duma were affiliated with the moderately liberal parties, yet suffered no punishment therefor.

Not long after the granting of this general permission, the Perm branch of the Union of the Russian People chose two monks, Iuvenalii and Serafim, as its delegates to the All-Russian Congress of Monarchists in Moscow. Both the leader of the local organization and Bishop Nikanor of Perm asked the Synod whether these monks might be permitted to attend in this capacity.[136] In answer, the Synod stated that the bishop of Perm might be permitted to release them from duty

---

[132] Sv. Sinod, 1906, portfolio 775, sheets 1–3.
[133] Ibid., sheets 12–13.   [134] Ibid., sheet 17.
[135] Ibid., sheets 19–20.   [136] Ibid., sheets 22–24.

in the monastery for this purpose.[137] The Synod also informed Archbishop Nikolai of Vladimir that he might consecrate the regalia of the local branch of the Union of the Russian People and might keep them in the church, if the banners met with his approval.[138]

Other requests for clarification of the Synod's position respecting political organizations were soon made. In August, 1907, a congress of monarchical organizations of the province of Astrakhan asked the Synod's blessing "for those priests and laymen who enter patriotic organizations for the peaceful struggle against treason, which disturbs both church and state, and for the maintenance of the great foundations of Russian statehood—Orthodoxy, Autocracy, and Nationality." [139] To this appeal the governor of Ekaterinoslav added his voice. "I know that actually the Most Reverend Simeon, Bishop of Ekaterinoslav, strongly disapproves of the participation of the clergy in the party of the Union of the Russian People, thus depriving this party of many intelligent and useful workers who might lend it invaluable support." [140] In answer, the ruling body of the church decided to "advise the Most Reverend Bishop of Ekaterinoslav that the Synod blesses the participation of the clergy of Ekaterinoslav in the activity of the local Union, as long as the Union remains in conformity with the rules of the Orthodox Church and its hierarchy, and serves to benefit our Fatherland." [141]

Thus in several instances the Synod showed a benevolent attitude toward this organization. However, the Synod had not yet taken an open stand on the matter; its approval had not been made public. The Union of the Russian People felt that this absence of official Synod approbation hampered its cause, for on March 11, 1908, the All-Russian Congress of the Union sent a letter to the Synod, asking for an open expression of its approval. The reason for the request was that many of the clergy refused to join the Union without the express permission of their bishops or of the Synod itself.[142] Once more the Synod gratified the counter-revolutionaries; on the fifteenth of March it was decreed "to inform the bishops for their careful attention that they should permit and bless the participation of the Orthodox clergy

[137] *Ibid.*, sheet 26.
[138] *Ibid.*
[139] *Ibid.*, sheet 27.
[140] *Ibid.*, sheets 28–29.
[141] *Ibid.*, sheet 30.
[142] *Ibid.*, sheet 36.

under them in the activities of the Union of the Russian People and of other monarchical patriotic societies as long as they remain in conformity with the rules of the Orthodox Church and serve the interests of.the Fatherland." [143]

It should be added that not even this pronouncement was entirely satisfactory to the members of the Union of the Russian People. Not long after the above interchange of letters, the Chief Council of the organization sent a complaint to the Synod, to the effect that a number of the bishops had interpreted the discretionary directions given to them in a manner unfavorable to the Union and had forbidden their clergy to join its ranks. To remedy this situation, the Chief Council proposed that "the highly authoritative voice of the company of ruling hierarchs of the Russian Church should state firmly and definitely how the clergy should act toward the Union of the Russian People." [144] To this the Synod apparently made no answer; it perhaps felt that the earlier expressions of opinion were sufficient indication of the Synod's approval of this counter-revolutionary party.

In still another fashion the authorities of the church showed their sympathy with the Union of the Russian People. In 1908 the Fourth Missionary Congress at Kiev passed, and the Synod approved, a resolution that if the missionaries found their efforts blocked, they should "resort to coöperation with the political parties that inscribe on their banners the defense of the Orthodox Faith, namely, the Union of the Russian People and the Union of the Archangel Gabriel [another reactionary group]." [145]

In the eyes of the liberals of the period, it was in the highest degree compromising for the ruling body of the church to approve the Union of the Russian People. Mention has already been made of the vehement anti-Semitic propaganda which this party disseminated in its newspapers and in pamphlet form. Its agents were widely regarded as instigators of pogroms, and liberals and radicals believed that true Christians should feel only horror at the mention of the Union of the Russian People. An article published on January 18, 1907, in the

[143] Sv. Sinod, 1906, portfolio 775, sheet 38.   [144] *Ibid.*, sheet 45.
[145] Gosudarstvennaia Duma, *Stenograficheskie Otchety*, III Duma, Session II, Part 3, col. 2255.

liberal ecclesiastical journal, *Tserkovnyi Vestnik,* expressed its repugnance for some of the actions of the counter-revolutionaries:

The Hebrew pogroms, at first breaking out now here, now there, in 1905 and 1906 swept over all Russia in a hurricane. The soul shuddered at the news of the bestialities which occurred; but the "Truly Russian Men" of all ranks and names rejoiced and celebrated "the victory over the revolutionaries." That is, over some aged women—revolutionaries, forsooth—and youths with nails driven into their skulls![146]

In its issue of September 24, 1906, *Pravo* (*The Law*), a law review of far from radical tendencies, discussed the leading party of the extreme Right in an editorial of the same tone:

. . . As the relations of the government to the Union of the Russian People became more clearly defined, the impudence of the Black Hundred organizations grew and grew, and the carrying out of the second part of the program [of reforms] became more and more difficult. This especially refers, of course, to the reform of the position of the Jews, against whom the members of the Union rose in arms with all the strength of their bloodthirsty hatred, their unreasoning wish to annihilate.[147]

In the Third Duma, in 1909, an interpellation was proposed concerning several murders or attempted assassinations of members of the Duma, which were alleged to have been actions of the Union of the Russian People. The government was asked to explain its supposed connection with these outrages. The proposal was sponsored largely by the parties of the Left and the Left Center. However, it was signed not only by members of these groups, but also by three priests who belonged to the Progressive party, and by Counts Uvarov and A. Tolstoi, who were not affiliated with any party.[148] Professor Miliukov, the leader of the liberal Cadet party, denounced the support of the Union by high officials of the government, and said that the Bishop of Chirigin had been elected as an honorary member of the Union and had consented to accept his title and a certificate of membership; likewise, that the bishop of Ekaterinoslav had taken part in a ceremony of the Union, although the clergy of his diocese

[146] *Tserkovnyi Vestnik,* Jan. 18, 1907, col. 83.
[147] *Pravo,* Sept. 24, 1906, col. 2922.
[148] Gosudarstvennaia Duma, *Prilozheniia k Stenograficheskim Otchetam,* III Duma, Session II, Vol. 2, No. 461.

were reported to have abstained from participation.[149] The most damaging testimony during the debate on the Union of the Russian People was given by the Progressive, Fedorov. He told of forming an acquaintance, during the period of the Second Duma, with Dezobri, leader of the St. Petersburg "fighting band" of the Union. Dezobri had openly admitted that he was the leader of this fighting band and had declared that he received two bags of revolvers from the military commandant of the capital.[150] Other speakers against the Union of the Russian People were Count Uvarov, and Protopopov, who became Minister of Internal Affairs under the Tsar shortly before the Revolution of 1917. As a result of these denunciations, the Duma voted, 131 to 87, to interpellate the government concerning its relations with the Union.[151] Inasmuch as the electoral law of 1907 had greatly strengthened the voting power of the wealthy classes at the expense of the poorer peasants and the city workers, it seems probable that public opinion in Russia would have been even stronger in its condemnation of the Union of the Russian People if the people themselves had had an opportunity to give free expression to their views.

The vote of the Third Duma may be taken as proving that the liberals of the time were generally of the opinion that the Union of the Russian People was an organization that deserved the condemnation and not the support of the church. This belief was an important fact in itself; but fortunately for the student of today, the strong suspicions of 1906 and 1907 were verified in full by the testimony of former members of the Imperial government and of members of the Union, given before the investigating commission of the Provisional government in April, 1917. Not only did members of the Union of the Russian People admit that they had belonged to armed "fighting bands" organized by the Union, but the secretary of the editorial staff of the reactionary newspaper *Russkoe Znamia* testified that these bands had been formed in order to combat political opponents, to kill personal enemies, and to cause riots, looting, and killing.[152] Further

---

[149] Gosudarstvennaia Duma, *Stenograficheskie Otchety,* III Duma, Session II, Part 4, cols. 2239–40.

[150] *Ibid.,* cols. 2338–40.

[151] *Ibid.,* cols. 2298–2304 and 2336–38; col. 2368.

[152] P. E. Shchegolev, ed., *Padenie Tsarskogo Rezhima,* I, 320; II, 354–55; A. Chernovskii, ed., *Soiuz Russkogo Naroda,* pp. 33, 40–45, 50–53, 57, 62–63.

evidence concerning the fighting bands of the Union of the Russian People is given in a series of telegrams to the Minister of Internal Affairs from the commandant of gendarmes in Odessa, in the spring and summer of 1907. The officer of gendarmes testified to the provocative conduct of the members of the local fighting band, their attempts to start a pogrom in Odessa, and the series of attacks which they made upon individuals, both Russians and Jews, on the streets of the city. "As repeated police reports have stated, this band for the most part consists of youths without regular occupation, and among them some charged with theft, and even some known to the police as *souteneurs* living off the takings of prostitutes." [153]

This information concerning the Union of the Russian People has been introduced to show the nature of this political party. In the testimony which has been studied on the subject of the fighting bands, there is no word directly implicating the church or the clergy; none the less, the evidence is damaging for the church. It is impossible not to realize that this Union was an organization which violated the fundamental teachings of the Christian faith. It is likewise difficult to believe that the members of the Synod of the Russian Church did not know the nature of the Union to which they gave their open support; its actions and the nature of its propaganda were too well known at the time for the churchmen to plead ignorance. And indeed by their utterances from the pulpit and by their printed words a considerable number of the higher clergy showed that their sympathies were with the counter-revolution, and some were even inclined to countenance violence.

However, while many of the higher clergy were strongly conservative, it appears that the bulk of the parish clergy did not follow their lead. Like the outspoken liberals from the ranks of the priesthood, the clerical reactionaries were far from representing the mass of their fellows. According to the statements of a number of observers, including several from the ranks of the clergy, most of the parish priests refused to declare themselves on political matters. There is reason to believe that this failure to take sides was due in part to fear of arousing dangerous enmity on one side or the other. As one priest wrote to *Tserkovnyi Vestnik,*

[153] Chernovskii, *op. cit.,* pp. 216, 225, 227, 230–31.

If a priest does not act in the spirit of the Union of Russian Men, the "lords" threaten, and the religious authorities also. If you are on the side of this Union, the peasants pass resolutions not to give anything to the pope [the village priest], they threaten to loose the "red cockerel" [fire], to wreck his home, and even to kill him. What then is to be done? [154]

Whether this is the chief cause is something that cannot be determined, but certainly many observers remarked upon the neutrality of the priests. A number of articles in the liberal *Tserkovnyi Vestnik* proclaimed this as a fact,[155] as did the comment of three other ecclesiastical publications, two of them in the conservative camp.[156] Hence there is a strong probability that during the revolutionary years most of the lower clergy refrained from taking sides.

While many of the lower clergy doubtless tried to preserve their neutrality, the Synod, as has been shown, was definitely opposed to the "liberative movement." Nevertheless, there is evidence to show that the support which the administration of the church rendered to the government was not so effective as the latter might have wished. During the Revolution of 1905 the influence of the clergy seems to have been limited. Several observers commented on the indifference of many of the members of the educated classes. Vasilii Rozanov, whose articles were printed in the conservative *Novoe Vremia*, reported his observations when attending church both in St. Petersburg and in the provinces. "Nowhere does an official, a judge, a naval officer, a general, a journalist, a doctor, or a statesman stand among the people and worship fervently. Everywhere—only the humble people. . . . This is much more distressing than the books of Strauss and Renan." [157] Even more serious for the church was the alienation of the masses reported by the official *Tserkovnyia Vedomosti*. "From all sides are heard complaints . . . that the clergy do not command the minds of the people. Prejudice against the clergy did not begin

[154] Oct. 12, 1906, cols. 1327–28.

[155] Feb. 3, 1905, cols. 138–41; March 10, 1905, cols. 295–96; March 17, 1905, cols. 334–36; May 5, 1905, col. 567; Sept. 29, 1905, col. 1221; Jan. 26, 1906, col. 106.

[156] *Pravoslavnyi Sobesednik*, April, 1905, pp. 661–63; *Missionerskoe Obozrenie*, Oct., 1905, pp. 759–61; *Tserkovnyia Vedomosti*, Feb. 10, 1907, pp. 240–44.

[157] V. Rozanov, *Okolo Tserkovnykh Sten*, I, 330.

yesterday; it has simply succeeded in taking root in society."[158] This article went on to cite supporting evidence from several of the diocesan publications—those of the dioceses of Podolia, Kaluga, and Kursk.[159] Much the same thing was said by *Khristianskoe Chtenie* (*Christian Reading*).[160]

A number of reasons were assigned by members of the clergy for the low level of priestly influence. "A Village Priest," in the *Orel Diocesan News*, laid it to a lack of seriousness on the part of the clergy, as evidenced by their mechanical manner of saying the service.[161] A pastor of Kishinev declared that the priests lacked energy.[162] Priestly formalism and servility before the authorities were the reasons given by a pastor of Orenburg;[163] while a priest of Iaroslavl wrote, "In our parish, especially among the young, real unbelief is evident. . . . How to cure the evil I do not know."[164] Another writer blamed the weakness of religious influence on the fact that for years the best sons of the clergy had been turning to civil life, so that "of late the mental and moral level of the village clergy has been declining."[165] To make matters worse, he said, many of those who took holy orders found themselves faced with such discouraging ignorance and poverty in the villages that they lost their morale.[166] An enlightening item was reprinted from the *Diocesan News* of Simbirsk. The author stated that the clergy were not satisfied with their lot. They wanted to be permitted to wear civilian dress, to cut their hair and to shave their beards, to remarry if they became widowers, to send their sons to the universities without entrance examinations, and the like.[167]

Still other reasons were given for the disturbing phenomenon. The district priests, according to the *Don Diocesan News*, stated that the local priests offended their parishioners by their hasty and mechanical performance of prayers when visiting the peasants' homes for the collection of donations.[168] Much more serious was the charge made in the diocesan journal of Nizhnii Novgorod, which stated that there

[158] Dec. 2, 1906, pp. 3051–52.　　　[159] *Ibid.*
[160] Nov., 1906, pp. 627–29.
[161] *Tserkovnyi Vestnik,* Oct. 19, 1906, col. 1372.
[162] *Ibid.*　　　[163] *Ibid.*　　　[164] *Ibid.*
[165] *Pravoslavnyi Sobesednik,* Jan., 1905, p. 156.　　　[166] *Ibid.*
[167] *Tserkovnyia Vedomosti,* Dec. 16, 1906, pp. 3126–27.
[168] *Tserkovnyi Vestnik,* July 20, 1906, col. 957.

were priests "who do not hesitate to declare openly that they do not recognize any special sanctity in pastoral service," and that such cases were far from exceptional.[169] A writer in the weekly publication of the Kazan Religious Academy affirmed that among the pastors of the church were men who did not believe in the sacraments of the church and who denied the sanctity of its rites. The author referred especially to a former classmate at the religious seminary, who "mocked at the sacrament of the Eucharist in such terms that my readers would not believe them if they were made public."[170]

By other ecclesiastics the weakness of priestly influence was ascribed to failure to side with the peasants against the landowners, an attitude which at times became almost slavishness before the great and the near-great. "Who has not noticed what humbleness and even servility the ministers of the church display before some local bigwig —a landlord, an official, or merely a rich merchant—and with what offensive scorn they treat the poor man?" These words came, not from a journal of the Left, but from the official church publication, *Tserkovnyia Vedomosti,* which reprinted them from the pages of the *Polotsk Diocesan News.*[171] Another issue of *Tserkovnyia Vedomosti* reprinted an article from the *Kiev Diocesan News* entitled, "Why Don't They Believe Us?" In this passage the author explained that the failure of the clergy to control the outcome of the elections to the Second Duma was due to "the distrust of the peasants [for the priests], which was no less than their distrust of the landlords."[172]

In July, 1905, the first of two All-Russian Peasant Congresses met in Moscow. This body contained delegates from only about half of the provinces of European Russia, and even these delegates had not been chosen in a uniform manner. Moreover, the congress was attended by some Social Democrats and Socialist Revolutionaries, although these outsiders were not allowed to vote for the executive committee.[173] None the less, the decisions of the congress possess considerable interest as an indication of what some of the peasants were thinking. The delegates agreed that Russia should have complete freedom of

[169] *Tserkovnyi Vestnik,* Nov. 16, 1906, col. 1512.   [170] *Ibid.*
[171] *Tserkovnyia Vedomosti,* July 14, 1907, p. 1139.
[172] *Ibid.,* Aug. 26, 1906, p. 2479.
[173] G. T. Robinson, *Rural Russia under the Old Regime,* p. 161.

conscience, as well as freedom of speech, of the press, and of assembly. A constituent assembly should be called to establish a new form of government; this assembly should be elected by near-universal suffrage, limited by the exclusion of certain minor categories of persons: those who should be deprived of the vote were criminals convicted by courts of the people, members of the police, officials of the government, and the clergy. The congress voted unanimously that all land, including that of the churches and the monasteries, should be nationalized without compensation. In addition, all schools should be secular in character. Religious instruction in the schools should be given only with the consent of the parents. Only three votes were cast for compulsory religious education.[174]

The second Peasant Congress, which met in November, 1905, had delegates from twenty-seven of the fifty provinces of European Russia and in other respects was little more representative than the first.[175] Moreover, the second gathering was much more interested in the tactics to be used against the landlords than in discussing objectives, so that its decisions had but little relation to the Orthodox Church. However, the second Peasant Congress voted that all land must be made common property of the whole people; also it insisted that the franchise be given to members of all creeds alike.[176]

Neither of the Peasant Congresses was a truly representative body. This does not mean, however, that their attitude toward the church was more extreme than that of the mass of the peasants. In economic matters, at least, a considerable part of the village populace seems to have been more radical than the Peasant Congresses: while the congresses were *talking* about a constituent assembly and the nationalization of all land, if necessary by seizure, the peasants of many villages were *actively engaged* in seizing the property of the landlords and in burning manor houses.[177] If the attitude of the villages toward the church differed in similar fashion from the attitude of the congresses, the friends of the church could draw little comfort from the unrepresentative character of these gatherings.

[174] Vserossiiskii Krest'ianskii Soiuz, *Postanovleniia S'ezdov Krest'ianskogo Soiuza*, pp. 1–4.
[175] Robinson, *op. cit.*, p. 171.
[176] Vserossiiskii Krest'ianskii Soiuz, *op. cit.*, p. 6.
[177] Robinson, *op. cit.*, p. 173.

To what lengths the distrust of the clergy sometimes went was strikingly shown by reports of peasant activity during 1905 and 1906. When peasants were burning the buildings on the estate of Count Bobrinskii, in the province of Tula, one of the local priests tried to restrain them, but they jeered at him and threatened to throw him into the fire.[178] In a village of Orel the peasants, after wrecking the home of a landowner, plundered the house of their priest and drove him out. Later, when he was preaching in the church, he was interrupted by shouted insults and threats to drag him out of the church if he did not stop speaking.[179] Peasants of the village of Chemeevo, in Kazan, rose, drove out the police from their village, refused to pay taxes, and demanded that the priest should leave the village.[180] In another locality, after the priest had preached a sermon on the dissolution of the Duma, the peasants wrecked his home and conducted him and his family to the boundary of the parish.[181] A wave of arson in the county of Voronezh destroyed not only the property of landowners, but also the hay barn of a priest, valued at one thousand rubles, and the buildings of another, of eight hundred rubles' value.[182] In fact so great was the hostility to some of the priests that in the province of Penza several of them asked the county police inspector for permission to buy weapons, as they were afraid of personal attack; but the consistory of the diocese ruled against their proposal.[183]

Perhaps more significant, although less violent, was the communal action taken by some villages against the clergy. There were a number of decisions to revoke the agreements to pay salaries to the priests,[184] and several of the meetings voted to take over the church land used by their pastors. In several cases these proposals were actually carried out, and the meadows of the priests were mowed, and their fields plowed, by the peasants.[185] This action was caused in part by the feeling that the need of the peasants was greater than that of

[178] M. N. Pokrovskii, ed., *1905—Materialy i Dokumenty*, Vol. 5-i, p. 127.
[179] *Ibid.*, p. 169.   [180] *Ibid.*, p. 488.
[181] *Tserkovnyi Vestnik*, Oct. 12, 1906, col. 1319.
[182] Pokrovskii, *op. cit.*, Vol. 5-i, p. 331.
[183] *Vera i Razum*, May, 1907, p. 424.
[184] *Tserkovnyia Vedomosti*, Jan. 19, 1908, p. 140, and March 22, 1908, p. 596; *Pravo*, Sept. 3, 1906, col. 2783.
[185] *Pravo*, July 30, 1906, col. 2495; *ibid.*, Dec. 17, 1906, col. 3997; Pokrovskii, *op. cit.*, Vol. 5-i, p. 420.

the clergy; but resentment at failure to support their cause also animated the peasantry. This sentiment was expressed in picturesque terms at a peasant meeting in Viatka in 1905: "Here, you see, the authorities sit at the table, and we sit under the table; the priests stand at the corners with their crosses. We wish to look up at the light from under the table, but the priests poke us in the teeth with their crosses and force us down." [186]

The monasteries which possessed large tracts of land occasionally felt the wrath of the peasants during the troubled years. In 1906, during the sessions of the First Duma, there were passed "thousands of peasant resolutions desiring or demanding the confiscation of the lands and the property of the monasteries for the benefit of the working population"—so said *Tserkovnyi Vestnik* in 1906.[187] Some of the peasants were not satisfied with mere words, for there were a few reports of arson on monastery property. [188] Another sign of the beleaguered position of the monastic institutions was given by their requests that the government grant them the right to maintain armed police on their properties at their own expense. The monasteries and convents had begun to obtain this privilege in 1903 and 1904, with three instances in each year. Three more institutions were granted the protection of special constables during 1905, none in 1906, and two in 1907.[189] Here were signs that some of the peasants of Russia were coming to feel that among their enemies were numbered some of the clergy.

The composition of the Second Duma, which represented the people of Russia more truly than did any of the other Dumas, gives an indication of the views held by the Tsar's subjects concerning the Orthodox Church. In this legislative body there were 65 Social Democrats, whose program included "separation of the church from the state and the school from the church," as well as the confiscation of monastery and church property.[190] The 37 Socialist Revolutionaries were only

[186] Pokrovskii, *op. cit.*, Vol. 5-i, pp. 29–30.

[187] *Tserkovnyi Vestnik*, Oct. 19, 1906, col. 1363.

[188] *Pravo*, Aug. 20, 1906, col. 2659; Sept. 3, 1906, col. 2784.

[189] *Sobranie Uzakonenii i Rasporiazhenii Pravitel'stva*, 1905, Nos. 858, 1732, 1827; 1907, Nos. 277, 1006.

[190] *Polnyi Sbornik Platform Vsekh Russkikh Politicheskikh Partii*, pp. 15–18. For the numbers of the parties in the Duma, see Gosudarstvennaia Duma, *Ukazatel' k Stenograficheskim Otchetam*, II Duma, pp. 27–33.

slightly less radical in their proposals.[191] The People's Socialist party had 16 deputies; unfortunately their program is not available, but doubtless it was not favorable to the privileges of the Orthodox Church. The *Trudovik* (Labor) Group and the Party of the All-Russian Peasant Congress, which worked together and formed the largest group in the Duma, displayed hostility to the maintenance of the church's prerogatives; the Peasant Congresses of 1905, which have been discussed above, demanded complete freedom of religion, secularization of education, and the confiscation of church and monastery lands. The platform of the *Trudovik* Group contained provisions which were almost identical. The Polish *Kolo*, with 46 members, and the Mussulman party, with 30, can hardly have been protectors of the Russian Orthodox Church. Even the Cadet (Constitutional Democratic) party, while more moderate than the three chief parties of the Left, stood for complete religious freedom—". . . the Orthodox Church and the other faiths must be free from state control." Moreover, this party, the second largest in the Duma, with 98 members, proposed that the lands of the monasteries be given to the peasants, and that education be controlled by the local governments.[192] Thus all parties from the Social Democrats to the Cadets, with a total membership of 396 deputies, represented opposition to the privileges of the Orthodox Church.

The supporters of the church in the Second Duma were much less numerous. At the extreme right were 10 Rightists and Monarchists, who were avowed defenders of Orthodoxy. Next came 44 Octobrists and Moderates, who advocated freedom of religious profession, but made no direct attack on the privileges of the church.[193] Other groups which may or may not have been supporters of the Orthodox Church were 50 non-party deputies, the Cossack Group with 17, and the Party of Democratic Reforms with one. Thus even if all these undeclared deputies be included in the ranks of the partisans of the Orthodox Church, the church's defenders numbered only 122, against 396 opponents of the most important privileges of the church. Inasmuch as the Second Duma had not been freely elected by universal manhood suffrage, but by a complicated system intended to aid the supporters

[191] *Polnyi Sbornik Platform*, pp. 25–27.
[192] *Ibid.*, pp. 60–67.   [193] *Ibid.*, pp. 97–101.

of the government, the people of the Russian Empire were probably even more strongly opposed to the privileged position of the Orthodox Church than these figures indicate.

Indeed while the evidence is far from complete, the available facts seem to show that by 1907 large numbers of people had been alienated from the leaders of the church. Of course Russian Orthodoxy was not the only denomination which had experienced hostility; Marxian socialism, the rise of a materialistic spirit, had produced individuals in considerable numbers who were out of sympathy with *all* organized religion. But in addition to those who as a matter of principle were opposed to religion in general, by the end of the Revolution of 1905 many of the subjects of the Tsar had apparently come to the realization that a considerable and highly influential number of the Russian clergy were firm in their support of the Russian autocracy in its conflict with the revolutionary masses, even while the government resorted to harsh measures of repression. Moreover, the people could see that a relatively small number of hierarchs, including some of the highest figures of the church, were willing to use their influence to further such devices of the reactionaries as anti-Semitism and pogroms. In the sharp conflicts of the Revolution of 1905, an increasing number of peasants as well as of urban workingmen were coming to feel that the church as an institution, and not a few of its individual members, were following policies which were sharply opposed to what many of the people considered to be their own interests. Although the Revolution of 1905 ended in a storm of floggings and executions, the critical attitude of many humble folk obviously contained the possibility of danger for the church in the future. Only if the attitude of these people toward the church were to change during the years following the Revolution of 1905 would a serious threat be averted.

PART IV

The Interval between
Revolutions
1908-17

CHAPTER VII

The Years of Neglected Opportunity

IN 1906 the Pre-*Sobor* Conference had been formed to prepare the agenda and the general rules for the coming church council. It left a series of concrete proposals, but nothing was to come of them. The Emperor Nicholas II had promised to call the *Sobor* when "a favorable time" might come, but as the months passed the favorable moment seemed to fade further and further into the future. In 1906 and 1907 there were strikes, peasant uprisings, and other disturbances; the First and Second Dumas met and were dissolved in an atmosphere too heated to promise dispassionate consideration, in the proposed *Sobor*, of the problems of the Orthodox Church. To be sure, with the development of forcible repression and the summoning of the Third Duma with its limited responsibility, there ensued a period of relative quiet. By this time the revolutionary wave had spent its force. Reform was no longer in the air and, as the government was doubtless suspicious of representative assemblies, it was in no hurry to call the *Sobor*. Moreover, the Over Procuratorship changed hands frequently after Pobedonostsev's dismissal, and the changes brought to the office several men who knew little concerning the problems of the church. Their need to familiarize themselves with these problems doubtless helped to delay the calling of the *Sobor*. It was not summoned during the years following the Revolution of 1905, and, if one may judge by the absence of articles on the subject in the religious periodicals of the time, there seemed to be no reason to expect it in the near future.

By 1912, however, interest in the *Sobor* had to some extent revived. The editor of *Tserkovnyi Vestnik* insisted on the necessity of a church council,[1] and shortly after he had expressed this view the Synod announced the formation of a new conference to study the findings of the Pre-*Sobor* Conference of 1906 and to revise its recommendations in the light of contemporary conditions.[2] Moreover, in 1911 there had occurred the scandalous case of Bishop Hermogen of Saratov—concerning which more anon—which created a great uproar in church circles. Many loyal sons of the Orthodox faith felt that the need for a new dispensation was very great and raised their voices to demand a *Sobor*. The spokesman for the Third Duma's Committee on the Affairs of the Orthodox Church, V. N. Lvov, an Independent Nationalist (moderate conservative), voiced the unanimous proposal of his committee that "the All-Russian Church *Sobor* be called. We do not see . . . [anything] in the labors of the Pre-*Sobor* Conference [of 1912] which might bring us nearer to the long desired *Sobor*." [3] In his address to the Duma he added:

I must say that the position of all those who love the Orthodox Church is at the present moment exceedingly sad. We are like persons who stand at the threshold of their native home and see how, before their eyes, this native nest is falling apart. The evil position of the Orthodox Church has compelled us to speak; it might be that we wished to keep silent, but to keep silent is a crime, for . . . we would be like persons who in the guise of allies act as most dangerous enemies in destroying the foundations of our Orthodox Church.[4]

Lvov went on to characterize the maneuvers of the officials of the church in no flattering fashion. He said:

Actually, when we turn to the Administration [of the Orthodox Faith —the official title of the central administration of the church] and say, "The position of the church, beginning with the parish and the religious consistory and finishing with the Synod administration, is to such a

[1] *Tserkovnyi Vestnik*, Jan. 19, 1912, cols. 73–77.

[2] *Tserkovnyia Vedomosti*, March 3, 1912, official part, pp. 53–54. The second Pre-*Sobor* Conference held meetings for some years after its formation, but accomplished little. Its proceedings were never published, and to a great extent its deliberations were kept a secret from the general public. See: A. Osetskii, *Pomestnyi Sobor—Svobodnyi Opyt Organizatsii*, p. 7.

[3] Gosudarstvennaia Duma, *Stenograficheskie Otchety*, III Duma, Session V, Part 3, col. 55.

[4] *Ibid.*, col. 56.

degree abnormal and frightful, to such a degree filled with the miasma of the old order, that reform cannot be delayed," what do they answer? "Wait for the *Sobor*." When we say, "When, then, will there be a *Sobor* —in the near future?"—they answer, "The *Sobor* would not now be timely." When we again bring up the question: "When will there be reform?" they reply, "Wait for the *Sobor*." [Laughter from the Left and the Center.] [5]

Another speaker before the Third Duma, N. D. Sazonov, likewise from the ranks of the Independent Nationalist party, also saw urgent need for a *Sobor*. After describing the troubled condition of the church, a state of affairs so serious that many saw no cause for hope, he declared, "We must certainly turn again to that anchor of salvation which V. N. Lvov saw in the speedy summoning of a church *Sobor*." He added that if this were not done, "owing to the condition, to the half-paralyzed condition in which our church affairs are, even more dangerous consequences may threaten us in the future." [6] However, in spite of these and other warning voices, the *Sobor* was not called in 1912.

Hope still remained at the beginning of 1913. Some persons felt that the emperor would take advantage of the celebration of the tercentenary of the accession of the House of Romanov to issue a summons for the eagerly awaited church council. These hopes were not realized. "Persons close to higher church spheres, so the newspapers state, declare that the calling of the *Sobor* cannot be expected in the near future. These tidings, *The Voice of Moscow* remarks, cannot fail to cause distress to lovers of the church." So wrote the editor of *Tserkovnyi Vestnik* (*Church Messenger*) in the issue of March 28, 1913.[7] When Sabler, Over Procurator of the Synod, was asked how soon the *Sobor* would meet, he replied, on April 26, 1913, "Regarding the question as to when the *Sobor* will be, I, not possessing the gift of prophecy, cannot answer definitely." He was pressed by members of the Duma Budget Commission to state whether it would be in five years or ten, but only answered, "I am glad to explain those questions

[5] *Ibid.*   [6] *Ibid.*, cols. 81–82.
[7] *Tserkovnyi Vestnik*, March 28, 1913, cols. 391–92; also, Jan. 3, 1913, col. 4; Jan. 31, 1913, col. 145; March 14, 1913, cols. 325–26; also May 30, July 25, Aug. 23, 1913.

which are within the limits of my knowledge. I may say, that special attention has been given to the question of the desirability of the *Sobor.* . . ."[8]

In spite of this disappointment, interest in the *Sobor* did not die down. *Tserkovnyi Vestnik* printed frequent editorials on the subject and excerpts from other periodicals and from newspapers. Vain hopes! Sabler remarked before the Budget Commission of the Duma in 1914, "When will this *Sobor* take place? It will take place when it shall be pleasing to His Imperial Majesty to call it; and when this will be, is entirely unknown to me."[9] Not long after this the armies of the Tsar marched against the Austrians and the Germans, so that expectations of extensive church reform were largely laid aside until the war should be won. But even in the midst of the war a petition was presented by all the priests in the Fourth Duma, asking for the immediate reform of the Orthodox diocese and of the parish. In order to execute this, the petition said, the *Sobor* was needed, for only its action could free the church from arbitrary control and from outside influences.[10] In 1916 the Duma embodied in its recommendations on the Synod's budget a request for the summoning of the *Sobor* "as soon as possible,"[11] but by this time there had been so many disappointments that not a few felt that the *Sobor* would not be held. A devoted son of the church among the deputies of the Fourth Duma, V. P. Shein, a member of one of the parties of the Right, from the rostrum voiced his feeling of disillusionment:

Yes, in the first years of our activity we naïvely believed . . . that the *Sobor* would be called, . . . and we waited patiently. It may be, of course, that in the first years of the activity of the Duma [it was impossible], and it may be that now, in view of internal and external complications, it is still impossible to undertake such a great work—but peaceful years went by, gentlemen, and more than one; and none the less the *Sobor* was not summoned. . . . Does the suggestion of the *Sobor* not seem like a mere screen, like a convenient pretext, like a plausible at-

---

[8] Gosudarstvennaia Duma, *Doklady Biudzhetnoii Kommissii*, IV Duma, Session I, No. 4, Stenogram of the sessions of the Budget Commission, p. 23.

[9] *Ibid.*, Session II, No. 4, Stenogram, p. 5.

[10] *Missionerskoe Obozrenie*, Oct., 1915, pp. 292–95.

[11] Gosudarstvennaia Duma, *Stenograficheskie Otchety*, IV Duma, Session IV, Part 2, col. 2373.

tempt to divert the attention, in order [that the heads of the church] . . . might avoid doing what the *Sobor* itself should do? And I see considerable evidence for my supposition.[12]

Whether Shein was right in his hypothesis is a matter for conjecture, but one thing is certain: the ruling powers of the church missed the golden moment for undertaking reform, and the church was to meet its hour of trial with most of its weaknesses still uncured. When the *Sobor* was finally convened, it was at the most unfavorable moment that the twentieth century had yet brought to the church—late in 1917, when the Bolsheviks were about to seize power.

Thus the Imperial government missed its opportunity. Consequently, with minor exceptions all the faults of the central administration of the church which had given rise to the campaign for immediate ecclesiastical reform in 1905 and 1906 remained uncorrected. The authority of the Over Procurator was still great. Bishops were still transferred from one diocese to another, and apparently the membership of the Synod remained quite as much a matter of the Over Procurator's choice as before.[13] In 1912 Father Titov, a member of the Progressive party, declared before the Duma that the members of the Synod rarely knew of any new business before it was placed before them for decision at their meetings, so that they often had no chance to study the details; if, by some chance, said Father Titov, the members made some decision which was not pleasing to the Over Procurator, it "withered away and remained . . . unexecuted." [14] In fact, it appeared in 1912 that the authority of Over Procurator Sabler was almost as all-embracing as that of Pobedonostsev had ever been. Sabler's handling of the reorganization of the theological academies and of the seminaries occasioned caustic criticism in the Duma, on the ground that it was done in arbitrary, bureaucratic fashion,[15] and the formation of the new Pre-*Sobor* Conference was announced without consulting the body of the church.[16] Moreover the abrupt dis-

---

[12] *Ibid.*, col. 2226.

[13] Sv. Sinod, *Vsepoddanneishii Otchet Ober-Prokurora . . . za 1910 God,* pp. 14–16; statement by the Synod, *Russkiia Vedomosti,* Jan. 29, 1912.

[14] Gosudarstvennaia Duma, *Stenograficheskie Otchety,* III Duma, Session V, Part 3, cols. 186–87.

[15] *Ibid.*, cols. 154–57.

[16] *Tserkovnyia Vedomosti,* March 3, 1912, official part, pp. 53–54.

missal of Bishop Hermogen and his exile to a monastery in disgrace, all of which was done without the formality of a trial,[17] caused many loyal sons of the church to murmur, no matter how much they had disliked the past actions of the bishop. Father Tregubov, a member of the conservative wing of the Duma, in 1916 declared, "I would answer, yes, the helm of authority is firm in the hands of the Over Procurator." He went on to cite cases to prove that "the power of the Over Procurator in the Most Holy Synod is everything." For example, the Synod had authorized Sabler to introduce into the Duma a bill on the organization of the parish. The bill was introduced and then, "without the knowledge and consent of the Most Holy Synod," it was withdrawn by the Over Procurator. Again the Duma expressed a wish that the diocese of Kiev retain its separate fire-insurance system for church property. The Synod considered the matter and instructed Sabler to introduce a bill in accordance with the wishes of the Duma. The bill was introduced; but, again without the knowledge and consent of the Synod, the Over Procurator withdrew the bill. On another occasion the Council of Ministers asked the Synod for its views concerning a bill on freedom of conscience, then under consideration in the Duma, and the Synod duly drew up a statement of its position. However, this statement was not in conformity with the views of the Over Procurator, and consequently the latter published in the name of the Most Holy Synod a statement which was contrary to what the Synod had decided on the question. "This is the authority the Over Procurator has in the Most Holy Synod, and what the Over Procurator can do."[18]

The testimony on the power of the Over Procurator for good or for evil was supplemented in 1916 by N. V. Zhilin, a member of the Right party of the Duma. He declared to the Duma that "truly the members of the Most Holy Synod have become 'martyrs'" beneath the "scorpions" of the Over Procurator. Here he referred to the latter's power to name the members of the Synod and to choose those for attendance at the summer or the winter session, or both, or neither. "Refractory and undesired members are thrown overboard without

[17] *Tserkovnyia Vedomosti,* Jan. 21, 1912, pp. 20–24.
[18] Gosudarstvennaia Duma, *Stenograficheskie Otchety,* IV Duma, Session IV, Part 2, cols. 2234–36.

noise or unpleasantness. . . ." If this were insufficient, "if this scorpion did not disarm the refractory holy one, then there was still another scorpion—transfer from one diocese to another. . . . The members of the Synod were permitted merely to pray, to bow, and to give thanks." [19] Furthermore, the machinery of the Synod chancery remained as fully in the hands of the Over Procurator as before; a detailed description of the operation of the central administration of the church published in 1916 [20] differed in no significant manner from the accounts written before 1905.

Thus the Over Procurator remained supreme within the realm of church administration. Yet in one important particular the situation had changed markedly since the fall of Pobedonostsev. The latter occupied his position for more than twenty years and exercised such strong influence over two tsars that he was troubled only slightly by outside interference in the affairs of the church. After this great figure retired from public life, there appeared a succession of Over Procurators who rose and fell as the tides of political influence swirled and eddied, so that a consistent church policy was lacking. First came Prince Obolenskii, and then Shirinskii-Shikhmatov, who was followed by Izvol'skii and Luk'ianov. In 1911 V. K. Sabler received the Over Procuratorship, a post which he held until 1915. He was replaced by Samarin, who was followed by Volzhin; and Volzhin in turn gave way to Raev. Thus there was considerable instability in the Over Procuratorship; but the evidence presented shows that the church was not able to achieve independence of the civil power during this period, but, as before, remained subject to the political influences which dominated the state.

In the field of diocesan administration, matters were not in a much better state. Reforms were instituted, but they were not far-reaching. In 1910 the consistories were ordered by the Synod to simplify their procedure by the elimination of unnecessary words and formalities in their documents; in minor matters they were to act without consulting the bishops, and routine business was to be left to the chancery officials. All this tended to increase the efficiency of the consistories;

[19] *Ibid.*, cols. 2308–9.
[20] P. V. Verkhovskoi, *Uchrezhdenie Dukhovnoi Kollegii i Dukhovnyi Reglament*, I, 599–600, footnote.

but in one important respect the changes did not remedy, but rather intensified, the evils against which there had been many protests. The secretary of the consistory, who had long been regarded by reformers as a perilously powerful figure in the diocesan administration, was not only not shorn of his authority but was even endowed with greater prerogatives. He was given full power to appoint the clerks and the officials of the chancery and, although he was instructed not to quarrel with the members of the priestly consistory if they failed to heed his suggestions,[21] he remained second in power only to the bishop, if indeed the latter was not under his control. ". . . These little Over Procurators," said N. D. Sazonov before the Duma in 1912, "work great and endless evil within the sphere of their influence. . . ."[22] Consequently the Synod's reform, which did not strike at the power of the consistorial secretaries and did not remove the fundamental evils of the diocesan administration, was termed by the Cadet Lipiagov in the Duma a mere "patch on worn-out clothing."[23]

That reform of the diocesan administration was still considered necessary by many was shown by the fact that the Duma in 1910 and again in 1911 urged this reform, at the time of voting the Synod's budget.[24] Moreover, Kovalevskii, spokesman for the Duma Budget Commission, declared in his report in 1912 that "on a question exceedingly important, difficult, and burdensome—the improper condition of the local church administration and the unsatisfactoriness of the religious consistories—we have moved forward somewhat, but unfortunately only a very little." He added: "We here once again emphasize the real necessity for the Administration [of the Orthodox Faith] to hasten with this work, as otherwise the movement away from Orthodoxy, which has become strong of late, may make the very organization of the parish unnecessary."[25]

These were strong words, but they seem to have had little effect. The next year Sabler, the Over Procurator, is found before the Duma Budget Commission declaring "As for the question of the full reform

[21] *Tserkovnyia Vedomosti,* Aug. 21, 1910, official part, pp. 333–35.

[22] Gosudarstvennaia Duma, *Stenograficheskie Otchety,* III Duma, Session V, Part 3, col. 80.

[23] *Ibid.,* col. 153.

[24] *Ibid.,* Session III, Part 2, cols. 1640–41; Session IV, Part 2, cols. 2605–6.

[25] *Ibid.,* Session V, Part 3, cols. 38–39.

of the consistories, I am in complete agreement with the view that the consistories need such reformation. But the question is, how to do it." [26] Apparently the question was not quickly solved, for in August, 1915, the Duma clergy in their manifesto declared that in spite of the promises made to the Duma, the Code of Religious Consistories and the religious courts still needed basic reform.[27] And in 1916 the Duma voted the necessity of "the realization of the reformation, demanded by life, of the higher and the local church administrations." [28]

While the control of the secretary of the consistory over diocesan affairs was one of the items that was frequently pointed to as needing change, there were a number of other sides of the administration of the diocese which were also much criticized. Sazonov, who was a member of one of the parties of the Right, in 1912 alleged the existence of graft in the consistories [29]—a charge which had been made more than once in the past. And in 1916 the diocesan administration was again criticized in the Duma, with an analysis of the conditions which gave rise to its failings.[30] The handling of judicial matters by the consistories was another weakness to which reference was again made. Corruption, formalism, and antiquated procedure were among the faults denounced in 1908 by Father Rozhdestvenskii, a noted churchman.[31] In 1914 Father Filonenko, a member of the Center party in the Duma, told the same story. "Do you know, gentlemen, that any of our priests at any moment, as a result of a denunciation, even when anonymous (when I was a religious investigator, I had to make an investigation because of an anonymous denunciation, written in pencil) —any priest may find himself on trial?" [32] In April, 1915, a certain Father Popov, writing in the conservative *Missionerskoe Obozrenie* (*Missionary Survey*), declared that the term "jurisprudence" must be

[26] Gosudarstvennaia Duma, *Doklady Biudzhetnoi Komissii,* IV Duma, Session I, No. 4, Stenogram, p. 21.

[27] *Missionerskoe Obozrenie,* Nov., 1915, p. 293.

[28] Gosudarstvennaia Duma, *Stenograficheskie Otchety,* IV Duma, Session IV, Part 2, cols. 2368–71.

[29] *Ibid.,* III Duma, Session V, Part 3, col. 80.

[30] *Ibid.,* IV Duma, Session IV, Part 2, cols. 2223–24.

[31] *Bogoslovskii Vestnik,* Nov., 1908, pp. 378–79.

[32] Gosudarstvennaia Duma, *Stenograficheskie Otchety,* IV Duma, Session II, Part 3, col. 1328.

used with mental quotation marks when speaking of the judicial procedure of the diocesan authorities; this fact was evident, according
to the author, to "each and everyone who is not deprived of vision.
The periodical press . . . beats the never-silent alarm; the weighty
volumes of the Pre-*Sobor* Conference, and the present Pre-*Sobor*
meetings are also concerned with it." The chief reason, he stated, was
that the authorities "have thrown overboard . . . the Code of Religious Consistories, and as a simpler anchor of safety use liberal
amounts of arbitrary judgment and blind guesses." [33] Thus Father
Popov added to the chorus of criticism; much more, equally sharp in
tone, was uttered by Potulov, spokesman of the Duma Budget Commission in 1916,[34] as well as by the clerical members of the Fourth
Duma in their manifesto of August, 1915.[35]

The Duma clergy declared that both the Code of Religious Consistories and the religious courts needed basic reform. "Almost every
session of the Duma ends with the expression of a wish for an immediate start upon this reform, as the representatives of the Religious Administration have kept making promises to begin this work
in the very near future; but those wishes and those promises up to
now have produced nothing." As for the bishops, the Duma clergy
were not disposed to mince words. The well-being of the church demanded that the power of the bishops be curbed. No longer should
they have the power to shift priests from one parish to another, nor
shut them up in monasteries without trial. (Although imprisonment
in the Suzdal and Solovetskii Monasteries was officially ended in
1905, by order of the Tsar, the bishops still retained the right to
send priests to monasteries "for penance.") Trials should not be
started without proper grounds. Said the Duma clergy, "The present
practice of shifting priests from one parish to another is a great evil
for the priesthood"; this practice, they said, had assumed "an epidemic character." In one diocese, they stated, a new bishop had made
forty changes in seven days; in another, at the end of a three-year
period, not one priest remained in the parish which he had originally

[33] *Missionerskoe Obozrenie,* April, 1915, p. 497.
[34] Gosudarstvennaia Duma, *Stenograficheskie Otchety,* IV Duma, Session IV, Part 2, col. 2168.
[35] *Missionerskoe Obozrenie,* Nov., 1915, p. 293.

served. The shifting of priests was taking place in all dioceses; furthermore, in almost all of them priests were brought to trial merely because of rumors, gossip, and the like.[36]

Examples of the practice of transferring priests were given by individual members of the Duma clergy. In 1912 Father Titov of Perm declared that in some places among the clergy "such terror, such falling asunder and decay, exist, that the priests can only weep and trust that the Lord will come and save them by a miracle. . . ." As proof he cited the "casting out" of the clergy of the diocese of Perm. In the 436 parishes of this diocese there were 512 transfers in 12 months; moreover, there was an influx of deacons and psalmists from other dioceses, many of whom were raised to the rank of priest and installed in the places of those removed. This led to hostility between the newcomers and the original priests, which expressed itself in slander and intrigue. "As a result, we see that in this same diocese, within a very short time, three priests were suicides, and two lost their minds." [37] Father Filonenko in 1914 stated that in the diocese of Minsk the clergy affirmed that not one priest could be sure of his position; what was worse, he added, many changes were due to outside influence. Not only the governor of a province, but any county official or landlord could obtain the transfer of a priest.[38]

Another charge sometimes leveled against the bishops was that the diocesan congresses of the clergy were no longer granted that limited influence over the affairs of the diocese which they had previously enjoyed. That there was some justification for the charge was shown by the fact that in 1911 Bishop Aleksii of Pskov summoned the district priests to confer on the affairs of the diocese, instead of representatives of the parish clergy, who were usually convened. Bishop Aleksii gave three reasons for this course: first, that the district priests knew more about the affairs of the diocese; secondly, that they had greater authority, owing to their rank; but in the third of his reasons lay what was probably the crux of the matter—it was that his appointed district priests did not talk so much as did the elected delegates

[36] *Ibid.*
[37] Gosudarstvennaia Duma, *Stenograficheskie Otchety,* III Duma, Session V, Part 3, cols. 196–98.
[38] *Ibid.,* IV Duma, Session II, Part 3, cols. 1329–32.

of the clergy, "who often waste precious time in useless debates and even in attacks upon the representatives of the diocesan administration."[39] Moreover, in 1912 Count Uvarov, a man deeply interested in church affairs, told the Duma that in a certain matter of importance its wishes had not been respected: certain diocesan congresses of the clergy had not been given full power to distribute the money voted as salary increments for the priests. The Count told of receiving a letter from some of the clergy of the diocese of Smolensk, who asked him not to publish their names and to burn the letter. In it they told him that the diocesan congress had voted to place the parish of Dmitrovets in the thirty-first place on the list of those to receive salary increments, as there were thirty parishes more in need than this one. But the diocesan authorities had intervened, and after their interposition the name of the parish of Dmitrovets led all the rest. Count Uvarov added that in the diocese of Saratov the same thing happened—a fact which he feared might lead a number of Duma members to join the peasant deputies in voting against salary increases for the clergy.[40]

Apparently these instances were not unique, for in their manifesto in 1915 the Duma clergy declared that "pastoral gatherings of the clergy, which are permitted by the Most Holy Synod, now have ceased almost everywhere, most frequently because of the bishops' lack of sympathy for them." The priests urged that in order that the church might function more normally, these congresses be held regularly and that they be given wider powers, instead of having their competence limited to the financial matters of the diocese. Furthermore, the priests asked that the congresses be given the right to elect the district priests, who almost everywhere were appointed by the bishops.[41]

In making these requests the clergy of the Duma displayed a certain hostility to the authorities of the church, and this feeling was never more in evidence than in the passage dealing with the bishops as a group or class. The Duma priests denounced the current practice of making monks out of young students in the academies and of promoting them rapidly, so that at twenty-five or twenty-six they became

[39] *Vera i Razum,* Jan., 1912, pp. 271–72.
[40] Gosudarstvennaia Duma, *Stenograficheskie Otchety,* III Duma, Session V, Part 3, cols. 137–38.
[41] *Missionerskoe Obozrenie,* Nov., 1915, p. 295.

rectors of seminaries; such rapidly rising young men, who often became bishops, tended, they said, to forget their humble origin and to become haughty and arrogant. Moreover, the pronouncement declared that the majority of those students who took the vows did so because they were susceptible to the appeal of easy promotion and high ecclesiastical rank; they took them "not for heaven but for earth, for advantage in life." "This is why the academy students who are not always the best in a mental sense, nor in a religious and moral sense, enter monastic life; considerations of a far from idealistic nature often play the deciding part." [42]

Quite often the bishops were haughty and overbearing to the clergy beneath them. The manifesto declared:

. . . [The Duma clergy]cannot but grieve when they see that the bishops have taken too haughty an attitude, too far from their co-workers in church matters—from the parish priests. The clergy do not receive paternal guidance from Their Lordships; their guidance consists of cold, official, and largely written, communications. Often Their Lordships are averse to association with the pastors, even when the most favorable circumstances exist. . . . The fact that the clergy everywhere and always utter complaints against their inferior position with respect to the bishops shows that these complaints have some grounds. Sometimes a layman of very humble position enjoys more attention from a bishop than the most respected and deserving pastor.[43]

That the attitude of the bishops toward their priests had been more supercilious in the past was suggested by the fact that in 1907 *Tserkovnyi Vestnik* reported that several of the bishops were holding talks with their priests for an hour or more—even Metropolitans Antonii of St. Petersburg and Flavian of Kiev had done so. Furthermore, several of the hierarchs, notably Archbishop Tikhon of Iaroslavl, had forbidden their clergy to prostrate themselves before their bishops; the article said that this time-honored practice was almost extinct.[44] Nevertheless, in their journeys around their dioceses the bishops still traveled in ceremonial style. In 1914 Father Stanislavskii declared before the Duma Budget Commission that he had often ridden with his bishop on journeys around the diocese, for which ten horses or more were needed. The bishop had to travel in a closed car-

[42] *Ibid.*, p. 289.   [43] *Ibid.*, pp. 291–92.
[44] *Tserkovnyi Vestnik,* July 12, 1907, col. 911.

riage, which required three horses; he took with him a deacon, a sexton, and, as he often performed services on his trips, vestments and utensils, which all required horses. Consequently Father Stanislavskii felt that ten animals were far from excessive.[45] Some bishops demanded a great deal of ceremony on their visits to the villages of their dioceses. In 1916 the following decree, alleged to have come from one of the Siberian dioceses, was read in the Duma; its authenticity was not challenged, even by the extreme partisans of the church on the benches of the Right:

> It is desirable that the reception [of the bishop] should be ceremonious, with four priests and two deacons present; moreover, the school children and the teachers should be at the church, waiting at the churchyard gate; let there be priests and deacons in vestments; banners; crucifixes; welcoming exclamations, as is fitting; service in the church. . . . When His Reverence arrives and goes to the priest's house, to the school, to the psalmist's house, the bells should peal. My protodeacons and hypodeacons never demand anything, but I have no objection to voluntary gifts to them.[46]

As has been suggested, to the lower clergy the hierarchs still seemed like dangerously powerful overlords, to be placated at all costs. However, the unfortunate position of the parish priests was but one side of the woeful state of affairs in the parishes. It was widely agreed that the Orthodox parish was in urgent need of reform; mention has already been made of the strong movement for the reconstruction of the parish in 1905 and 1906. Hopes for parish reform did not die, even after the postponement of the *Sobor* to the Greek Kalends. Many felt that while the *Sobor* was not imminent, this vital reform could be effected, or at least begun, through the Duma. In 1906 the emperor commanded that this work be undertaken, and the Pre-*Sobor* Conference adopted a set of proposals for the new parish. A new imperial decree in 1907 commanded the hastening of this work, but it was not until 1908 that the Synod approved a revised version of the rules adopted by the Pre-*Sobor* Conference and instructed the Over Procurator to introduce a suitable bill into the Duma and the Council

---

[45] Gosudarstvennaia Duma, *Doklady Biudzhetnoi Komissii*, IV Duma, Session II, No. 4, Stenogram, p. 28.

[46] Gosudarstvennaia Duma, *Stenograficheskie Otchety*, IV Duma, Session IV, Part 2, col. 2343.

of State. In October, 1908, the bill was placed before the Council of Ministers for preliminary consideration. However, shortly afterward changes occurred in the church administration. Luk'ianov was named Over Procurator, and at once the bill for the reconstruction of the Orthodox parish was withdrawn. On November 24, 1910, the bill, once more revised, was approved by the Synod and was introduced into the Council of Ministers; but in 1911 Sabler was named Over Procurator, the bill was again withdrawn, and the Synod was asked to prepare a third project for reforming the parish. The disillusioned Father Titov, speaking in the Third Duma, said, "A fourth version has been written [by the Over Procurator?], but apparently we shall not see the parish code here [in the Duma]—and will the Most Holy Synod ever see it again?" [47]

Father Titov's suspicion was correct. In 1912 the Third Duma ended its session without having seen the bill on the parish; and in 1915 the Duma clergy urged in their petition that conditions in the parish necessitated fundamental change.[48] No legislation on this matter was presented to the Duma in 1916; consequently the February Revolution was to find the Russian Orthodox parish in a condition but little different from that of the unreformed parish of 1900.

While no general legislation on the parish was adopted, an attempt was made to grant to the laymen more rights in the affairs of the parish. A decree of the Synod on October 18, 1905, provided for the optional institution of parish councils of not more than twelve men, to be elected by the parishioners and to act under the guidance of the priest, who was to preside. The purpose of these parish councils was to unite the parishioners for the devising of means of "satisfying the religious, charitable, and educational needs of the parish, and of coöperating with the priest." [49] However, the parish councils never proved to be strong. In 1908 *Kolokol* (*The Bell*), the semiofficial newspaper of the Over Procurator, said, "The ruling clergy have passed judgment upon the new work—make haste slowly"; [50] and *Tserkovnyia Vedomosti* mentioned in the same year that the parish

[47] *Ibid.*, III Duma, Session V, Part 3, col. 184.
[48] *Missionerskoe Obozrenie*, Nov., 1915, pp. 295–97.
[49] *Tserkovnyia Vedomosti*, Nov. 26, 1905, official part, pp. 523–25.
[50] Cited in *Pravoslavnyi Sobesednik*, June, 1909, p. 712.

Neglected Opportunities

councils "were lagging." [51] In December there was a gathering of priests in Kazan, at which the question was raised whether they should try to stimulate the development of these councils or should allow them to develop naturally. Out of the fifty priests in attendance, not more than five advocated the active furthering of this work.[52]

This attitude on the part of the clergy helps to explain the general failure of the parish councils. Additional light was shed on this failure by the *Report* of the Over Procurator for 1908 and 1909. Here it was stated that only the diocese of Orel had made a serious attempt to start these councils, and that even here serious objections to them had been noted. In this diocese misunderstandings often arose between the parishioners and the priests over the functions of the councils, so that frequently the parishioners became indifferent toward these bodies; and the clergy were quite apt to hold aloof from the parishioners with whom they were to coöperate. Very possibly the reason for this hostility of the priests to the parish councils was that the laymen of these bodies had often gone to extremes and had acted as if they were complete masters of the church property, at times even refusing to make required payments from parish funds, establishing very low rates of remuneration for the ministrations of the priests, and the like. Nevertheless, the Over Procurator's *Report* went on to say that in cases where the priests and the people coöperated, the parish councils were able to accomplish much good, especially in raising money to repair and adorn the churches, as well as in establishing parish libraries, improving the choirs, and combating drunkenness and immorality.[53] However, this statement seems to have been unduly optimistic, for in 1914 *Tserkovnyia Vedomosti* stated that the parish councils had turned out to be infertile seed.[54]

The chief weakness of the organization of the Russian parish had long been recognized to be the lack of popular participation in the parish affairs. The institution of the councils had been a half-hearted gesture toward granting a voice to the parishioners, but apparently that was not enough. As the Over Procurator's *Report* stated, the parishioners wanted the right to dispose of the donations which they

[51] *Pravoslavnyi Sobesednik,* June, 1909, p. 712.   [52] *Ibid.,* footnote.
[53] Sv. Sinod, *Vsepoddanneishii Otchet,* 1908–9, pp. 354–62.
[54] *Tserkovnyia Vedomosti,* Jan. 18, 1914, p. 143.

made to the parish, and to administer the expenditures devoted to its needs. But inevitably the interests of the parishioners in spending the parish funds on parish needs would conflict with well-established interests of the diocesan and the central church authorities. Each Orthodox parish was required to make fixed contributions for the diocesan school in the county town, for the maintenance of the consistory, for subscribing to the official publications, for maintaining the chancery of the district priest, and the like. In many parishes almost one-third of the money offerings made by the people were used for these purposes. In addition to these regular levies there were many special collections made with the consent of the Synod—collections for the extension of Orthodoxy in the Caucasus, for the needs of the Orthodox mission in Jerusalem, for the Orthodox of Galicia, for the starving, and the like. "The requirement of such advances out of parish collections in vital fashion affects meeting the needs of the church itself, so that necessary reforms have to be postponed, the vestments cannot be renewed, and a whole series of other essential requirements remain unsatisfied." [55] The Council of State in 1914 expressed a wish that the Synod "should take proper measures for restricting within the limits of extreme necessity the levies upon the churches for any need whatever not connected with satisfying directly the needs of the church itself and of religious worship, . . ." and should abolish all special collections which were not absolutely necessary.[56] Moreover, the Budget Commission of the Fourth Duma, "like the Third Duma, declared its unchanging demand that the local collections should be used for the needs of the parishes themselves." [57]

The manifesto of the Duma clergy in 1915, to which reference has been made, touched on this thorny problem. It declared that the Orthodox parish was in need of more charitable work and of more facilities for education, but this was impossible, as long as the many levies and collections from the parishes deprived them of the necessary funds. In order to have parish charities, it would be needful to make sure that "donations of parishioners to the parish church . . .

[55] Gosudarstvennyi Sovet, *Stenograficheskii Otchet,* Session IX, June 9, 1914, cols. 2703–4.

[56] *Ibid.,* col. 2710.

[57] Gosudarstvennaia Duma, *Doklady Biudzhetnoi Komissii,* IV Duma, Session II, No. 4, p. 46.

do not go to maintain [diocesan] religious educational institutions and consistories, to pay district priests, to subscribe for books ordered by the diocesan authorities but not needed by the clergy," and so on. The Duma clergy added, "already in the parishes sharp voices are heard speaking against the improper use of church revenues, and we may expect that in the not distant future the protest may appear in more definite forms. . . ." Not surprisingly, the clergy reported that the constant collections were very bad for the moral influence of the pastors; the parishioners were alienated by the frequent requests to give.[58]

Substantial data were given in the Budget Committee's report to the Duma in 1914 on the income of the Orthodox parishes of the empire and on their disbursements. Their gross income was nearly 39,000,000 rubles; of this sum, 13,000,000 or about one-third, went for purposes which were not directly connected with the needs of the parish churches as such. What the other levies meant to an ordinary village church in central Russia is shown by the following table. The chief deductions were

	Rubles	Kopecks
For the diocesan girls' school	9	90
For the [county] religious school	49	35
25 percent of taper income	26	60
To buy official blanks	17	65
	103	50

There were also other levies to the amount of 55 rubles 78 kopecks, to say nothing of the special collections authorized by the Synod, of which there were fifteen in a period of not more than nineteen months. Thus from this particular parish, which had a gross income of about 600 rubles, at least 159 rubles 28 kopecks were drained off by the diocesan and the higher authorities for uses not immediately necessitated by the needs of the parish church itself.[59]

Quite possibly these apparently burdensome levies were one of the chief reasons for the low level of activity in the Orthodox parish,

[58] *Missionerskoe Obozrenie*, Nov., 1915, pp. 295–96.
[59] Gosudarstvennaia Duma, *Doklady Biudzhetnoi Komissii*, IV Duma, Session II, No. 4, pp. 44–45.

although certainly other factors were present. But whatever the cause, agreement was quite general that parish life was sluggish. *Tserkovnyi Vestnik* (*Church Messenger*), a journal devoted to the interests of the parish clergy, gave much space to the question of reviving the interest of the people in the affairs of their parishes. Among the means suggested were the selling of religious books at low prices, sessions of community oral reading from both secular and religious books, more inspiring sermons, and especially more attractive singing in the churches.[60] Much attention was paid to this last item by the above journal in 1913. Judging from the articles reprinted from other religious periodicals, it was a subject for considerable thought in the dioceses of Kiev, Moscow,[61] and perhaps in many others. However, these expedients do not seem to have improved the condition of the parish, for in 1914 the official *Tserkovnyia Vedomosti* admitted that "for various historic reasons the spontaneous life of the parish has of late years been extinguished. Although here and there there are heartening examples, they are exceptions. In general in the parish each one lives in his family circle and there is no care of the parish for the parish." [62]

Thus most of the problems of the Orthodox parish remained unsolved. Only in one respect was appreciable headway made—namely, in providing all the clergy with partial support from the treasury. As will be shown later, the Duma appropriated considerable sums for paying the priests, but so numerous were the clergy to be taken care of and so limited the funds available that large numbers of them remained without aid from the state.

The religious seminaries also continued to present serious problems to the authorities of the church. For some time before 1905 the seminaries had been filled with dissatisfied students, and the reformers of 1905 and 1906 had given seminary reform a prominent place on their schedule of needful changes. The Pre-*Sobor* Conference in 1906, especially, had dealt with the question at some length. The resolutions adopted left no doubt that it regarded seminary reform

---

[60] *Tserkovnyi Vestnik*, Jan. 19, 1912, cols. 83–85.

[61] *Ibid.*, Nov. 29, 1912, cols. 1520–21; Feb. 7, 1913, col. 172; May 23, 1913, col. 642; Aug. 15, 1913, cols. 1009–12.

[62] *Tserkovnyia Vedomosti*, Jan. 18, 1914, p. 142.

as a pressing matter. But actually little was done to transform the seminaries into institutions from which the church might derive new strength and new life, and when the great test came the men who had entered the priesthood since 1905 were hardly more valuable additions to the church than the often admittedly unsatisfactory contingents of priests graduated before the Revolution of 1905.

This is not to say that the church authorities utterly neglected the problem. Several decrees were issued by the Synod, and its subordinate institutions issued several sets of rules to deal with the problems of the seminaries, but these new pronouncements were far from attempting the basic reform which was demanded and were rather intended to quiet the situation by insisting on stricter discipline and more effective punishment for offenders. In August, 1908, a set of rules for all the seminaries was promulgated by the Synod. The teaching staffs were ordered to set fitting examples for the youths under their guidance, who were to be required to perform the necessary religious observances; a scornful or unbelieving attitude on the part of students was not to be tolerated. The masters were to "instill in the students the qualities, habits, and knowledge necessary for . . . pastors . . . respectful of the authorities established by God, and loyal to their people and to the Fatherland." The instructors were especially warned that "it will be necessary to struggle determinedly with the materialistic teachings which are seizing the youths." As a precaution against dangerous propaganda, the students should study and read under observation. Furthermore, "the secret cliques," which had become so common and had "fallen under the influence of revolutionary elements," were to be prosecuted with severity and the students at their heads expelled. Secret organizations, libraries, or meetings, and the presentation of collective demands, were unconditionally forbidden. Finally, the following failings were to be regarded as causes for expulsion: poor work; antisocial attitudes; theft; drunkenness, if habitual or manifested in extreme fashion; immorality; insubordination and provocation thereof; antireligious attitudes; and the like.[63]

Late in 1909 the Synod issued a decree dealing with the educational side of seminary life. Instead of dividing the seminary horizontally

[63] Sv. Sinod, *Vsepoddanneishii Otchet,* 1908–9, pp. 549–59.

into two schools, one giving general education for the less mature
students and the other providing a higher theological course for those
who wished to enter the priesthood, the new decree provided that
theological education was to be given in all the classes, so that "the
students throughout their course of study . . . will recognize that
they are students of a real theological school"; in other words, the
Synod wished "to keep chiefly in mind the pastoral problem of the
religious school." On the other hand, the Synod hoped so to arrange
the course of study that those who finished the full ten-year course
of the seminary would be in a position, in case they did not feel a call
to enter the priesthood, to continue their education in the higher
secular educational institutions.[64] Thus the Synod in dealing with the
problem of the religious seminaries attempted to carry water on
both shoulders; there was no fundamental reform, although for years
it had been demanded as vitally necessary. The Russian religious
seminary remained essentially in its former condition.

This condition was not good. The Educational Committee of the
Synod, after reading reports on some of the seminary disorders which
had flourished under apparently peaceful surfaces, mentioned two
troublesome incidents. One seminary rector, on November 11, 1909,
spoke of complete quiet among his students, only to be faced a few
days later with disturbances which ended with the expulsion of the
first four classes. The rector of another seminary stated that on November 12 of the same year the attitude of his students was most
peaceful and quiet; but from a letter from the Assistant Minister of
Internal Affairs in charge of the secret police, it was learned that on
the initiative of the students of this same seminary a meeting had
been held which decided "to agitate for a strike with the aim of
improving the existing seminary regime." [65]

Whether the new measures were sufficient to establish firm discipline in the seminaries cannot be stated, but it is certain that they were
far from solving the problems and correcting the serious failings of
seminary life. In fact Lipiagov, a member of the Cadet party, told the
Duma in 1912 that the changes made in the arrangement of the course
would make matters worse than before. For those students who had
no desire to enter the priesthood, the general six-year course would

[64] *Ibid.*, pp. 567–69.   [65] *Ibid.*, pp. 560–61.

not provide a sufficient preparation for the secular institutions of higher learning. Consequently many who could not afford two additional years in some other secondary school would feel constrained to stay in the seminaries and to prepare for a priestly career for which they felt no calling.[66] This view was perhaps unduly gloomy, but certainly the measures of the Synod were far from making sweeping reforms in the seminaries.

The faults found with the seminaries were many and various. One criticism was that the students were deprived of the means of acquiring broad general culture through the restrictions placed upon the content of the seminary libraries. In 1913 *Tserkovnyi Vestnik* said, "Even now (unless we are mistaken) there is in effect a circular forbidding the inclusion of *Rudin, A Noble's Nest,* and the works of Turgenev in general, Goncharov's *Obryv,* Tolstoi's *Anna Karenina,* and the poems of Nekrasov, in the libraries for seminary students"; that is, as *Tserkovnyi Vestnik* pointed out, standard works of great Russian writers, which were widely read in the secular schools, were barred to the seminarists. The article commenting on this prohibition went on to point out the harm which it did to the education of pastors, who were often called upon to disprove doctrines hostile to the church —deism, materialism, evolution, and the like—and expressed the hope that the time would come when the seminaries would turn out broadly educated men.[67]

Another complaint frequently heard was that the seminaries were filled largely with sons of the clergy, while boys of peasant or working-class origin rarely entered. To be sure in March, 1909, the Synod removed the restriction on children whose fathers were not priests nor deacons.[68] This restriction had limited the number of children from non-clerical families to 10 percent of the student body.[69] Nevertheless, in September, 1909, out of 20,772 native students, 17,618 were from clerical families; [70] during the academic year 1910–11, of the 21,507

[66] Gosudarstvennaia Duma, *Stenograficheskie Otchety,* III Duma, Session V, Part 3, col. 157.

[67] *Tserkovnyi Vestnik,* June 20, 1913, col. 756.

[68] *Tserkovnyia Vedomosti,* March 7, 1909, official part, p. 74.

[69] Sv. Sinod, *Smeta Dokhodov i Raskhodov Vedomstva Sviateishago Sinoda na 1913 g.,* p. cvii.

[70] Sv. Sinod, *Vsepoddanneishii Otchet,* 1910, p. 202.

seminary students, 18,267 were of priestly origin.[71] In 1915 the Budget Commission of the Duma was told that while in theory the children of peasants were admitted to the religious schools, actually few of them entered. In the seminary of Tver, out of 818 students only 21 were the sons of peasants; in Kostroma, 10 out of 472; and similar figures were quoted for a number of other schools. In all the seminaries there were 1,293 peasants' sons, out of a total enrollment of 21,850.[72] One possible reason for the failure of the non-clerical classes to take advantage of the lowering of the barriers against them was the fact that in certain respects the sons of the clergy were given the advantage. If the number of vacancies in a given seminary were limited, preference was given to them; they were relieved of the payment of tuition fees; and in the distribution of state stipends, diocesan scholarships, and admission to dormitories, they were given first consideration.[73] Perhaps here lies the major explanation of the fact that while there were many who felt that the clergy should draw new blood and new vigor from other social groups, actually the priesthood received few seminary graduates from non-clerical families.

The most serious charge against the Russian religious seminaries, however, was that they failed to provide the church with a sufficient number of pastors. "The flight of the seminarists from the priesthood," which had been noticed before the Revolution of 1905, continued. This movement away from the church began even before the youths matured. In 1906 Father Kozlovskii told the Pre-*Sobor* Conference that in the diocese of Mogilev, out of 530 priests about 150 were educating their sons in secular secondary schools.[74] The religious periodicals of the time not infrequently contained articles discussing the attempts of the sons of priests to enter the universities or to obtain secular employment without higher education—attempts which caused a lack of priests to fill vacancies in several dioceses.[75] In his *Report* for 1911 and 1912 the Over Procurator remarked on "the

[71] Sv. Sinod, *Smeta Dokhodov,* pp. cvii–cviii.

[72] Gosudarstvennaia Duma, *Doklady Biudzhetnoi Komissii,* IV Duma, Session IV, No. 4, Stenogram, p. 36.

[73] Sv. Sinod, *Smeta Dokhodov,* p. cviii.

[74] Sv. Sinod, *Zhurnaly i Protokoly . . . Predsobornago Prisutstviia,* II, 496.

[75] *Tserkovnyi Vestnik,* Oct. 1, 1909, col. 1236; *Vera i Razum,* July, 1913, pp. 255–56.

movement, noted over a whole series of years, of the seminary students away from the pastorate." [76] In 1912 *Tserkovnyi Vestnik* declared that the clergy of the city parishes had almost completely dispensed with the religious schools and seminaries and were placing their sons in gymnasia and other secular schools. If the youths were placed in the seminaries, they did not stay to the end of the full course, but left at the end of the fourth year, in order to avoid the theological courses of the fifth year and to enter secular educational institutions.[77]

Interesting statistics for the year 1911 were given in 1913 by V. P. Shein, Progressive Nationalist (conservative) member of the Duma. Of the 2,148 men graduating from the seminaries in 1911, only 574, or 26 percent, entered the priesthood directly; an additional 189 entered the theological academies, while the rest "did not wish to enter the service of the church." [78] In 1915 the manifesto of the Duma clergy declared that the flight of the seminarists into civil life continued and that even those bishops who had sons before entering monastic life educated them in secular institutions; moreover, the declaration warned, "No compulsory measures will stop this flight; if access to the civil institutions of higher education is closed to seminary graduates, the clergy will strain themselves beyond their strength and will educate their sons in the gymnasia." [79] Finally, in November, 1916, Father Butkevich informed the Council of State that the students "flee from the seminaries . . . flee into civil institutions— they flee into excise offices, they flee into the agrarian commissions, they flee into railroad offices, anywhere, except into the church." [80]

Here was a serious situation. Quite as serious was the fact that apparently those who did enter the service of the church were not always candidates for parishes from sincere conviction, but at times because they had no choice. In 1909 a certain Father Gorain wrote an article for *Vera i Razum* (*Faith and Reason*) entitled "Why Do Priests' Sons Leave the Clerical Life?" In it he listed a number of

[76] *Tserkovnyia Vedomosti,* Feb. 8, 1914, p. 318.

[77] *Tserkovnyi Vestnik,* Sept. 13, 1912, col. 1162.

[78] Gosudarstvennaia Duma, *Doklady Biudzhetnoi Komissii,* IV Duma, Session I, No. 4, Stenogram, p. 48.

[79] *Missionerskoe Obozrenie,* Nov., 1915, p. 287.

[80] Gosudarstvennyi Sovet, *Stenograficheskii Otchet,* Session XIII, Nov. 26, 1916, cols. 221–22.

causes. First came family influence—the poverty of the priestly fathers, and their infection with the ideas of the times, which induced dissatisfaction with their lot. Allied with this there was the dependence of the average priest upon the peasants, his economic insecurity, and the like. Additional reasons were the decline of idealism in society, the increasing materialism, the desire for worldly well-being, all evidenced by the fact that both secular and religious literature portrayed the priests, the clergy, and clerical life in an unfavorable light. Finally, there was the influence of school life—the prevalence of liberal and radical ideas; the widespread practice of seminary students of avoiding attendance at divine services, and the complete lack of reading of the Bible, which had been superseded by the works of Kautsky, Gorkii, Marx, and Bebel; the ridicule heaped upon those who did take an interest in religion, who were termed Pharisees and hypocrites by their fellows.[81] Thus the environment in which the seminarist grew up did not tend to make him desire the priesthood and, although numbers of the seminary students did take the priestly vows, none the less with such a preparation some of them must have regretted the necessity of taking this step and must have entered their life of service sorrowfully or even sullenly. In 1912 N. D. Sazonov, of the Independent Nationalist party (of the Right), declared in the Duma:

Those who from their origin could perhaps very well be molded into ideal pastors of the church, in the last analysis in those very schools lose their predilection [for religious life] and become thoroughly unpromising for that high service for which they have from the first prepared themselves. For an extreme example I point to the men who, on finishing the seminary and receiving parishes, have gone thither with feelings of bitter regret and displeasure; their interests have not corresponded to those problems which they were to solve in life as spiritual pastors. . . .[82]

And the manifesto of the Duma clergy in 1915 in guarded terms declared, ". . . the present-day seminaries do not know how to nourish in their students real faith and sincere love for the church."[83]

The failure of many of the seminary students to enter the priesthood inevitably led to a scarcity of priests. At the Pre-*Sobor* Con-

[81] *Vera i Razum,* April, 1909, pp. 117–26.
[82] Gosudarstvennaia Duma, *Stenograficheskie Otchety,* III Duma, Session V, Part 3, cols. 78–79.
[83] *Missionerskoe Obozrenie,* Nov., 1915, p. 289.

ference in 1906 Bishop Arsenii of Pskov stated that there were not enough candidates for vacant parishes, so that some bishops had even come to take the step of consecrating as priests the graduates from teachers' seminaries and other persons not fully qualified.[84] In 1907 the bishop of Riazan printed an appeal to the teachers of church schools and to psalmists who had had some seminary training to become priests or deacons, as there were ten vacancies of each category in the diocese.[85] A writer in *Tserkovnyia Vedomosti* (*Church News*) in 1908 stated that the bishops were occasionally filling priestly vacancies by appointing less well-trained men—not only deacons, but also laymen; clerks, even railroad conductors, were consecrated as priests.[86] The lack of priests continued, however. In 1912 *Tserkovnyi Vestnik* reprinted an article from the *Diocesan News* of Volhynia, which mentioned the existence of thirty vacancies for priests under Aleksii, Bishop of Saratov—places which "doubtless will be filled with deacons, who, in the words of the same bishop, are so little educated that they cannot read the Gospel without mistakes." The article stated that this phenomenon was not unique; parishes were known to be vacant in the dioceses of Polotsk, Poltava, Chernigov, Ufa, Orel, Kiev, and many others. "Yes, and with us in Volhynia. . . ."[87]

The central authorities of the church were not slow in adopting the expedients of the local churchmen. In 1909 a conference on the needs of the church in the newly settled regions of Siberia decided that there were not enough priests available to meet the needs of the settlers, and consequently a special course was begun at the Znamenskii Monastery, in Moscow, under the famous missionary, Dean Vostorgov, where teachers from parish schools were given training for six months. The graduates were then ordained and sent out to the dioceses beyond the Urals, with the understanding that they might not take positions in European Russia for five years.[88]

The "Vostorgov courses" proved, however, to be unpopular, in

[84] Sv. Sinod, *Zhurnaly i Protokoly*, II, 492.

[85] *Tserkovnyi Vestnik*, Nov. 1, 1907, col. 1422.

[86] *Tserkovnyia Vedomosti*, Sept. 27, 1908, pp. 1917–21.

[87] *Tserkovnyi Vestnik*, Dec. 20, 1912, col. 1621.

[88] Gosudarstvennaia Duma, *Prilozheniia k Stenograficheskim Otchetam*, IV Duma, Session I, Vol. I, No. 100, pp. 1–4.

Duma circles at least. The Fourth Duma was asked to appropriate a small amount for the Synod, so that the latter, which had borrowed money from an insurance fund in order to bestow traveling allowances on a group of graduates from these courses, might repay what it had borrowed. However, the Duma displayed an exceedingly critical attitude, in part due to displeasure over the improper use of insurance funds and partly because of dislike of the low standard of the courses. One speaker charged that the priests sent out from the Vostorgov school included many ignorant clerks, bankrupt storekeepers, and the like, and that the priests made of this material were almost illiterate and were thoroughly unsatisfactory to the peasants to whom they were to minister. The *Omsk Diocesan News* was cited as evidence to this effect.[89] Another speaker declared that actually the courses were only four months in length instead of six, and pointed out that after five years these priests would be free to return to the dioceses of European Russia.[90] To these arguments the defenders of the Synod's actions answered by insisting that the qualifications of those attending the courses were carefully considered, and that moreover the need was pressing and that this was the best way to solve the problem at a reasonable cost.[91] The Duma refused to grant the rather small amount requested.[92]

This was not the last of the Vostorgov courses, however. In December, 1915, the spokesman of the Budget Commission of the Duma stated that on the pretext of a lack of seminary graduates to fill vacancies "an attempt has been made to lower the level [of the standard of education of priests], pastoral courses like the so-called 'Vostorgov courses' in Moscow have been started, pastoral courses have begun in Zhitomir and in Orenburg." This, he added, produced priests with standards considerably below the former educational qualifications of the clergy. Moreover, he pointed out, the general level of education in Russia had risen greatly since 1905, so that the effect of reducing the educational standards of the priesthood would most certainly be harmful.[93] Thus if it is possible to believe these critics

[89] Gosudarstvennaia Duma, *Stenograficheskie Otchety*, IV Duma, Session I, Part 1, cols. 1884–89.
[90] *Ibid.*, cols. 1890–93.   [91] *Ibid.*, cols. 1893–1904.
[92] *Ibid.*, col. 1909.   [93] *Ibid.*, Session IV, Part 2, col. 2169.

of the seminary policy of the Synod—and most of them were apparently sincerely religious persons, who spoke because they feared for the church—the seminaries were not providing the church with the proper number of adequately trained priests, while the expedients adopted by the Synod in dealing with the problem made matters worse instead of better.

In still another field of church life—the monastic—no vital reforms were instituted, although it was widely believed that the need for reform was great. Of course the question of monastery reform directly affected far fewer people than did the great problems of the parish and the seminaries, but inasmuch as the monastic institutions were traditionally the acme of holiness in Russia, the question has significance.

At the Fourth All-Russian Missionary Congress, held at Kiev in 1908, Bishop Nikon of Vologda discussed the failings of the Orthodox monasteries. The resolutions adopted on the subject were serious enough to lead to the holding of a national congress of representatives from the monasteries to consider the questions raised. One of the foremost problems on the agenda was the use of spirituous liquors by monks. The monastic congress addressed a suggestion to the heads of the church that a pledge of total abstinence be required of the monks, as the monastic vows implied the renunciation of the lusts of the flesh. "If this is not possible, then cannot the regaling of monks with liquor at the refectory table and in the cells of the superiors be forbidden; and in general, what measures should be taken to instill in the monks aversion to this shameful and destructive vice?" [94] Other questions referred to the uncalled-for traveling about of monks and novices from one monastery to another, and the allied problems of the need for more thorough religious education, better discipline, and the like. Furthermore, "a sore spot in monastic life is the question of what to do with those monks who have long since discarded their vows, and who live shamefully, who subject themselves to monastic discipline only so far as they have to in order to have their cells and board free, and are a foul spot in their unrighteousness." The suggestion was advanced that there should be some easy way of returning such monks to civil life, as "they have long since ceased to be monks." The assembled monastics also denounced the practice of many superiors of

[94] *Tserkovnyia Vedomosti*, July 11, 1908, p. 1295.

passing these undesirables along to other institutions without warning as to their true character.[95]

Other points which the congress found in need of attention included the practice of having female servants on the monastery farms—cow girls, laundresses, and the like—as well as the employment of men as watchmen or doorkeepers at convents. Exact accounting of the funds of the monasteries was urgently needed. The practice of appointing as abbots persons who had never served novitiates and who had never before lived in monasteries was also condemned. Finally, the practice of sending forth monks with holy ikons to collect donations was brought to the attention of the gathering.[96]

In 1910 the Synod took action on the proposals of the monastic congress by condemning most of the practices cited.[97] However, an article published by Bishop Nikon of Vologda in 1912 gave an indication that all was not yet well with the Russian monasteries. This hierarch had been one of the bishops who took a leading part in the discussion of monasticism at the Missionary Congress in 1908; in 1912, in spite of the reforming efforts of the intervening period, his words bore the same burden as in the earlier year. He said, "Many monasteries there are in Holy Rus, and not a few monks; but . . . the life of the monastics has declined in righteousness; the superiors complain that there is no one to consecrate as deacon or senior monk; the bishops complain that there is no one to name as abbot." Further on in his article he said:

Of course, there always were weaknesses among the monastics, the vices of drunkenness, of slavery to the flesh, of love for money; of course, there are true saints in our monasteries today—the holy seed; but unfortunately there have now been added to the former weaknesses a sort of spirit of opposition, a spirit of egotism, an unlimited love of honors, and a waywardness, which have agitated those living in the monasteries. Even their activities and their deeds have taken on a special character; there are those who wear fetters, but are infected by a spirit of pride; there are those who fast, but are ruled by intolerant personal opinions; there are those who are strict with themselves, and merciless with others. Of late there have appeared in monasteries persons who give

---

[95] *Ibid.*   [96] *Ibid.*, pp. 1295–96.

[97] Sv. Sinod, *Obzor Nekotorykh Storon Deiatel'nosti Dukhovnago Vedomstva za 1910 g.*, pp. 17–18.

grounds for suspecting them of sectarianism, of *Khlystyism*—one of the most destructive, anti-Christian sects. . . .[98]

The economic condition of monastic affairs also provoked criticism. In 1908 the metropolitan of St. Petersburg complained of the twenty-five diocesan hotels, or *podvor'es,* in the capital, to say nothing of the Synodal and the metropolitan *podvor'es.* Said Metropolitan Antonii:

> The chief purpose of the *podvor'es* springing up in St. Petersburg is the financial, economic one—i. e., the gaining of funds for the monasteries in whose names they were built. The *podvor'es* degrade the holy work of spiritual and moral inspiration to the satisfying of the religious demands of the local flock by the mere external performance of rituals. The ritual performances in them become a business enterprise for securing funds for institutions outside the boundaries of the diocese.

Other objections raised by the metropolitan to the diocesan *podvor'es* in St. Petersburg were that while the monks who lived there were outside the jurisdiction of their bishops, they could not easily be controlled by the authorities in the capital; and further, that these monks hampered the educational and charitable work of the St. Petersburg parishes by diverting income that otherwise would have gone to the churches of the capital.[99]

A criticism which affected the monasteries themselves was made by the Synodal auditors who examined the monasteries of the diocese of Smolensk. The auditors found that in almost all the monasteries the agricultural operations were carried on by hired workers, or else the lands were rented for cash payments, "which gives ground for thinking that the monasteries do not need their lands, as physical labor and work in agriculture are favorite occupations of energetic and healthy monks, and distract them from the lures of vices not proper for monastics." In view of these findings, the religious consistory of the diocese ordered the abbots of the monasteries to discharge all hired laborers but those who did tasks which the monks themselves were not able to perform.[100]

In 1912 *Tserkovnyi Vestnik* printed an illuminating article on the causes of the mutual hostility between the white and the black clergy.

---

[98] *Tserkovnyia Vedomosti,* May 20, 1912, pp. 820–21.
[99] Sv. Sinod, *Vsepoddanneishii Otchet,* 1908–9, pp. 81–82.
[100] *Vera i Razum,* Dec., 1909, p. 699.

One reason was the age-long practice of sending parish priests to the monasteries for discipline: "Of course those subject to imprisonment can have no special love for their places of involuntary confinement, as . . . the superiors of the monasteries show special strictness toward them." Next, an economic reason: "There is an undoubted grain of truth in the charges that the monasteries are too interested in material matters, in improving economic operations, to the detriment of the development of the soul." Furthermore, the parish clergy disapproved of the monastic fund-collectors, "who, after the end of the harvest work, appear in large numbers in the villages and make collections" which the monasteries could well do without. "Not without ground, too, the clergy refer to the faults of monastic life, to the decline of discipline in the monasteries, and so on, although these accusations are frequently exaggerated." [101] Father Vostokov, a noted priest of Moscow, in his journal *Otkliki na Zhizn'* (*Responses to Life*), declared that the disorders of church life were creating a favorable soil for socialist propaganda. "The cloisters, for example, are now adorned with holy relics, miracle-working ikons; but in order to approach the sanctuaries kept in the monasteries, it is difficult to avoid being disturbed in your soul. 'A whole ring of worldly things surrounds the place of holiness.'" [102]

Much less was heard concerning evils in the life of the Russian convents. As stated in an earlier chapter, they seem in general to have been much poorer than the men's institutions. Nevertheless, in 1910 the Synod issued a decree prescribing rules for their governance. Greater care was to be used in investigating the past of prospective nuns. There was to be close supervision over the lives and the cells of the sisters, so that no luxury might creep in; simple and modest dress was to be the rule. Moreover, because of the unfortunate results of sending nuns and novices out from the convents on journeys to collect donations from patrons, this practice was absolutely forbidden. In addition the Synod voted, "with the aim of immediate abolition of disorders in the women's institutions, to entrust to all diocesan bishops the making, through especially trustworthy persons appointed by them, of a careful investigation of the inner conditions in the con-

[101] *Tserkovnyi Vestnik*, March 8, 1912, cols. 312–13.
[102] Cited in *Tserkovnyi Vestnik*, Nov. 14, 1913, cols. 1436–37.

vents, [and] of their economy and capital," and ordered that they should advise the Synod concerning the results of this investigation.[103]

With the following citation the present account of the movement for ecclesiastical reform after the Revolution of 1905 comes to a close. The results of the hopes and strivings of many intelligent and sincere sons of the church can best be summed up in the words of the report of the Budget Commission of the Duma at the end of 1915:

> When we study the reports of the Most Holy Synod, our attention is drawn to the regularly recurring phenomenon that, even with the agreement of the legislative institutions, of the Pre-*Sobor* Conference, and in part of the Most Holy Synod, on the necessity of certain reforms, these reforms have not been realized; the institutions remain as archaic as before, and the condition of things continues to be exceedingly unsatisfactory, even hopeless. . . .
>
> . . . But to live longer in this fashion is impossible. We must heal ourselves of this paralysis, we must become active, weakness and lack of purpose must be replaced by energy and strength. For this it will be necessary, . . . with the united, simultaneous efforts of the whole church, of all its members, to move it from that dead center on which it has stood for many centuries.[104]

Unfortunately, the hour was already late. These words were written on the eve of the Revolution.

[103] Sv. Sinod, *Vsepoddanneishii Otchet,* 1910, pp. 71–73.

[104] Gosudarstvennaia Duma, *Doklady Biudzhetnoi Komissii,* IV Duma, Session IV, No. 4, pp. 8–10.

CHAPTER VIII

Plus Ça Change

IN THE preceding chapter it was shown that the movement for ecclesiastical reform failed to change the church in any significant fashion between the Revolution of 1905 and the Revolution of 1917. There were some slight shifts in direction, and some new developments occurred, but in the main the old course was followed. Above all, in spite of the greater freedom given to the non-Orthodox religions, the church remained closely connected with the state and showed willingness to support it.

In one important particular, however, the attitude of both the church and the government did change after 1905. Mention has already been made of the wooing of the Old Believers by the Orthodox Church and by the government, and also of the unsatisfactory response to these overtures. But although the Old Believers did not show a disposition to accept the proposals, the authorities of the Orthodox Church persisted in their conciliatory gestures. On November 29, 1907, both Bishop Mitrofan and Father Nikonovich urged from the rostrum of the Duma that the Old Believers of all sorts make peace with the official church. ". . . We extend . . . to you the hand of our fraternal union," said Father Nikonovich.[1] However, F. E. Mel'nikov, a noted member of the Old Believers, wrote, ". . . I think it [union of the churches] will be possible only if the church attains a system of conciliar control and admits laymen to participation in church affairs." [2]

In spite of this rebuff, official circles in Russia continued to view the

---

[1] Gosudarstvennaia Duma, *Stenograficheskie Otchety*, III Duma, Session I, Part 1, cols. 727–30 and 738.

[2] *Missionerskoe Obozrenie*, June, 1909, p. 876.

Old Believers as erring brothers who might soon return to the fold. In 1910 the Minister of Internal Affairs stated that, unlike the sectarians, the Old Believers were considered by the government as Orthodox, but "with a mistaken view, historically formed, of the uncanonical nature of the Ruling Church." This description, the minister said, applied to all varieties of Old Believers.[3] In March, 1912, Archbishop Antonii of Volhynia issued a long message urging the Old Believers to unite with the church, or with *Edinoverie,* the Orthodox Uniat Church, against their mutual foes, the revolutionists and the atheists.[4] The appeal was answered by the great Moscow industrialist, A. I. Morozov, who was an Old Believer. The reply was evidently in the negative, for soon afterward Archbishop Antonii accused him and his followers of being "concealers of the truth." [5] Yet the official organ of the Orthodox domestic missions repeatedly expressed hopes that the Old Believers would seize the occasion of the canonization of Patriarch Hermogen, or the celebration of the three-hundredth anniversary of Mikhail Romanov in 1913, to unite with the ruling church.[6] However, by January, 1914, even the missionary publication had become disillusioned. In an article at the beginning of that year the editor stated that the Old Believers were not drawing closer to the official church, but were moving further from it, under the influence of "Jewish Freemasonry." The Old Believers, said the editor, had displayed their hostility to both church and government at the time of the Beilis case (an important "Jewish ritual murder" trial), at the canonization of Hermogen, and at the Romanov tercentenary. According to this article, the Old Believers were, in fact, moving so far to the left that they were taking up Christian socialism.[7] Apparently the authorities of the Orthodox Church now felt that there was no chance of union with the "schismatics," for the official church publications printed nothing more on the subject for some time.

The Russian government was not entirely consistent in its attitude toward the Old Believers. While advances were made to them from

[3] *Missionerskoe Obozrenie,* June, 1910, p. 897.
[4] *Tserkovnyia Vedomosti,* March 10, 1912, pp. 395–403.
[5] *Ibid.,* June 14, 1912, pp. 1143–50.
[6] *Missionerskoe Obozrenie,* June, 1913, pp. 309–16.
[7] *Ibid.,* Jan., 1914, pp. 158–74.

time to time, there were occasional instances of unwillingness to make slight concessions, and of hostile acts. Thus Prugavin, a well-known writer on subjects pertaining to the Old Believers and the sectarians, alleged that in June, 1909, the police in a county of the province of Saratov had forbidden the Old Believers to hold prayer meetings, and had even obliged them to sign pledges not to do so. Also the author alleged that the governor of Vladimir had sent to the county police officials a circular saying that ". . . public religious processions, in church vestments, by the followers of Schism, are forbidden by law, . . ." an order which was at once forwarded to the local authorities for "proper action." Thus the Old Believers were suddenly deprived of a legal right which they had been enjoying for several years.[8] At the Old Believer Peasant Congress in 1909 several of the delegates complained that they had been oppressed in various ways. One group had been forbidden to organize a campaign to collect money for building a house of prayer; others had been obliged to contribute toward the building of churches for the local Orthodox parishes, to pay part of the cost of a house for an Orthodox priest, and so on.[9] On the other hand, P. P. Stremoukhov, governor of Saratov in 1911, states that on one occasion in that year he paid a visit to the local Old Believer bishop in his monastery, kissed his Old Believer cross in reverence, and ate dinner with the bishop in the latter's quarters.[10]

One instance of the official restrictions to which the Old Believers were subject was reported in 1910 by *Missionerskoe Obozrenie* (*Missionary Survey*, published by the official church). In this case the Minister of Internal Affairs stated that it had been learned that the pastors of Old Believer congregations had failed to observe the rules governing the admission of persons of the Orthodox faith to membership in their congregations. Moreover, the provincial authorities in many cases had noted in the passports and the other official docu-

[8] A. S. Prugavin, "Raskol i Biurokratiia," *Vestnik Evropy*, 1900, No. 6, pp. 171–72. Prugavin, a well-known authority on the sects and the Old Believers, was decidedly disposed in their favor.

[9] Sovet Vserossiiskikh S'ezdov Staroobriadtsev, *Sel'sko-khoziaistvennyi i Ekonomicheskii Byt Staroobriadtsev*, pp. 272–74.

[10] P. P. Stremoukhov, "Moia Bor'ba s Episkopom Germogenom i Iliodorom," *Arkhiv Russkoi Revoliutsii*, 1925, XVI, 42–44.

ments of persons born into Orthodoxy that they were Old Believers, although these persons had not complied with the formalities required by law and hence in the eyes of the law were still of the Orthodox faith. Consequently the Minister of Internal Affairs ordered the provincial authorities not to list Orthodox persons as Old Believers in official documents unless the proper formalities had been observed. Moreover, the local officials were to require the religious leaders of the Old Believers to refuse to accept into their denomination any Orthodox persons who had not complied with the formalities of the law.[11]

In the field of elementary education the Old Believers still remained at a disadvantage. In 1912 the noted manufacturer Morozov asked the Council of Ministers to have the state contribute to the building of parish schools for the Old Believers, as the children educated there would learn piety and patriotism and true loyalty to Tsar and Fatherland. The Council of Ministers referred the question to the Most Holy Synod, which rejected the request.[12] Nor was this the only denial of equality in educational privileges with which the Old Believers met; on January 13, 1914, the Minister of Education issued a circular forbidding the acceptance of Old Believers as teachers in the public schools.[13]

As has been said, the official attitude toward the Old Believers wavered between friendly overtures and insistence on special privilege for the official church. In connection with two important bills before the Duma—the bill regulating changes from one faith to another, and the bill regulating the congregations of the Old Believers —both church and government showed that the time-honored principle of special rights for Orthodoxy and restrictions for other denominations was still the official policy, and that the scheme for *rapprochement* with the Old Believers was conceived not out of fondness for the erring brothers, but out of a desire to strengthen the official church.

In 1909 the Ministry of Internal Affairs introduced a bill to regulate changes in religious adherence in accordance with the imperial decree of October 17, 1906. No new privileges to the non-Orthodox

[11] *Missionerskoe Obozrenie,* Feb., 1910, p. 356.
[12] *Ibid.,* March, 1913, pp. 489–91; *Tserkovnyia Vedomosti,* Dec. 15, 1912, p. 2030.
[13] *Missionerskoe Obozrenie,* Jan., 1916, p. 152.

were granted by the ministerial bill; however, it was greatly revised in the Duma's Commission on Questions of Religious Belief, so that the version placed before the Duma was much more liberal than the original. The bill which came out of the commission provided that all persons over twenty-one years of age should be granted the right to change their religious adherence to ". . . any religious denomination or cult, adherence to which is not punishable by criminal procedure." Children who had not attained their fourteenth year were to change their faith when their parents changed, while older minors were to be granted the right of independent choice of faith only with the consent of both parents, if living, or of their guardians. All such changes were to be officially registered by the police within forty days after the handing in of the proper petition by the person changing his faith. Moreover, when anyone wished to join any lawful denomination, ". . . no one under any pretext may prevent the fulfillment of this desire." [14]

The bill concerning changes from one faith to another, which applied to all non-Orthodox denominations, caused heated debates in the Duma. The terms of the bill were approved by the moderates of the Octobrist party, especially Barons Meiendorf and Rosen from Livonia.[15] The Orthodox Bishop Mitrofan, of the Right, declared that ". . . at present the bill under consideration is unacceptable and pernicious in its frightful consequences, for it opens the door for seduction into those sects and those other beliefs, which have nothing in common with the spirit of Christian faith." [16] The Orthodox Father Ganzhulevich, of the Nationalist Group, proclaimed, ". . . we cannot deprive Orthodoxy of the protection of the laws in our Orthodox Russian state; we cannot but protect the sons of our Orthodox Church from violence to their religious conscience." [17] On the other hand, the parties of the Left Center and the Left—the Cadets, and especially the *Trudoviks* (Labor Group) and the Social Democrats—were eager for full religious freedom, and opposition was voiced to the forty-day period preliminary to registration, during which, they said, the Ortho-

---

[14] Gosudarstvennaia Duma, *Stenograficheskie Otchety*, III Duma, Session II, Part 4, cols. 1745–52.

[15] *Ibid.*, cols. 1777–80; 1829–34; 1868–73.

[16] *Ibid.*, col. 1789.   [17] *Ibid.*, col. 1937.

dox clergy would have ample time to learn of the petitioner's intention and to use strong pressure to restrain the erring son of the church. Bulat, a Polish *Trudovik,* even declared that the Orthodox bishops ". . . preach that their Orthodox faith—I say *theirs*—not that which is professed by the majority of the Duma—their Orthodox faith can be protected only by prisons, arrests, *nagaikas* [Cossack whips], and bayonets," and his speech received considerable applause from the Left.[18] Karaulov, a Cadet, followed with a speech in which he stated that the people of the district of Kholm had been turned from the Catholic Uniat faith ". . . not by Orthodox preaching, but by the *nagaikas* of dragoons [applause from the Left, and voices, "True!" Voices from the Right, "That's a lie!" Uproar; the bell of the presiding officer]." [19]

Further antagonism was aroused on the Right by Miliukov, leader of the Cadet party, who spoke eloquently for freedom of religion and declared that many of the Old Believers, the sectarians, and the non-believers made citizens of the best type; moreover, he affirmed that it was useless to try to keep apostates in the church by preventive measures.[20] However, his studied words were very much outdone by the *Trudovik* Miagkii of Tomsk, who said:

. . . The bureaucratic clergy have made the church an enemy of freedom, and a defender of oppression [uproar from the Right; the bell of the presiding officer].

. . .

We see that the majority of the higher pastors blessed the pogrom banners and were not rarely present at these pogroms. The heart of every man who believes in anything would shudder if he passed before the monument in Tomsk where hundreds of people were burned alive; but the heart of the aged pastor who bore high religious authority [Bishop Makarii of Tomsk] did not shudder, and he looked calmly on that pyre where hundreds of Christians burned. . . .[21]

Another striking speech was made by Markov, a noted deputy of the extreme Right. In his remarks he said:

"The right is to be granted" to fall away from that church which, from the standpoint of the government, is uniquely true, uniquely holy. I

---

[18] Gosudarstvennaia Duma, *Stenograficheskie Otchety,* III Duma, Session II, Part 4, cols. 1820–23; cols. 1863–67; col. 1804.

[19] *Ibid.,* col. 1885.   [20] *Ibid.,* cols. 1900–10.   [21] *Ibid.,* cols. 1866–67.

understand that the state tolerates the weaknesses of mankind; it tolerates mistakes, it tolerates certain vices, . . . it tolerates drunkenness, even immorality; the state tolerates houses of immorality. . . . Hence they call them houses of toleration. But from all this, gentlemen, it should not follow that the state . . . is obliged to legalize the visitation of houses of toleration. These, gentlemen, are two entirely different things: to tolerate something, and to legalize it. [Rozanov, from his seat, "A cynical comparison!"] . . . In the bill it says, "The right is granted" to fall away from Orthodoxy. . . . This is exactly as if a law were published granting the right to enter liquor saloons and to get drunk [voices from the Left, "That is cynicism!"].[22]

The excitement over the debate reached its height, however, with the speech of Bishop Evlogii of Kholm. After denouncing the Polish Catholics for accusing the Orthodox of oppressing them, when it was the Poles who had oppressed the Orthodox Russians, he said he realized that the Poles spoke as interested parties, "but when our Russians second them, . . . I can call that nothing but most revolting Pharisaism, unlimited hypocrisy, and a mockery of the truth; and I say [turning to the Left] shame upon you, gentlemen! [prolonged applause and voices from the Right, "Correct! Bravo!"]." [23]

For this he was rebuked by the presiding officer, the Orthodox Baron Meiendorf, whereupon the deputies on the Right raised such an uproar that the session was temporarily suspended. When it was renewed the Right parties absented themselves from the hall in protest against the action of the presiding officer. Consequently the bill was speedily passed in their absence, without amendment.[24] However, it was a fruitless victory for the liberal parties. The Synod, which had already branded the moderate bill introduced by the Minister of Internal Affairs as a violation of the Fundamental Laws, opposed the revised bill even more strongly in the Council of State. The bill was once more amended by the removal of several of the provisions upon which the Duma had insisted and all attempts to compromise the differences between the two chambers failed.[25]

A second conflict developed over the bill introduced by the Ministry of Internal Affairs to regulate the formation of Old Believer congre-

---

[22] *Ibid.*, col. 1954. [23] *Ibid.*, col. 1926.
[24] *Ibid.*, col. 1926; cols. 2102–18.
[25] *Ibid.*, Session V, Part 3, cols. 150–51.

gations—or, more exactly, over the amendment introduced by the Commission on Old Believer Affairs granting the right of propaganda and of using clerical titles. Speeches in opposition to the amended bill were made by Bishop Evlogii, who declared that the Orthodox monopoly of propaganda must be preserved, by Kryzhanovskii, Assistant Minister of Internal Affairs,[26] and by several others. However, the Octobrists and the Cadets, represented by Kamenskii, Baron Feldkerzam, Count Uvarov, Miliukov, and Karaulov, as well as the parties of the extreme Left, spoke in defense of the right of propaganda for the Old Believers.[27] Likewise the spokesman for a minority group of the Duma clergy, Father Ispollatov, declared that his following favored the bill as amended. Although himself a member of the ruling church, Father Ispollatov declared that the prohibition of propaganda by the opponents of the church was not in harmony with the teachings of Christ and moreover was "not worthy of the dignity and the righteousness of the Holy Orthodox Church, which . . . does not need the help of external repressive measures for its defense against attacks from non-Orthodox proselytizing. . . ." [28] Father Balalaev and several others of the Right failed to agree with these arguments, and Kryzhanovskii frequently interrupted to object to the amended version of the bill; none the less, it was triumphantly passed amid stormy scenes.[29] Once more it was an empty victory, however. The Council of State refused to accept the liberal provisions introduced into the bill by the Duma; the Duma refused to accept the Council of State's edition of the bill; and so it died. The sole result of these attempts at legislation on religious matters was to leave a heritage of bitter feeling.[30]

The government had failed in its attempt to secure legislation satisfactory to it on the status of the Old Believers and the sectarians. As there seemed to be little hope that the Duma would pass a bill acceptable to the Synod, the government was obliged to fall back on administrative decrees to delimit the legal position of the Old Believers and the sectarians. Consequently, several such decrees were

---

[26] Gosudarstvennaia Duma, *Stenograficheskie Otchety*, III Duma, Session II, Part 4, cols. 1263 and 1023–29.

[27] *Ibid.*, cols. 1041–49; 1395–1401; 1060–65.

[28] *Ibid.*, col. 1398.   [29] *Ibid.*, cols. 1049–55; 1403–19; 1421.

[30] G. Iurskii, *Pravye v 3-ei Gosudarstvennoi Dume*, pp. 54–60. This author is a strong partisan of the Right and of the church authorities.

issued in 1909 and 1910, to clarify questions which had arisen. Thus in October, 1909, the Ministry of Internal Affairs issued rules to govern cases in which persons expressed a desire to join the Old Believers or a legally recognized sect, or any other legal non-Orthodox faith. In such case the person was to apply to the governor of the province through the county police, who were required, in the case of an Orthodox person, to notify his parish priest immediately.[31] The clergy were at once to admonish the erring member; but the police were instructed that this was no concern of theirs; their duty was to verify the age of the person desiring to change and then to issue the proper certificate of adherence to the new faith before a thirty-day period had elapsed.[32] However, while the police were to interpose no ultimate obstacles in the way of those adults who wished to change their faith, they were told that the law still prohibited any attempt to win converts from the ranks of Orthodoxy; the law still considered it illegal for a Catholic priest to confess Orthodox children, or for a sectarian to instruct them in his catechism, to teach them sectarian prayers and hymns, or to take them to sectarian religious services. These provisions, the police were instructed, were to apply even to Orthodox children whose parents had become sectarians.[33]

The prohibition of propaganda by the non-Orthodox, and especially by the sectarians, imposed duties on the police that at times must have proved burdensome. For example, in the circular cited above they were instructed that for a convert to use a printed blank in applying for registration as a member of his adopted faith was permissible, but the authorities were advised "to investigate whether the appearance of the printed blanks is not a result of propaganda not permitted by law, or of conscious action, on the part of someone, designed to lead to the unwitting transfer of Orthodox persons into a sect." If this were so, the authorities were to start criminal prosecution against the distributors of the blanks.[34] Furthermore, the rules against propaganda forbade the distribution, to non-members of the congregation, of summonses or invitations to attend prayer meetings, as well as the use of posters, placards, and similar announcements. Orthodox persons

---

[31] *Missionerskoe Obozrenie,* June, 1910, pp. 897–900.
[32] *Ibid.,* June, 1911, p. 454.
[33] *Ibid.,* p. 453.   [34] *Ibid.,* pp. 454–55.

were privileged to attend religious services of sectarians and Old Believers, but if they did so, the police were warned to see "that the sectarian preachers at the time of preaching do not denounce the teachings or the precepts of the Orthodox Church, or call upon the Orthodox to join their faith; in case they do perform such acts, [the police were] to start criminal proceedings against them." [35]

Another important decree of the Ministry of Internal Affairs relating to religious meetings, congregations, and the like, was issued on October 4, 1910. One significant section of the circular declared that neither the rules contained in the circular on the congresses of the non-Orthodox denominations nor the rules of the present circular were to apply to the Old Believers: "i. e., those who recognize the dogmas of the Orthodox Church but not its rituals, and who perform service according to the old-style books." [36]

The new rules for the prayer meetings of the sectarians, held in licensed houses of prayer, provided that they might be held without special permission for each meeting, but the police were to be notified of the time of the meetings. As for meetings outside the recognized buildings, more formality was required. At least twenty-five adults had to be members of the congregation holding the meeting; the police were to be notified at least two weeks in advance as to the time and place of the meeting, the names of the organizers of the meeting, and other details. Three days before the time set for the gathering, the local authorities were to inform the sectarians whether or not the meeting would be permitted to take place, with their reasons in case of refusal. Persons who were not members of the congregation were permitted to preach and to perform the service, except in the case of foreigners, who were required to obtain special permission from the Ministry of Internal Affairs for each occasion. While religious services in the recognized buildings of the sectarians were not to be restricted, gatherings for conversation, reading, and discussion were not to be tolerated in their religious buildings; moreover, gatherings of societies of youths, meetings for evangelizing or catechizing the young, and for performing rites "signifying their adherence to the sectarian faith" were prohibited. At prayer meetings and services not held in

[35] *Missionerskoe Obozrenie,* June, 1910, pp. 899–902.
[36] *Tserkovnyia Vedomosti,* Feb. 26, 1911, official part, p. 42.

the regular buildings, collections of money were not to be made without proper permission. To ensure that these rules were obeyed, the police authorities were to detail a competent representative to attend each prayer meeting of each sectarian congregation. If he should find that the meeting was not of the type announced in the original application to the police, the constable was instructed to close the meeting, if after two warnings the sectarians persisted in their course, while if the sectarians cast abuse or ridicule on the dogmas and rites of the Orthodox Church, or urged Orthodox persons to abandon their faith, he was instructed to draw up a warrant and begin criminal proceedings against the offenders. If the sectarians desired to hold non-religious meetings, readings, or discussions, they were to obtain permission from the governor of the province in each case. Funerals were to be held without obtaining permission; but services out of doors, ritual processions, and prayer meetings or services for children of sectarian families were to be matters for the special decision of the Ministry of Internal Affairs after proper petitions had been submitted by the sectarians.[37]

In the same year the Ministry issued rules to govern the holding of congresses of sectarians. In explaining his decree the minister declared that the sectarians had been abusing the privileges of holding congresses. Not only had they held their meetings in large towns far from the centers of their denominations, but also at times foreign subjects had been present at these meetings. The congresses, moreover, instead of being the business sessions they were intended to be, often had turned into religious festivals at which large numbers of converts from Orthodoxy were obtained. Hence rules were issued that before each congress the elected delegates of at least twelve congregations must petition the ministry, submitting the program of the meeting, which was to be confirmed and strictly adhered to—and also a list of all persons entitled to take active part in proceedings. Two types of congresses were to be permitted—religious and business gatherings—but they were to be kept separate and distinct. Furthermore, a representative of the Ministry of Internal Affairs was to be present at each meeting, to see that the rules were obeyed, that only adults attended,

[37] *Ibid.*, pp. 43–44; Gosudarstvennaia Duma, *Prilozheniia k Stenograficheskim Otchetam,* III Duma, Session IV, Vol. I, No. 68, 1910, pp. 7–8.

that no foreigner took any active part in proceedings, that no collections of money were made, and that business meetings were not transformed into religious sessions, and vice versa. Only under these conditions was each sectarian congregation entitled to participate in one business session and one religious session a year.[38]

In addition to these lengthy circulars relating to the sectarians which the Ministry of Internal Affairs promulgated, a number of minor regulations were issued. In December, 1909, it was proclaimed that in future the solemn christenings of Baptists under the open sky were to be looked upon as religious processions, not as integral features of their faith to which the law gave full sanction. Hence, in order to have the privilege of holding these ceremonies, they were to ask special permission from the ministry before each occasion.[39] In 1913 the Senate decided that only pastors of regularly organized congregations were to be permitted to preach—a decision which deprived unorganized groups of sectarians of instruction by the circuit riders who had previously ministered to them.[40] And a little later in the same year, the Minister of Internal Affairs extended the principle of this ruling still further by issuing a general public prohibition of the sale of gramophone records of sermons of sectarian preachers. According to the minister, records reproducing the sermons of the Baptist Stepanov on "Living and Dead Faith" and on "Bowing to God in Spirit and in Truth" were eagerly bought in some localities, and were often played in tea rooms, drinking places, lodging houses, and private homes. Inasmuch as "the aforesaid means of propaganda of false sectarian teachings appears to be exceedingly dangerous for the Orthodox population," the minister ordered the governors to take immediate steps to halt the sale of all such records.[41]

As an indication that some of the local inhabitants were not loath to restrict the sectarians, the writer Iasevich-Borodaevskaia cited a number of instances in which sectarians were reported to have been hampered in the enjoyment of religious rights. The members of a congregation of Baptists found themselves obliged to petition the

[38] *Tserkovnyia Vedomosti*, May 1, 1910, official part, pp. 146–48.
[39] *Missionerskoe Obozrenie*, June, 1910, pp. 899–902.
[40] *Ibid.*, Oct., 1913, p. 342.
[41] *Tserkovnyia Vedomosti*, June 20, 1913, p. 1350.

Minister of Justice for redress: certain of their fellow members, after "having been subjected to a multitude of all kinds of persecutions both by the local police and by the Orthodox clergy," were brought before the court of the *zemskii* chief (a powerful local official) for holding some sort of prayer meeting which actually had never taken place. The *zemskii* chief was severe with the defendants, and sentenced thirteen persons to pay fines of twenty-five rubles each, or serve a two-months' term of imprisonment.[42] The attempt of the Baptist Kuz'ma Smorgun to bury his daughter in the community cemetery "led to strong protests from the local priest, before whose eyes there occurred the 'chastisement,' the beating and maltreatment, of Timofei Stukal, who accompanied the body of the child." [43]

Iasevich-Borodaevskaia was a witness whose sympathies were certainly with the sectarians, so that her testimony of itself is not convincing. However, it is considerably strengthened by reports appearing in official church publications, which show that at least some of the local authorities were taking action against the sectarians. *Missionerskoe Obozrenie* in 1910 reported that General Dumbadze, Commandant at Ialta, "after noticing political agitation among the local 'Evangelicals,' had ordered several of them to move out of the city of Ialta." [44] And in 1913 a Baptist congregation at the village of Tsarskaia Milost', in the province of Ekaterinoslav, complained to the Ministry of Internal Affairs that when they had held a solemn baptismal ceremony in public the priest of the village had successfully urged the police to issue orders against the repetition of such ceremonies in future. However, these last complainants obtained no satisfaction from the ministry; instructions were sent to the local governor to inform the sectarians that the police had acted correctly, as the privilege of performing in the open air this rite, ". . . which is not an indispensable consequence of the teachings of the Evangelical Christians, does not derive from the essence of the freedom of conscience granted to the sectarians by the Will of the Monarch." [45]

Additional evidence on the treatment of sectarians after 1907 was

[42] V. Iasevich-Borodaevskaia, *Bor'ba za Veru*, p. 386.
[43] *Ibid.*, p. 385.
[44] *Missionerskoe Obozrenie*, Feb., 1910, p. 352.
[45] *Vera i Razum*, Aug., 1913, No. 16, pp. 573–74.

given by a question signed by fifty members of the Duma in 1913—deputies of the parties of the Left Center and the Left—Progressives, Cadets, Laborites, and Social Democrats. In the complaint a series of incidents were cited, involving action by the local authorities. The first episode had occurred on November 13, 1911, when a police inspector with several constables broke into a Baptist house of prayer, drove out the congregation, and arrested many. "None of your business. I know what I'm doing," he said in answer to the protest of the preacher. In Nikolsk-Ussuriisk at the end of 1912 the house of prayer belonging to the Evangelical Christians was closed without explanation, although it had been in use for five years. "The closing occurred at the demand of the recently arrived missionary, the Orthodox priest Sergii Tolpygin." Further it was stated that early in the year 1913 the police of Odessa had closed a meeting of Evangelical Christians, one of *Subbotniki* (Adventists), and another of Baptists. In February, 1913, the prayer meetings of the Baptists in Ekaterinodar were closed without explanation. Not long after this they were permitted to reopen, but with the condition that "the Baptists should read only the Gospel and should not dare to utter one thought of their own. The police officer attending the meeting watches over the strict fulfillment of this condition."

These instances of persecution were supplemented with a number of additional cases, all described fully, with names, times, and places.[46] The Commission on Questions (of the Fourth Duma) reported these statements of fact to be true, and denounced the actions of the local authorities as unlawful.[47] The representatives of the ministry who were interpellated refused to answer the questions asked and did not deny the truth of the allegations.

All of the above instances involved the older sects, chiefly the *Molokane* and the Stundists, who had formed an alliance in 1906 and were known respectively as Evangelical Christians and Baptists. The positions of several of the newer groups, notably *Novyi Izrail* (New Israel) and the Abstainers, left much more to be desired. The law gave equal rights to all sects except those guilty of "superstitious or

[46] Gosudarstvennaia Duma, *Prilozheniia k Stenograficheskim Otchetam*, IV Duma, Session I, No. 222.
[47] *Ibid.*, Session II, No. 447.

grossly immoral acts," which in 1906 included only the *Skoptsy* and the *Khlysty*. In 1910 the Minister of Internal Affairs issued a decree naming *Novyi Izrail* as a ". . . superstitious and immoral, . . ." and therefore criminal denomination.[48] In 1911 a second circular was issued, stating that while the charges of superstition and immorality were not to be pressed, no new registrations of congregations of this sect were to be made. According to charges made in the Duma, in the question addressed by the Left Center and the Left to the Ministry of Internal Affairs, the formation of the congregations of *Novyi Izrail* had been stopped after the orders of the ministry, and long-established meetings of the sect were closed in the Terek, Kuban, and Don regions, and in the provinces of Voronezh, Stavropol, and Chernomorie.[49] Prugavin, a noted writer on sectarian affairs, declared that several closings were accompanied by beatings at the hands of Orthodox neighbors, and that many of the sectarians were arrested on charges of blasphemy and sacrilege, at the urging of Orthodox missionaries. Administrative exile and imprisonment were the fate of others, and even after they moved to the Caucasus in search of greater religious freedom, their condition was little better, so that twenty thousand of them were planning to follow the example of the *Dukhobortsy* by emigrating to America.[50] Prugavin's claim that the sect was moral, loyal, and devout was sharply disputed by Professor Golubev of the St. Petersburg Religious Academy; however, the professor made no denial that the sect had received harsh treatment.[51]

The Abstainers were groups of people both in Moscow and St. Petersburg who attempted to win redemption from the prevalent curse of drunkenness by turning to religion. Professor Miliukov told the Fourth Duma of the difficulties experienced by these people at the hands of the Orthodox clergy. Miliukov cited the official testimony from the trial of the Abstainer Churikov in St. Petersburg: "I am

[48] Prugavin, "Religioznyia Goneniia pri Obnovlennom Stroe," *Vestnik Evropy,* Aug., 1911, p. 123.

[49] Gosudarstvennaia Duma, *Prilozheniia k Stenograficheskim Otchetam,* IV Duma, Session I, No. 222.

[50] Prugavin, "Religioznyia Goneniia," pp. 125–30.

[51] *Tserkovnyia Vedomosti,* Aug. 27, 1911, pp. 1471–75; Sept. 7, 1911, pp. 1576–79; Sept. 24, 1911, pp. 1612–15; Oct. 1, 1911, pp. 1666–69; Oct. 8, 1911, pp. 1726–28; Nov. 22, 1911, pp. 1833–36.

Orthodox," said Churikov. "I have gone to church for twenty years, confessed, and received Communion." But the Orthodox missionary answered, "No, thou are a sectarian, a *Khlyst.*" "Why a *Khlyst?*" And the reply of the missionary, expressed in the condescending second person singular, was: "Because thou illuminest thy whole life with religion; because thou performest healing, not by hypnosis, not by medicine, but through faith in God. Because thou talkest not merely of morality, but of the Scriptures, and thou interpretest the Scriptures in thine own words." According to Professor Miliukov, the cases were tried in closed courts and, although the missionaries were forced to base their case upon hearsay evidence, the leaders of the Abstainers, who had long been deprived of the right of preaching, found that their efforts to promote temperance were largely curtailed.[52] The well-known Octobrist, E. P. Kovalevskii, testified that he had visited the factory region of St. Petersburg, where thousands of people had attended the temperance meetings of the Abstainers, and had found the results to be excellent. None the less, the police had prohibited the meetings, ". . . under the influence, unfortunately, of the religious authorities; and the reason alleged was suspicion of *Khlysty* tendencies in those who attended—note, not their actions, not their crimes, not their beliefs, but only a tendency to fall into error." [53]

To return to the Old Believers: from the evidence already presented it is apparent that both the law and the practice of the government had become quite favorable to them, at least when compared with the treatment meted out to the schismatics before 1905. In spite of the fact that the government was not willing to extend to the Old Believers the right of propaganda enjoyed by the state church, the official policy was now one of wooing the Old Believers and of reducing to a minimum the restrictions upon them. The major sects also enjoyed considerably wider privileges than before the Revolution of 1905, in that they might build prayer houses, form congregations, register their marriages and births, with comparative ease. None the less, the authorities, both ecclesiastical and secular, remained hostile to the sectarians, and in spite of the changed conditions, continued to make

[52] Gosudarstvennaia Duma, *Stenograficheskie Otchety*, IV Duma, Session II, Part 3, col. 1340; cols. 1281–82.
[53] *Ibid.*, Session I, Part 2, col. 1390.

trouble for them. However, there are indications that the methods employed by the churchmen and the government against the sectarians were not attended by great success. For one thing, in many cases the sectarians seem to have enjoyed a considerable advantage over their rivals. Even *Missionerskoe Obozrenie*, in discussing the "Pharisaic righteousness" of the sectarians in claiming that they were free from drunkenness and that they excelled in charity, one to another, admitted, ". . . we must, however, recognize that the admirable features of their life undoubtedly surpass the virtues of the Orthodox. . . ." [54] The same story was told by *Tserkovnyi Vestnik* in 1913. It declared that the chief reason for the success of the sectarians in winning converts from the Orthodox was that the latter on joining the Baptists "feel relief from their former moral confusion and an undisciplined life." For

the Baptists state with pride that they spend their free time in reading the New Testament and in prayer, that their children love sacred reading and do not run on the streets, are not ill-mannered, and do not curse; that the Orthodox, who curse them as Stundists, spend their holidays in drinking bouts at home and in grogshops, in ribaldry, in fights, and in other uncouthness. When a missionary visited one old Baptist for discussion, the latter asked in wrath, "Where were you these thirty years, when I was rolling drunkenly under hedges, when I was tormenting my wife and children?" [55]

That the missionary work of the church was not winning the sectarians was shown by the official figures for conversions in 1910, 1911, and 1912. While in each of these years the church reported more conversions than losses, and while the conversions from the Old Believers slightly exceeded the losses to them, the conversions from the sectarians were only 1,059, 1,140, and 1,140 for those three years, while the losses to the sects were declared to be 4,019, 4,476, and 4,915.[56] In their petition to the new Over Procurator in 1915 the Duma clergy declared,

Further, it is necessary to point to the unfortunate condition of missionary work. The institution of diocesan missionaries, who frequently

---

[54] *Missionerskoe Obozrenie*, May, 1910, p. 770.
[55] *Tserkovnyi Vestnik*, Oct. 10, 1913, col. 1276.
[56] *Missionerskoe Obozrenie*, Jan., 1914, pp. 154–55.

are without religious rank, is not only a fruitless, but even in some cases a harmful one. They have a police function rather than a religious and enlightening one. The diocesan missionaries can do nothing toward converting those who have strayed, and at the same time they often hamper the activity and the energy of the pastors, the only proper missionaries in the parishes.[57]

Thus the missionary activity of the Orthodox Church tended to follow the policies and the methods used in earlier years. In still another respect certain members of the clergy showed little evidence of having undergone a fundamental change. Many of the upper clergy retained their former attitude toward the revolutionaries, and the Jews, whom they coupled with the radicals. To be sure, there was a decline in the active preaching of anti-Semitism after the Revolution of 1905 had spent its force; however, the Synod and the hierarchy never disowned the tie with the extreme Union of the Russian People. Moreover, while the central authorities of the church did not give open support to the counter-revolutionary anti-Semites, one of the dioceses was still violent in its hatred of the Jews. This was Saratov, on the far-off lower Volga, where the monk Iliodor and his protector, Bishop Hermogen, fulminated in the manner of the Union of the Russian People. The character of Bishop Hermogen can be illustrated by excerpts from an article written by him in denunciation of the Third Duma, which appeared in his journal, *Bratskii Listok* (*Fraternal Leaflet*). After denouncing the members of the Duma as "downright traitors, and despisers of the soul of the nation," as "enemies of the Orthodox Russian people," as "robbers and thieves who stop at nothing," he urged, ". . . cast out this Mongol band! . . . They, together with the revolutionaries, the Jews, the Poles, and other foreign races, are preparing for Russia the planned coming of a new frightful . . . Time of Troubles." [58]

As for Iliodor, he became head of a monstery in Tsaritsyn and organizer of the local branch of the Union of the Russian People. His outbursts grew in intensity and became more and more outrageous, so that after a breach with the local governor he was exiled to a monas-

[57] *Missionerskoe Obozrenie*, Oct., 1915, pp. 297–98.
[58] Gosudarstvennaia Duma, *Stenograficheskie Otchety*, III Duma, Session II, Part 3, cols. 2189–90.

tery in Tula. However, he soon returned to Tsaritsyn in disguise and defied the Synod. The latter took steps to punish him, but Bishop Hermogen was on his side and eventually, on April 1, 1911, the Tsar wrote a resolution, "To leave the monk Iliodor in Tsaritsyn in response to the wishes of the people; and I propose that the Most Holy Synod consider the matter of imposing penance." [59] Stremoukhov, governor of Saratov at the time, repeatedly urged Sabler to discipline Iliodor, but without success. Later, in a talk with Stolypin, the head of the government, Stremoukhov explained the victory of the Hermogen-Iliodor group as follows: "I have definite information that Hermogen and Iliodor act in close conjunction with Rasputin [the dissolute "holy man" who had won favor with the Tsar and the empress]. As evidence of this I present to you a group [photograph] of this honorable company." [60]

After the Synod had voted to allow him to stay in Tsaritsyn and had freed him from performing penance "because of the approach of Easter and Holy Week," [61] Iliodor became more audacious than ever. In June, 1911, he went by Volga steamer on a pilgrimage to a monastery, accompanied by seventeen hundred pilgrims, mostly women. When he stopped at Kazan and Nizhnii Novgorod reactionary demonstrations took place, and near a village on the Volga he made a speech before a local band of the Union of the Russian People, in which he proclaimed the necessity of uniting the people in order to throw off the hated Jewish yoke and that of the Russian rebels and traitors, and to purify Russia of them; moreover, he urged all to take up "the great and merciless struggle with all enemies of Faith, of Tsar, and of the Russian People." On another occasion the monk declared that he would load up all the Jews and their Russian dupes and drown them in the Black Sea.[62]

In August, 1911, Iliodor's agitation reached such heights that the governor of the province reported that business was disrupted, owing to the fear of a pogrom among the Jews and the local intelligentsia. To this Iliodor answered with a sermon filled with incitement:

---

[59] Report of a police agent sent to investigate Iliodor, "Pokhozhdeniia Iliodora," *Byloe*, 1924, No. 24, p. 192.
[60] Stremoukhov, "Moia Bor'ba s Episkopom Germogenom," pp. 38–40.
[61] "Pokhozhdeniia Iliodora," *loc. cit.*   [62] *Ibid.*, pp. 196–201.

. . . they curse you as hooligans, they insult your wives and daughters, and abuse you in all sorts of ways. They say that Iliodor is inciting you to a pogrom. No! Iliodor has never urged you to that. . . . But if there should be a pogrom, then, not Iliodor will be to blame, but the Jews and the Russian atheists.

. . . Look here, then, atheists, when the Russian people turn on you— I say this openly, in the presence of the police and the gendarmes—it will go hard with you; but the guilt will not rest on Iliodor—he warned you—but you yourselves will be to blame. To you . . . I speak: don't mock the simple Russian people, don't drink their blood, or it will go hard with you, and you will suffer.[63]

Finally matters in the diocese of Saratov reached such a point that a group of deputies of the Duma proposed a question to the government concerning Bishop Hermogen, for ". . . in general, the bishop of Saratov, instead of pacifying, everywhere promotes hostility and conflict." [64] The case of these notorious churchmen soon came to a head. Late in 1911 Bishop Hermogen was summoned to the Synod. He was instructed to bring Iliodor to discipline, and at first promised fulfillment of the Synod's commands. However, he soon came into conflict with the Synod—according to the official accounts, over the institution of deaconesses in the church and over the question of prayers for those who had died outside the Orthodox communion. Hermogen denounced both of these practices as uncanonical, although the Synod had approved them.[65] When the Synod attempted to silence his denunciations, he refused to submit, and after a long dispute, which was spread on the pages of the newspapers, a special imperial order had to be issued depriving him of his diocese and sending him off in disgrace to the Zhirovitskii Monastery near the Polish frontier.[66] Iliodor fled, but was arrested and taken to another monastery,[67] where he stayed until he left the religious life.

The disciplining of Hermogen and Iliodor quieted much of the reactionary uproar in Tsaritsyn and was a decided blow to the Union of the Russian People. Before the bishop was exiled, the Moscow branch of this organization sent a delegation to St. Petersburg to

[63] "Pokhozhdeniia Iliodora," pp. 204–7.
[64] Gosudarstvennaia Duma, *Prilozheniia k Stenograficheskim Otchetam,* III Duma, Session II, No. 59.
[65] *Tserkovnyia Vedomosti,* Jan. 21, 1912, pp. 20–24.
[66] *Russkiia Vedomosti,* Jan. 24, 1912.   [67] *Ibid.,* Jan. 28, 1912.

express sympathy with him,[68] and several of the reactionary newspapers were strong in their support of him. *Moskovskiia Vedomosti* (*Moscow News*) declared that his punishment was uncanonical,[69] and an issue of *Svet* (*The World*) was confiscated, because of an editorial supporting the disgraced bishop.[70] However, while the reactionaries were displeased by this action of the Synod, many of the liberals did not regard it as a rebuke to the extremists of the Right, but as the result of a struggle between unsavory influences behind the scenes in the capital. Liberal newspapers and liberals in the Duma ascribed the punishment of Hermogen and Iliodor not to a revulsion in authoritative circles against the reactionary policies of the two, but to a quarrel between them and the powerful Rasputin, favorite of the Tsar.[71]

In 1913 new evidence appeared that many of the higher churchmen were still in sympathy with the anti-Semitism of the Union of the Russian People. This was the famous Beilis case, which developed as a result of the death of the young Andrei Iushchinskii in Kiev, in 1913. He was found with about forty wounds in his body, and at once the rumor was circulated that he had been the victim of a "Jewish ritual murder." Beilis, a Jewish resident of Kiev, was arrested and tried for the crime, although there was no direct evidence implicating him. The chief efforts of the prosecution were directed toward showing that Iushchinskii had been slaughtered by Jews in order that his blood might be used in a religious ceremony. However, in spite of a battery of "expert testimony," Beilis was acquitted, much to the disgust of the reactionaries. How some of the heads of the church stood in this case was shown by several facts. One was a telegram sent to the leading witnesses and the prosecutor of the government's case; it "expressed a unanimous desire to greet" these proponents of the ritual-murder theory "for their well-born civic courage and the high moral worth of unbribed independent Russian men." The telegram bore several names, secular and clerical, and among the latter those of Metropolitan Flavian of Kiev, Archbishop Nikon, and Dean Lo-

---

[68] *Ibid.*, Jan. 21, 1912.   [69] *Ibid.*   [70] *Ibid.*, Jan. 19, 1912.

[71] *Ibid.*, editorial, Jan. 21, 1912; Gosudarstvennaia Duma, *Stenograficheskie Otchety*, III Duma, Session V, Part 3, cols. 583–84, speech of Guchkov, leader of the Octobrists.

khotskii.[72] Moreover, several of the religious periodicals of the time contained articles declaring that in the past Jews had been guilty of ritual murders. *Tserkovnyi Vestnik,* for example, printed a long editorial in which it was stated that the killing of Iushchinskii bore all the earmarks of a ritual murder. The article further declared, on the authority of Archbishop Sergii of Finland, that it was possible that Jews did occasionally perpetrate ritual murders, although in the present case there was no direct evidence against them. However, the article urged that all Jews should not be condemned because of what might be done by a few of their number.[73] *Missionerskoe Obozrenie* also printed a long article—"The Sacrament of Blood among the Jews"—referring specifically to the Beilis case.[74] Finally the Synod took an official stand on the matter; early in 1914 the metropolitan of Kiev asked, and received from the Synod, permission to build a church in commemoration of Andrei Iushchinskii,[75] thereby showing that the Synod held that the lad was a martyr.

Thus some of the noted churchmen showed that they were still hostile to the Jews. In similar fashion, although more openly, a number of the higher clergy displayed their eagerness to support the autocratic regime of the House of Romanov. Before the elections to the Third Duma, the clergy were urged in the pages of *Tserkovnyia Vedomosti,* the official organ of the Synod, to organize and to take active part in the elections, in order that candidates sincerely loyal to Church and Fatherland might be chosen.[76] Moreover, in addition to printing the above, the Synod's publication reproduced a sermon of Bishop Innokentii of Tambov, in which he instructed the voters in a fashion favorable to the government.[77] The church authorities apparently did not devote so much energy to the elections to the Third Duma as they had to those preceding the Second, but the greatly revised electoral law in force in 1907 did much to reduce to a minimum the chances of the liberals and radicals, whether lay or clerical. The results of the elections must have been satisfactory to churchmen of conservative views.

[72] P. E. Shchegolev, ed., *Padenie Tsarskogo Rezhima,* II, 395.
[73] *Tserkovnyi Vestnik,* Oct. 10, 1913, cols. 1265–66.
[74] *Missionerskoe Obozrenie,* Dec., 1913, pp. 559–97.
[75] *Tserkovnyia Vedomosti,* March 1, 1914, p. 521.
[76] *Ibid.,* Aug. 4, 1907, pp. 1283–87.   [77] *Ibid.,* Oct. 27, 1907, pp. 1843–45.

The clergy in the Third Duma were found almost exclusively in the conservative parties. There were 4 Orthodox priests in the Progressive party, and the Union of October 17, which was moderate in its policies, contained 9 more—a small fraction of this party's 148 members. In the Moderate Right party the clerical members were more significant, both in numbers and in relative strength. This group included 13 priests and Bishop Evlogii of Kholm—14 out of a total membership of 69. The National Group had 2 priests in its ranks, while the Right party, most conservative of all, had 16 clergy among its total membership of 49; one of this number was Bishop Mitrofan of Mogilev. Thus the Third Duma had as deputies 45 Orthodox churchmen,[78] most of whom could be counted on to support the policies of the government, and none of whom could be considered really radical.

However, this clerical contingent was not enough to guide the Duma to the satisfaction of the conservatives among the higher clergy. In the voting on some important measures affecting the church, notably the bill relating to the Old Believer congregations and the bill regulating the changing of one's religion, the actions of the Duma were contrary to the wishes of the government and of the dominant hierarchy. Hence when the elections for the Fourth Duma drew near in 1912, the clergy were urged by powerful members of the church and the government to take a very active part,[79] supporting the Octobrists and the parties further to the Right.[80] In many dioceses the clergy were advised to take part in the election campaign; reports to this effect came from the dioceses of Polotsk, Podolia, Kishinev, Kherson, Tver, and Simbirsk.[81] These were not isolated examples, for an editorial in *Tserkovnyi Vestnik* declared that "as is well known," almost all of the bishops were busy with the coming elections, writing circulars, giving instructions and advice, visiting election gatherings of the clergy, and so on; the lower clergy were also active in forming

[78] Gosudarstvennaia Duma, *Ukazatel' k Stenograficheskim Otchetam*, III Duma, Session I, pp. 13–18.

[79] V. Skvortsov, *Tserkovnyi Svet i Gosudarstvennyi Razum*, I, pp. vi–viii. Skvortsov was chief missionary of the church, and a noted conservative.

[80] V. N. Kokovtsov, *Iz Moego Proshlago*, II, 109.

[81] *Tserkovnyi Vestnik*, May 24, 1912, col. 650; Aug. 2, 1912, cols. 971–73; *Vera i Razum*, May, 1912, pp. 575–80.

leagues, holding meetings, and working for the nomination of candidates. "Undoubtedly one of the most characteristic features of the present election campaign," this journal said, "is the wide participation of the clergy." [82]

In the passages cited above no mention is made of the specific parties for which the bishops were working; in several other instances, however, it is possible to show that they supported the parties of the Right. This was the case in the dioceses of Kiev, Kursk, Ufa,[83] Viatka, Riazan, Irkutsk,[84] and the Don,[85] while in Ekaterinoslav, Bishop Agapit felt that the Octobrists were not conservative enough and denounced them as those "who sold Christ." [86] Another indication of the coöperation between the church and the government was given by Count Kokovtsov, who kept a record of the disbursement of the government's election fund of three million rubles. Among the recipients were a number of laymen, including the leaders of the Union of the Russian People, and "some bishops with their unions of enlightenment," and "a publication of the Pochaevskaia Monastery." [87]

These methods brought results. Numbers of priests were chosen as electors in the preliminary voting in many of the provinces, so that in the elections to the Fourth Duma the clergy played an important part. Actually, however, when it met in 1913, the Fourth Duma contained forty-six deputies from the ranks of the clergy, one more than the Third Duma. In the Right party there were nineteen priests and two bishops; the Russian Nationalists in combination with the Moderate Right had nineteen priests; while the Center party, the Octobrists, and the Progressives had two priests each. As for the Cadets and the parties of the Left, they had no clerical members.[88] In comparison with the clerical delegates in the Third Duma, the clergy in the Fourth Duma were concentrated further to the Right. The Right parties in

[82] *Tserkovnyi Vestnik*, Aug. 9, 1912, col. 995.

[83] *Ibid.*, Feb. 16, 1912, col. 222; April 5, 1912, cols. 428–29; May 24, 1912, col. 651.

[84] *Russkiia Vedomosti*, May 16, 1912.

[85] *Vera i Razum*, May, 1912, pp. 575–76.

[86] M. V. Rodzianko, *The Reign of Rasputin*, p. 90.

[87] Kokovtsov, *op. cit.*, II, 11.

[88] Gosudarstvennaia Duma, *Ukazatel' k Stenograficheskim Otchetam*, IV Duma, Session I, pp. 19–24.

the Fourth Duma contained forty clerical deputies; in the Third the same groups had had thirty-two members from the clergy. On the other hand, in the Fourth Duma the moderate parties had a total of six clerical members; in the Third they had had thirteen.

However, while the Fourth Duma held only one more cleric than the Third, the clergy were widely believed to have had considerable influence in securing the election of many laymen from the conservative parties, thus arousing the enmity of many lay members of the Duma, who in 1913 proposed a question to the government on this score. During the heated debate, statements were made that "the church and its ministers were reduced to the level of political tools," and that the government handled the clergy "like slaves"; N. N. Lvov, a Progressive, stated that they had been forced to play "the degrading rôle of assistants to the police." [89] Another speaker read from the rostrum the words of *Novoe Vremia* (*The New Time*), a powerful newspaper of the Right, that "no heresy or schism ever brought so much harm to the church and so damaged the authority of the clergy in the eyes of the population as the degrading rôle which was imposed upon the priests in the last elections." [90] Many instances were cited in which bishops had prevented liberal clergy from attending the election meetings, as well as several cases where stringent means had been used by the hierarchs to force all the "trustworthy" clergy to do their part. Sermons of a number of bishops were referred to as showing their firm support of the authorities.[91] Many of the clergy in the Duma defended the part of the church and its members in the elections, but to no avail. The interpellation was voted by an overwhelming majority.[92]

Another method by which the church lent its support to the government was that of celebrating glorious days of the nation's past. In 1909 Metropolitan Antonii of St. Petersburg issued a special message in which he proclaimed the two-hundredth anniversary of the battle

[89] Gosudarstvennaia Duma, *Stenograficheskie Otchety*, IV Duma, Session I, Part 3, cols. 407 and 416.

[90] *Ibid.*, col. 408.

[91] Gosudarstvennaia Duma, *Prilozheniia k Stenograficheskim Otchetam*, IV Duma, Session I, No. 7, and No. 25, pp. 17–23.

[92] Gosudarstvennaia Duma, *Stenograficheskie Otchety*, IV Duma, Session I, Part 3, col. 2173.

of Poltava; in his message he called the battle a great victory for Orthodoxy, and exalted the warriors who there fought "for Faith, Tsar, and Fatherland." [93] The centenary of the battle of Borodino, fought in 1812, was made by the Synod the occasion for special ceremonies throughout the country, and many sermons were preached in honor of Russia's brave stand in defense of Holy Moscow against the French.[94] Not long after, on October 11, 1912, the evacuation of the ancient capital by the French was widely celebrated, upon order of the Synod.[95] However, the festivities on these occasions, impressive as they doubtless were, were completely overshadowed by the three-hundredth anniversary of the accession of the House of Romanov.

In preparation for this event, which was celebrated on February 21, 1913, the Synod ordered the preparation of a special ikon for sale to the populace. An elaborate scroll was sent forth, in which it was proclaimed to the people that the Tsar and the Ruling House were holy and blessed by God, and that the authority of the emperor was of divine origin.[96] Moreover, the Synod sent to the diocesan authorities a decree explaining how the parish schools were to observe the occasion. Before the great day, the teachers were to instruct their charges in the history of Church and Fatherland and in the glorious significance of the event to be celebrated. All the pupils were ordered to attend the solemn requiem on February 20, and on the next day they were to gather at the school, from which they were to march to the church with the teachers at their head. When possible a lantern-slide lecture was to be given after the *Te Deum* in the church, and the whole celebration was to be concluded with the reading of verses from the Bible and the singing of the national anthem.[97] The same procedure was to be followed by the heads of the diocesan schools, the theological seminaries, and the other educational institutions of the church.[98]

As for the celebration of the anniversary in St. Petersburg, it was a momentous event. It was made the occasion for pardoning all per-

[93] *Tserkovnyia Vedomosti*, July 4, 1909, pp. 1213–14.
[94] *Ibid.*, Sept. 1, 1912, official part, p. 336.
[95] *Ibid.*, June 9, 1912, official part, p. 240.
[96] *Ibid.*, Jan. 5, 1913, official part, p. 4; Feb. 21, 1913, pp. 37–38.
[97] *Ibid.*, Dec. 22, 1912, official part, pp. 486–87.
[98] *Ibid.*, Jan. 5, 1913, p. 5.

sons convicted of minor religious offenses, if committed out of ignorance or carelessness.[99] To give proper sanctity to the celebration, the
miracle-working ikon of the Virgin of the Pochaevskaia Monastery
was brought to the northern capital, where it was met at the railroad
station by high church dignitaries and was carried at the head of a
solemn procession through the streets to the sanctuary where it was
to stay.[100] On the final day of the celebration it was taken to the great
Kazan Cathedral, where processions from the Fortress of Peter and
Paul, from the Aleksandro-Nevskaia Monastery, and from the Synod
Chapel converged for the *Te Deum* performed by the patriarch of
Antioch, the three Russian metropolitans, and a host of lesser dignitaries.[101] Thus in a ceremony unrivaled for its pomp and magnificence,
the Russian Orthodox Church once more placed the seal of holiness
upon the last reigning Romanov Tsar.

These efforts to impress on the people the holiness of the Tsar and
the sanctity of the subjects' duty to obey him combined with other
evidence to show the continued strength of the connection between
the Orthodox Church and the Imperial government. The economic
bond between the two showed no slackening, and in fact became
stronger and tighter. While the church had drawn on the imperial
treasury for many years, its receipts from this source showed an unprecedented rate of increase in the years when the Third and the
Fourth Dumas were sitting in the Tauride Palace. The estimates
which the Over Procurator submitted mounted year after year; year
after year the Duma passed them almost without change. Thus while
all the deputies of all except the parties of the Right were becoming
increasingly critical of the *administration* of the church, almost all
except the Cadets and the extreme Left valued the continued existence
of the official church sufficiently to support it with increasing open-
handedness. The following table shows the amounts assigned to the
Synod in the official budgets approved by the Tsar for the years 1908
to 1914:[102]

[99] *Ibid.*, March 9, 1913, p. 113.

[100] *Tserkovnyi Vestnik*, Feb. 7, 1913, col. 174.

[101] *Ibid.*, Feb. 28, 1913, col. 275; *Tserkovnyia Vedomosti*, March 2, 1913,
pp. 386–92; Rodzianko, *The Reign of Rasputin*, p. 75.

[102] Gosudarstvennyi Kontrol, *Otchet*, 1908, p. 262; 1909, p. 264; 1910, p.
302; 1911, p. 304; 1912, p. 302; 1913, p. 308; 1914, p. 312.

Year	Rubles
1908	29,739,152
1909	31,663,444
1910	34,195,217
1911	37,535,478
1912	40,129,979
1913	44,219,759
1914	53,093,225

In 1915, owing to the financial stringency caused by the war, the amount asked by the Synod (49,189,350 rubles) was less than the total appropriated for the preceding year; however, in the budget which was finally adopted the Synod was allotted 52,564,695 rubles. In 1916 the Synod asked for an increase over the amount appropriated to it in 1915; its request was for the modest increment of 1,401,072 rubles. The Budget Commission of the Duma, however, was much more generous. It recommended that the Synod be given nearly 10,-500,000 more than its 1915 appropriation. The Duma approved the increased amount without change; the budget officially adopted by the Duma, the Council of State, and the Tsar gave the Synod 62,920,-835 rubles.[103] The projected budget of the Synod for the year 1917 was still greater, with a total of 66,796,000 rubles; [104] it was never adopted, as the Revolution of 1917 intervened before the Duma could act upon it. It should be noted, however, that while the totals of the Synod appropriations mounted rapidly in 1915 and 1916, the purchasing power of these totals was adversely affected by the war inflation. None the less, the increasing strength of the financial tie between church and state had been clearly shown in the years before the war.

Two items of expenditure accounted for most of the increases in the budgets of the Synod—the salaries of the clergy, and the sums devoted to the expansion and improvement of the church's educational system. The first of these items had been a favorite project of Alexander III, but great difficulty had been experienced in finding funds for

[103] Gosudarstvennaia Duma, *Doklady Biudzhetnoi Komissii,* IV Duma, Session III, Part II, pp. 15–18; Session IV, No. 4, pp. 59–60; *Sobranie Uzakonenii i Rasporiazhenii Pravitel'stva,* 1915, No. 385; *ibid.,* 1916, No. 763.

[104] Ministerstvo Finansov, *Proekt Gosudarstvennoi Rospisi Dokhodov i Raskhodov na 1917 god,* Part I, p. 99.

salaries. By 1900 the amount appropriated by the government for the support of the town and village clergy and the missionaries was 10,263,396 rubles, all but a few hundred thousand of which went to the parish clergy.[105] By 1905 this item of the budget had increased to 12,116,103 rubles;[106] but by 1908 it had risen only to 12,564,563 rubles.[107] Beginning with 1909, however, there was a large annual increase; from 1910 on, the increase was at least 500,000 rubles a year, and in 1914 the increase over 1913 was 2,536,499 rubles in this single item, making the total devoted to this purpose 17,932,283 rubles.[108] In 1915 the amount for salaries was decreased slightly; however, in 1916 the advance was resumed, with a total for priestly salaries and missions of 18,830,308 rubles.[109]

As has been said, the value of the appropriation for 1916 was considerably reduced by the inflation; however, even the substantial increases in the pre-war years were far from satisfying what the church felt to be the needs of the clergy. It was held by many that as long as the priest had to depend to a considerable extent upon the payments made by the peasants for ministrations and on voluntary contributions, his income would be uncertain and insufficient and the collection of donations would lead to unseemly disputes. Hence his position and his authority would be secure only when the state should provide him with a full salary. However, the realization of this desire did not appear imminent. It was pointed out in 1912 that only 30,237 of the more than 44,000 parishes in the empire received state funds for salaries, and in a number of these parishes the payments were below the desired minimum set by the Synod—300 rubles for the priest, 150 for the deacon, and 100 for the psalmist. If the current rate of increase continued—namely, 500,000 or 600,000 rubles per year—nearly twenty years would elapse before the clergy of all the existing parishes received the minimum salaries. Furthermore, the special commission appointed by the Synod in 1912 set the desired minimum for the clergy in the central Russian provinces at 1,200 rubles for the priest, 800 for the deacon, and 400 for the psalmist. In

---

[105] Gosudarstvennyi Kontrol, *Otchet,* 1900, p. 230.
[106] *Ibid.,* 1905, p. 196.   [107] *Ibid.,* 1908, p. 258.
[108] *Ibid.,* 1909, p. 260; 1910, p. 298; 1911, p. 300; 1912, p. 298; 1913, p. 302; 1914, p. 306.
[109] *Sobranie Uzakonenii,* 1915 and 1916, *loc. cit.*

order to provide the clergy with incomes of this size, it would be necessary to supplement the 34,000,000 received in 1912 by the parish clergy from all sources (from church lands, from interest on church investments, from the treasury, from payments for services, from voluntary contributions, and so on) with 41,000,000 more, to come either from the imperial treasury or from a special local tax.[110] The gains already made were thus far short of the estimated needs.

The clergy seemed almost unanimous in their desire for state salaries. They wrote frequent articles for *Tserkovnyi Vestnik* and for *Vera i Razum*, as well as for other periodicals, urging the extension of payments to all the clergy.[111] All the priests who spoke on this question in the Duma in 1908 were in favor of state support.[112] However, opposition was voiced by some of the other deputies. It is not surprising to find that in 1908 the Social Democrats were opposed to an increase of 600,000 rubles in state subsidies to the parish clergy; it is, however, significant to find that some of the members of the Center and even of the Right raised voices of protest in no uncertain fashion. The Octobrist Udovitskii, a peasant, declared that the priests were much better off than the peasants, who deserved consideration before the clergy. While he did not actually oppose the payment of salaries to the priests, he did believe that if this were done they should be deprived of their land and be required to perform their ministrations gratis.[113] Storchak of Kherson, a peasant Cadet, declared that many of the clergy were rich—he knew a priest who had lent 1,500 rubles to the Jews, and was noted for never lending money to the poor. Furthermore, he complained that the Duma discussed the interests of the clergy too much, while it said nothing about the needs of the poor peasants.[114] Two peasant members of the Moderate Right party, Kuchinskii and Amosenok, also spoke, and in a manner contrary to the general policies of their party; like Udovitskii, they believed that state salaries should be paid to the clergy only if they were deprived

[110] Gosudarstvennaia Duma, *Doklady Biudzhetnoi Komissii,* III Duma, Session V, No. 19, pp. 26–27.

[111] *Tserkovnyi Vestnik,* Feb. 2, 1912, col. 150; June 28, 1912, cols. 803–5; July 19, 1912, col. 902, etc.; *Vera i Razum,* Aug., 1908, pp. 399–401.

[112] Gosudarstvennaia Duma, *Stenograficheskie Otchety,* III Duma, Session I, Part 3, col. 1074 ff.

[113] *Ibid.,* cols. 1098–99.   [114] *Ibid.,* cols. 1103–4.

of their land and if payment for ministrations were abolished.[115] It is interesting to find that, while peasants of the Right parties joined peasants of the Left in speaking against the payment of state salaries to the clergy, there were no peasants among those who spoke in defense of such appropriations. However, the Duma voted to appropriate the sum requested.[116]

In 1911 another bill to increase the salaries of the clergy came before the Duma, and again several peasant deputies spoke against it. The non-party peasant, Gul'kin, declared that Bishop Evlogii and Father Kuz'minskii had pigeonholed the progressive tax bill introduced by the peasants, and hence the latter would vote against the bill favoring the clergy. A note of bitterness crept into his words when he stated, ". . . the little fathers . . . continue to fleece the peasants more grievously than the police, more than the commissary agents [of the Army]." [117] Amosenok, who had spoken on the same topic in 1908, repeated his arguments that the clergy should receive support only if they gave up their land and their payments for ministrations. He declared that these salaries would in the last analysis come from the pockets of the peasants, who never received any money from the Duma.[118] But in spite of these arguments and those of the Social Democrats and the Laborites the Duma again voted the increases.[119]

A much more hotly contested question was that of the support of the educational facilities of the church. Here, too, although friends of the church complained that its schools were treated shabbily as compared with those under the Minister of Education, rapid increases were made, especially under the Fourth Duma. The following table shows the amounts of the appropriations to the Synod for its elementary schools: [120]

Year	Rubles
1905	10,091,916
1906	10,091,052

---

[115] *Ibid.*, cols. 1106–8.   [116] *Ibid.*, col. 2113.

[117] *Ibid.*, III Duma, Session IV, Part 2, col. 1722.

[118] *Ibid.*, cols. 1722–23.   [119] *Ibid.*, col. 1723.

[120] Gosudarstvennyi Kontrol, *Otchet*, 1905, p. 198; 1906, p. 200; 1907, p. 228; 1908, p. 260; 1909, p. 262; 1910, p. 300; 1911, p. 302; 1912, p. 300; 1913, p. 304; 1914, p. 308.

Year	Rubles
1907	9,433,145
1908	9,533,145
1909	10,683,145
1910	12,516,053
1911	15,151,365
1912	16,946,723
1913	20,233,219
1914	22,254,486

There was a slight decline in 1915, but in 1916 the total again mounted, although in depreciated currency; for the parish schools 30,442,834 rubles were appropriated.[121] For 1917 the proposed amount was 33,-191,000 rubles.[122]

The appropriations for the other schools of the church—the seminaries, the diocesan schools, and the academies—also increased rapidly. In 1908 the amount was 2,833,799 rubles; [123] in 1914 it was 7,434,087 rubles,[124] and in 1916, 7,432,572.[125]

These were substantial sums; they were not gained, however, without a struggle. On December 15, 1907, a bill was placed before the Duma to appropriate 4,003,740 rubles for the building and equipping of new parish schools and for the salaries for the necessary teachers. The Duma refused to vote the priority for this measure which had been asked,[126] and some months later it was sent to the Commission on Public Education for consideration.[127] It was not until November, 1908, during the Second Session of the Third Duma, that the bill was favorably reported out of the Commission and came up for consideration in the Duma. At once a bitter conflict developed. The parties of the Right were strongly behind the bill; the Left, however, was quite as strongly opposed. The keynote of the opposition was sounded by the Cadet Voronkov: "I say only that the governmental schools

[121] *Sobranie Uzakonenii*, 1915, No. 385; 1916, No. 763.

[122] Ministerstvo Finansov, *Proekt Gosudarstvennoi Rospisi*, p. 99.

[123] Gosudarstvennyi Kontrol, *Otchet*, 1908, p. 258.

[124] *Ibid.*, 1914, p. 306.   [125] *Sobranie Uzakonenii*, 1916, No. 763.

[126] Gosudarstvennaia Duma, *Stenograficheskie Otchety*, III Duma, Session I, Part 1, col. 1095.

[127] *Ibid.*, Part 2, col. 785.

must be unified, and must be subject to the Ministry of Public Education. The parish school was brought into being by the law of 1884 for the struggle against the *zemstvo* schools, the struggle against the enlightenment of the country [Purishkevich from his seat, "Bosh!" Voices from the Right, "Untrue!"]." [128] N. N. Lvov, a Progressive, said, ". . . gentlemen, the school of the Religious Administration [the Synod] is really a product of the 1880's, of the epoch of reaction; and actually, through this school a blow has been delivered to the *zemstvo* institutions [applause in the Center and from the Left]"; and he declared that if the Duma approved this appropriation, it would mean tilting the scale in favor of "that side which has always been the opponent of the *zemstvo* and of the social principle." [129]

In the Duma there were many able defenses of the church schools by both clerics and laymen of the Right parties; Bishop Mitrofan urged that the Duma give the parish schools the same support as that given to the secular schools, and a speaker declared, "We laymen are still only beginners in the work of public education. . . . Our Orthodox Church and our Orthodox pastorate have been working uninterruptedly and unpaid in this field for a thousand years." [130] However, no speech exceeded in interest the hostile declaration of the Progressive Lukashin, of Riazan. He stated that he spoke in the name of fifty-three peasant deputies of various parties, both Right and Left, who, with forty-one nonpeasant deputies, had signed a manifesto against the church schools. In their declaration, which the speaker read, they stated that they regarded the parish schools as institutions "which do not serve the cause of public education as much as the material and careerist interests of those who administer them and teach in them. . . ." [131] Under pressure from the Right, however, Lukashin admitted that many of the peasants had withdrawn their signatures from this document. [132]

The action of the Duma on this bill reflected some of the hostility voiced by the speakers, for it was voted to send the bill back to the commission for revision, the reason for this being "the necessity for reforming the parish and for the participation of the parish in the

[128] *Ibid.*, Session II, Part 1, col. 704.
[129] *Ibid.*, col. 1132.
[130] *Ibid.*, col. 722; col. 730.
[131] *Ibid.*, col. 1420.
[132] *Ibid.*

control of the schools. . . ." [133] When the bill again came before the Duma, it was for an appropriation of only one million rubles, instead of more than four million.[134] Even this relatively modest request did not pass unchallenged; the deputy Shevtsov of the Right party declared that the peasants who had elected him wanted schools under one jurisdiction, not under two. However, the bill passed; but the method provided by the Duma for distributing the money was a further disappointment to the religious authorities.[135]

The fate of this bill was very important to the church, for the action of the Duma in this case set a precedent for the general policy of the latter toward the parish schools. The Synod authorities had hoped that the expansion of the church schools would occur at approximately the same rate as the growth of the secular schools; hence the Duma's action in delaying the bill and forcing the Synod to reduce the amount of its request was a severe blow to the hopes of the church authorities.

In 1910 another conflict arose over religious education. The Over Procurator asked 232,000 rubles for salary increases for the teachers and the professors of the church's educational institutions. The bill was favorably reported except for the item of 46,760 rubles for the academy professors; this was opposed by the Budget Commission on the grounds that the new Code of Religious Academies had been adopted by the Synod without submitting it to the Duma. The Duma showed its displeasure by rejecting not only the sum for the academy professors, but the whole bill, by a vote of 83 to 65.[136]

Another difference of opinion arose in the Duma in 1912 over the question of appropriating 1,550,000 rubles to increase the salaries of the teachers in the parish schools. The Synod asked for this sum outright, but the Budget Commission approved this appropriation only on condition that it be added to the general budget of the church by the passing of enabling legislation.[137] When the original bill came up for consideration in the house there were appealing speeches made by several of the priests and the bishops of the Right, and the Over

[133] Gosudarstvennaia Duma, *Stenograficheskie Otchety*, III Duma, Session I, Part 1, col. 1422.

[134] *Ibid.*, Part 4, cols. 2447–56.

[135] *Ibid.*, cols. 2469–72.   [136] *Ibid.*, Session III, Part 4, cols. 3547–59.

[137] Gosudarstvennaia Duma, *Doklady Biudzhetnoi Komissii*, III Duma, Session V, No. 19, p. 43.

Procurator also spoke in favor of the bill. Nevertheless, the chamber voted, 113 to 79, to make the appropriation conditional upon the passing of the necessary enabling legislation.[138] Almost immediately upon this rebuff the Over Procurator submitted a bill embodying the necessary legislation; it was referred to the Budget Commission, which did not report on it until the last weeks of the session.[139] Moreover, when its consideration drew near, Rodzianko, President of the Duma, found the temper of this body so hostile, owing to a speech in which the Tsar had denounced the critical attitude of the Duma, that it seemed best to remove the measure from the agenda so that no untoward incident should occur.[140] The bill for 1,550,000 rubles came up in the Fourth Duma in 1913, but it was now for the benefit of the Council of Ministers rather than the teachers, for while the Duma was not in session the ministers had paid the teachers out of moneys at the disposal of the government. Once more the bill failed, by a vote of 112 to 109.[141] Its failure was due, however, to hostility not so much to the church schools as to the ministry, for a week later the Duma passed a bill granting 1,425,000 rubles for the teachers of the church's schools.[142] Even on this occasion some hostile words were uttered against the parish schools. On May 15, 1913, the Nationalist Tarutin, a peasant deputy from Vladimir, declared that the alarming wave of hooliganism then prevalent was due to the lack of education of the people, a lack which the parish schools did little to remedy, for "the parish schools are useful rather for those zealous persons who reward us with them, than for those for whom they are [supposedly] intended. There will be wildness and evil among the people, gentlemen, until they are given proper light." [143]

But while occasional voices were raised to denounce the parish schools, and while the Third and Fourth Dumas rejected some of the Synod's minor requests for appropriations for its schools, the Dumas continued to vote to the parish schools subsidies which increased with some rapidity. Nevertheless, the Duma gave much more liberally to

[138] Gosudarstvennaia Duma, *Stenograficheskie Otchety*, III Duma, Session V, Part 3, cols. 864–71.

[139] *Ibid.*, Part 4, col. 1504.   [140] Rodzianko, *op. cit.*, pp. 64–65.

[141] Gosudarstvennaia Duma, *Stenograficheskie Otchety*, IV Duma, Session I, Part 3, cols. 2206–18.

[142] *Ibid.*, cols. 2410–13.   [143] *Ibid.*, Part 2, cols. 1424–25.

the Ministry of Public Education. In 1907 the ministry was granted 9,681,061 rubles for elementary education, while the appropriation to the Synod's schools was almost as large—9,433,145 rubles.[144] There followed increases to the ministry at the rate of at least 6,000,000 a year, and in 1911, of over 10,000,000; at the same time, the increases to the church schools averaged considerably below 2,000,000 rubles a year. By 1912 the appropriation of the central government to the public schools amounted to 48,905,983 rubles a year, while the grant to the Synod for parish schools was 16,946,723 rubles.[145] During this period the number of parish schools actually declined, owing to the abandonment of many of the makeshift "schools of literacy"; and while the number of pupils showed an increase, in 1911 there were only 60,000 more pupils in the parish schools than in 1907.[146] A one-day school census was taken on January 18, 1911; it showed that the ministerial schools comprised 59.6 percent of all the schools of the empire, and had 68 percent of the pupils; the Synod had 37.7 percent of the schools, but only 1,792,941 pupils, or 29 percent of the total.[147]

In 1912 Bishop Evlogii of Kholm, assuming the position of spokesman for the clergy in the Duma, summed up the relations between the Duma and the church. He said, ". . . we, the representatives of the church, express warm thanks to the Duma for appropriating needed funds for the institutions of the church and for the poor village clergy . . ."; and he thanked the Duma, too, for its efforts to push the summoning of the *Sobor;* nevertheless, he said, the urging of "unlimited freedom of religious profession, and also the difficult position of, and the restriction of the activity of, the church schools, . . . will be held to be great sins of the Third Duma against the Holy Orthodox Church." [148] Moreover, Father Stanislavskii, a member of the Right party, stated to his fellow deputies that "not one department is subjected to such harsh and merciless criticism, amounting even to abuse, at [the time of] the consideration of its estimates, as

[144] Gosudarstvennyi Kontrol, *Otchet,* 1907, pp. 228 and 382.
[145] *Ibid.,* 1912, pp. 300 and 462.
[146] *Tserkovnyia Vedomosti,* Feb. 2, 1913, pp. 244–45.
[147] *Ibid.,* June 4, 1911, p. 988.
[148] Gosudarstvennaia Duma, *Stenograficheskie Otchety,* III Duma, Session V, Part 3, col. 582.

the Administration of the Orthodox Faith. The pearls of hellish elo-
quence are literally poured out of the horn of plenty upon the Administration . . .";[149] and Father Tregubov said the same thing in
slightly milder terms.[150] To this the well-known Octobrist E. P.
Kovalevskii made answer. "I shall not deny that there were, of course,
various speeches which gave rise to undesirable polemics, but was
the Duma to blame that the clergy were drawn into the sharp political
conflict, which definitely undermined . . . the harmony between the
more enlightened ranks of the populace and the clergy?"[151]

However, Bishop Evlogii's charge that the Duma had "sinned
against the church" is actually unwarranted by the facts. The Duma
did urge much more religious freedom than the leaders of the church
were willing to concede; but it did not restrict the activity of the
parish schools. The Duma consistently voted increased amounts to
the schools of the church; it is only when these grants are compared
with the appropriation to the secular schools that the funds given to
the parish schools seem niggardly.

None the less, there was a good deal of criticism of the church by
the Center and by the moderate Left, as well as downright hostility
from the parties of the extreme Left. It was not surprising, of course,
that the Social Democrats and the Laborites were enemies of the
official church, but what was decidedly ominous was that moderates
—Constitutional Democrats, Progressives, and Octobrists—and even
a few members of the Right, should find so much to criticize. If the
Third and Fourth Dumas, which were packed with members of the
propertied classes, contained such and so many outspoken critics and
even enemies of the official church regime, it boded ill for the church
when the masses of the population should have an opportunity to
make themselves felt. Moreover, the *zemstvos*, which also were more
representative of the landowners than of the peasants, were critical,
not of the church itself, but of the activity of the church which affected
them directly—the parish schools. Through the county school boards,
the *zemstvos* controlled the distribution of state subsidies to the
parish schools, and irritated many churchmen by refusing funds to a

[149] *Ibid.*, col. 178.　　　　　　　　[150] *Ibid.*, col. 125.
[151] *Ibid.*, IV Duma, Session I, Part 2, col. 1393.

number of parishes—for example, in the province of Saratov not one church school was ruled eligible for state funds.[152] A congress of representatives of the *zemstvos* met in Moscow in August, 1910, and voted that the parish schools ought to be removed from church control and placed under *zemstvo* administration.[153] In 1911 this policy began to bear fruit; *Tserkovnyi Vestnik* reported that a number of provincial and county *zemstvos* had refused to give subsidies from their funds to the church schools to which they had previously contributed.[154] Moreover, according to a churchman who was a strong partisan of the parish school, the newspapers, of which "a huge majority" opposed these schools, "in their articles, correspondence, and news about parish schools, tried to place the clergy in a very unfavorable light, ascribing to them a lack of education, and moral weakness, and consequently a sort of unfitness for social, and, in particular, educational activity —in a word, tried to discredit the clergy in the eyes of society" in order to force them out of the field of education.[155] Of course an attack on the schools of the church was far from being an attack upon the Orthodox faith; none the less, it was not an encouraging sign for the clergy.

Another unfavorable sign for the authorities of the church was the reaction of the Duma to the famous Mt. Athos incident. Some of the monks of the Russian monasteries on Mt. Athos in northern Greece, who for decades had been supported by donations from the Synod and by the gifts of Russian pilgrims, came under the influence of a monk preaching heretical doctrines. Those who became his followers were excommunicated by the patriarch of Constantinople; when this failed to bring them to submission, the Russian authorities were appealed to and drastic action was begun against the heretical monks. First, their representatives were arrested in Odessa, where they had come to buy food in 1913; but to no avail. Next, in the summer of that year, Archbishop Nikon of Vologda was sent to Mt. Athos by Sabler, the Over Procurator, to reason with them, also without success. He regarded the stubborn monks as rebels against the Russian government,

[152] I. S. Berdnikov, *Kratkii Kurs Tserkovnago Prava*, pp. 1383–84.
[153] *Tserkovnyia Vedomosti*, Nov. 26, 1911, pp. 2089–91.
[154] *Tserkovnyi Vestnik*, Jan. 12, 1912, col. 63.
[155] I. V. Preobrazhenskii, *Dukhovenstvo i Narodnoe Obrazovanie*, pp. 75–76.

and appealed to the Russian ambassador for help. Soldiers of the Tsar were sent against them, and, when most of the monks remained obdurate, they were drenched with fire hoses for about an hour, dragged from their hiding places with fire hooks, and taken down ladders to the vessel awaiting them. They were then transported to Odessa, where, to the number of 629, they were imprisoned in the police stations and in a monastery. Many made their peace with the authorities by renouncing their forbidden doctrines; the others were kept in prison for periods averaging 53 days, during which time they were forced to wear civilian clothing and were deprived of their long hair and their money. Finally, most of those who remained unrepentant were sent back as peasants to the villages from which they had come long years before; [156] 25 of the monks were tried for heresy by the Moscow Synod Office.[157] A question concerning the incident was addressed to the government by members of the Duma in 1914. The interpellation was voted, on April 30; but the government failed to answer.[158] It is interesting to note that two years later many of the monks were still in disgrace; on March 3, 1916, the Tsaritsa wrote to the Tsar: "Here is a petition fr. the *Athos* monks living at Moscou. I send it you, hoping you will forward it to *Volzhin* [Over Procurator in 1916] with a strong resolution upon it, that you insist (once more) that all are to be allowed to take Holy Communion. . . ." [159]

During the period between the two revolutions, when large sections of the Duma and many of the *zemstvos* were decidedly critical of certain aspects of the church's life, several factors were acting to weaken its sway over the people. One of these was the influence of rich and powerful individuals in church matters. Before the diocesan congress of the clergy of Kaluga a priest stated that one reason for the lack of influence of the priests was that many of them were dominated by their parish *starostas* [elders], "before whom they are wont to bow low." The bishop confirmed this fact, and said that laymen

---

[156] Gosudarstvennaia Duma, *Prilozheniia k Stenograficheskim Otchetam*, IV Duma, Session II, No. 332.

[157] Gosudarstvennaia Duma, *Doklady Biudzhetnoi Komissii*, IV Duma, Session II, No. 4, Stenogram, pp. 38–39.

[158] Gosudarstvennaia Duma, *Stenograficheskie Otchety*, IV Duma, Session II, Part 3, col. 1580.

[159] *Letters of the Tsaritsa to the Tsar*, p. 284.

often interfered in parish affairs—several merchants had even asked
their priests not to preach on Sundays, so that they and their custom-
ers might get to the bazaar earlier; and the priests had complied.[160]
Many pastors, according to a writer in the official *Tserkovnyia Vedomosti,* showed partiality to rich parishioners in order to obtain
more income; at Easter these priests gladly ate at the rich man's
table, but rarely at that of the poor parishioner.[161] The bishop of
Poltava found it necessary to order the clergy to stop the practice of
letting rich parishioners have special seats in the chancels, where
they often did not conduct themselves reverently during the service.[162]

Another slow poison which was destroying the interest of many in
religious life was the absence of popular participation in the affairs
of the parish. Much has been said about this in an earlier chapter, and
does not need repeating. Still another reason assigned for the sad
state of religious life was the inadequate religious instruction im-
parted by the priests. One pastor wrote: "It is said that the people
do not know the truths of the Orthodox faith which they have been
professing for a thousand years, that they know the prayers im-
perfectly and thus perhaps say them incorrectly—all this is true. . . .
It is said that the clergy in the schools give very few lessons in religion. And this is true." The writer went on to say that the reason for
these failings of the clergy was lack of time—"our day has only 24
hours and not 120"[163]—but whatever the cause, the effects were bad
for the church. Much the same thing was said in 1915 by a meeting
of teachers of religion from the diocese of Voronezh.[164]

Whatever may have been the factors or the combination of factors
which caused it, the weakness of religious authority was reported
from all sides. It was noticed especially among the young. The sons
of the clergy tried desperately to avoid following in their fathers'
footsteps, and instead sought to obtain positions in civil life. A member of the Duma reported in 1915 that according to his past experience
the students in the diocesan girls' schools, on returning home to the
villages, "are very discontented, and say that not for anything will

[160] *Vera i Razum,* Aug., 1908, pp. 559–60.
[161] *Tserkovnyia Vedomosti,* Oct. 3, 1909, pp. 1889–90.
[162] *Vera i Razum,* May, 1909, p. 561.   [163] *Ibid.,* March, 1908, p. 671.
[164] *Missionerskoe Obozrenie,* Nov., 1915, pp. 483–84.

they marry priests' sons. . . ." [165] As for the students in the Russian universities, a certain Dean Kondrat'ev, writing in the official *Tserkovnyia Vedomosti* in 1911, asserted that "a believing student is a very rare case. . . . Not less than nine-tenths of the students are indifferent or complete unbelievers, and of the few believers the majority are of sectarian views." [166] This statement seems unduly pessimistic; but inasmuch as Dean Kondrat'ev had read it as a report before a meeting of teachers of religion, it cannot be lightly dismissed.

Even in the villages many of the younger generation were "frightfully infected with the poison of hooliganism"; they insulted priests on the street, lighted cigarettes from the church tapers, applauded the deacon's chant, and otherwise displayed irreverence.[167] This phenomenon was so noticeable that in 1913 the Synod sent a circular to the bishops requesting information about the threatening growth of hooliganism. They were asked to state: (1) to what extent this evil had developed in their dioceses; (2) the causes of its growth; (3) the measures taken by the clergy to combat it and to encourage morality among the Orthodox population.[168] Further evidence of widespread unbelief among the young was given by their ". . . precocious disillusionment, apathy, moral weariness—the natural result of this appears to be mass suicides of the students, even of those below ten years of age. The statistics of the Minister of Public Education convince us of the progressive growth of suicide among the young"; so said *Tserkovnyi Vestnik* in 1913.[169]

Moreover, among the older peasants, of whom the men of the church loved to speak—"the hundred million Christ-loving Orthodox peasants"—there were occasional voices raised against the priests. In the Duma, in 1912, the Octobrist Kovalevskii quoted a letter from a priest who wrote, "We would not wish even our worst enemy to live through the burdensome tragedy of contemporary pastorship. . . . There is rapidly arising the type of parishioner who, instead of the usual fifty kopecks, gives only ten for a christening, and this with the

[165] Gosudarstvennaia Duma, *Doklady Biudzhetnoi Komissii,* IV Duma, Session IV, No. 4, Stenogram, pp. 12–13.

[166] *Tserkovnyia Vedomosti,* Dec. 17, 1911, p. 2203.

[167] *Vera i Razum,* July, 1913, pp. 283–88.

[168] *Tserkovnyi Vestnik,* April 11, 1913, cols. 460–61.

[169] *Ibid.,* Dec. 20, 1913, col. 1598.

remark, 'Thank God I give thee this money, or thou'lt get nothing; no one obliges us to pay thee for ministrations.' " [170]

At times, as in the above instances, the hostility to the priest was over economic matters. In the Duma, in 1912, the nonparty peasant deputy Gul'kin declared, ". . . in my province the priests take twenty rubles for a wedding; they even take for things forbidden by the rules of the Holy Fathers and of the Holy Apostles—they charge for every ministration, and they not only charge, but they fleece the population." He continued, "If the police take bribes, they are at least hampered by the fear that someone will see, but the little father fleeces the peasants before your eyes in the light of day. . . . The little fathers in our district live better than lords. . . ." [171] Speeches of this nature led the Progressive, Count Uvarov, to declare to the Duma:

> You know—and this has great symbolic significance, and especially draws general attention—that the most uncompromising opponents, the most fiery foes of voting salaries to the clergy are those peasants, those deputies from the peasants, to whom the clergy constantly refer, affirming that "behind us there come the many millions of the Russian peasantry"; moreover, when there . . . arises the question of assigning the least salary to the clergy, you will not find, either on the Right benches or on those of the Left, one peasant deputy who will defend that appropriation. [172]

Count Uvarov was not an impartial witness; on several occasions he had been a leader in the attack upon the privileges of the Orthodox Church. Yet there was more than a little truth in his statement; many of the peasant deputies were outspoken opponents of appropriations for the clergy and the parish schools, while few were the peasants who spoke in favor of such grants.

At times the hostility to the clergy was personal, as in the case of the peasants of Volhynia who sent a message to Archbishop Antonii saying that if he did not remove their priest and give them a better one, they would change to another faith—to which the archbishop's answer was to send a police inspector to arrest the peasant delegates

[170] Gosudarstvennaia Duma, *Stenograficheskie Otchety*, IV Duma, Session I, Part 2, cols. 1392–93.

[171] *Ibid.*, III Duma, Session V, Part 4, col. 4261.

[172] *Ibid.*, Part 3, col. 136.

who had presented the message.[173] More often, however, it appears to have been impersonal dislike of priests in general. Father Gepetskii, a strong defender of the church in the Duma, complained in 1912:

Allow me to say to you that the attacks, the abuse, the accusations of cupidity which are poured forth from this rostrum, and on the pages of the hooligan press, and even in shouts on the street, those frightful affronts which wither one's ears—tell me, do not these degrade the moral authority, do they not paralyze the force, of the pastors of today? [174]

Missionerskoe Obozrenie (*Missionary Survey*) was able to cast a ray of light into the gloom by citing the reports of Bishop Andrei, who in his journeys to the wild backwoods villages of Kazan had found the peasants most religious. However, the periodical continued with the statement that in the southern dioceses the priest was dubbed "pope" (a slightly contemptuous popular term for a priest), and was regarded as a parasite. In some cases the people refused to support their clergy, so that the bishops had had to close the churches and to remove the priests from these unruly parishes.[175] The diocesan congress of Poltava declared in 1912 that ". . . since the time of the liberation movement [the Revolution of 1905] in the villages there have appeared not a few persons inspired by some inexplicable hostility to the clergy . . ."—which feeling they expressed by making all sorts of complaints against the priests, even to the Synod, ". . . with the aim of frightening, blackening, and undermining the pastors whom they dislike, although the former are often very worthy pastors of the church." [176]

The same story was told in 1914. In that year the official organ of the Synod, *Tserkovnyia Vedomosti,* cited an article from the diocesan journal of Volhynia, which complained "The people do not listen to us, they laugh at us, they revile us, they cast all sorts of insults at us, they drive us out; in a word, they in all ways degrade those persons who serve as the leaders, guides, and sanctifiers of Christian life." In his comments on this quotation, the editor expressed a hope that mat-

[173] *Tserkovnyia Vedomosti,* April 18, 1909, p. 717.

[174] Gosudarstvennaia Duma, *Stenograficheskie Otchety,* III Duma, Session V, Part 3, col. 602.

[175] Feb., 1908, pp. 296–97.

[176] *Tserkovnyi Vestnik,* Oct. 4, 1912, cols. 1265–66.

ters had not actually reached such a pass: "but at the same time one cannot close his eyes to the undoubted fact, remarked by all diocesan journals, that of late there has been observed a decline of pastoral authority among the people—that 'deep, conscious loyalty to the pastor is now a very rare phenomenon.' " [177] These words were published just nine weeks before the outbreak of the World War.

To the hostility to the village clergy there must be added some hostility to the monasteries. In 1908 four monastic institutions were granted the protection of policemen, who were quartered there at the expense of the institutions. [178] In 1909 four more received this protection. [179] Including the famous Troitsko-Sergieva Monastery near Moscow, which was to enjoy the security furnished by one senior officer and six of junior rank, [180] four monastic institutions were granted police protection in 1910, [181] and in 1911, one. [182] Possibly these precautions were caused by a general increase in crime, rather than by a special feeling against the monasteries; none the less, the need for special police protection suggests the coming of evil days for the church.

It must not be supposed that the church did nothing in the face of these threatening manifestations. During the period after the Revolution of 1905 it encouraged its clergy to engage in social and charitable enterprises to a much greater extent than before. A large part of this activity centered in a campaign against drunkenness. In 1909 the Synod sent out a message to the church urging energetic work in the parishes—the formation of brotherhoods, temperance societies, special temperance libraries, and the like, as well as the exertion of influence by the priests through sermons and through personal example. [183] Thanks largely to this encouragement, the number of temperance societies under church auspices grew rapidly, especially after 1908. In 1905 there were only 770 such organizations; by 1911 the number had risen to 1,767, with 498,685 members. [184] Temperance work was actively pushed in 1912 and 1913 in a number of dioceses, includ-

---

[177] *Tserkovnyia Vedomosti*, May 17, 1914, p. 920.
[178] *Sobranie Uzakonenii*, 1908, Nos. 837, 877, 1376, 1564.
[179] *Ibid.*, 1909, Nos. 829, 1700, 2017, 2177.   [180] *Ibid.*, 1910, No. 2126.
[181] *Ibid.*, Nos. 1124, 1521, 1600.   [182] *Ibid.*, 1911, No. 2129.
[183] *Tserkovnyia Vedomosti*, June 13, 1909, official part, pp. 242–45.
[184] *Ibid.*, Nov. 12, 1911, pp. 1961–63.

ing St. Petersburg, Moscow, Perm, Polotsk, Astrakhan, Kursk, and the Don; [185] and in April, 1914, the Synod set aside August 29 to be the annual Temperance Day of the church.[186] Another helpful endeavor of the clergy was the encouragement of coöperative credit and consumers' societies, in which priests acted as presidents or directors, with valuable increase in their prestige. They also took part in the famine relief committees in the Volga and Ural provinces in 1911. In 1914 a number of diocesan journals favored social work as a valuable means of gaining popular sympathy for the clergy.[187]

Some of the reports in the ecclesiastical journals were decidedly hopeful of the future. In 1908 a certain Father Nikolenko wrote to say that the priests still enjoyed the confidence of the people; they were chosen to head committees for building churches and for other responsible positions.[188] Kolokol (The Bell), widely believed to be the personal organ of the Over Procurator, asserted in 1909 that the churches were again filled with people, that the intelligentsia were coming to confession, and that in St. Petersburg students were to be seen among the churchgoers.[189] In 1912 an observer noted churches filled with worshipers, and harmonious relations between priests and parishioners; crowds of communicants during Lent, long processions of pilgrims; and new parishes, new schools, new almshouses.[190] Undoubtedly the church was still a strong influence in the lives of many; but in spite of occasional hopeful reports, the general tone of the observations of both laymen and ecclesiastics was that the portents boded ill for the church.

Far more typical than the cheerful statements just cited were the findings of a certain A. Vvedenskii, who, in 1911, wrote to a number of newspaper subscribers asking them to express their religious convictions. He received answers from about eight hundred persons—doctors, lawyers, priests, engineers, workers, and peasants; 95 per-

---

[185] Tserkovnyi Vestnik, Oct. 24, 1913, col. 1340; Oct. 31, 1913, col. 1374; Nov. 7, 1913, col. 1408; Dec. 20, 1913, cols. 1604–6; Tserkovnyia Vedomosti, Jan. 25, 1914, pp. 171–76.

[186] Tserkovnyia Vedomosti, April 19, 1914, official part, p. 125.

[187] Ibid., Feb. 8, 1914, pp. 322–23; July 5, 1914, pp. 1213–17.

[188] Vera i Razum, Sept., 1908, pp. 824–28.

[189] Ibid., April, 1909, pp. 280–81.

[190] Missionerskoe Obozrenie, May, 1912, pp. 106–7.

cent stated that they did not believe in God.[191] Even as early as 1908 the diocesan periodicals of Perm, Viatka, Novgorod, Vladivostok, Kostroma, Orenburg, and Voronezh complained of the low level of religious belief.[192] In 1912 Father Emilian Berdega stated the same sad fact: the upper strata of Russian society and all the intelligentsia and half-intelligentsia, with minor exceptions, were, he thought, entirely unbelieving, while the masses themselves were beginning to be affected by the existing lack of faith in educated circles—"among them also there is now noted a trend toward weakness of faith and even toward unbelief. Indifference to the obligations imposed by the Orthodox Church is met with over and over again among the plain people." [193]

Several priests declared that preaching no longer had much hold over the people, and that "unfortunately, in contemporary parish life a silent pulpit is a fairly common thing." As their reasons for omitting sermons, these pastors stated that "the people do not love sermons, and when the preacher even enters the pulpit, the congregation crowds out of the church." [194] The *Poltava Diocesan News* reported the same condition: ". . . the preacher of today has to appear before a public which is of a critical and even unfriendly frame of mind, whose father and pastor he can be called only in a . . . figurative sense; on entering the pulpit he risks having to see his hearers turn their backs." [195]

Finally, even many of those who were still imbued with faith were falling away from the Orthodox Church. After the Romanov jubilee in 1913 had failed to lead to the summoning of a *Sobor*, the liberal *Tserkovnyi Vestnik*, published by a group of professors of the Religious Academy of St. Petersburg, printed the following warning, quoted from *Golos Moskvy* (*The Voice of Moscow*):

We cannot close our eyes to the hitherto unheard-of enormous falling away of the people from their native Orthodoxy into different sects, into Schism, and other faiths, especially Lutheranism (in the west of Russia) and even into Catholicism (in both our capitals). The Russian Orthodox

---

[191] *Vera i Razum*, Feb., 1912, p. 530.

[192] *Tserkovnyia Vedomosti*, Aug. 9, 1908, pp. 1552–55.

[193] *Ibid.*, May 6, 1912, p. 743.   [194] *Ibid.*, June 28, 1914, p. 1157.

[195] *Tserkovnyi Vestnik*, Aug. 15, 1913, col. 1024.

people in many places literally run from their "state" church, as they call it, or else, under the influence of strongly developed religious feeling, . . . rush in crowds after various Iliodors and Innokentiis, after Abstainer brothers and similar persons at the head of religious movements.[196]

This was written in 1913, before the blood bath of the World War had begun to shake Russian confidence in authority, and before the corrosive influence of Rasputin had penetrated very deeply into the minds of the people. The church had failed to change its ways in fundamental fashion in response to the danger signal of 1905, and in most respects its old defects remained uncorrected. Now years of great trial and danger were approaching; how would the church meet the test?

[196] *Ibid.*, March 28, 1913, cols. 391–92.

CHAPTER IX

The Sway of Rasputin

WHILE in most respects the Russian Church in the years after the Revolution of 1905 failed to present significant changes from its previous condition, there was arising an important new factor—a phenomenon which was to have dire consequences for the church. This factor bore the name of Grigorii Rasputin. He was born in 1872 in the village of Pokrovskoe, in the Siberian diocese of Tobolsk. At first known as Grigorii Novyi (The New), he later was dubbed Rasputin (The Dissolute) by his fellow peasants, because of his debauched life. His religious career apparently began with a visit to the monastery of Verkhotur'e, from which he returned to Pokrovskoe claiming to be a *starets,* or holy man. He seems to have won a following among the folk of the neighborhood, although his scandalous practices continued.[1] However, the local priest heard of his activities and reported the rumors to the bishop, who ordered an investigation, apparently about 1902.

Nevertheless, during Lent, 1903, according to Iliodor, who at the time was a monk in the Religious Academy of St. Petersburg, Rasputin was brought to the capital by Abbot Khrisanf, who believed him to be a holy man of the people. Abbot Feofan, a devout monk who was inspector of the academy, was especially taken with the Siberian peasant, and at Easter, 1905, told Iliodor that he and Rasputin had just come from the palace of the Grand Duke Peter and his Montenegrin wife. Moreover, Feofan mentioned that he had on

[1] P. Gilliard, *Le Tragique Destin de Nicolas II et de sa famille,* p. 46. Gilliard was tutor to the imperial children from 1905 until after the Revolution of 1917. His book is a careful and highly credible piece of work, especially useful for determining the chronology of events.

several occasions taken Rasputin to the imperial palace at Tsarskoe Selo. The "holy man" was for a time made much of by members of the highest society of St. Petersburg, so that it was not hard for the adventurer to gain access to the household of the Tsar.[2]

In passing, it should be noted that Rasputin was not the first charlatan to be accepted in Russian court circles. Their Imperial Majesties were eager for mystical religious experiences, and had patronized in turn the French spiritualist Philippe, Papus, a sort of astrologer, and the half-insane mute Mitia, a peasant from Kaluga. Much the same atmosphere existed in certain other fashionable circles, in which several religious salons flourished, notably those of Countess Ignat'eva, Baroness Korff, Mme Pistolkors, and others close to the court. In their search for religious satisfaction, these ladies tended to turn from the accepted theology of the church to the more primitive and emotional religion of the peasants. In this hospitable atmosphere the earthy figure of Rasputin found a haven, and it was not long until, with the support of Feofan, now a bishop, the peasant was accepted by the Tsar and his German-born consort and made "the emperor's lamp-keeper," with the duty of tending the lamps burning before the ikons in the palace.[3] Once inside the palace, Rasputin was able to convince the imperial couple that he was a man sent from God. Being fortunate enough to possess a soothing influence over the Tsarevich, who was a victim of the dread haemophilia, he claimed credit for the improvement in the boy's condition which occurred after more than one crisis. The empress was firmly convinced that the fate of her adored son depended on the "holy man"; the emperor was tolerant of his spouse's favorite, so that the latter's position became very

[2] S. M. Trufanov [Iliodor], *Sviatoi Chort*, pp. 3–7. Iliodor was not a stable person, and when he wrote was hostile to the Rasputin party; however, while his work is sensational, it is useful for the early period of Rasputin's activity, and agrees with the other evidence available. Also, N. D. Zhevakhov, *Vospominaniia*, I, 267. Zhevakhov was Assistant Over Procurator during the last months of the Rasputin regime. He tries strongly to exculpate himself, and on controversial points must be used with caution.

[3] M. V. Rodzianko, *The Reign of Rasputin*, pp. 1–7. A chamberlain of the imperial court, and President of the Duma, Rodzianko had opportunities to learn what was happening. He was strongly hostile to Rasputin, but, judging by the other evidence, did not distort the facts. Also, Zhevakhov, *op. cit.*, I, 248 ff.

strong. Indeed he was allowed to call the imperial couple "Papa" and "Mama," and in return was "Our Friend" to the empress.[4]

It was well for Rasputin that he was strong at court, for the investigation begun at Pokrovskoe had not been dropped when he left for the capital, and eventually Bishop Antonii of Tobolsk ordered that criminal charges, on the ground of gross immorality and superstition, be brought against him. However, the case was never pressed; according to Rodzianko, President of the Duma, Bishop Antonii was given his choice of withdrawing the charges and accepting promotion to the see of Tver, or of retiring to a monastery. He chose the former alternative, and the prosecution was dropped.[5] Moreover, the priest of Rasputin's parish was replaced by one who did not deny the latter's righteousness, and as considerable sums were lavished on his parish church by Rasputin's protectors, all danger from that quarter was averted.[6]

In 1909 Iliodor, who was in disgrace because of his conflict with the governor of Saratov, was ordered by the Synod to go to the diocesan home in Minsk. Instead, the monk hastened to St. Petersburg to ask his friend Bishop Feofan to intercede for him. In his account, published in 1917, Iliodor stated that while he was closeted with Feofan, Rasputin entered and offered to arrange for Iliodor's return to his monastery in Tsaritsyn, in spite of the orders of the Synod. While waiting for the matter to be arranged, Iliodor was much in company with Rasputin, and with him was received by the empress. In September of the same year Rasputin paid a visit to Iliodor's superior, Bishop Hermogen, in Saratov, and in November Hermogen and Rasputin visited Iliodor's monastery in Tsaritsyn, where the friendship of the three was cemented.[7]

However, while Rasputin's power grew, his conduct became more

[4] P. E. Shchegolev, ed., *Padenie Tsarskogo Rezhima*, IV, 500–2, Beletskii. Beletskii was head of the Dept. of Police from 1912 to 1915, and Assistant Minister of Internal Affairs, September, 1915, to February, 1916. His testimony is exceedingly detailed, as he turned state's evidence, apparently hoping to escape punishment. Although many of his statements are highly sensational in character, Beletskii's deposition tallies with the other evidence on all vital points. For an estimate of Beletskii see S. A. Korenev, in *Arkhiv Russkoi Revoliutsii*, VII, 20.

[5] Rodzianko, *op. cit.*, pp. 56–58. [6] Shchegolev, *op. cit.*, IV, 505, Beletskii.
[7] Trufanov, *op. cit.*, pp. 10–19.

brazen. Drunken orgies and debauches, even with ladies of the world of society, became characteristic features of his life. The trusting Bishop Feofan came reluctantly to realize that Rasputin was not a worthy companion for the children of the Tsar. In 1910 the bishop complained to the emperor, but was coldly received, and not long after was removed from his position as confessor to the empress and as head of the Religious Academy of St. Petersburg, and was sent off to the diocese of Simferopol, in the Crimea.[8]

Near the end of the same year another unsuccessful attempt was made to end the influence of the dissolute Rasputin at court. Mlle Tucheva, governess of the Tsar's daughters, complained to the empress of the danger of having such a man near the grand duchesses. The governess was so insistent that Rasputin was forbidden the floor on which the girls slept; but the empress continued to revere him, and before long Mlle Tucheva resigned her position.[9] Rodzianko, President of the Duma, relates a story which was probably current at court, that the nurse of the imperial children hastened to Metropolitan Antonii who was taking the baths at Kislovodsk, and besought the prelate "to save the little Tsarevich from the clutches of the devil." On his return to the capital early in 1911, the metropolitan sought an audience with the Tsar, and, according to Rodzianko, recounted what he knew of Rasputin's actions. Nicholas heard him with evident displeasure, remarking finally that the affairs of the imperial family did not concern the Most Reverend Antonii. The latter persisted, but the Tsar again silenced him, and abruptly terminated the interview.[10]

About the same time Stolypin, President of the Council of Ministers, felt compelled to intervene. Luk'ianov, the Over Procurator of the Synod, gathered all available material on the "holy man" and presented it to the Tsar, and Stolypin supported Luk'ianov in insisting that Rasputin must go.[11] Perhaps because of these attacks, the adventurer started on an extended pilgrimage to Jerusalem in March, 1911, returning only in the fall.[12] Almost at once he became more notorious than before. In September, 1911, Stolypin was assassinated

[8] Rodzianko, *op. cit.*, pp. 12–15.
[9] Gilliard, *op. cit.*, p. 49.
[10] Rodzianko, *op. cit.*, pp. 27–28.
[11] *Ibid.*, pp. 23 ff.
[12] Gilliard, *op. cit.*, p. 49.

and Luk'ianov resigned. He was succeeded by V. K. Sabler, an official who soon turned out to be a supporter of Rasputin. Almost immediately the Synod was confronted by a proposal to appoint Abbot Varnava as bishop of Kargopol. Varnava, a former gardener of Archangel, was reputed to be almost illiterate; when his name was proposed in the Synod in 1911 by Bishop Nikanor, the Synod, usually complaisant, balked. However, the emperor insisted, and Sabler, Over Procurator, threatened to resign if the Synod did not acquiesce in the appointment. Archbishop Antonii of Volhynia wrote to his friend, Metropolitan Flavian of Kiev, "It has come out that Rasputin pushed Varnava into the episcopate. The Synod named him on the basis of the written request of Bishop Nikanor, but it [the request] was almost forced through by Damanskii [Assistant Over Procurator]. Rasputin . . . is a *Khlyst* and takes part in orgies. . . ."[13] This appointment was the subject of debates in the Third Duma in 1912. Count Uvarov declared from the rostrum that several members of the Synod had told him that in the beginning they had declared that under no circumstances should Varnava be made a bishop, but that when orders came from above they gave way. The count added, "This gardener, made bishop, is a great friend and partisan of the 'holy man' Rasputin, and was designated for this position at the wish of this same Rasputin."[14] More sensational events soon followed. In October, 1911, Bishop Hermogen of Saratov, and Iliodor came to the capital—the bishop to attend the Synod, and Iliodor, so *Russkiia Vedomosti* (*The Russian News*) suggested, in order to receive promotion to the rank of abbot.[15] However, Hermogen incurred the enmity of Sabler, the new Over Procurator, by denouncing the weakness of the Synod in submitting to domination in the case of Varnava. He also had the temerity to object to the creation of an Order of Deaconesses, on the grounds that such an establishment had been forbidden by one of the great church councils; the wishes of the Grand Duchess Elizabeth, sister of the emperor, did not sway the obstinate

[13] "V Tserkovnykh Krugakh pered Revoliutsiei," *Krasnyi Arkhiv*, 1928, No. 31, pp. 211–12.

[14] Gosudarstvennaia Duma, *Stenograficheskie Otchety*, III Duma, Session V, Part 3, cols. 784 and 858.

[15] *Russkiia Vedomosti*, Oct. 8, 1911.

bishop.[16] His disgrace soon followed; but there were insistent reports that his fall was not due to these questions, but to his break with Rasputin.

According to Rodzianko, who heard the story from Colonel Rodionov, a witness to the scene, Bishop Hermogen sent for Rasputin and, when he came, upbraided him in the following words: "You pose as a 'holy man,' while leading an unclean and shameful life. You duped me in the past. . . . I adjure you in the name of the Living God to cease troubling the Russian People by your presence at court." Rasputin's answers were insolent, and a violent scene followed. Hermogen anathematized him, whereupon Rasputin made a violent attack upon the bishop. However, others present seized the angry peasant, and he escaped only after having been roughly handled.[17]

Rasputin vowed vengeance as he fled and he was not long in getting it, for Hermogen was ordered to return to his diocese at once, and to take Iliodor with him. However, they refused to go. Instead, representatives of the press were called in, and Hermogen announced to them that he was being disciplined, not because he objected to the Order of Deaconesses, but because Rasputin had turned against him.[18] The Synod at once issued a hasty denial of the allegations; [19] but the matter could not be so easily ended. The incident was widely discussed in St. Petersburg—in the newspapers, in official circles, in high society, and in the Duma. ". . . [It] attracted still more attention to the personality of Rasputin"—so writes Count Kokovtsov in his memoirs.[20]

Undoubtedly the denial of the Synod was disingenuous. Kokovtsov relates that Makarov, Minister of Internal Affairs, went to the imperial court in the hope of mitigating the vengeance against Bishop Hermogen, so that further scandal might be avoided, but met with no success. "On the same day, about six o'clock, he told me on the tele-

---

[16] Rodzianko, *op. cit.*, pp. 18–19.　　[17] *Ibid.*, pp. 16–17.

[18] Gosudarstvennaia Duma, *Stenograficheskie Otchety*, III Duma, Session V, Part 3, col. 175, speech of Bishop Mitrofan.

[19] *Tserkovnyia Vedomosti*, Jan. 21, 1912, official part, pp. 20–24.

[20] V. N. Kokovtsov, *Iz Moego Proshlago*, II, 28. The author, a conservative statesman of the better type, was President of the Council of Ministers at the time. His statements are valuable evidence.

phone that he had met with a definite refusal, that all sympathy was on the side of Rasputin, 'whom they had attacked as robbers attack, in the forest, first luring their victim into a trap.'"[21] The order for Hermogen's punishment, instead of being revoked, was made more severe; after a considerable delay he was packed off to the Zhirovitskii Monastery near Poland, and Iliodor was also sent to a distant monastery. For some time the excitement continued: "In society, in the Duma, and in the Council of State they talked only about this, and all this disgusting business kept me in a nervous condition"—so writes Count Kokovtsov.[22] The dismissal of these two famous churchmen was widely discussed in the newspapers, and liberal papers like *Russkiia Vedomosti* (*The Russian News*) upheld the theory that it was the work of Rasputin.[23]

In the Duma likewise this opinion was voiced. Guchkov, leader of the Octobrists, headed the attack on Rasputin on March 9, 1912, with these words: "It may be that he is a superstitious sectarian doing his dark work; it may be, a scoundrelly impostor performing his shady tricks. By what paths did this person attain his dominant position, seizing such influence that the higher authorities of church and state bow before it? [voice from the Left: "Kiss the little hands!"]." Guchkov continued with a word of warning, "No revolutionary and antichurch propaganda over a whole series of years, could have done as much as has been accomplished by the events of the last few days [voices: "True!"]. . . ."[24] Even more outspoken was Purishkevich, noted as a leader of a reactionary monarchist organization: ". . . the affair of Bishop Hermogen is that nightmare which now hangs over all the great Russian Empire, tormenting in the same degree the souls of all Russians, whether they be strong or weak in their faith." The official explanation of the matter he ridiculed, declaring that no one believed what the Synod stated as to the facts of the case. The climax of his long and forceful denunciation of the leaders of the church (of which the monarchist parties claimed to be the special protectors) was greeted with laughter and applause:

[21] V. N. Kokovtsov, *Iz Moego Proshlago*, II, 28.   [22] *Ibid.*
[23] *Russkiia Vedomosti*, editorial, Jan. 21, 1912; also citations from *Birzhevyia Vedomosti*, in issue of Jan. 17, 1912.
[24] Gosudarstvennaia Duma, *Stenograficheskie Otchety*, III Duma, Session V, Part 3, cols. 583–84.

I am deeply convinced, and I say to you, that not one revolutionary of the years of disorder has done so much evil in Russia as the recent happenings in the Orthodox Church; no disturbance of 1905, no attack on the foundation of the nation, produced such internal unsettlement, such relations on the part of different classes of society, as the latest developments in the Orthodox Church have done. If at the present moment you were to ask to whom the Left would wish to set up a monument in the Russian Empire, all the Left would answer, to V. K. Sabler [the Over Procurator].[25]

In still another fashion the Third Duma took notice of Grigorii Rasputin. On January 25, 1912, forty-eight members of the Octobrist party introduced a question addressed to the Minister of Internal Affairs, asking why recent issues of two conservative newspapers, *Golos Moskvy* (*The Voice of Moscow*) and *Vechernee Vremia* (*The Evening Time*), had been confiscated by the authorities for printing a letter on Rasputin. The letter, written by Novoselov, editor and publisher of the *Religiozno-Filosofskaia Biblioteka* (*Religious and Philosophical Library*), denounced both the "holy man" and the authorities of the church who allowed him to work evil without check; the denunciation began with the words of Cicero to Catiline:

Quousque tandem abutere patientia nostra.
These words of indignation involuntarily burst forth from the breasts of Orthodox Russian men, addressed to the sly plotter against sanctity and the church, the base corrupter of human souls and bodies, Grigorii Rasputin, who boldly covers himself with that very sanctity of the church.
Quousque tandem abutere patientia nostra.
With sorrow and bitterness the sons of the Orthodox Church are compelled to call upon the Most Holy Synod with these words when they see the dreadful complaisance of the highest administration of the church in respect to the said Grigorii Rasputin.

. . .

Why does it [the Synod] keep silent and do nothing when the command of God—to guard the flock from the ravening wolves—must, it would seem, have spoken with irresistible force in the hearts of arch-pastors, who are called "rightly to administer the word of truth."
Why do the bishops keep silent, to whom the activity of the bare-faced deceiver and corrupter is well known?
Why do they, "the watchmen of Israel," keep silent, when in letters to

---

[25] *Ibid.*, cols. 68–78.

me several of them openly call this servitor of lies a *Khlyst,* an eroto-maniac, a charlatan? [26]

Guchkov, leader of the Octobrists, spoke in behalf of the interpella-tion. In his speech he declared that ". . . dark symbols of the Mid-dle Ages have arisen before us," and praised the press for doing what had not been done ". . . by the protectors of these holy things, of the sanctity of the altar and the throne." The voices of the prelates and of the state authorities had not spoken, but "now our press has performed that duty, and we perform it today, when we introduce and support this interpellation." He received applause from the Left, the Center, and the Right.[27] V. N. Lvov followed with remarks of the same tenor, while defense of the government and of the church authorities was lacking. The interpellation was voted, with the priority asked for. It produced no direct results, however, as the term of the Third Duma expired shortly after and the government did not take up the chal-lenge.

Echoes of this debate were heard in the press, which continued to display the sensational news, to the dismay of the government. Ras-putin's court connections, his influence in the Synod's appointments, and "transparent allusions to certain ladies of St. Petersburg who accompanied him to the village of Pokrovskoe"—all this and more appeared in the columns of the newspapers, especially the Cadet organs *Rech* (*Speech*) and *Russkoe Slovo* (*The Russian Word*). Several attempts to influence the newspapers failed to stop these re-ports; even Count Tatishchev, head of the government Bureau on Affairs of the Press, was not able to still the clamor.[28] Kokovtsov him-self tried to bring an end to the unfavorable articles by calling in Suvorin, editor of *Novoe Vremia* (*The New Time*), a newspaper which was generally regarded as an unofficial mouthpiece of the gov-ernment. However, the editor pointed out that the other papers were printing these articles, and Kokovtsov could not bring him to promise not to print them. "It was clear to me that even in the editorial staff

[26] Gosudarstvennaia Duma, *Prilozheniia k Stenograficheskim Otchetam,* III Duma, Session V, Vol. 2, No. 249.

[27] Gosudarstvennaia Duma, *Stenograficheskie Otchety,* III Duma, Session V, Part 2, cols. 1015–16.

[28] Kokovtsov, *op. cit.,* II, 19–21.

of *Novoe Vremia* some hand was already doing its evil work and that the influence of this editorial board upon its brothers of the pen could not be counted on." [29]

This storm of disapproval did not have the effect of making the government or the Synod disavow Rasputin, but it did lead to his temporary eclipse. Early in 1912 Rodzianko, President of the Duma, denounced Rasputin to the Tsar.[30] Somewhat later Count Kokovtsov also urged the emperor to rid himself of this unsavory person.[31] The emperor was not entirely convinced, but saw the need for a concession to public opinion; consequently, Rasputin left for Siberia, where he stayed for many months, with only occasional returns to the court. None the less, through letters and telegrams to Mme Vyrubova, who was an intimate friend of the empress, he kept in touch with the imperial family, and his influence continued strong.[32]

The absence of Rasputin caused the gradual disappearance of his name from the newspapers. In the spring of 1914, however, there was a new flare-up in the Duma, when the Cadets, led by Prince Mansyrev and Professor Miliukov, once more attacked the influence of Rasputin in the church. Miliukov trained his fire upon the recent appointment of Varnava, previously vicar of Kargopol, to the independent post of Bishop of Tobolsk, and said that Varnava's predecessor, Bishop Aleksii, who had once been accused of heresy, had been moved from Tobolsk to the very important post of exarch of Georgia at the wish of Rasputin.[33] Miliukov also read a passage written by Iliodor before his fall from grace: "Sabler and Damanskii are appointees of Grishka [Rasputin]," who had said that "Sabler bowed down at his—Grishka's—feet, because the latter made him Over Procurator." [34] Another salvo came as a result of an item in *Kolokol* (*The Bell*), a newspaper close to the ruling circles of the church, in the issue of December 13, 1913: "It is affirmed that the declaration of war with Turkey hung by a thread, and our preserver from most senseless bloodshed is said to be an inspired 'holy man,' a sincere prophet, who dearly loves Russia,

[29] *Ibid.*

[30] Rodzianko, *op. cit.*, pp. 41–47.

[31] Gilliard, *op. cit.*, p. 51.

[32] *Ibid.*, pp. 51–52.

[33] Gosudarstvennaia Duma, *Stenograficheskie Otchety*, IV Duma, Session II, Part 3, col. 1345.

[34] *Ibid.*, col. 1346; see also Iliodor's memorandum, in S. P. Beletskii, *Grigorii Rasputin*, p. 98.

and is, moreover, close to the helm of our highest politics, and who, by his beneficent influence, held us back from the frightful step." [35] To Miliukov this was an outrage, and he asked how, under such conditions, there could be any talk of reform of the church, and how the church could have any moral or spiritual influence over the people. He closed with the words, "No, gentlemen, first free the state from slavery to adventurers, the hierarchy from slavery to the state, and the church from slavery to the hierarchy [applause from the Left], and then think of reforms [prolonged applause from the Left]." [36] Sabler, the Over Procurator, made answer with a denial of the validity of the sources quoted by Miliukov, and a declaration that he (Sabler) bowed only to God; the Over Procurator did not, however, mention Rasputin by name or deny that he had had dealings with him. [37]

Interesting testimony as to the reason for the rise of Varnava was given under oath in 1917 by Prince Andronikov, a journalist of poor repute, who held a minor office under the Synod and was a member of Rasputin's inner circle. The Prince declared that Varnava, a strait-laced though calculating monk, disliked Rasputin for his manner of living, but that the latter asked the Tsar to name Varnava as bishop, first of Kargopol, and later of Tobolsk, so that when Rasputin returned to his native village in that diocese "he could misbehave, interfere in things, more easily than under another bishop. Rasputin thought that Varnava would wink [at his misdeeds], and, on occasion, support him—that is, not expose all his wickedness, as a whole series of governors and bishops had done." The Prince added, "In his soul Varnava hated him, but for the sake of Tsarskoe Selo [the court] he excused him much: *il fermait son bec.*" [38]

Rasputin again became a topic of excited conversation in July, 1914. When he arrived in his native village early in July, he was attacked by a young woman, supposedly one of his former mistresses, and received a dangerous knife wound in the abdomen. However, his abundant vitality saved him; he was taken to a hospital, a specialist was sent from St. Petersburg, and in eight days the sufferer was out

[35] Gosudarstvennaia Duma, *Stenograficheskie Otchety,* IV Duma, Session II, Part 3, col. 1347.

[36] *Ibid.*   [37] *Ibid.*

[38] Shchegolev, ed., *Padenie Tsarskogo Rezhima,* I, 385.

of danger.[39] Nevertheless, sensational as this incident was, it was soon lost to sight amid the excitement aroused by the war. Although Rasputin returned to the capital from Siberia in September, 1914, he played little part in events until the late spring of 1915. He opposed the war and, as the Tsarevich suffered no attacks during this period, Rasputin was not called on to exert his supposed power to save the child.[40] Russia was engaged in a deadly struggle with the Central Powers, and for a time at least politics were forgotten, while the energies of church and state were thrown into the fray.

As soon as war was declared, the Synod issued a proclamation stating that Russia had been unexpectedly drawn into the conflict in defense of "our brothers in faith" (i. e., the Serbs). The appeal continued: "Russian warriors! Go with God to the field of battle. May God hallow our arms with victory! . . . Brothers and sisters in Christ! Be courageous, be firm in faith, be ye all as one. . . ." The message closed with the words, "Let us pray to the Creator and Giver of all, the King of Kings and Lord of Lords, that He may give to us and to our allies victory over the enemy, that He may by His almighty power stop the present great conflict of peoples, that He may bring to their senses our enemies and all those who hate us, and may send to our land speedy peace and happiness. . . ." The Synod decreed that this message, as well as the Imperial Manifesto on the war, was to be read in all Orthodox churches, and that after it special prayers for victory were to be said.[41] New prayers for the emperor and for the men in the field of battle were recommended to the clergy and, after the entry of the Turks into the war, solemn prayers for victory.[42] In August, 1914, a special chant was sent to the dioceses, with the refrain, "Most Gracious Lord, crush the enemy beneath our feet!"[43] Sermons were preached urging the people to support the war, and later, after the first great defeats of the Russian arms, telling them to bear the fortunes of war as God's will.[44] Parish priests were told to urge their people to coöperate with the government in every way possible to win the war, and were themselves commanded to collect

[39] Gilliard, op. cit., pp. 80–81.   [40] Ibid., p. 105.

[41] Tserkovnyia Vedomosti, July 26, 1914, official part, pp. 346–48.

[42] Ibid., Aug. 2, 1914, official part, p. 359; Oct. 25, 1914, official part, p. 490.

[43] Ibid., Aug. 23, 1914, p. 1541.   [44] Ibid., Sept. 1, 1914, pp. 1545–52.

supplies for the troops.[45] The regimental chaplains were advised to seize all opportunities "to exert their pastoral influence in maintaining in the soldiers a courageous spirit, faith in God, and esteem for His laws." To this end the chaplains were instructed to hold frequent talks with the rank and file, to encourage desirable tendencies, and to discourage those which promised evil. The Synod made clear the meaning of these injunctions when it expressed a hope that the chaplains would perform their duty and "show their love for Tsar and country."[46]

The activity of the clergy during the war was not confined to words. Many of them took an active part in Russia's war effort. On August 9, 1914, the Synod urged all Orthodox monasteries and churches to contribute toward relief for the wounded and aid for the widowed and the orphaned. The monasteries and convents were told to establish hospitals as well.[47] In Smolensk a Diocesan War Committee was set up, in order to maintain hospitals and perform other war services; the funds for its operations were supplied by a 5 percent levy on the income of churches.[48] In another diocese the clergy established a hospital and organized a home for crippled soldiers, and plans were laid for setting up an asylum for 1,000 children whose fathers had been killed in the war; moreover, a religious mission was sent to the front to help the soldiers. The funds for these activities in this diocese were provided by self-taxation; one ruble was levied for every *desiatina* of church land, a tax which gave nearly 40,000 rubles a year; moreover, the clergy of each parish of this diocese contributed 4 rubles and 50 kopecks for the religious missions at the front. According to Father Gepetskii, who told of this work, it was not an exceptional case; many dioceses were doing likewise, he said.[49] Furthermore, parish trusteeships had been established in all dioceses by order of the Synod, and were taking a very active part in the relief work. They cared for the families of dead or wounded soldiers, and organized hospitals and shelters for the wounded and for refugees. About

[45] *Tserkovnyia Vedomosti*, Nov. 8, 1914, official part, pp. 515–18.
[46] *Ibid.*, Nov. 8, 1914, p. 1882.
[47] *Ibid.*, Aug. 9, 1914, pp. 1413–14.
[48] *Ibid.*, Aug. 16, 1914, p. 1465.
[49] Gosudarstvennaia Duma, *Doklady Biudzhetnoi Komissii*, IV Duma, Session IV, No. 4, Stenogram, p. 43.

250 priests were at the front as regimental chaplains, or as chaplains with sanitary detachments and the like; many others visited the front from time to time, taking gifts to the troops.[50] However, in 1915 the Duma clergy indicated that all was not well with the war work of the church. In their manifesto they urged that the monasteries take part in extensive charitable work, in order to disprove the increasingly frequent charges that these institutions did not display sufficient zeal, even in the work of caring for sick and wounded soldiers. The manifesto recognized that the accusations were often greatly exaggerated; "nevertheless, it cannot but be wished that the monasteries rendered more service to society through works of mercy and love. This would increase the importance of the monasteries in the eyes of the Orthodox people, and would restore to them the influence which they enjoyed in times past." [51]

In still other ways religious inspiration was given to the populace and to the soldiers. On July 22, 1914, Archbishop Antonii of Khar'kov wrote to his friend, Metropolitan Flavian of Kiev, "We have collected 40,000 little crosses for the whole garrison of Khar'kov, and from the twenty-eighth on we shall begin to bestow them upon the soldiers and to say inspiring words to them. . . ." [52] Many miracles were reported to the newspapers from the front—cases of the miraculous escape of congregations of soldiers when churches were hit by shells, instances when men were hit by bullets or shell splinters, but escaped injury because of the fact that the projectiles struck ikons or crosses worn around their necks, dreams of miraculous appearances of the Virgin or of saints, cases of marvelous cures of blinded soldiers—all of them believed to show divine intervention on behalf of the Russian arms. In August, 1914, after the defeat of General Samsonov's army at the Masurian Lakes, the wonder-working ikon of the Mother of God, painted on a board from the coffin of St. Sergii, was sent "by Imperial command" to the front, from the Troitsko-Sergieva Monastery, and it was remarked that almost immediately after this, news was received of a Russian victory near Lvov and of the Allied victory at the Marne.[53] On June 15, 1915, the Tsar wrote to the empress, "I spoke

---

[50] *Ibid.*, p. 13.   [51] *Missionerskoe Obozrenie*, Nov., 1915, p. 297.
[52] *Krasnyi Arkhiv*, 1928, No. 31, p. 212.
[53] I. V. Preobrazhenskii, *Velichaishaia iz Velikikh Voin za Pravdu Bozhiiu*, pp. 7–71.

to Shavelsky [Head Chaplain of the forces] about arranging, for some day or other, *krestny khod* [the procession of the cross] all over Russia. He thought it a very good idea, and suggested for it the 8th of July, the day of the Mother of God of Kazan, which is celebrated everywhere." [54]

After the first few months, however, signs appeared that the moral support given by the church to Russia's war effort was growing less active and less effective. In the autumn of 1914 several of the regular religious periodicals ceased to devote much space to the war; some of them, like *Missionerskoe Obozrenie, Vera i Razum,* and *Pravoslavnyi Sobesednik,* no longer printed sermons and items on the war; their pages during 1915 and 1916 presented almost no evidence that a desperate conflict was in progress. However, the official *Tserkovnyia Vedomosti* continued to devote a part of its space to the war. In its issue of September 5, 1915, there was an article advising that false rumors about the war should not be believed, as they were quite as dangerous in their effect as poisonous gases. The author, Archbishop Nikon, went on to complain that the people were becoming skeptical in matters of religion, because of the influence of the Jews and of the "Jewish press"; for example, the people failed to credit the accounts of miracles which were reported from the tomb of St. Serafim, at the monastery of Sarov. In this Archbishop Nikon saw the influence of the enemies of the church, who were following the tactics used in 1905; "the firing has begun, the attack is being prepared." [55] Another article in the same issue, by Father A. Rozhdestvenskii, was entitled "A Summons to Fasting and Repentance." In it he spoke of Russia's enemies, domestic and foreign, who were numbered in millions; however, he declared, if the Russians were true sons of the Orthodox Church, God would save them.[56] But articles of this nature were rare in the unofficial ecclesiastical press.

Although the religious periodicals dedicated but little space to Russia's war effort after the first few months had passed, the government considered the church organs sufficiently important to grant them financial support. In 1914 the governmental "reptile fund" (secret

[54] *Letters of the Tsar to the Tsaritsa,* p. 59.
[55] *Tserkovnyia Vedomosti,* Sept. 5, 1915, pp. 2001–5.
[56] *Ibid.,* pp. 2005–6.

press fund) bestowed 28,500 rubles for propaganda purposes on churchmen and church periodicals; 23,500 rubles were distributed in 1915; and in 1916, 105,000 rubles. This last sum included a payment of 60,000 rubles made to *Russkaia Zhizn'* (*Russian Life*), a secular newspaper, at the request of Archbishop Antonii of Khar'kov (formerly of Volhynia).[57]

If one may judge by the attitude revealed by the speeches of the clergy in the Duma and in the Council of State, the church continued to support the war. In July, 1914, Archbishop Arsenii made a patriotic speech in the Council of State, in which he proclaimed that ". . . we . . . believe with never a doubt that in this war the Lord is and will be with us. This war must be looked upon as a holy crusade." He declared that the conflict had been forced upon Russia, which was fighting for true Russian and Slavic ideals. His closing words were, "The heart of the Tsar is in the hand of God. The summons of the Tsar is His holy law, to which we must unconditionally submit. In this union of the Tsar with the people is the pledge of glory and well-being, to which He leads great Russia. 'Save Thy people, O Lord, and bless Thine inheritance.'"[58] In January, 1915, Father Gepetskii, acting as the accredited spokesman of the clergy in the Duma, declared that Russia was the victim of the plots of her enemies, but ". . . with sword in hand and cross in heart we carry on the struggle for the principles of truth and peace. . . . May the Lord God protect our Fatherland, and the Tsar, our Supreme Commander, and may the blessing of God remain with our army."[59] A year later Father Mankovskii demanded in the Duma that all peoples beneath the yoke of Austria-Hungary should be freed. *"Germania vero delenda est*—Germany must indeed be destroyed. . . . Victory will be brought to us by our splendid invincible army with its supreme leader, Lord of the Might of Russia, at its head. Eternal truth will give us this victory, . . . this victory God Himself will give us. Submit, ye heathen, for God is with us!"[60]

[57] *Krasnyi Arkhiv*, 1925, No. 10, pp. 334–42.
[58] Gosudarstvennyi Sovet, *Stenograficheskii Otchet*, IX Session, July 20, 1914, cols. 5–6.
[59] Gosudarstvennaia Duma, *Stenograficheskie Otchety*, IV Duma, Session III, cols. 24–28.
[60] *Ibid.*, Session IV, Part 2, cols. 1537–38.

During the war the government also looked to the clergy for aid in its campaign against the liberal elements in the Duma. Father Filonenko, speaking in February, 1916, told the chamber, "You will remember, gentlemen, how half a year ago there appeared a whole series of high religious persons who thundered from the pulpit against the Duma, and that this coincided almost exactly with its dismissal in September." [61] In 1916 the government began to form plans for the election of a Fifth Duma, which was to take place in 1917. A conference composed of the head of the cabinet, Stürmer, and two members of the Right parties in June, 1916, drew up an elaborate program for a secret election campaign, which was to include the lavish use of funds from the treasury, the publication of pamphlets, and the active coöperation of all branches of the government. The conference concluded: "The government should, as in the last campaign, rely on the Orthodox clergy, which will be possible only if the bishops of the dioceses are impressed with the seriousness of the state problem assigned to them. The clergy should be used chiefly as electors; it is desirable to elect to the Duma not more than eighty priests (on the average, one to a province)." [62] In a summary of the election possibilities, province by province, Khvostov, Minister of Internal Affairs, made the following statements: "The province of Kiev . . . is in a favorable condition, having a united clergy and, in general, successful marshals of nobility. . . ." "Vitebsk has a united Russian landowners' group. . . . This group has strengthened its position in the *zemstvos,* and, in alliance with the clergy, can carry the election." In Grodno, "The Russian landowners' group is not strong, but, in alliance with the clergy and under the guidance of the governor, it may elect nationalist men." "In Vologda there is a group of Rightist landowners, and the full coöperation of the Most Reverend Alexander may also be counted on." In Orel, ". . . there are many conservative nobles who, in league with the clergy, can defeat the Leftist party." And in a number of other provinces the clergy were regarded as a mainstay of the government. [63]

It is interesting to note, however, that some of the clergy in the

[61] Gosudarstvennaia Duma, *Stenograficheskie Otchety,* IV Duma, Session III, col. 2299.

[62] V. P. Semennikov, ed., *Monarkhiia pered Krusheniem,* p. 243.

[63] *Ibid.,* pp. 229–41.

Duma were not as "trustworthy" as the government might have wished. In November, 1916, when N. E. Markov made a violent scene by abusing the Presiding Officer of the Duma to his face, Father Filonenko declared it was shameful that the clergy belonging to the parties of the Right had followed Markov from the hall as an expression of their sympathy; Father Filonenko urged them to leave the Right parties. "You are bearers of the image of the meek, kindly Christ—and do birch rods and *nagaikas* [Cossack whips] on the one side, and the Cross and the Gospel on the other, have anything in common?" "Before you is the odious affair of Rasputin [applause from the Left and the Center] and you are silent, you do not speak, you sell your apostolic heritage for a mess of pottage [applause from the Left and the Center]."[64] This appeal was followed by an announcement from six of the clergy of the Right that they considered the attack of Markov upon the Presiding Officer an attack upon the Duma itself, and that they therefore seceded from the Right party, which had approved the attack.[65] Not long after, however, eleven priests of the Right, five of them members of the original six, denounced this disavowal. Their reasons were that Father Filonenko's speech was a political oration, filled with intolerance. They declared that the clergy should avoid politics and should confine themselves to being "guardian angels to the people."[66] None the less, a number of the clergy in the Duma refused to countenance the provocative attack made by Markov.

The government was never able to make use of the services of the clergy in elections to a Fifth Duma, for the Revolution of 1917 intervened and the elections were not held; nevertheless, from Samuel Hoare, who was in Russia on a British secret service mission, we learn that the Synod was serving the government well through its secret service, operating chiefly among the Jews, the Baltic minorities, the Poles, and the Mohammedan subjects of the Tsar. ". . . I had the uneasy feeling that it was not they [the secret services of the Army and the Navy] who chiefly mattered in Russia, but that the real Intelligence that interested the Government was the Intelligence obtained

[64] Gosudarstvennaia Duma, *Stenograficheskie Otchety*, IV Duma, Session V, cols. 449–50.

[65] *Ibid.*, cols. 451–52.   [66] *Ibid.*, cols. 634–37.

by totally distinct organizations, the Secret Services of the Court, the Ministry of the Interior and the Holy Synod." [67]

Inasmuch as the government continued to depend to such an extent upon the support of the church, it was quite natural that the civil authorities should make strong efforts to support the church against its enemies, especially against the sectarians. Apparently the Old Believers were no longer regarded as dangerous. In an earlier chapter it has been shown that while between 1905 and 1914 many of their former disabilities remained, the government treated them with considerable liberality; their condition was much the same during the war years. The sectarians also continued to suffer the same restrictions as in the later pre-war years, but besides this, many of them, notably the Baptists and the Adventists, were also subjected during the war to repressive action on the grounds that they represented a form of German influence.

As early as November, 1914, Maklakov, Minister of Internal Affairs, obtained a decision from the Senate that the clergy of all sectarian denominations were to officiate only before the congregations to which they were accredited.[68] There soon began an attack upon many of the sectarians, owing to their alleged pro-German attitude. In its issue of March, 1915, *Missionerskoe Obozrenie* declared that wounded men had reported that Baptists and Evangelical Christians had preached, or talked in hospitals, against the war.[69] Before the Duma on August 3, 1915, Shcherbatov, Minister of Internal Affairs, said: ". . . I must say that among . . . [the Baptists], along with those who are sincere believers there are not a few undoubted tools of the German government. Concerning this there are facts beyond all doubt." [70] This statement led the Social Democrat Skobelev to condemn the attack upon the sectarians as an attempt to make them scapegoats. He stated that before the war the Synod had regarded Baptism as largely of English origin, but after the first volley this denomination was termed a German faith, a charge which was taken up by the various diocesan publications and by the missionaries. The result was that many noted leaders of the Baptists were exiled, houses

[67] S. Hoare, *The Fourth Seal*, pp. 52–53, 64.
[68] *Missionerskoe Obozrenie*, Nov., 1914, pp. 367–68.
[69] *Ibid.*, March, 1915, pp. 484–85.   [70] *Ibid.*, Jan., 1916, p. 137.

of prayer had been sealed up, and even hospitals organized by the Baptists had been closed. Now, he said, the campaign was being extended to cover all sectarians.[71]

The Social Democrats, of course, were enemies of the government and of the church, so that this evidence is not from an impartial source. Corroboration of some of Skobelev's statements soon came, however. Father Stanislavskii, a member of the Right party, rose to declare to the Duma that long before the war the Germans had recognized the unifying force of Orthodoxy. Forty years ago they had ". . . sent their preachers into our land, distributed their anti-Orthodox literature, and implanted . . . [their] teachings among us. . . ." He went on to tell of three conscripts who refused to serve, openly declaring that they hoped that the Germans would win, for then ". . . our faith, the true Evangelical faith, will flourish . . ."; and he mentioned other alleged cases in which sectarians had shown pro-German sympathies. He even charged that sectarian soldiers surrendered at the first opportunity. Moreover, he declared that when the sectarians raised money, ostensibly for hospitals, they actually sent it to the Germans. Father Stanislavskii stated that in view of these facts, the Right party proposed that the Duma adopt a resolution recognizing the Stundists, the Adventists, and the sect of *Novyi Izrail* (*New Israel*) as hostile to the state and a danger to its defense, and urging that their prayer meetings be closed.[72]

In December of the same year Skobelev again denounced the persecution of sectarians. He told how an Orthodox priest had so annoyed a hospital in Baku, maintained by the *Molokane,* that the sectarians had closed it. In Moscow the Baptists had had a hospital, which the authorities had evidently wanted to close. A series of demands had been made—that an ikon be hung on the wall, that a sign be removed from the front, and that the hospital be staffed by persons of the Orthodox faith. Although the Baptists had complied with the first two requests, the third was too extreme for ready acceptance, and attempts were made through the Union of Towns to exert influence at court so that the diocesan authorities of Moscow might be induced

[71] Gosudarstvennaia Duma, *Stenograficheskie Otchety,* IV Duma, Session IV, Part 1, cols. 406–7.

[72] *Ibid.,* cols. 420–25.

to withdraw this demand; but to no avail. Consequently the Baptists had dismissed all their denominational staff, with the exception of the manager. Inasmuch as they had raised the funds themselves, they claimed the right to have their own manager administer them, but the Orthodox authorities were adamant, suggesting that while they did not object to the raising of money by the Baptists, it must be spent by the Orthodox. Under such conditions, there was nothing left to do but close the hospital. These cases were described before the Budget Commission of the Duma; at the end of his discourse Skobelev asked Over Procurator Volzhin, who was present, whether he knew of these incidents. Volzhin's answer was, "We have no information about what happened. The Orthodox clergy have not been given the right to close the institutions of civil organizations." [73]

Charges of the same nature were made during 1916. On February 10, Miliukov, leader of the Cadets, declared to the Duma that certain forms of sectarianism were being persecuted, on the grounds that they were really a form of German influence. ". . . On unsupported charges, frequently based on malicious inventions, established, legally registered Evangelical congregations have been closed; their pastors, entirely innocent, have seen sent into remote regions and have been subjected to all sorts of privations." [74] In June a petition, signed by members of parties of the Left, was introduced into the Duma, based on the complaint of a congregation of Baptists in Omsk, who alleged that they had been persecuted as pro-German and that their congregation had been closed by the authorities, who had acted at the request of the Diocesan Brotherhood of Omsk. The Duma voted, in the closing minutes of the session, to question the government concerning these new charges. [75]

From this evidence it seems that the state was aiding the church by persecuting its sectarian rivals. However, by the summer of 1916 a much greater danger was threatening the church, so that it is doubtful whether such measures could do much to remedy the situation. Rasputin was once more in power. During the first months of the war, as

[73] Gosudarstvennaia Duma, *Doklady Biudzhetnoi Komissii*, IV Duma, Session IV, No. 4, Stenogram, p. 40.

[74] Gosudarstvennaia Duma, *Stenograficheskie Otchety*, IV Duma, Session IV, Part 2, col. 1313.

[75] *Ibid.*, Part 3, cols. 5764–66.

has been said, he was in eclipse and, although he returned from Siberia in the fall of 1914, he exerted little influence. Indeed for a time other influences, hostile to Rasputin, swayed the mind of the Tsar. In the summer of 1915, when the disasters of the great retreat were not yet ended, the emperor appointed several new ministers who were in sympathy with the Duma and with the Union of Towns and the Union of *Zemstvos*. The new Over Procurator of the Synod was Samarin, Marshal of the Moscow nobility, a sincere and honorable member of the church; he was chosen in spite of the Tsaritsa and of Rasputin (July 5, 1915). In his letter of June 15, 1915, the Tsar wrote to his wife, "Old Gorem., and Krivoshein and Shcherbatov have all told me . . . [that Sabler, Rasputin's Over Procurator, must go], and believe that Samarin would be the best man for this post. . . . I am sure that you will not like this, because of his being a Muscovite, but these changes must be brought about. . . ." [76] The empress was strongly opposed to the appointment of Samarin; on June 15 she wrote, "(. . . certainly *Samarin* wld. go against our Friend [Rasputin] & stick up for the Bishops we dislike—he is so terribly Moscovite & narrowminded). . . . He [Rasputin] gave over this message for you, that you are to pay less attention to what people will say to you, not let yourself be influenced by them but use yr. own instinct & go by that. . . ." [77] Her letter of the next day also expressed hostility to Samarin, in the following terms: "When Gr. [Rasputin] heard in town yesterday before He left, that *Samarin* was named, . . . He was in utter despair . . . & now the Moscou set will be like a spiders net around us, our Friend's enemies are ours. . . ." [78]

But great was the rejoicing in certain church circles over the fall of Sabler, Over Procurator since 1911. In August, 1915, the Duma members from the ranks of the lower clergy went in full force to Samarin, the new Over Procurator, and presented a petition. It began:

That our church life does not proceed in fully normal fashion there is scarcely need to say. Not only in educated circles, but also among the simple people, of old true to the principles of Orthodoxy and to the church, there is now noted coolness to the church, a decline of the religious

---

[76] *Letters of the Tsar to the Tsaritsa*, p. 60.

[77] *Letters of the Tsaritsa to the Tsar*, p. 95. The empress's letters, which were written in English, contain many mistakes in spelling and grammar.

[78] *Ibid.*, p. 97.

spirit, or an attraction to sectarian false teaching, so widely spread . . . over the face of the Russian land; in connection with this there is a decline in moral life. The authority of the religious pastors seems to diminish more and more, so that even the best and the most energetic of them sometimes fold their arms in helplessness and despair. All this—the decline of faith and morality and the weakening of pastoral authority—is a result of complex and numerous causes, which can scarcely be explained at the present moment. It should only be said that the blame does not always fall on the Orthodox clergy, who are powerless to counteract the corrupting spirit of the times, especially under those conditions under which they have to perform their great work.[79]

The petition continued with an exposition of the weaknesses of the church, and an affirmation that they could be cured only by a church council; the Duma clergy expressed a hope that the new Over Procurator would hasten the summoning of the *Sobor,* which had been so often promised, but never called.[80]

Many in addition to the clergy of the Duma hoped that better days for the church were coming. The reactionary *Moskovskiia Vedomosti* (*Moscow News*) was quoted as saying that when the news of the dismissal of Sabler was printed in the newspapers, "among the clergy it was like Easter Day. All joyfully congratulated one another." The Over Procurator, so the article stated, had made himself thoroughly feared by many of the clergy by assiduously collecting rumors and gossip, by placing his protégés in all the well-paid positions, and by his incessant dabbling in divorce cases.[81] Menshikov, editor of the conservative *Novoe Vremia* (*The New Time*), declared that under Sabler no great or even happy events in the life of the church had occurred, while there continued "the nihilist disorganization of the religious school, the flight of the seminary students in any direction but into the priesthood, the seminary riots, an epidemic of which seized all Russia, the general decline of the ancient class of ministers of the altar of God, the abandonment of many village parishes, and the weakening of belief among the people and the growth of indifference to the Church. . . ." Menshikov closed his indictment with the words, "All the great problems of restoring the church which V. K. Sabler inherited from the past, he left untouched. To his successor he

[79] *Missionerskoe Obozrenie,* Nov., 1915, p. 286.
[80] *Ibid.,* pp. 286 ff.   [81] *Ibid.,* Sept., 1915, p. 97.

handed unpacked baggage of good intentions and abandoned beginnings." [82] *Moskovskiia Vedomosti* made the remarkable statement that

Not one newspaper, Right, Left, or Moderate, has uttered one single word of approval for the dismissed dignitary. . . . This remarkable fact must be noted. Even those journals which were created by Sabler for his own personal ends are silent. Evidently, it is necessary either to speak the truth and to pronounce the same stern sentence that we read in the words of Menshikov, or . . . to keep silent. Positively, literally nothing good can be said.[83]

Under these circumstances, great hopes were entertained that a new era had dawned for Russia and for the church. A strong press campaign against Rasputin began almost immediately. On August 16, Paleologue, French Ambassador at St. Petersburg, wrote: "For the first time [since the beginning of the war] Rasputin has been attacked by the press. Hitherto the censorship and the police had protected him against all newspaper criticism. It is the *Bourse Gazette* [*Birzhevyia Vedomosti*] that leads the campaign." The *Gazette* ruthlessly exposed "the man's whole past, his ignoble beginnings, his thefts, his drunken bouts, his debaucheries, his intrigues, the scandal of his relations with high society, high officials, and upper clergy." It closed with the words, "Today Russia means to put an end to all this." [84]

However, Samarin's hold on power was brief. He soon crossed swords with Rasputin's friend and protégé, Bishop Varnava of Tobolsk. Varnava had apparently won the dislike of at least a part of his flock, for Sukhanov, a member of the Labor party in the Duma, stated that on July 11, 1915, a deputation of citizens of Tobolsk had presented a petition to the Over Secretary of the Synod then in their midst, asking that the bishop be transferred to another diocese. The reason given for the request was that their archpastor was under the influence of Rasputin, known to many in Tobolsk as a horse-thief and a *Khlyst*. Moreover, the complaint declared that many of Varnava's

---

[82] *Ibid.*, pp. 96–97.   [83] *Ibid.*, p. 97.

[84] M. Paleologue, *La Russie des tsars pendant la grande guerre*, II, 57. An invaluable source. Paleologue was hostile to the empress and to Rasputin, whom he blamed for much of Russia's ineffectiveness as an ally, but, none the less, his intimate contacts with the leading men of the time give his book great historical value.

sermons were so unbecoming that women and children had to be sent out of the cathedral when he preached. An expurgated version of one of his sermons was printed in the local diocesan periodical; Sukhanov, who described it to the Duma's Budget Commission, said that the bishop had explained the slaughter of Russian soldiers as God's punishment for the practice of abortion, introduced into Russia by the Germans. "We ask often: will this war soon end? But is it time to raise this question? Does the number of our dead sons equal the number of innocent babes who have been killed by their foolish mothers in their wombs?" [85]

While these reports must have held some interest for Samarin, the immediate reason for his action against Bishop Varnava was the issue, raised by the bishop, of the canonization of Archbishop Ioann Maximovich of Tobolsk, who died in 1715. Canonization of a saint customarily brought the rank of archbishop to the bishop in whose diocese the relics of the saint were found; moreover, it usually led to the coming of numerous pilgrims to worship at the shrine of the saint. The Synod began gathering data on the question of the canonization of Ioann of Tobolsk, but much too slowly, apparently, for Varnava. He began to use his influence with Rasputin, for on August 29 the Tsaritsa wrote to the Tsar, "Perhaps you better give Samarin the short order that you wish *Bishop Varnava to chant the laudation of St. John Maximovich* because *Samarin* intends getting rid of him [Varnava], because we like him & he is good to Gr. [Rasputin]." [86] The Tsar gave permission for the "laudation" of Ioann—an act which was a preliminary to canonization, but did not suffice to raise Ioann to sainthood. And, unbeknown to the Synod, Nicholas sent the order direct to Varnava, who thereupon performed the laudation without the consent of the Synod. [87]

Samarin had already shown his dislike of Varnava by calling him to Petrograd. The empress wrote to the Tsar that the Over Procurator "abused our Friend [Rasputin], & said that *Hermogen* had been the only honest man, because he was not afraid to tell you all against *Gregory* & therefore he was shut up, & that he, *Samarin,* wishes *Varnava* to

[85] Gosudarstvennaia Duma, *Doklady Biudzhetnoi Komissii,* IV Duma, Session IV, No. 4, Stenogram, pp. 16–17.

[86] *Letters of the Tsaritsa,* p. 128.   [87] Paleologue, *op. cit.,* II, 150.

go & tell you all against *Gregory.* . . ." Varnava refused. The indignant empress thereupon asked for the head of the Over Procurator: ". . . he does nothing in the *Synod* & only persecutes our Friend, i. e. goes straight against us both—unpardonable, & at such a time even criminal. He must leave." [88] Samarin rebuked Varnava with even greater vigor after he had learned about the laudation of Ioann of Tobolsk. The empress wrote to her husband, "I saw poor *Varnava* today my dear, its abominable how *Samarin* behaved to him in the hotel & then in the *Synod*—such cross-examination as is unheard of & spoke so meanly about *Gregory,* using vile words in speaking of Him." Another passage read:

Samarin said highest praise of *Feofan* & *Hermogen* [Hermogen had just returned from exile], & wants to put the latter in *Varnava's* place. You see the rotten game of theirs. . . . *Agafangel* [archbishop of Iaroslavl, a member of the Synod] spoke so badly . . . —he ought to be sent away *on the retiring list* & replaced [in the diocese of Iaroslavl] by *Sergei F.* [archbishop of Finland] who must leave and get out of the *Synod—Nikon* ought to be cleaned out of the *Council of the Empire,* where he is a *member* & also out of the *Synod,* he has besides the sin of *Mt. Athos* on his soul. . . .
. . . Let them see & feel that you are not a boy & [that] who calumniates people you respect & insults them—insults you, that they dare not call a Bishop to account for knowing *Gregory*—I cant repeat to you all the names they gave our Friend. . . . [89]

A few days after this appeal, the Tsaritsa wrote: "The article about *Varnava* in the papers is untrue, he gave exact answers to all questions and showed yr. telegram about the *salutation* [the ceremony performed before canonization]. . . . *Varnava* implores you to hurry with clearing out *Samarin* as he and the *Synod* are intending to do more horrors and he has to go there again, poor man, to be tortured." [90]

However, Varnava did not go to the Synod again, because, wrote the empress to her husband, "he will not hear yr. orders mocked at— the *Metropolitan* [Vladimir of Petrograd] calls yr. telegram 'foolish telegram.' " The empress implored the Tsar to "set yr. broom working & clear out the dirts . . . at the *Synod,*" and once more attacked Samarin, who had "told his set at *Moscou* that he took it [the Over

[88] *Letters of the Tsaritsa,* p. 146.   [89] *Ibid.,* pp. 150–51.
[90] *Ibid.,* pp. 153–54.

Procuratorship] only because he intends to get rid of *Gregory* & that he will do all in his power to succeed." [91] Although "the papers are furious that he wont appear," Varnava went back to Tobolsk on the advice of Rasputin, in defiance of Samarin and his supporters in the Synod.[92] Samarin determined to place the defiant bishop on the retired list, but instead fell from power himself. Already the empress had been suggesting possible successors to the emperor,[93] and when the Over Procurator attempted to obtain confirmation of the Synod's decree ousting Varnava, the Tsar refused, and almost immediately afterward Samarin's resignation was requested (the end of September, 1915).[94] The press took up the matter, and the evidence of the intervention of Rasputin in the affairs of the church was presented to the public in a manner which brought little profit to the church.[95]

Samarin's brief Over Procuratorship did not destroy Rasputin's influence at court; it did, however, lead the latter to go into hiding for a time. When Samarin had assumed office, he at once served notice on the Tsar that Rasputin must go. The peasant was, in consequence, instructed to leave Petrograd for a few weeks.[96] But he soon returned.

After the fall of Samarin, the hold of Rasputin upon the church soon grew even stronger than before. According to Beletskii, Rasputin, Khvostov, Varnava, and Rasputin's familiar, Prince Andronikov, decided on Volzhin, whom Paleologue, the French Ambassador, calls "an obscure and servile official," [97] as the next Over Procurator. Volzhin had won the favor of Rasputin by his promise to bring to a satisfactory end the canonization of Ioann of Tobolsk and by his willingness to cease the persecution of the monks expelled from Mt. Athos.[98] The empress thereupon received the successful candidate; she wrote to the Tsar that Volzhin had made a "perfect impression," and that he seemed "the right man in the right place." [99] He was appointed in October, 1915. This triumph was followed by the transfer of Metro-

[91] *Letters of the Tsaritsa*, p. 156.   [92] *Ibid.*, p. 159.   [93] *Ibid.*, pp. 146, 159.
[94] Paleologue, *op. cit.*, II, 150–51; G. Buchanan, *My Mission to Russia*, I, 249; Rodzianko, *op. cit.*, pp. 157–58.
[95] Gosudarstvennaia Duma, *Doklady Biudzhetnoi Komissii*, IV Duma, Session IV, No. 4, Stenogram, pp. 17–18.
[96] Buchanan, *op. cit.*, I, 247.   [97] Paleologue, *op. cit.*, II, 151.
[98] Shchegolev, *op. cit.*, IV, 164–67.   [99] *Letters of the Tsaritsa*, p. 193.

politan Vladimir of Petrograd, primate of the Russian Church, who had opposed Varnava in his conflict with Samarin,[100] to the lesser post of Kiev, and the installation in the see of Petrograd of Pitirim, who as bishop of Samara and later as exarch of Georgia had already proved himself to be Rasputin's friend.[101] On November 12, 1915, the Tsaritsa wrote that Pitirim was ". . . a worthy man, and a great *Worshiper*, as our Friend says. He forsees *Volzhin's* fright & that he will try to dissuade you, but begs you to be firm, as he [Pitirim] is the only suitable man." [102] The naming of Pitirim as metropolitan of Petrograd caused much excitement, not only because he was believed to owe his place to Rasputin, but also because the transfer of Metropolitan Vladimir was effected without asking the approval of the Synod.[103] V. P. Shein, a member of the moderate Right of the Duma, told the Budget Commission that ". . . not a hundredth part of what loud-mouthed rumor noises abroad in seeking the causes of this unexplained occurrence, has appeared in the press. . . ." [104] One result was that much sympathy was aroused for Metropolitan Vladimir—"expressed in the form of sometimes badly concealed protests." In the speeches made during the farewell ceremonies he was "termed a cross-bearer who carries on his shoulders a heavy burden. Verses were consecrated to him, in which . . . you may find such lines as, 'For thou didst not fear the strong.' " [105]

The current suspicions of the reason for the appointment of Pitirim were not without foundation. Even while he was archbishop of Samara, he was proved to be a supporter of Rasputin; when, in 1914, as has been related, the latter was stabbed by a former mistress in his native village, Pitirim sent him a telegram of condolence, expressing hopes that God would aid his recovery; this fact was told under oath in 1917 by A. Naumov, Minister of Agriculture under the Tsar.[106] According to A. Khvostov, Minister of Internal Affairs in 1915, ". . . Rasputin made Pitirim! He transferred him to the Caucasus (that was the time when there became known the telegram of Ras-

---

[100] *Ibid.*, p. 156; p. 159.

[101] Paleologue, *op. cit.*, II, 151; Shchegolev, *op. cit.*, I, 356, Andronikov.

[102] *Letters of the Tsaritsa*, p. 218.

[103] Gosudarstvennaia Duma, *Doklady Biudzhetnoi Komissii*, IV Duma, Session IV, No. 4, Stenogram, p. 31.

[104] *Ibid.*   [105] *Ibid.*   [106] Shchegolev, *op. cit.*, I, 335.

putin, 'The Siberian marmot to the Caucasus, and to us the blessing.'
. . . The telegram was transmitted by hand to the Duma. . . . 'To
us the blessing'—that is, move Varnava to Tobolsk: in Greek Varnava
means blessing)." [107] When in 1915 a metropolitan had to be named
in place of Flavian, Volzhin submitted the names of several possible candidates to the "holy man," Rasputin; however, the latter
threw out the name of Bishop Konstantin of Mogilev, Volzhin's
suggestion for the place, as this bishop was known to be openly opposed to Rasputin. He insisted on Pitirim, who was named to the see
of Petrograd in spite of Volzhin's unfavorable report to the Tsar.[108]

By this stroke Rasputin became supreme in the church. According
to the promise made to him by Volzhin, the affair of Bishop Varnava
was quickly ended. Not only did the bishop escape punishment, but
he was even honored by the award of a decoration from the emperor.[109]
Not long after that he was raised to the archepiscopal rank which he
had sought, and Ioann of Tobolsk was formally recognized by the
Synod as a saint.[110] Other friends of Rasputin sought, and many of
them received, favors in the realm of church affairs, while not a few
of those who had opposed him were humbled. Rasputin protected a
certain peasant, Vasilii, who stood regularly in front of the Kazan
Cathedral in Petrograd in monastic garb soliciting donations, although the bishop of his diocese wanted him unfrocked and sent away
from the capital, and the police had evidence that he was a law-
breaker.[111] Dean Vostorgov of Moscow, a friend of Rasputin, was
eager to become vicarian bishop of Moscow, while Metropolitan Pitirim suggested making him archbishop of Irkutsk, as he had been active in the missionary field. Beletskii asked Dr. Dubrovin, head of the
Union of the Russian People, for his opinion of Vostorgov; Dubrovin
produced an article in which Vostorgov had criticized Rasputin. This
evidence was sent to the "holy man," who at once disposed of the
hopeful candidate with the words, "Now it's the lid [*kryshka*] for
Vostorgov; he'll get nothing." [112] Archbishop Innokentii of Irkutsk
was removed from his see because the Department of Police had found

---

[107] Shchegolev, *op. cit.*, I, 25–26.   [108] *Ibid.*, IV, 191–96.
[109] *Ibid.*, III, 398, Beletskii.   [110] *Ibid.*; Paleologue, *op. cit.*, II, 200.
[111] Shchegolev, *op. cit.*, IV, 310, Beletskii.   [112] *Ibid.*, IV, 289–90, Beletskii.

a letter from him in which he freely spoke his thoughts concerning the destructive influence of Rasputin upon the church, his debasing effect upon the hierarchy, and the scandal of his relations with the imperial family. Beletskii related that Vyrubova, Volzhin, and Metropolitan Pitirim were informed of this correspondence, and the result was the removal of Archbishop Innokentii from his see. It proved necessary to take "a number of measures to obviate possible actions of a demonstrative character at the farewell of his flock and clergy to the bishop." [113]

Rasputin seems to have been especially anxious to harry out of the capital any men who might acquire an influence rivaling his own. A certain Father Mardarii, who was popular in the salons of Petrograd and often visited the palace, incurred his enmity. Although Father Mardarii had found a position in the capital as a teacher of religion, Rasputin had him appointed to the Caucasus, "in spite of all the entreaties of several ladies. . . ." On another occasion a barefooted religious wanderer came to the palace at Tsarskoe Selo, whereupon Rasputin became much upset, and had him sent away.[114]

Another example of Rasputin's power was presented when he drove Father Vostokov out of Moscow. This man, editor of the religious journal *Otkliki na Zhizn'* (*Responses to Life*), was very active in opposition to all that Rasputin represented. He directed scathing criticism against Bishop Varnava of Tobolsk,[115] and in addition to preaching sermons against Rasputin, printed in his periodical a petition which he and his parishioners signed, denouncing the powerful adventurer.[116] When Samarin was dismissed, the empress wrote to the Tsar, on October 3, 1915:

> So silly, in Moscou they want to give *Samarin* an address [of welcome] when he returns. . . .—it seems that horror *Vostokov* has sent him a telegram in the name of his two "*flocks*," *Moscou & Kolomna* [Father Vostokov had been sent from his Moscow parish to a suburban church]—so the dear little *Makari* [metropolitan of Moscow] wrote to the *Consistory* to insist upon a copy of *Vostokov's* telegram to *Samarin* & to know what

[113] *Ibid.*, IV, 291.   [114] *Ibid.*, IV, 309–10.

[115] Gosudarstvennaia Duma, *Stenograficheskie Otchety*, IV Duma, Session IV, Part 2, col. 2350.

[116] Shchegolev, *op. cit.*, IV, 288, Beletskii.

gave him the right to forward such a telegr.—how good, if the little Metropolitan can get rid of *Vostokov*, its high time, he does endless harm & its he who leads *Samarin*.[117]

A year later V. N. Lvov told the Duma: "In Moscow Father Vostokov was brought to trial by Metropolitan Makarii, merely because he permitted himself to criticize sharply, according to his priestly conscience, a foul person known to all. When Metropolitan Makarii demanded that Vostokov stop his attacks upon Rasputin, he refused." The stubborn priest was tried on the charge of heresy, which should have been prosecuted to the end; "but how lightly this accusation was made, was shown by the fact that when Bishop Andrei . . . took Father Vostokov into his diocese of Ufa, the attacks upon . . . [the latter] ceased immediately." An indignant comment on this case was made by the "esteemed Dean Arsen'ev" of Moscow, who declared before a diocesan congress that "the case of Vostokov is a shame for the clergy of Moscow." [118]

The chief source of Rasputin's power at this time was apparently the empress, who, as before, was convinced of his holiness. Of him she wrote to the Tsar, ". . . a man of God's near one gives the strength, faith & hope one needs so sorely." [119] Additional evidence of the part played by Rasputin in the life of the empress, and through her, in the affairs of Russia, was given at Easter, 1916. The French Ambassador Paleologue learned from a trustworthy source that the empress attended service in the Feodorovskii Cathedral in Tsarkoe Selo with her three older daughters; and behind them stood Rasputin with Mmes Vyrubova and Turovich. "When Alexandra Feodorovna advanced to the ikonostas to receive the eucharistic Bread and the precious Blood, she glanced at the *starets* [Rasputin], who followed her and took the sacrament immediately after her. Then, before the altar, they exchanged the kiss of peace, Rasputin kissing the empress on the forehead and she returning the kiss, on his hand." [120]

There is no reason to think that this was a guilty kiss. Few students of the period, even those numbered among the enemies of the imperial

[117] *Letters of the Tsaritsa*, p. 186.
[118] Gosudarstvennaia Duma, *Stenograficheskie Otchety*, IV Duma, Session V, cols. 612–13.
[119] *Letters of the Tsaritsa*, p. 443.　　　[120] Paleologue, *op. cit.*, II, 250–51.

regime, believe that the Empress Alexandra was anything but a true and loving wife to Nicholas II. Her letters to the Tsar are too full of sincere affection for any reader to be convinced that her relations with Rasputin were sinful.

The fact that she was on terms of such intimacy with this adventurer was enough to enhance his prestige greatly among those who wanted special favors which could not be obtained through normal channels. Consequently, he was surrounded by a shady crew of seekers after privilege, especially during the last year and a half of his life. Chaplin, an important official in the Ministry of Justice, testified in 1917 that he had been repeatedly bothered by some lady who was interested in a well-known law suit involving the Aleksandro-Svirskii Monastery—"an entirely hopeless case." She insisted that the matter would go through. "When, foaming at the mouth, I began to tell her that it would not, she said, 'You're too young to know how these things are handled.' " The case was repeatedly rejected, but she continued to press the suit and finally an imperial order was received to grant her wish. "She told me her power lay in the fact that she had known Rasputin when he was still needy and unknown; he always remembered this, and she invariably had success." [121]

A less successful intervention of the "holy man" took place in the case of Abbot Anatolii of Samara, who wished to become a vicar of that diocese. According to V. N. Lvov, Anatolii was almost entirely illiterate, so that even the Synod hesitated, and asked that he take an examination on the Scriptures in order to determine his fitness for the post. He made such a bad showing that Lvov raised in the Duma the question whether he was fit to be, not in charge of a diocese, but even in charge of a monastery.[122] Father Krylov of Samara, who spoke after Lvov, gave the Duma the following explanation of the candidacy of such a person: "This abbot, who did not know one Old Testament prophet, . . . in conversation with me disclosed his acquaintance with the well-known 'holy man' Rasputin [laughter], whom Abbot Anatolii considers a great ascetic sent down from on high, for the

[121] Shchegolev, op. cit., VII, 45. Chaplin was probably speaking about the well-known lawsuit involving the Aleksandro-Svirskaia Church, rather than of a monastery of that name.
[122] Gosudarstvennaia Duma, Stenograficheskie Otchety, IV Duma, Session V. cols. 614–15.

salvation of sinful Petrograd." [123] Abbot Anatolii failed to receive his coveted advancement.

However, the fate of lesser fry like Anatolii mattered little to Rasputin, as compared with his success in getting his partisan Pitirim made metropolitan of Petrograd. Once installed in his high post, Pitirim was most circumspect. He professed to have no dealings with Rasputin and, although the latter visited him frequently, the visits were secret.[124] The intimacy of Pitirim and Rasputin did not, however, long remain unknown. Prince Andronikov, a member of Rasputin's circle, testified in 1917 that ". . . when I returned [from a journey] Rasputin asked, 'Do you know Pitirim?' I said, 'No, I don't.' 'Then go and see him; he is a very fine man. He is ours.' " [125] Khvostov, Minister of Internal Affairs for a few months in 1915 and 1916, told in 1917 how he had gratified his curiosity as to whether the metropolitan was actually seeing Rasputin. General Komissarov, an officer of gendarmes then on duty in the capital, reported that Rasputin and Pitirim were intimates, and arranged for Khvostov to pay an unexpected visit to the metropolitan. "He arranged that I should come to Pitirim after a trip to Tsarskoe, [and] I went in without announcement and found them, with Pitirim sitting without his cowl, in very intimate conversation [with Rasputin]." [126] Komissarov described the incident somewhat differently; according to him, Khvostov arranged for Komissarov to bring Rasputin to the metropolitan, which he did. Rasputin and Komissarov were admitted to the monastery, and waited. "After a while Pitirim came out. Between them [Pitirim and Rasputin] it was 'thee' and 'thou' [in the Russian language, used only between intimates]. They kissed. I bowed, Pitirim blessed me. Then he raised his eyes and said, 'Who is this?' I said, 'General Komissarov, on special mission.' He [Pitirim] recoiled a step or two from me. Rasputin shouted at the top of his voice, and ran to Khvostov. . . . Pitirim had been stating to Khvostov that he never saw Rasputin. . . ." [127]

With the coming of Pitirim to the see of Petrograd Rasputin's hold over the church became very strong; at the same time, he also felt the

[123] Gosudarstvennaia Duma, *Stenograficheskie Otchety*, IV Duma, Session V, col. 620.
[124] Shchegolev, *op. cit.*, IV, Beletskii; *ibid.*, I, 25, Khvostov.
[125] *Ibid.*, I, 367.   [126] *Ibid.*, VI, 83.   [127] *Ibid.*, III, 168–69.

need to strengthen his influence over the civil government. On January 20, 1916, the aged Prime Minister Goremykin was replaced by Stürmer, a politician of indifferent reputation. What made this act in the game of "ministerial leapfrog" particularly distasteful to wide circles of society was that the appointment was ascribed to the influence of Pitirim and Rasputin. The testimony of Manasevich-Manuilov, a journalist of ill repute connected with *Novoe Vremia,* showed that there was some basis for this supposition. Before the Extraordinary Investigating Commission in April, 1917, he testified to a conversation with Pitirim before Goremykin's removal, on the subject of a successor to the aged Prime Minister, whose policies Pitirim feared. "I then put the question directly, 'Who is it to be?' Then Osipenko, the secretary . . . [of Metropolitan Pitirim] said, 'I know who' and he named Stürmer. . . . I said, "What—Stürmer?' He said, 'Yes, yes, I know it from trustworthy sources,' and Pitirim nodded his head, confirming the statement made to me by Osipenko." To this Manasevich-Manuilov added that Pitirim "was taking an undoubted part in the appointment of the President of the Council of Ministers. This was clear from my entire conversation with Pitirim, from everything that I heard there." [128]

The empress also was interested in the appointment of Stürmer. On January 7, 1916, she wrote to the Tsar, ". . . He [Stürmer] very much values *Gregory* wh. is a great thing." [129] Additional evidence as to the connection between Rasputin, Pitirim, and Stürmer, was given in 1917 by Rodzianko, President of the Duma. He declared that ". . . Stürmer did not need a salon in order to increase his political influence; he was so very strong at the Aleksandro-Nevskaia Monastery. Monks kept running to me and saying that Rasputin was constantly sitting there with Pitirim and Stürmer." [130] Moreover, Paleologue, the French Ambassador, who was following the course of events with keen interest, wrote in his diary on February 13, 1916:

Stürmer's growing and open favor with the empress and the confidence reposed in him by the emperor, are causing a lively agitation in the Holy Synod. The whole clan of Rasputin is rejoicing. Metropolitan Pitirim, and Bishops Varnava and Isidor already feel themselves masters of the

---

[128] *Ibid.,* II, 30–32.   [129] *Letters of the Tsaritsa,* p. 256.
[130] Shchegolev, *op. cit.,* VII, 150.

ecclesiastical hierarchy; they are announcing for the near future a radical purification of the higher clergy—in other words, the elimination of all the prelates, priors, and abbots who still refuse to bow before the mystic erotomaniac of Pokrovskoe, because they regard him as Antichrist. Lists of degradations and dismissals have been circulating for several days, and even lists of those destined for exile to the distant monasteries of Siberia. . . .[131]

The circle of Rasputin's supporters among the clergy, as this passage indicates, included others beside Varnava, and Metropolitans Makarii and Pitirim. Bishop Isidor of Viatka was another of his intimates. On October 1, 1916, the empress wrote to the Tsar, "Spent a quiet, peaceful evening 8-½-10-¼ with our Friend, Bishop Issidor— Bish. Melchizidek. . . ."[132] The latter was a young bishop recently brought to Kronstadt from the Caucasus. Another newcomer to the capital was Bishop Antonii, brought from the Caucasus and made vicar of Petrograd by Pitirim; according to Beletskii, Antonii was a visitor at Rasputin's home.[133] Rodzianko relates that while in process of drawing up, by order of the Tsar, a report on Rasputin, he was visited by Damanskii, Assistant Over Procurator, who asked him to drop the matter, as "a very exalted person," admittedly the empress, desired it. Damanskii was supported in this request by Dean Vasil'ev, teacher of religion to the Tsarevich; the priest was much taken aback when Rodzianko rebuked him for supporting such a scoundrel as Rasputin.[134]

On the other hand, a goodly number of prelates were known to be hostile to the "holy man." Metropolitan Vladimir of Kiev has already been mentioned as his enemy; Bishop Hermogen was released in 1915, and again became for a time a center of opposition to Rasputin.[135] Other hierarchs whom the empress regarded as hostile were Archbishops Nikon, Agafangel of Iaroslavl, Sergii of Finland,[136] and Antonii of Khar'kov (formerly of Volhynia).[137] However, after Pitirim had been installed in Petrograd, there was little that these malcontents could do without risking the overthrow of the regime, and

[131] Paleologue, *op. cit.*, II, 179.   [132] *Letters of the Tsaritsa*, p. 421.
[133] Shchegolev, *op. cit.*, IV, 199.
[134] *Ibid.*, VII, 160–61; Rodzianko, *The Reign of Rasputin*, pp. 53–55.
[135] *Letters of the Tsaritsa*, pp. 137, 148, 363–64.   [136] *Ibid.*, p. 151.
[137] Referred to as A. V. by the Empress, *ibid.*, p. 218.

they kept silent. Indeed, while individual prelates grumbled, the Synod as a body showed its subservience. On September 21, 1916, the empress wrote to her husband: "Fancy, the *Synod* wants to present me with a *Testimonial* & Image (because of my work for the wounnded, I think). . . . Since Catherine no Empress has personally received them alone, *Gregory* is delighted (I less so)—but strange, is it not, I, whom they feared & disapproved of always." [138] A few days later she wrote, "The *Synod* gave me a lovely old Image & *Pitirim* read a nice *paper*—I mumbled an answer." [139]

However, while Pitirim, Rasputin, and their supporters were dominant, the voices of the laymen who detested their authority grew louder and louder. In November, 1916, Miliukov, leader of the dominant Progressive bloc (which included all parties of the Duma except the extreme Right and the extreme Left), startled the Duma by citing the *Berliner Tageblatt* to show that Manasevich-Manuilov, Prince Andronikov, and Metropolitan Pitirim had been "participants, together with Rasputin, in the appointment of Stürmer [noise from the Left]. . . ." [140] On the twenty-ninth of the month Father Nemertsalov of the National Progressive party told the Duma, "Our obligation is to cry loudly, in the hearing of all, to all Orthodox Rus, 'The Orthodox Church is in danger: brothers, protect it!' " [141] In the Council of State the famous liberal, Prince E. N. Trubetskoi, began a speech with the words, "The ministers change, but Rasputin remains," and continued: ". . . I speak not as a representative of this or that political party, I speak far more as a believing Christian and as a true son of the Orthodox Church. For the church, this is an even worse evil, even a worse collapse, than for the state. Hence I am waiting. . . . I still have not lost hope that the silence of the pastors of the church, which so disturbs me, will end." [142] And Dean Butkevich of the same chamber praised Prince Trubetskoi's speech, saying, "He, as an Orthodox, believing Christian, has pointed out to us that frightening, gaping ulcer that threatens to infect the whole church organism,

[138] *Ibid.*, p. 406.   [139] *Ibid.*, p. 415.
[140] Gosudarstvennaia Duma, *Stenograficheskie Otchety*, IV Duma, Session V, col. 39.
[141] *Ibid.*, col. 621.
[142] Gosudarstvennyi Sovet, *Stenograficheskii Otchet*, Session XIII, cols. 122–23.

and I must only confirm the fact that, actually, this ulcer is frightful, that it may cause too great harm, not only to the church, but even to Orthodox people in general." [143]

Some of the prophets of disaster made their predictions in more specific fashion. As early as February 26, 1916, Father Gepetskii, a member of the Center party, declared to the Duma:

Here are the disturbing words of one of the deputies, spoken before the Budget Commission, that if matters continue thus, he fears that a catastrophe awaits us, that very many hierarchs and Orthodox persons will proclaim their independence of the Synod and will proclaim [its] uncanonical nature, and we shall see a division of the Orthodox Church— an unheard-of disgrace for the church. Of course this, God grant, will never be, but it is characteristic and symptomatic that such speeches are uttered in those circles of society which until now have been exceedingly restrained.[144]

Nine months later (November 29, 1916) V. N. Lvov declared to the Duma:

. . . I know that many noted prelates who cannot bear to see how the Synod is losing its authority are gathering bishops around them in their cells and are taking counsel how to end this church scandal. We, gentlemen, are on the eve of seeing part of the hierarchy raise a cry against this collapse of the church. . . . What if . . . there should occur . . . a split of the hierarchy into two parts—one, composed of those who stand for the Most Holy Synod [voice from the Left: "For Rasputin!"], and the other, of those who, seeing the lack of authority of the Most Holy Synod, may declare themselves in canonical fashion a free Council of hierarchs.[145]

Another highly significant warning to the church was uttered in December, 1916, by the Congress of the United Nobility, held in Moscow:

. . . Irresponsible dark forces strange to the lawful authorities are burrowing into the state administration. These forces have subjected to their power the supreme authority, and are infringing even upon the administration of the church. . . .

---

[143] Gosudarstvennyi Sovet, *Stenograficheskii Otchet*, Session XIII, col. 220.

[144] Gosudarstvennaia Duma, *Stenograficheskie Otchety*, IV Duma, Session IV, Part 2, col. 2315.

[145] *Ibid.*, Session V, col. 613.

The most worthy holy ones of the church are disturbed by the scandal occurring before the eyes of all. The church, the protectress of Christian truth, does not hear the freely spoken words of its bishops, but sees that they are oppressed. . . .[146]

With these examples before it, the press could not be restrained. Although Protopopov, Minister of Internal Affairs, ordered the censors to forbid articles attacking Metropolitan Pitirim,[147] the latter's friend, Prince Zhevakhov, wrote: ". . . [the newspapers] openly called Metropolitan Pitirim a Rasputinite, they spoke of his sympathies for the 'holy man.' . . . They said that the metropolitan received this high position thanks entirely to Rasputin. . . ."[148] Even the extremely conservative *Novoe Vremia* in December, 1916, printed editorials highly critical of the administration of the church. On December 2 a leading article, entitled "The Voice of the People," declared that the comments of the nobles, the Duma, and the Council of State represented public opinion concerning the church. "We see that laymen—ordinary Orthodox persons—have been forced to defend the church—and from what? From the hierarchs, and from the Synod. Is this not a disaster?"[149] On the eighteenth an article commenting upon an example of episcopal highhandedness closed with the words, "One wishes to exclaim, 'Well, did you ever hear of Christianity?' "[150]

Although no one could say a word of defense for the followers of Rasputin, these attacks had little effect upon his protectors. ". . . The only result is that the Emperor, by an act obviously intended to flout the Duma, issued on his Name Day a special Rescript, thanking the Metropolitan for his services."[151] On December 13, 1916, the empress wrote to the Tsar, praising his firmness in defiance of the Duma. "There were a lot of paris [bets] in the *Duma* that *Pitirim* wld. be sent away—now that he got the cross, they have become crushed & small (you see, when you show yourself the master). . . ."[152]

The attack on the supporters of Rasputin in church circles also fell on Prince Zhevakhov, on November 29, 1916. Over Procurator Volzhin had lost the favor of the empress, as he had become hostile to Ras-

---

[146] *Novoe Vremia*, Dec. 2, 1916.   [147] Shchegolev, *op. cit.*, IV, 40–41.
[148] Zhevakhov, *Vospominaniia Tovarishcha Ober-Prokurora*, I, 189–90.
[149] *Novoe Vremia*, Dec. 2, 1916.   [150] *Ibid.*, Dec. 18, 1916.
[151] Hoare, *The Fourth Seal*, p. 114.   [152] *Letters of the Tsaritsa*, p. 454.

putin's clique,[153] and on August 7, 1916, he had been dismissed; he was replaced by N. P. Raev, son of former Metropolitan Palladii, and known chiefly as head of a women's college.[154] Prince Zhevakhov, who had for some months been in the empress's favor, was made Raev's second assistant on September 15, 1916. Beletskii declared in 1917 that Zhevakhov received the post of Second Assistant Over Procurator over the heads of other candidates because Rasputin felt that it was desirable to have his supporter close to the Over Procurator.[155] However, there were signs that the Duma would object to the creation of this new administrative position without its consent, so Zaionchkovskii, who was already First Assistant Over Procurator, was relegated to the senate, and his post was given to Prince Zhevakhov.[156] V. N. Lvov led the debate on a proposed interpellation on this subject, on November 29, 1916, and declared that the creation of this "sinecure" had been only one more instance which "gives me the right to touch on and to sketch, with pain in my heart, . . . the picture of the ruin of all our Orthodox Russian Church." ". . . I add to that: the fatherland is in danger and the church is in danger." [157] Under such conditions, he declared, it was his duty to criticize the hierarchs of the church:

We see presiding over the Synod . . . Metropolitan Pitirim of Petrograd, who, instead of busying himself with his diocesan affairs, instead of watching over men's consciences, of acting as pastor, of forming proper judgments concerning the men entering the priesthood, travels to all the ends of Russia and takes a hand in appointments, not to the priesthood, but to the Council of Ministers and to administrative posts. Is it the work of the metropolitan of Petrograd to busy himself with politics, and not with church affairs? [158]

Lvov's philippic was followed by a speech from Father Budilovich, who also criticized the appointment of Prince Zhevakhov. His point of view was that this was another instance of the narrow, bureaucratic

---

[153] *Letters of the Tsaritsa*, pp. 256 and 364; Shchegolev, *op. cit.*, II, 65–66, Manasevich-Manuilov.
[154] Shchegolev, *loc. cit.*; *Letters of the Tsaritsa*, p. 364.
[155] Shchegolev, *op. cit.*, IV, 222–25.   [156] *Ibid.*
[157] Gosudarstvennaia Duma, *Stenograficheskie Otchety*, IV Duma, Session V, cols. 608–11.
[158] *Ibid.*, col. 612.

spirit in control of the church, a spirit which was out of harmony with the feelings of clergy and laymen.[159] Three other speakers also touched on Zhevakhov's appointment; of these, two were from the clergy. And yet, not one voice was raised in the Duma in defense of the authorities of the church. Priority was speedily voted for the interpellation, and it was passed by a large majority.[160]

With the Duma and the press in such a critical frame of mind, it was only natural that the authority of the church should suffer. Zhevakhov in his memoirs has pointed out that several members of the Synod were exceedingly hostile to Raev and to himself. "The chief cause of the opposition of the Synod . . . lay in the fact that we were both friends of Metropolitan Pitirim, toward whom the Synod continued to manifest intense hostility." [161] Likewise in society at large the subservience of the upper hierarchy to unsavory influences aroused hostility. "What is happening, and what is in store for us, is abominable," former minister Krivoshein told Paleologue in February, 1916. "The Most Holy Synod has never before sunk so low! If they wanted to destroy all respect for religion, all religious faith, they would not go about it in any other way. What will be left of the Orthodox Church ere long? When Tsarism, in danger, seeks its support, it'll find nothing left." [162] Paleologue reported in March, 1916, that Kokovtsov, former President of the Council of Ministers, "whose perspicacious patriotism and sound good sense I greatly admire," came to him in a very pessimistic mood. Much of this discouragement, the Frenchman found, arose from the demoralization of the Russian clergy. "In a grief-stricken tone, which occasionally made his grave voice tremble," Kokovtsov declared:

The religious forces of this country will not be able to withstand much longer the abominable strain upon them. The episcopate and the high ecclesiastical offices are now completely under the heel of the Rasputin clique. It's like an infamous disease, a gangrene which will soon have devoured all the higher organs of the church. I could shed tears of shame when I think of the ignoble traffic that goes on sometimes in the offices of the Holy Synod.[163]

---

[159] *Ibid.*, col. 623.   [160] *Ibid.*, cols. 608–26.
[161] Zhevakhov, *op. cit.*, I, 182–83; 190.
[162] Paleologue, *op. cit.*, II, 179–80.   [163] *Ibid.*, II, 230–31.

He went on to say that the attitude of the parish priests boded no good. They had always been poor, humble, and oppressed: "you've no idea what an accumulation of grief and bitterness there is in the hearts of some of our priests." And now, he declared, revolutionary propaganda was seeping into their minds, especially those of the sem inarians: ". . . their minds are only too ready to receive the seed of the socialist gospel; and, to complete their perversion, agitators excite them against the higher clergy by telling them of the Rasputin scandals." [164]

Apparently the stories concerning Rasputin were very widely current. Gilliard, tutor to the imperial children, wrote in 1916 that "all were agreed" on the need for breaking the power of Rasputin. "For many he was an emanation of Satan, the Antichrist whose heralded coming was to be the signal for the worst calamities." [165]

Rasputin was assassinated on December 16, 1916. Samuel Hoare reported to the British Intelligence, "The feeling in Petrograd is most remarkable. All classes speak and act as if some great weight had been taken from their shoulders. Servants, *izvoshchiks* [cabmen], working men, all freely discuss the event. Many say that it is better than the greatest Russian victory in the field." [166] Paleologue reported that the popular rejoicing was so great that people kissed each other on the streets, and many went to burn candles in the Kazan Cathedral. "When it was known that the Grand Duke Dmitrii was one of the assassins, there was a crush to light candles before the ikons of St. Dimitrii. The murder of Grigorii is the sole topic of conversation among the interminable queues of women who wait in the snow and wind at the doors of the butchers and grocers for the distribution of meat, tea, and sugar." Many of the people showed their satisfaction by quoting the proverb, "For a dog, a dog's death." [167]

However, while great things were expected as a result of this murder, no striking changes actually resulted in the church. The French ambassador reported on February 16, 1917 (new style), that the Rasputin party, albeit without a head, had survived the death of its leader. "Raev, the Over Procurator, . . . has just ordered Mgr. Basil, the bishop of Chernigov, who is the fine flower of Rasputinism, to

[164] Paleologue, *op. cit.*, II, 231.
[165] Gilliard, *Le Tragique Destin de Nicolas II*, p. 149.
[166] Hoare, *op. cit.*, p. 146.   [167] Paleologue, *op. cit.*, III, 131–32.

Petrograd. This prelate's mission will be to organize, with the support of the Minister of the Interior, a moral propaganda service; in other words, police supervision over the deportment of the clergy." [168] If one may judge by the items printed in the liberal *Russkiia Vedomosti* (*The Russian News*), Raev was able to maintain securely his position and that of his partisans among the hierarchy. Instead of news of sweeping removals of the supporters of Rasputin, this newspaper printed articles and editorials on Raev's improper actions in a current divorce case; according to excerpts cited, several other newspapers likewise took an interest in the case.[169] Another article in *Russkiia Vedomosti*, about two weeks before the beginning of the Revolution, remarked on the Over Procurator's arbitrary decision concerning the Central Taper Committee—a decision which was contrary to the vote of the Synod and which "produced an unfavorable impression in ecclesiastical circles." [170] And only a week before the Revolution began, Bishop Feofan, Rasputin's original sponsor, paid a visit to the empress and asked her to do something to check the growing demoralization of the people. Paleologue, who learned of the interview, stated that the bishop declared that "the men who return from the army, sick, wounded, or on leave, are giving utterance to abominable opinions; they affect unbelief and atheism, and go as far as blasphemy and sacrilege." [171] Apparently, in the two and a half months between the death of Rasputin and the fall of the empire, nothing was done to restore the lost prestige of the Russian Church.

After the stirring events of 1916 and 1917 it seems a far cry to the beginning of the twentieth century; and yet, in the close connection between the Orthodox Church and the Russian state—a connection which was very strong in the peaceful years just after 1900—there lay important causes of the later developments. The church possessed economic privileges of considerable importance; its rivals were hampered, and its own efforts aided, by the agents of the civil power. In return, the church, by its teachings and by its ceremonies and in other ways, rendered valuable aid to the autocracy. However, in spite of, and in part because of, the closeness of this connection, all was

[168] *Ibid.*, III, 194.   [169] *Russkiia Vedomosti*, Feb. 7, 10, 11, 23, 1917.
[170] *Ibid.*, Feb. 9, 1917.   [171] Paleologue, *op. cit.*, III, 211.

not well with the Russian Church. Important sections of the people were not firm in their allegiance to it; the intelligentsia and the factory workers could not be regarded as solidly loyal to the church of their fathers. Even the peasants were somewhat infected with distrust and aversion. The monastic clergy were believed often to be indifferent models of Christian virtue, and the parish priests did not enjoy as great an authority as many churchmen might have wished. In part this last condition was due to the unfortunate system of preparing men for the priesthood; in part, to economic friction with the peasants, and to the belief of many of the latter that the priests served the interests of those whom these peasants viewed as their enemies. Certain it is that on the eve of the Revolution of 1905 the Orthodox Church suffered from serious weaknesses and stood in need of important reforms.

For a time in 1905 and 1906 it appeared that these reforms would be realized. Pobedonostsev, the champion of the old order, was dismissed; the position of the Old Believers and the sectarians was much improved; and the many liberals among the clergy were gratified by the steps taken toward the calling of the *Sobor*. However, the forces of reaction were too strong. Many of the upper clergy were exceedingly hostile to liberalism in all its forms, and they proved able to turn the organization of the church to the support of the reactionary government. The *Sobor* was indefinitely postponed, and hope that the church would achieve internal reform through its own efforts faded away. During the period of the Third and Fourth Dumas repeated attempts were made by the liberal parties to induce the central administration of the church to institute the needed reforms, but all these efforts came to naught.

During the period between the Revolution of 1905 and the World War the connection between church and state remained strong. Although the Old Believers enjoyed considerable toleration, the sectarians were still persecuted; many of their disabilities had been removed, but many still remained. Through its impressive participation in several state festivals the church showed that it supported the government of the Tsar. Moreover, the Mt. Athos incident and the Beilis case demonstrated that the partnership was still a reality. During these years before the war, however, there were many signs suggesting that the church failed to command the hearts of many of the Russians; the old weaknesses of its organization still remained almost unchanged, and in the notorious case of Bishop Hermogen there was an indication of a more dangerous evil which in the succeeding years was to fasten itself upon the administration of the church.

The Rasputin scandal was already coming to the attention of large sections of the populace before the war; the Duma and the newspapers had taken notice of it as early as 1912. For a period during the early months of the war the church seemed free of the influence of Rasputin; the Synod supported the Russian arms, and numbers of the churchmen aided the efforts of the fatherland. In 1915, however, the influence of Rasputin once more grew strong; the conflict between Samarin and Bishop Varnava brought it to the attention of the public and, when the Over Procurator fell, the enslavement of the Russian Church to the dissolute peasant was accomplished. His creature, Pitirim, became the foremost metropolitan of the Russian Church and, although other prelates might grumble, few of them dared make public their protests. The general public waxed indignant, and already warnings were heard that a split in the church was imminent; but no purification of the hierarchy took place, and until the end the Russian Church remained fettered to a state controlled by a tottering government. When that state collapsed in ruins, its fall would inevitably drag its handmaid, the church, to the edge of the abyss.

Bibliography

Archive Documents

Among the valuable materials used in this study are a number of documents preserved in the Leningradskoe Otdelenie Tsentral'nogo Istoricheskogo Arkhiva (Leningrad Division of the Central Historical Archive). These documents are arranged in several "funds," each of which contains items deriving from one part of the administration of the church or of the government. The following funds were drawn upon:

The fund of the Kantseliariia Sinoda (Chancery of the Synod). All available materials were consulted with reference to the finances of the Church and of its parts during the period under consideration. This fund also furnished a number of significant documents bearing on specific instances of relations between the clergy and the government, the Synod and the government, and the Synod and the political parties, especially during the Revolution of 1905. All such materials contained in this fund were studied.

The fund of the Kantseliariia Ober-Prokurora (Chancery of the Over Procurator). Here are found items of the same sort as those in the preceding fund. All pertinent materials in this fund were studied.

The fund of the Departament Dukhovnykh Del Inostrannykh Ispovedanii Ministerstva Vnutrennikh Del (Department of Religious Affairs of the Foreign Confessions of the Ministry of Internal Affairs). This fund contains documents pertaining to the application of restrictions upon the Old Believers and the sectarians, for the years 1900–5. Extensive use was made of selected items, many of them chosen as typical examples of important categories of documents in this fund.

Printed Materials

The following bibliography contains only works actually used in the writing of this volume, and cited in the footnotes.

Abbreviations used below:
 N. Y. for New York
 St. P. for St. Petersburg
 P. for Petrograd
 L. for Leningrad
 M. for Moscow

Bibliography

Agafangel, Volynskii. Plenenie Russkoi Tserkvi: Zapiski Preosviashchennago Agafangela Volynskago Aleksandru II (Captivity of the
Russian Church: Memoir of the Most Reverend Agafangel of Volhynia to Alexander II). M., 1906.

Aksakov, I. Article in *Russkii Arkhiv* (*Russian Archive*), No. 4 (1886),
St. P.

Arsen'ev, K. K. Svoboda Sovesti i Veroterpimost', Sbornik Statei (Freedom of Conscience and Religious Toleration, Collection of Articles).
St. P., 1905.

Barsov, T. V. Sbornik Deistvuiushchikh i Rukovodstvennykh Tserkovnykh i Tserkovno-grazhdanskikh Postanovlenii po Vedomstvu
Pravoslavnago Ispovedaniia (Collection of Effective and Guiding
Church and Church-Civil Decrees Concerning the Administration of
the Orthodox Confession). St. P., 1885.

Beletskii, S. P. Grigorii Rasputin. P., 1923.

Belokonskii, I. P. "Chernosotennoe Dvizhenie ili Tainaia Russkaia
Kontr-revoliutsiia" ("The Black Hundred Movement or the Secret
Russian Counter-Revolution"). *Obrazovanie* (*Education*), (1906),
St. P.

Berdnikov, I. S. Kratkii Kurs Tserkovnago Prava (Short Course of
Church Law). Revised edition, Kazan, 1913.

———— "K Voprosu o Preobrazovanii Eparkhial'nago Upravleniia"
("On the Question of Reforming the Diocesan Administration").
Pravoslavnyi Sobesednik (*Orthodox Companion*), (Jan., 1906),
Kazan.

Birzhevyia Vedomosti (*Bourse News*). Daily, St. P.

Blagovidov, F. V. K Rabote Obshchestvennoi Mysli po Voprosu o
Tserkovnoi Reforme (Toward a Consideration of Public Opinion on
the Question of Church Reform). Kazan, 1905.

Bogoslovskii Vestnik (*Theological Messenger*). Monthly, Sergiev Posad.

Boldovskii, A. Vozrozhdenie Tserkovnago Prikhoda (Obzor Mnenii

Pechati) (The Regeneration of the Church Parish, Survey of the Opinions of the Press). St. P., 1903.

Brodskii, L., editor. Mneniia, Otzyvy i Pis'ma Filareta, Mitropolita Moskovskago i Kolomenskago po Raznym Voprosam za 1821–1867 gg. (Opinions, Statements, and Letters of Filaret, Metropolitan of Moscow and Kolomna on Different Questions from 1821 to 1867). M., 1905.

Buchanan, G. My Mission to Russia, and Other Memories. 2 vols., London, 1923.

Butmi, G. Vragi Roda Chelovecheskago. Posviashchaetsia Soiuzu Russkago Naroda. (Enemies of the Human Race. Consecrated to the Union of the Russian People). St. P., 1906.

Chernovskii, A., editor. Soiuz Russkogo Naroda po Materialam Chrezvychainoi Sledstvennoi Komissii Vremennogo Pravitel'stva 1917 g. (The Union of the Russian People according to the Materials of the Extraordinary Investigating Commission of the Provisional Government of 1917). M., 1929.

Conybeare, F. C. Russian Dissenters. Cambridge, Mass., 1921.

Cross, S. H. The Russian Primary Chronicle. Cambridge, Mass., 1930.

Derviz, V. D. K Voprosu ob Ekonomicheskom Polozhenii Byvshei Troitse-Sergievoi Lavry (On the Question of the Economic Position of the Former Troitse-Sergieva Monastery). Sergiev, 1926.

Dixon, W. H. Free Russia. 2 vols., London, 1870.

Dzhivelegov, A. K., and others, editors. Velikaia Reforma (The Great Reform). 6 vols., M., 1911.

Fortescue, A. The Eastern Orthodox Church. 2d edition, London, 1908.

Gilliard, P. Le Tragique Destin de Nicolas II et de sa famille. Paris, 1921.

Golubinskii, E. E. Istoriia Kanonizatsii Sviatykh v Russkoi Tserkvi (History of the Canonization of Saints in the Russian Church). M., 1894.

———— Istoriia Russkoi Tserkvi (History of the Russian Church). 2 vols. in 4, M., 1900–17.

———— O Reforme v Byte Russkoi Tserkvi (Concerning Reform in the Life of the Russian Church). M., 1913.

Gorchakov, M. I. Tserkovnoe Pravo: Kratkii Kurs Lektsii (Church Law: A Short Course of Lectures). St. P., 1909.

Gosudarstvennaia Duma (State Duma). Doklady Biudzhetnoi Komissii (Reports of the Budget Commission). III Duma, 10 vols., St. P., 1908–12; IV Duma, 11 vols., St. P. and P., 1913–16.

———— Prilozheniia k Stenograficheskim Otchetam (Supplements to the Stenographic Reports). III Duma, 18 vols., St. P., 1908–12; IV Duma, 21 vols., St. P. and P., 1913–16.

———— Stenograficheskie Otchety (Stenographic Reports). I Duma, St. P., 1907; II Duma, St. P., 1907; III Duma, 17 vols., St. P., 1908–12; IV Duma, 13 vols., St. P. and P., 1913–17.

———— Ukazatel' k Stenograficheskim Otchetam (Index to the Stenographic Reports). I Duma, St. P., 1907; II Duma, St. P., 1907; III Duma, 5 vols., St. P., 1908–12; IV Duma, 3 vols., St. P. and P., 1913–16.

Gosudarstvennyi Kontrol' (State Comptrol). Otchet Gosudarstvennago Kontrolia po Ispolneniiu Gosudarstvennoi Rospisi i Finansovykh Smet (Report of State Comptrol on the Fulfillment of the State Budget and the Financial Estimates). Annually, St. P., 1866–1914.

Gosudarstvennyi Sovet (Council of State). Stenograficheskii Otchet (Stenographic Report). Sessions I–XIII, 13 vols. in 12, St. P. and P., 1906–17.

Gradovskii, A. D. Sobranie Sochinenii (Collection of Works). 9 vols., St. P., 1899–1907.

Grass, K. K. Die russischen Sekten. 3 vols., Leipzig, 1905–14.

Hecker, J. Religion under the Soviets. N. Y., 1927.

Hoare, S. The Fourth Seal; the End of a Russian Chapter. London, 1930.

Iakovlevin. Russkaia Revoliutsiia i Evreiskaia Sotsial-Demokratiia (The Russian Revolution and Jewish Social Democracy). Khar'kov, 1905.

Iankovskii, Protohierarch F. I. "O Preobrazovanii Russkoi Pravoslavnoi Tserkvi" ("Concerning the Reformation of the Russian Orthodox Church"). *Khristianskoe Chtenie* (*Christian Reading*), (Nov., 1906), St. P.

Iasevich-Borodaevskaia, V. Bor'ba za Veru. Istoricheskо-bytovye Ocherki i Obzor Zakonodatel'stva po Staroobriadchestvu i Sektantstvu v Ego Posledovatel'nom Razvitii, s Prilozheniem Statei Zakona i Vysochaishikh Ukazov (The Struggle for the Faith. Historical Sketches Descriptive of Life, and a Survey of the Legislation on Old Belief and Sectarianism in Its Subsequent Development, with an Appendix of Articles of the Law and Imperial Ukazes). St. P., 1912.

Istoricheskoe Opisanie Sviato-Troitskoi Sergievoi Lavry (Historical Description of the Holy Troitsko-Sergieva Monastery). Sviato-Troitskaia Sergieva Lavra, 1910.

Istoriia Rossii v XIX Veke (History of Russia in the Nineteenth Century). 9 vols., St. P., n. d.

Iurskii, G. Pravye v 3-ei Gosudarstvennoi Dume (The Rightists in the Third State Duma). Khar'kov, 1912.

Iuzov, I. Russkie Dissidenty. Starovery i Dukhovnye Khristiane (Russian Dissenters. The Old Believers and the Spiritual Christians). St. P., 1881.

Ivanovskii, N. Rukovodstvo k Istorii i Oblicheniiu Staroobriadcheskago Raskola (Handbook for the History and the Unmasking of the Old Believers' Schism). Kazan, 1895.

——— "Sudebnaia Ekspertiza o Sekte Khlystov" ("Expert Testimony in Court Concerning the Sect of Khlysty"). *Zhurnal Ministerstva Iustitsii* (*Journal of the Ministry of Justice*), No. 1 (1896), St. P.

Ivantsov-Platonov, A. M. O Russkom Tserkovnom Upravlenii (Concerning Russian Church Administration). St. P., 1898.

Kapterev, N. F. Kharakter Otnoshenii Rossii k Pravoslavnomu Vostoku v XVI i XVII Stoletiiakh (Character of the Relation of Russia to the Orthodox East in the Sixteenth and Seventeenth Centuries). 2d edition, Sergiev Posad, 1914.

——— Patriarkh Nikon i Tsar' Aleksei Mikhailovich (Patriarch Nikon and Tsar Aleksei Mikhailovich). 2 vols., Sergiev Posad, 1909–12.

Karpov, N., editor. Krest'ianskoe Dvizhenie v Revoliutsii 1905 Goda v Dokumentakh (The Peasant Movement in the Revolution of 1905 in Documents). L., 1925.

Kel'siev, V. I. Sbornik Pravitel'stvennykh Svedenii o Raskole (Collection of Governmental Information about the Schism). 4 vols. in 3, London, 1860–62.

Khristianskoe Chtenie (*Christian Reading*). Monthly. St. P.

Kil'chevskii, V. Bogatstvo i Dokhody Dukhovenstva (The Wealth and the Income of the Clergy). 2d edition, St. P., 1908.

Kliuchevskii, V. O. Kurs Russkoi Istorii (Course of Russian History). Vols. I–II, 2d edition, M., 1906. Vol. III, M., 1908. Vol. IV, M., 1910. Vol. V, M., 1921.

Koeppen, P. Deviataia Reviziia. Izsledovanie o Chisle Zhitelei v Rossii v 1851 godu (The Ninth Census. An Investigation of the Number of Inhabitants in Russia in 1851). St. P., 1857.

Kokovtsov, V. N. Iz Moego Proshlago. Vospominaniia 1903–1917 gg. (Out of My Past. Recollections of 1903–1917). 2 vols., Paris, 1933.

Kolokol (*The Bell*). Daily. St. P.

Korenev, S. A. "Chrezvychainaia Komissiia po Delam o Byvshikh

Ministrakh" ("The Extraordinary Commission on the Affairs of Former Ministers"). *Arkhiv Russkoi Revoliutsii (The Archive of the Russian Revolution)*, Vol. VII (1922), Berlin.

Kornilov, A. A. Kurs Istorii Rossii XIX Veka (Course in the History of Russia in the Nineteenth Century). 3 vols., M., 1912–14.

Krasin, P. "Vospitanie v Dukhovnoi Seminarii" ("Training in the Religious Seminary"). *Trudy Kievskoi Dukhovnoi Akademii (Works of the Kiev Religious Academy)*, (Aug.–Sept., 1906), Kiev.

Krasnyi Arkhiv (The Red Archive). Bi-monthly. M.

Kuznetsov, N. D. Preobrazovaniia v Russkoi Tserkvi. Razsmotrenie Voprosa po Ofitsial'nym Dokumentam v Sviazi s Potrebnostiami Zhizni (Reformation in the Russian Church. Survey of the Question According to Official Documents in Connection with the Demands of Life). M., 1906.

Leroy-Beaulieu, A. The Empire of the Tsars and the Russians. 3 vols., N. Y., 1902–3.

The Letters of the Tsaritsa to the Tsar, 1914–1916. London, 1923.

The Letters of the Tsar to the Tsaritsa, 1914–1917. London, 1929.

Lisenko, S. "Chernaia Sotnia v Provintsii" ("The Black Hundred in the Provinces"). *Russkaia Mysl' (Russian Thought)*, No. 2 (1908), M.

Liubinetskii, N. A. Zemlevladenie Tserkvei i Monastyrei Rossiiskoi Imperii (Landholding of the Churches and the Monasteries of the Russian Empire). St. P., 1900.

Makarii, Mitropolit Moskovskii (Makarii, Metropolitan of Moscow). Istoriia Russkoi Tserkvi (History of the Russian Church). 12 vols., M., 1868–1883.

Maslov, P. Agrarnyi Vopros v Rossii (The Agrarian Question in Russia). 2 vols., St. P., 1905.

Materialy k Istorii Russkoi Kontr-revoliutsii (Materials for the History of the Russian Counter-Revolution). St. P., 1908.

Maude, A. A Peculiar People. London, 1905.

Mel'gunov, S. P. "Epokha Ofitsial'noi Narodnosti i Krepostnoe Pravo" ("The Epoch of Official Nationalism and the Serf Right"). In Vol. III: Dzhivelegov, A. K., and others, editors, Velikaia Reforma (The Great Reform). 6 vols., M., 1911.

——— Iz Istorii Religiozno-obshchestvennykh Dvizhenii v Rossii XIX Veka. Staroobriadchestvo. Religioznyia Goneniia (From the History of the Religious-Social Movements in Russia in the Nineteenth Century. Old Believerdom. Religious Persecutions). M., 1919.

Mel'gunov, S. P. "Mitropolit Filaret—Deiatel' Krest'ianskoi Reformy" ("Metropolitan Filaret—a Worker in the Peasant Reform"). In Vol. V: Dzhivelegov, A. K., and others, editors, Velikaia Reforma (The Great Reform). 6 vols., M., 1911.

—————— Staroobriadchestvo i Osvoboditel'noe Dvizhenie (Old Believer-dom and the Liberative Movement). M., 1906.

Mel'nikov, P. I. Polnoe Sobranie Sochinenii (Complete Works). 2d edition, 7 vols., St. P., 1909.

Ministerstvo Finansov (Ministry of Finance). Proekt Gosudarstvennoi Rospisi Dokhodov i Raskhodov na 1917 god (Project of the State Budget of Revenues and Disbursements for 1917). P., 1916.

Ministerstvo Finansov, Departament Okladnykh Sborov (Ministry of Finance, Department of Direct Taxes). Mirskie Dokhody i Raskhody za 1905 g. po 50-ti Guberniiam Evropeiskoi Rossii (Mir Income and Disbursements for 1905 for the 50 Provinces of European Russia). St. P., 1909.

Ministerstvo Narodnago Prosveshcheniia (Ministry of Public Education). Statisticheskiia Svedeniia po Nachal'nomu Obrazovaniiu v Rossiiskoi Imperii, Dannyia 1898 goda (Statistical Information on Elementary Education in the Russian Empire, Data of 1898). St. P., 1902.

Ministerstvo Torgovli i Promyshlennosti, Otdel Promyshlennosti (Ministry of Trade and Industry, Division of Industry). Svod Otchetov Fabrichnykh Inspektorov za 1903 god (Digest of Reports of the Factory Inspectors for 1903). St. P., 1906.

Minsterstvo Vnutrennikh Del (Ministry of Internal Affairs). Sbornik Postanovlenii po Chasti Raskola (1875–1904 vkliuchitel'no), Sostavlen v Departamente Obshchikh Del, Ministerstva Vnutrennikh Del (Collection of Decrees Dealing with the Schism, 1875–1904 Inclusive, Compiled in the Department of General Affairs, of the Ministry of Internal Affairs). N. p., n. d.

Ministerstvo Vnutrennikh Del, Departament Obshchikh Del (Ministry of Internal Affairs, Department of General Affairs). Opis' Del I-ago Stola (Po Chasti Raskola) III Otdeleniia (A List of the Portfolios of the First Table [on the Subject of the Schism] of the III Division). St. P., 1905.

Missionerskoe Obozrenie (Missionary Survey). Monthly. St. P.

Moeller, W. History of the Christian Church. 3 vols., N. Y. and London, 1893–1900.

Moskovskiia Tserkovnyia Vedomosti (Moscow Church News). Monthly. M.

Myshtsyn, V. Po Tserkovno-obshchestvennym Voprosam (On Church-Social Questions). Sviato-Troitskaia Sergieva Lavra, 1906.

Nikanor, Arkhiepiskop. Besedy i Slova (Discussions and Sermons). Odessa, 1903.

Nikol'skii, N. M. "Raskol i Sektantstvo vo Vtoroi Polovine XIX Veka" ("The Schism and Sectarianism in the Second Half of the Nineteenth Century"). In Vol. V: Istoriia Rossii v XIX Veke (History of Russia in the Nineteenth Century). 9 vols., St. P., n. d.

——— "Raskol v Pervoi Polovine XIX Veka" ("The Schism in the First Half of the Nineteenth Century"). In Vol. IV: Istoriia Rossii v XIX Veke (History of Russia in the Nineteenth Century).

Novitskii, O. M. O Dukhobortsakh: Ikh Istoriia i Veroucheniia (Concerning the Dukhobors: Their History and Religious Teachings). Kiev, 1832.

Novoe Vremia (The New Time). Daily. St. P.

Novorusskii, M. V. "Dushespasitel'noe Khoziaistvo" ("Pious Economy"). Sovremennyi Mir (The Contemporary World), (Sept., 1907), St. P.

Novyi Put' (The New Path). Monthly. St. P.

Œconomos, L. La Vie religieuse dans l'empire byzantin au temps des Comnènes et des Anges. Paris, 1922.

Ognev, N. V. Na Poroge Reform Russkoi Tserkvi i Dukhovenstva (On the Threshold of Reform of the Russian Church and of the Clergy). St. P., 1907.

Opisanie Valaamskago Monastyria i Skitov Ego (Description of Valaam Monastery and Its Hermitages). St. P., 1897.

Opyt Izsledovaniia ob Imushchestvakh i Dokhodakh Nashikh Monastyrei (An Attempt at Investigating the Property and the Income of Our Monasteries). St. P., 1876.

Osetskii, A. Pomestnyi Sobor. Svobodnyi Opyt Organizatsii (The Local Sobor. A Free Attempt at Organization). P., 1917.

Paleologue, M. La Russie des tsars pendant la grande guerre. 3 vols., Paris, 1921–22.

Palibin, M. N., editor. Ustav Dukhovnykh Konsistorii, s Dopolneniiami i Raz'iasneniiami Sviateishago Sinoda i Pravitel'stvuiushchago Senata (Code of the Religious Consistories, with the Supplements and the Explanations of the Most Holy Synod and of the Governing Senate). 2d edition, St. P., 1912.

Palmieri, A. La Chiesa Russa, le sue odierne condizioni e il suo riformismo dottrinale. Florence, 1908.

Palmieri, A. "The Russian Dukhobors and Their Religious Teachings." *Harvard Theological Review*, No. 8 (1915), Cambridge, Mass.

Pobedonostsev, K. P. Moskovskii Sbornik (Moscow Compendium). St. P., 1896.

——— Pis'ma Pobedonostseva k Aleksandru III (Letters of Pobedonostsev to Alexander III). M., 1925.

Pochaevskiia Izvestiia (*Pochaev News*). Daily. Pochaevskaia Lavra.

Pochaevskii Listok (*Pochaev Leaflet*). Weekly. Pochaevskaia Lavra.

"Pokhozhdeniia Iliodora" ("The Adventures of Iliodor"). *Byloe* (*The Past*), No. 24 (1924), L.

Pokrovskii, M. N., editor. 1905—Istoriia Revoliutsionnogo Dvizheniia v Otdel'nykh Ocherkakh (1905—History of the Revolutionary Movement in Separate Sketches). 3 vols. in 4, M., 1925–26.

——— 1905—Materialy i Dokumenty (1905—Materials and Documents). 8 vols., M., 1925–28.

Polnoe Sobranie Zakonov Rossiiskoi Imperii (Complete Collection of Laws of the Russian Empire). Sobranie Vtoroe (Second Collection). Dec. 12, 1825–Feb. 28, 1881. 55 vols. and Index, St. P., 1830–84.

——— Sobranie Tretie (Third Collection). March 1, 1881–Dec. 31, 1913. 33 vols., St. P., 1885–1916.

Polnyi Sbornik Platform Vsekh Russkikh Politicheskikh Partii (Complete Collection of the Platforms of All the Russian Political Parties). St. P., 1906.

Popov, Sviashchennik Semeon (Priest Semeon Popov). "Pravda o Praktike Zemlevladeniia Dukhovenstvom" ("The Truth about the Practice of Landholding by the Clergy"). *Missionerskoe Obozrenie* (*Missionary Survey*), (June, 1906), St. P.

Pravitel'stvennyi Vestnik (*Governmental Messenger*). Daily. St. P.

Pravo (*Law*). Weekly. St. P.

Pravoslavnyi Sobesednik (*Orthodox Companion*). Monthly. Kazan.

Preobrazhenskii, I. V. Dukhovenstvo i Narodnoe Obrazovanie (The Clergy and Public Education). St. P., 1900.

——— Konstantin Petrovich Pobedonostsev: Ego Lichnost' i Deiatel'nost' v Predstavlenii Sovremennikov Ego Konchiny (Konstantin Petrovich Pobedonostsev: His Personality and Activity According to the Representations of Contemporaries of His Demise). St. P., 1912.

——— Tserkovnaia Reforma: Sbornik Statei Dukhovnoi i Svetskoi Periodicheskoi Pechati po Voprosu o Reforme (Church Reform: Collection of Articles of the Religious and Secular Periodical Press on the Question of Reform). St. P., 1905.

———— Velichaishaia iz Velikikh Voin za Pravdu Bozhiiu (The Greatest of the Great Wars for the Truth of God). P., 1916.

Prodolzhenie Svoda Zakonov Rossiiskoi Imperii (Continuation of the Code of Laws of the Russian Empire). 6 vols., St. P., 1906.

Provolovich, A. Sbornik Zakonov o Monashestvuiushchem Dukhovenstve (Collection of Laws Concerning the Monastic Clergy). M., 1897.

Prugavin, A. Monastyrskiia Tiur'my v Bor'be s Sektantstvom (Monastery Prisons in the Struggle with Sectarianism). 2d edition, M., 1906.

———— "Raskol i Biurokratiia" ("The Schism and the Bureaucracy"). *Vestnik Evropy (The Messenger of Europe)*, No. 259 (1909), St. P.

———— "Religioznyia Goneniia pri Obnovlennom Stroe" ("Religious Persecutions under the Reformed Regime"). *Vestnik Evropy (The Messenger of Europe)*, No. 8 (1911), St. P.

———— Staroobriadchestvo vo Vtoroi Polovine XIX Veka (Old Believerdom in the Second Half of the Nineteenth Century). M., 1904.

———— Vopiiushchee Delo (A Flagrant Case). M., 1906.

Reisner, A. Dukhovnaia Politsiia v Rossii (Religious Police in Russia). St. P., 1907.

Revoliutsionnaia Rossiia (Revolutionary Russia). Monthly. Paris.

Robinson, G. T. Rural Russia under the Old Regime. N. Y., 1932.

Rodzianko, M. V. The Reign of Rasputin. An Empire's Collapse. London, 1927.

Rozanov, V. Okolo Tserkovnykh Sten (Near Church Walls). 2 vols., St. P., 1906.

Rozhdestvenskii, A. Iuzhno-russkii Stundizm (South-Russian Stundism). St. P., 1889.

Russkiia Vedomosti (Russian News). Daily. M.

Russkoe Znamia (The Russian Banner). Daily. St. P.

Samarskiia Eparkhial'nyia Vedomosti (Samara Diocesan News). Semi-monthly? Samara.

Sanktpeterburgskiia Vedomosti (St. Petersburg News). Daily. St. P.

Saratovskiia Eparkhial'nyia Vedomosti (Saratov Diocesan News). Semi-monthly? Saratov.

Schaff, P. History of the Christian Church. 7 vols., N. Y., 1858–1910.

Semennikov, V. P., editor. Monarkhiia pered Krusheniem (The Monarchy before the Crash). M., L., 1927.

Shchegolev, P. E., editor. Padenie Tsarskogo Rezhima (The Fall of the Tsarist Regime). 7 vols., M., L., 1925–27.

Skvortsov, D. I. Sovremennoe Russkoe Sektantstvo (Contemporary Russian Sectarianism). M., 1905.

Skvortsov, V. Tserkovnyi Svet i Gosudarstvennyi Razum. Opyt Tserkov-no-Politicheskoi Khrestomatii (Church Light and Governmental Reason. An Attempt at a Church-Political Anthology). 2 vols., St. P., 1912–13.

Smirnov, A. Kak Proshli Vybory vo 2-uiu Gosudarstvennuiu Dumu (How the Elections to the Second State Duma Took Place). St. P., 1907.

Smirnov, P. Nastavlenie v Zakone Bozhiem (Instruction in the Law of God). St. P., 1895. Izdanie Pervago Uchilishchago pri Sviateishem Sinode Sovieta (Publication of the First School Board under the Most Holy Synod).

Sobranie Uzakonenii i Rasporiazhenii Pravitel'stva (Collection of the Legislation and the Enactments of the Government). St. P. and P., 1863–1917.

Soiuz Russkago Naroda (Union of the Russian People). Zagovor protiv Rossii (The Plot against Russia). St. P., 1906.

Soiuz Russkikh Liudei (Union of Russian Men). Pravoslavnoe Bratstvo v Bor'be za Veru Pravoslavnuiu i Russkuiu Narodnost' (The Orthodox Brotherhood in the Struggle for the Orthodox Faith and Russian Nationalism). M., 1906.

Sokolov, V. K. "Nashi Episkopy i Samoderzhavie" ("Our Bishops and the Autocracy"). *Vestnik Prava (The Messenger of Law)*, (1906), St. P.

—— "Predstoiashchii Vserossiiskii Tserkovnyi Sobor" ("The Coming All-Russian Church Council"). *Bogoslovskii Vestnik (Theological Messenger)*, (May, 1906), M.

Solov'ev, S. M. Istoriia Rossii s Drevneishikh Vremen (History of Russia from the Most Ancient Times). 2d edition, 29 vols. in 6, St. P., n. d.

Sovet Vserossiiskikh S'ezdov Staroobriadtsev (Council of the All-Russian Congresses of Old Believers). Sel'sko-khoziaistvennyi i Ekonomicheskii Byt Staroobriadtsev (po Dannym Ankety 1909 goda) (Agricultural and Economic Life of the Old Believers, According to the Investigation of 1909). M., 1910.

Spisok Izdanii (List of Publications). Izdatel'stvo "Vernost' " (Publishing House "Fidelity"). N. p., n. d.

Staroobriadcheskii Vestnik (The Old Believer Messenger). Monthly. M.

Stremoukhov, P. P. "Moia Bor'ba s Episkopom Germogenom i Iliodorom" ("My Struggle with Bishop Hermogen and Iliodor"). *Arkhiv Russkoi*

Revoliutsii (*Archive of the Russian Revolution*), Vol. XVI (1925), Berlin.

Suvorov, N. V. Uchebnik Tserkovnago Prava (Textbook of Church Law). 3d edition, M., 1912.

Sviateishii Pravitel'stvuiushchii Sinod (Most Holy Synod). Obzor Deiatel'nosti Vedomstva Pravoslavnago Ispovedaniia za Vremia Tsarstvovaniia Imperatora Aleksandra III (Survey of the Activity of the Administration of the Orthodox Confession for the Period of the Reign of Emperor Alexander III). St. P., 1901.

———— Obzor Nekotorykh Storon Deiatel'nosti Dukhovnago Vedomstva za 1910 g. (Survey of Some Aspects of the Activity of the Religious Administration for 1910). St. P., 1913.

———— Otzyvy Eparkhial'nykh Arkhiereev po Voprosu o Tserkovnoi Reforme (Statements of the Diocesan Bishops on the Question of Church Reform). 3 vols., St. P., 1906.

———— Pravila i Progammy dlia Tserkovno-prikhodskikh Shkol i Shkol Gramoty (Rules and Programs for Church-parish Schools and Schools of Literacy). 2d edition, St. P., 1894.

———— Raskol i Sektantstvo (Schism and Sectarianism). St. P., 1901.

———— Smeta Dokhodov i Raskhodov Vedomstva Sviateishago Sinoda na 1913 g. (Estimate of the Income and the Disbursements of the Administration of the Most Holy Synod for 1913). St. P., 1912.

———— Tserkovnyia Shkoly Rossiiskoi Imperii 13 Iiunia 1894–1903 g. (Church Schools of the Russian Empire, June 13, 1894–1903). St. P., n. d.

———— Ustav Dukhovnykh Konsistorii (Code of Religious Consistories). St. P., 1883.

———— Vsepoddanneishii Otchet Ober-Prokurora Sviateishago Sinoda po Vedomstvu Pravoslavnago Ispovedaniia (Most Humble Report of the Over Procurator of the Most Holy Synod Concerning the Administration of the Orthodox Confession). St. P., 1845–1914.

———— Zhurnaly i Protokoly Zasedanii Vysochaishe Uchrezhdennago Predsobornago Prisutstviia (Journals and Protocols of the Sessions of the Imperially Established Pre-*Sobor* Conference). 4 vols. in 2, St. P., 1906.

Sviatlovskii, V. K Voprosu o Sud'bakh Zemlevladeniia v Rossii (On the Question of the Fate of Landowning in Russia). St. P., 1907.

Svod Zakonov Rossiiskoi Imperii (Code of Laws of the Russian Empire). 1832 edition, 15 vols., St. P.; 1857 edition, 15 vols. in 21, St. P.; the parts of this Code were reissued at various times from 1862 to 1916, 16 vols. in 19, St. P.

Temnikovskii, E. K Voprosu o Kanonizatsii Sviatykh (On the Question of the Canonization of Saints). Iaroslavl, 1903.

Titlinov, B. V. Tserkov' vo Vremia Revoliutsii (The Church in the Time of the Revolution). P., 1924.

Titov, A. Odin iz Zakliuchennykh v Suzdal'skoi Kreposti (Delo O. Zolotnitskago) (One of the Prisoners in the Suzdal Fortress [The Case of Father Zolotnitskii]). M., 1904.

Troitskii, P. S. Tserkov' i Gosudarstvo v Rossii: Otnosheniia Gosudarstva k Tserkvi po Vozzreniiam Naibolee Vidnykh Nashikh Pisatelei i Obshchestvennykh Deiatel'ei (Church and State in Russia: Relations of the State to the Church According to the Opinions of Our Most Noted Writers and Public Figures). M., 1909.

Trudovaia Gruppa v Gosudarstvennoi Dume (The Labor Group in the State Duma). M., 1906.

Trufanov, S. M. [Iliodor]. Kogda-zhe Konets? (When Will There Be an End?). M., 1907.

———— Plach na Pogibel' Dorogogo Otechestva (Lament over the Destruction of the Dear Fatherland). M., 1907.

———— Sviatoi Chort (The Holy Devil). M., 1917.

———— Videnie Monakha (The Vision of a Monk). M., 1907.

Tsentral'nyi Statisticheskii Komitet (Central Statistical Committee). Ezhegodnik Rossii za 1905 god (Yearbook of Russia for 1905). St. P., 1906.

———— Naselenie Imperii po Perepisi 28-go Ianvaria 1897 goda po Uezdam (The Population of the Empire According to the Census of January 28, 1897, by Counties). St. P., 1898.

———— Raspredelenie Naseleniia Imperii po Glavnym Veroispovedaniiam. Po Dannym Pervoi Vseobshchei Perepisi 1897 g. (Distribution of the Population of the Empire According to the Chief Religious Faiths. According to the Data of the First General Census of 1897). St. P., 1901.

———— Raspredelenie Staroobriadtsev i Sektantov po Tolkam i Sektam (Distribution of Old Believers and Sectarians According to Creeds and Sects). St. P., 1901.

———— Statistika Zemlevladeniia 1905 g. Svod Dannykh po 50-ti Guberniiam Evropeiskoi Rossii (Statistics of Landowning for 1905. Abstract of Data for the 50 Provinces of European Russia). St. P., 1907.

Tserkovno-obshchestvennaia Zhizn' (*Church-Social Life*). Weekly. Kazan.

Tserkovnyia Vedomosti (*Church News*). Weekly. St. P. The periodical was issued in two parts: the "Official Part," containing decrees and orders of the Synod and the like, and the "Supplement," containing editorials and articles. Where *Tserkovnyia Vedomosti* has been cited in the present volume, the citations refer to the "Supplement," unless the words *official part* are expressly used.

Tserkovnyi Vestnik (*Church Messenger*). Weekly. St. P.

Vasiliev, A. A. Histoire de l'empire byzantin. 2 vols., Paris, 1932.

Veche. Daily. M.

Vera i Razum (*Faith and Reason*). Monthly. Khar'kov.

Verkhovskoi, P. V. Uchrezhdenie Dukhovnoi Kollegii i Dukhovnyi Reglament (The Establishment of the Religious College and the Religious Regulation). 2 vols., Rostov-on-Don, 1916.

Ves' Peterburg (All St. Petersburg). St. P., 1904.

Voennoe Ministerstvo (Ministry of War). Svod Voennykh Postanovlenii 1869 g. (Code of Military Decrees of 1869). 24 vols., St. P., 1869–1913.

Vserossiiskii Krest'ianskii Soiuz (All-Russian Peasant Union). Postanovleniia S'ezdov Krest'ianskago Soiuza 31 Iiulia–1 Avgusta i 6–10 Noiabria 1905 g. (Resolutions of the Congresses of the Peasant Union of July 31–August 1 and November 6–10, 1905). St. P., 1905.

"V Tserkovnykh Krugakh pered Revoliutsiei" ("In Church Circles before the Revolution"). *Krasnyi Arkhiv* (*The Red Archive*), No. 31 (1928), M.

Zaozerskii, N. O Nuzhdakh Tserkovnoi Zhizni Nastoiashchago Vremeni (Concerning the Needs of Present Church Life). Sergiev Posad, 1909.

Zav'ialov, A. A., editor. Tsirkuliarnye Ukazy Sviateishago Pravitel'stvuiushchago Sinoda 1867–1895 gg. (Circular Ukazes of the Most Holy Governing Synod for 1867–1895). St. P., 1896.

Zharinov, D. A. "Krest'iane Tserkovnykh Votchin" ("The Peasants of the Church Estates"). In Vol. I: A. K. Dzhivelegov and others, editors. Velikaia Reforma (The Great Reform). M., 1911.

Zhevakhov, N. D. Vospominaniia Tovarishcha Ober-Prokurora Sviateishago Sinoda (Recollections of an Assistant Over Procurator of the Most Holy Synod). 2 vols., Munich, 1923.

Znamenskii, P. V. Rukovodstvo k Russkoi Tserkovnoi Istorii (Handbook of Russian Church History). 2d edition, Kazan, 1876.

Index

Index